If you're wondering why you should buy this new edition of *Public Personnel Management,* here are six good reasons!

1. This edition analyzes the effects of underlying economic conditions with an updated section on the increasing and unpredictable health-care costs and variations in the pension system.

2. A newly focused chapter on performance-based pay weighs the dilemmas regarding individual- versus team-based performance assessment and rewards.

3. New emphasis on the effects of twenty-first-century information and communications technologies on recruitment, selection and outsourcing.

4. New focus on the legal and financial liability issues for employers, as well as on the balance between risk and cost containment on the one hand and training costs on the other.

5. Discussions on the relationship between immigration and diversity within the job market analyze the uneasy relationships of cultural, historical, and ethnic divisions.

6. Coverage of bioterrorism, terrorism, and communicable diseases addresses the conflicts among employee rights, organizational risk management and health care cost containment.

PEARSON

Sixth Edition

PUBLIC PERSONNEL MANAGEMENT

CONTEXTS AND STRATEGIES

Donald E. Klingner
University of Colorado

John Nalbandian
University of Kansas

Jared Llorens
Louisiana State University

Longman
New York San Francisco Boston
London Toronto Sydney Tokyo Singapore Madrid
Mexico City Munich Paris Cape Town Hong Kong Montreal

Editor-in-Chief: Eric Stano
Marketing Manager: Lindsey Prudhomme
Production Manager: Wanda Rockwell
Project Coordination, Text Design, and Electronic Page Makeup: Integra Software Services Pvt. Ltd.
Creative Director: Jayne Conte
Cover Illustration/Photo: George Hammerstein/Veer/Corbis
Printer and Binder: Courier Companies/Westford
Cover Printer: DPC

Library of Congress Cataloging-in-Publication Data

Klingner, Donald E.
Public personnel management: contexts and strategies/Donald E. Klingner, John Nalbandian, Jared Llorens.—6th ed.
p. cm.
Includes bibliographical references and index.
ISBN-13: 978-0-13-602688-4 (alk. paper)
ISBN-10: 0-13-602688-5 (alk. paper)
1. Civil service—Personnel management. I. Nalbandian, John, II. Llorens, Jared. III. Title.
JF1601.K56 2010
352.6—dc22

2009018336

1 2 3 4 5 6 7 8 9 10—12 11 10 09

Longman
is an imprint of

PEARSON

www.pearsonhighered.com

ISBN-13: 978-0-13-602688-4
ISBN-10: 0-13-602688-5

CONTENTS

Part IV Development

PREFACE

Originally published in 1980, *Public Personnel Management: Contexts and Strategies* continues to inform students and professionals in the United States and abroad. We are gratified that readers and reviewers confirm its strengths so much so that we have published the book in other languages for international use.

Much has changed since the original publication of this book, and every few years we find it beneficial to our audience to update our text with current references; illustrations; new cases that reflect the social, economic, political, and technological changes in the field; as well as changes in law and organizational policy and practice. The values and fundamentals found in previous editions remain. Here are some of the changes you will see:

- Chapter 2 introduces a sixth stage for the delivery of public services, emphasizes issues of third-party government (contracting) and the use of volunteers or NGOs for service delivery, and discusses the prerequisites for contracting out (in both developing and developed countries).
- Chapter 3 introduces and expands the discussion of competencies for various HRM functions and activities, focusing on the link to workforce planning and their necessity in all personnel systems. It also includes a discussion of the IPMA competency-based certification model for HRM professionals, and of local government HRM training through ICMA University.
- Chapter 4 emphasizes the importance of the larger political context in general, and the cycling of planning, budgeting, and evaluation in particular, to HRM policies and practices. It also introduces accountability based on traditional political/administrative models and defines and focuses on performance measurements as an organizational variable.
- Chapter 5 emphasizes the role of competency-based job descriptions and job design to regulate (internally and externally) budget and HR inputs in civil service systems. It also emphasizes the use of flexible classification systems, volunteers, work teams, independent contractors, and temporary/part-time/reemployed annuitant employees.
- Chapter 6 includes a new focus on performance-based pay and dilemmas regarding individual versus team-based performance assessment and rewards. It also discusses increasing and unpredictable health-care costs and variations in the pension system.
- Chapter 7 adds coverage on the uneasy relationship between immigration and diversity in terms of job markets, competencies, and cultural/historical/ethnic divisions.
- Chapter 8 includes new emphasis on the use of technology in recruitment and selection, and new coverage of outsourcing.
- Chapter 9 adds new emphasis on the "hollow state" concept.
- Chapter 10 focuses more on the legal/financial liability issues for employers as well as balance between risk and cost containment on the one hand and training costs on the other.
- Chapter 11 includes additional coverage of the tensions between individual assessments and merit pay and team-based performance and gain-sharing.

- Chapter 12 includes coverage of the issues of bioterrorism, terrorism, and communicable diseases and the conflict between preventative health care and the need to contain health-care costs.
- Chapter 13 adds coverage of the changing role of federal agencies in enforcement.
- Chapter 14 discusses conflicts that are likely to occur due to differential terms and conditions of employment in different sectors, with two-tier wage and benefit systems.

Perhaps the most obvious addition to this edition is that of Jared Llorens' name on the front cover. Jared studied at the University of Georgia and now teaches public administration at Louisiana State University. Along with his academic expertise, Jared also brings first-hand knowledge from working at both the U.S. Office of Personnel Management and U.S. Department of Labor.

We hope that you will find this book useful and a significant improvement over previous editions. As always, we invite you to share your comments and concerns with us.

ACKNOWLEDGMENTS

To my parents Ruth and Evans, who have shown by their own live's work how the twin professions of social work and accounting can contribute to public administration. To my wife Janette, who has defined with me the meaning of dual careers. To my colleagues throughout the world, who have helped me understand why public personnel management is so vitally tied to building democratic institutions. And to my children, who are all that will survive, other than my writings, beyond this life.

Don Klingner
Colorado Springs, CO

This is a very special dedication to my wife of 42 years, Carol. In her humble way, she encourages and nurtures, and she gives strength by the courageous yet unassuming way she leads her life.

John Nalbandian
Lawrence, KS

I want to first thank Don and John for providing me with the opportunity to join them in composing this new edition. Their sincere dedication to the study and practice of personnel management is inspiring and I have truly valued their friendship throughout the writing process. I would also like to thank my wife Elizabeth. Her patience, support and understanding have undoubtedly kept me going this past year. Last but not least, I would like to acknowledge my parents, Jim and Glenda. Their continuous dedication to public service serves as a constant reminder of why I entered the field of public administration.

Jared J. Llorens
Baton Rouge, Louisiana

PART **ONE**

Introduction

CHAPTER 1

The World of Public Personnel Management

Throughout the world, **public personnel management** (also known as **human resource management** or **HRM**) is widely recognized as essential for effective government. Increasingly, as we come to view the shared role of governments, private corporations, and international development organizations (**governance**) as the key to sustainable development, we recognize that throughout the world, human resources are potentially available yet, in practice, wasted. Interrelated global conditions—economic, political, social, and environmental—define the new millennium. Some are positive: Economic development and increased government capacity in countries like Brazil, Russia, India, and China raise hopes of a global trend toward stable, transparent, and representative governance. Others are negative: Global climate change, endemic poverty in sub-Saharan Africa, endemic violence in "hot spots" like Chechnya and Pakistan, and the continued fragility of Middle Eastern states threaten complex and fragile governance networks. Whether positive or negative, these conditions substantially affect administrative culture, and thus how HRM systems develop in practice.

By the end of this chapter, you will be able to:

1. Define the functions needed to manage human resources.
2. Explain why public jobs are scarce resources.
3. Describe the four traditional values that underlie the conflict over public jobs.
4. Discuss some consequences of these emergent HRM practices on state civil service reform efforts and traditional values.
5. Describe the history of public personnel management in the United States as one of conflict and compromise among competing personnel systems and values.
6. Explore the relationship between economic development and governance capacity, and propose an agenda for strengthening merit systems in transitional or fragile states.

TABLE 1-1 Human Resource Management Functions

Function	Purpose
Planning	Budget preparation, workforce planning; performance management, job analysis, and pay and benefits
Acquisition	Recruitment and selection of employees
Development	Training, evaluating, and leading employees to increase their willingness and ability to perform well
Sanction	Maintaining expectations and obligations that employees and the employer have toward one another through discipline, health and safety, and employee rights

HUMAN RESOURCE MANAGEMENT FUNCTIONS

First, HRM comprises the four fundamental functions needed to manage human resources in public, private, and nonprofit organizations. These functions, designated by the acronym **PADS**, are planning, acquisition, development, and sanction. Table 1-1 presents them along with the personnel activities that comprise them.

PUBLIC JOBS AS SCARCE RESOURCES

Second, public jobs are scarce resources. Public jobs include private- or nonprofit-sector jobs funded through government contracts. Tax revenues limit them. Their allocation is enormously significant for public policy making. Because jobs are how we measure economic and social status and because public jobs are scarce and important, individuals and groups compete for them.

THE FOUR TRADITIONAL VALUES

Third, public personnel management is the continuous interaction among fundamental **values** that often conflict because they reflect key differences over who gets public jobs and how, and over job security. While most prominent in hiring and separation decisions, these value considerations affect any personnel action that allocates scarce resources or opportunities. Traditionally, conflict in the United States has centered around four values:

- **Political responsiveness** and **representation**—an appointment process that considers personal loyalty and political support as indicators of merit.
- **Efficiency**—making staffing decisions based on applicants' and employees' abilities and performance.
- **Employee rights**—protecting employees from political interference or arbitrary treatment that may threaten their job security or interfere with their job performance.
- **Social equity**—adequately representing all groups in the workforce and managing this diverse workforce to maintain productivity and a positive organizational culture.

THE FOUR TRADITIONAL PUBLIC HRM SYSTEMS: PATRONAGE, CIVIL SERVICE, COLLECTIVE BARGAINING, AND AFFIRMATIVE ACTION

Fourth, public HRM comprises systems. These are the laws, rules, organizations, and procedures used to fulfill the four personnel functions in ways that express abstract values. There are four traditional systems: patronage, merit (civil service), **collective bargaining**, and affirmative action. Civil service is the predominant traditional system and the only complete system because it includes all four functions and can incorporate all four competing values. It dominates HRM culture in countries that have invested heavily in economic development.

Political Patronage

Public jobs in the United States were initially shared among elite leaders—the small group of upper-class property owners who had led the American Revolution, which won independence from England, and established a national government in 1789. The passing of this generation of "founding fathers" led to the emergence of a political system based around political parties. By the 1830s, this in turn created a patronage system that rewarded party members and campaign workers with jobs once their candidate was elected. This "**spoils system**" expanded as the size and functions of government grew after the Civil War (1861–1865). Political patronage means legislative or executive approval of individual hiring decisions, particularly for policy-making positions, based on the applicant's personal loyalty to the appointing official, or political support among stakeholders the appointing official represents. The elected officials who nominate political appointees may also fire them at any time. While the patronage system does not necessarily result in the selection of highly qualified employees or provision of efficient government services, it does enable elected officials to achieve political objectives by placing loyal supporters in key positions in administrative agencies. Moreover, it increases political responsiveness because elected officials get reelected by providing stakeholders with access to administrative agencies during the policy-making process. As an example of how patronage systems work in practice, the General Accountability Office (GAO) publishes the ***Plum Book***—a listing of U.S. government policy and supporting positions—immediately following each presidential election.[1] The White House also has an online application process for political appointments.[2]

Civil Service (Merit) Systems

In the United States, the period between 1883 and 1937 is important in the development of public personnel administration based on merit principles. With increased pressures for rational and transparent government and increased demands for more effective delivery of public services to meet the needs of an industrializing economy came increased dissatisfaction with patronage-based personnel systems. First, in progressive state governments like New York and then in the federal government, voters and reform organizations such as the National Civic League demanded merit-based HRM. The assassination of newly inaugurated President Garfield by an unsuccessful office-seeker in 1881 was a defining event that led Congress to approve the **Pendleton Act** (1883), marking a fundamental shift from patronage to merit systems.[3] The principles in Table 1-2 reflect the civil service

TABLE 1-2 Merit System Principles[4]

1. Recruitment should be from qualified individuals from appropriate sources in an endeavor to achieve a workforce from all segments of society, and selection and advancement should be determined solely based on relative ability, knowledge and skills, after fair and open competition that assures that all receive equal opportunity.
2. All employees and applicants for employment should receive fair and equitable treatment in all aspects of personnel management without regard to political affiliation, race, color, religion, national origin, sex, marital status, age, or handicapping condition, and with proper regard for their privacy and constitutional rights.
3. Equal pay should be provided for work of equal value with appropriate consideration of both national and local rates and by employers in the private sector, and appropriate incentives and recognition should be provided for excellence in performance.
4. All employees should maintain high standards of integrity, conduct, and concern for the public interest.
5. The workforce should be used efficiently and effectively.
6. Employees should be retained based on the adequacy of their performance; inadequate performance should be corrected; and employees who cannot or will not improve their performance to meet required standards should be separated.
7. Employees should be provided effective education and training in cases in which such education and training would result in better organizational and individual performance.
8. Employees should be:
   a. protected against arbitrary action, personal favoritism, or coercion for partisan political purposes.
   b. prohibited from using their official authority or influence for interfering with or affecting the result of an election or a nomination for election.
9. Employees should be protected against reprisal for the lawful disclosure of information which the employees reasonably believe as evidences:
   a. a violation of any law, rule or regulation.
   b. mismanagement, a gross waste of funds, an abuse of authority, or a substantial and specific danger to public health or safety.

ideal—the belief that a competent, committed workforce of career civil servants is essential to the professional conduct of the public's business.[5]

While the Pendleton Act affirmed that merit principles were the basis for making public personnel decisions, the tools to achieve these in reality did not emerge until the application of **scientific management** principles to administration during the 1920s. The cornerstone of public personnel management was position classification—grouping jobs by occupational type and skill level and paying them equitably based on the competencies needed to perform the job. It translates labor costs (for pay and benefits) into impersonal grades that can be added, subtracted, averaged, and moved about to create organizational charts. The legislature or the chief executive can limit personnel expenses to the total pay and benefits for all positions. They can set personnel ceilings to limit or preclude hiring. They may assign units an average allowable position grade, thus ensuring that they will not become top heavy. It clarifies career ladders and aids in the recruitment, selection, training, and assessment processes by specifying duties and qualifications for each position. More than any other personnel function, it epitomizes the connection between efficiency and the elimination of politics from administration, and suggests that public personnel management can be conducted in a routine and politically neutral fashion. At the same time, it can minimize political or administrative abuse and protect **individual rights**. Each employee's job duties are specified in his or her job description. Pay rates are tied to positions so individual favorites cannot be paid more than others can. Thus, hiring people at a high salary and asking them to assume few if any responsibilities—something that occurs frequently in **political patronage systems**—is minimized.

Intense conflict sometimes marks the relationship between political patronage and civil service systems because both represent powerful and legitimate values. For example, the tremendous economic, military, and social problems confronting the United States during the New Deal and World War II (1933–1945) brought about the emergence of **administrative effectiveness**, which combines administrative efficiency with **political responsiveness**. This combination required that civil service personnel cover most positions, but that political appointees fill sensitive or policy-making positions. It resulted in programs consistent with elected officials' philosophy and vision of government, and with administrators' ability to make operational plans and manage resources efficiently. Inevitably, this hybrid of politics and efficiency created strains in the merit-based model of public personnel management. The merit model viewed public HRM as a neutral administrative function; the effectiveness model viewed it as a management-oriented function under the direction of the executive branch.

Given the obvious need for politically responsive agency management, one might wonder why merit system advocates are so paranoid about protection from political influence.[6] The reason is that despite elected officials' assertions in support of merit system values, frequent incidents indicate that they consider political loyalty the most important criterion for selection regardless of the consequences. Thus, merit system proponents have learned to be extremely vigilant in detecting and preventing harassment or discharge of political appointees for reasons that seem to be based more on politics than on performance. A recent controversy was Attorney General Alberto Gonzalez' forced resignation (2007) over the Justice Department's alleged discharge of several U.S. Attorneys General for investigative or prosecutorial policies that ran counter to the White House's partisan political interests.[7]

We can view much of the history of public personnel management as efforts to reconcile civil service and patronage systems at an operational level. The Pendleton Act (1883) created the civil service system at the federal level, leading eventually to the development and implementation of civil service systems for a majority of professional and technical positions. The **Civil Service Reform Act (CSRA) of 1978**, passed almost a century later, was designed to maintain bureaucratic responsiveness but still protect the career civil service from political interference. It created a **Senior Executive Service (SES)** of high-level administrators who voluntarily elected to leave their civil service positions in return for multi-year performance contracts, in exchange for the possibility of higher salaries and greater career challenge and flexibility. Recognizing the fundamental conflict between protecting employee rights and maintaining management oversight over personnel policies within federal agencies, the CSRA split the old U.S. Civil Service Commission into two agencies, the **Merit Systems Protection Board (USMSPB)**, and the **Office of Personnel Management (USOPM)**. The MSPB is responsible for hearing appeals from employees alleging that their rights under civil service system laws and rules have been violated;[8] the OPM is responsible for developing, implementing, and evaluating personnel policies within federal agencies. However, in recent years, a number of federal agencies have sought and received OPM exemptions from Title V of the U.S. Code (which captures the federal government's personnel regulations) to create civil service systems designed with their own agency's needs in mind.

Collective Bargaining and Affirmative Action Systems

Under collective bargaining, contracts negotiated between management and unions set the terms and conditions of employment. This is in contrast to the patronage system, where they are set and operationally influenced by elected officials, or the civil service system, where they are set by law and regulations issued by management and administered by management or an outside authority (such as a civil service board). Public sector collective bargaining has many of the same procedures as its private sector counterpart, such as contract negotiations and grievance procedures. However, fundamental differences in law and power outweigh these similarities. Public sector unions never have the right to negotiate binding contracts with respect to wages, benefits, or other economic issues. This is because only legislative bodies (such as the city council, school board, or state legislature) have the authority to appropriate money to fund contracts. Therefore, both labor and management realize that ratification of negotiated contracts is more critical than negotiation of them and set their political strategies accordingly. Civil service systems include all public employees covered by collective bargaining agreements.

During the same period, **affirmative action systems** arose as a direct result of the civil rights movement of the 1960s and the women's rights movement of the 1970s. They represented the value of social equity through recruitment and selection practices to correct the underrepresentation of veterans, minorities, and women in the workplace. They reflected the fundamental beliefs that a **representative bureaucracy** was essential for government to function as a democracy; and that other personnel systems had not been effective at ensuring this.[9] In fact, all these systems had perpetuated—often inadvertently and always for different reasons—the dominance of white males in public employment. Because most elected officials are white males, appointment of white males to patronage jobs has been the rule. Because white males traditionally have had greater access to higher education and job experience, merit systems have tended to perpetuate the exclusion of women and minorities. The seniority systems favored by collective bargaining tend to perpetuate these biases.

TWO EMERGENT SYSTEMS: PRIVATIZATION AND PARTNERSHIPS

Privatization emerged as an identifiable public HRM system at the end of the 1970s when Jimmy Carter campaigned against public agencies and employees as a Washington "outsider." Following his election, he proposed the Civil Service Reform Act of 1978 on grounds that included poor performance in the public service and difficulty in controlling and directing bureaucrats. Beginning in 1981, the Reagan administration, though it held fundamentally different values and policy objectives, continued to cast government as part of the problem. Consequently, increasing reliance on market-based forces rather than on program implementation by government agencies and employees as the most efficacious tools of public policy marked this paradigm shift. The emphasis on economic perspectives and administrative efficiency reflected the intense pressures on the public sector to "do more with less." This caused governments to become more accountable through such techniques as program budgeting, management by objectives, program evaluation, and management information systems. It also resulted in efforts to lower expenditures through tax and expenditure ceilings, deficit reduction, deferred expenditures, accelerated tax collection, service fees and user charges, and a range of legislative and judicial efforts to shift program responsibilities and costs away from each affected government.

Because most public expenditures are for employee salaries and benefits, efforts to increase accountability and cut costs focused on HRM functions. The shift continued the trend set in previous eras such as the 1930s and the 1960s, emphasizing program outputs and rationally tying program inputs to outputs (e.g., program budgeting, HR forecasting, job evaluation, management by objectives, objective performance appraisal, training needs assessment, cost-benefit analysis, and gain sharing/productivity bargaining). Moreover, the information systems revolution expanded access to information formerly used by management for coordination and control, resulting in organizational restructuring and the downsizing of mid-managerial positions.

The 1990s brought continued efforts to increase government responsiveness and effectiveness, or to "shrink the beast" and put more resources in the hands of individuals and businesses. These were exemplified by Vice President Gore's **National Performance Review**,[10] aimed at creating a government that "works better and costs less" through fundamental changes in organizational structure and accountability, epitomized by the terms "reinventing government" or "New Public Management."[11] These trends decentralized most HR functions to operating agencies and thus reduced OPM's functions and authority; it also reduced federal civilian employment, particularly staff positions (personnel, budget, auditing, and procurement) and middle managers with no direct relationship to productivity increases.

The Republican Party gained control of Congress in 1994 and again in 2002 because of a shift toward three emergent nongovernmental values: personal accountability, limited and **decentralized government**, and **community responsibility** for social services. Proponents of **personal accountability** expect people to make individual choices consistent with their own goals and accept responsibility for the consequences of these choices, rather than passing responsibility for their actions on to society. Proponents of limited and decentralized government believe that people should fear government for its power to arbitrarily or capriciously deprive them of their rights. They also believe that public policy, service delivery, and revenue generation can be controlled more efficiently in a smaller unit of government. Some want to reduce the size and scope of government because they prefer individual freedom and prefer to spend less of their personal income on taxes.

A belief in community responsibility supplemented this preference for limited and decentralized government and personal accountability. The most significant consequence of this, at least as far as public HRM is concerned, was the delivery of local governments' social services through **nongovernmental organizations** (NGOs) funded by taxes, user fees, and charitable contributions. Third-party social service provision became more complex with an ideologically driven emphasis that directed contracting strategies toward faith-based organizations (FBOs). With the passage of the "charitable choice" component of the Personal Responsibility and Work Opportunity Reconciliation Act of 1996,[12] charitable choice has expanded to include a range of federal programs, such as Temporary Assistance to Needy Families (1996); Welfare-to-Work Formula Grants (1997);[13] Community Services Block Grants (1998);[14] and drug abuse treatment programs (2000).[15] The establishment of the White House

Office of Faith-Based and Community Initiatives and five similar offices in the Departments of Education, Justice, Health and Human Services, Labor, and Housing and Urban Development enabled these federal agencies to contract with **faith-based organizations (FBOs)** nationwide.[16] According to a study conducted by the Rockefeller Institute of Government (2003), this also occurred at the state level.[17] As of the date of that study, 32 states had contracted with FBOs to provide some social services, and eight states had enacted legislation requiring the inclusion of FBOs in contracting. State Departments of Labor also received directives from the U.S. Department of Labor (DOL) office of Faith-Based Initiatives requiring them to develop state DOL strategic plans aimed at increasing the number of FBO grantees by providing these organizations with training and technical assistance as they competed for service provision contracts.

This emerging ***partnerships*** system rests on the same values of personal accountability, limited and decentralized government, and community responsibility for social services that characterized privatization, with an added strategic emphasis on cooperative service delivery among governments, businesses, and NGOs. The partnership paradigm is undergirded by the belief that concrete results in public service delivery can only be achieved by the skilled deployment of human assets regardless of the framework within which it occurs. Its advocates also argue that the deployment of human assets is best accomplished outside of the traditional civil service model or third-party service delivery options. However, two concerns remain. First, reliance on NGOs to deliver public services assumes—often erroneously—that they have the organizational capacity to do so.[18] In addition, using NGOs as contractors can lead to the marketization of the nonprofit sector, thereby weakening the civil society they constitute.[19]

THIRD-PARTY GOVERNMENT AND NONSTANDARD WORK ARRANGEMENTS

While public agencies continue to meet most of their employment needs through traditional **public personnel systems** like civil service, the rise of privatization and partnerships has had a significant impact on the way government agencies deliver public services. Two trends are apparent: (1) **third-party government** (using alternative organizations or mechanisms for providing public services) and (2) **nonstandard work arrangements (NSWA)** such as temporary and part-time employment.

Third-Party Government

Purchase-of-service agreements with other governmental agencies and **NGOs** have become commonplace.[20] They enable counties and larger cities to sell services within a given geographic area, utilizing economies of scale. They offer smaller municipalities a way of reducing capital costs, personnel costs, the political issues associated with collective bargaining, and legal liability risks. Moreover, the use of outside consultants and businesses (hired under fee-for-service arrangements on an "as-needed" basis) increases available expertise *and* managerial flexibility by reducing the range of qualified technical and professional employees that the agency must otherwise hire to provide training.

Privatization may result in the abolition of the agency (sometimes as an intended ideological goal). Privatization offers all the advantages of service purchase agreements but holds down labor and construction costs on a larger scale. Privatization has become commonplace in areas such as solid waste disposal, where there is an easily identifiable "benchmark" (standard cost and service comparison with the private sector), and where public agency costs tend to be higher because of higher pay and benefits.[21]

Franchise agreements often allow private businesses to monopolize a previously public function within a geographic area, charge competitive rates for it, and then pay the appropriate government a fee for the privilege. Examples are cable TV and private jitneys as a public transit option. Municipalities often encourage the procedure because it reduces their own costs, provides some revenue in return, and results in a continuation of a desirable public service.

Subsidy arrangements enable private businesses to perform public services funded by either user fees from clients or cost reimbursement from public agencies. Examples are airport security operations (provided by private contractors and paid for by both passengers and airlines), some types of hospital care (e.g., emergency medical services provided by private hospitals and reimbursed by public health systems), and housing (subsidizing rent in private apartments occupied by low-income residents as an alternative to public housing projects).

Vouchers enable individual recipients of public goods or services to purchase them from competing providers on the open market. Under proposed educational voucher systems, for example, parents would receive a voucher that could be applied to the cost of education for their child at competing institutions (public or private), as an alternative to public school monopolies.

Volunteers provide contributed services otherwise performed by paid employees, if any. These include neighborhood crime watch programs operated in cooperation with local police departments, tutoring by volunteer teachers' aides in many public schools, and community residents who volunteer services as individuals, or through churches and other nonprofit service agencies. Frequently, such contributions are required to "leverage" a federal or state grant of appropriated funds. Although they would probably not consider themselves volunteers, inmates are often responsible for laundry, food service, and prison facilities maintenance.

Regulatory and **tax incentives** are typically used to encourage the private sector to perform functions that might otherwise be performed by public agencies with appropriated funds. These include zoning variances (for roads, parking, and waste disposal) granted to condominium associations. In return, the condominium association provides services normally performed by local government (security, waste disposal, and maintenance of common areas).

Nonstandard Work Arrangements

Increasingly, public employers reduce costs and enhance flexibility by supplementing full-time civil service hiring with temporary or part-time employees.[22] A main though often unstated reason for the use of these contingent workers is that they are not included in the "head count" of agency employees, giving the appearance of reducing the agency's workforce.[23] They *usually* receive lower salaries and benefits than their career counterparts and are *certainly* unprotected by due process entitlements or collective bargaining agreements.[24] Conversely, where commitment and high skills are required on a temporary basis, employers may seek to save money or maintain flexibility by using contract or leased employees to positions exempt from civil service protection. While contracts may be routinely renewed with the approval of the employee and the employer, employees may also be discharged at will in the event of a personality conflict, a change in managerial objectives, or a budget shortfall. Managerial and technical employees hired into these types of contracts usually receive higher salaries and benefits than can be offered to even highly qualified civil service employees, and they allow management to trim personnel costs easily if necessary, without having to resort to the bureaucratic chaos precipitated by the exercise of civil service "bumping rights" during a layoff.

CONSEQUENCES OF PRIVATIZATION AND NSWA

Civil Service Reform in the States

Several state governments have attempted to combine the advantages of traditional civil service employment with those of third-party government and NSWA. We have seen two types of reforms: *modernization*, meaning incremental structural and technical reforms to improve government performance, and *radical reform*, meaning wholesale efforts to dismantle existing civil service systems and replace them with systems more like those found in the private sector.[25] Hays and Sowa describe and classify each state's reform experience by comparing the degree of centralization, number of at-will employees, the range of grieveable issues, gubernatorial activism, and perceived decline in job security.[26] Based on their assessment, most states, including Arizona,[27] California,[28] New York,[29] South Carolina,[30] and Wisconsin,[31] have reformed incrementally. Several states have introduced reforms that are more radical:

- In 1996, Georgia mandated "at-will" status for all new state employees, decentralization of authority for personnel policy and administration, and a new performance management system built largely on performance-based pay.[32]
- In 2001, Florida initiated "Service First," a comprehensive effort to change the civil service by reforming recruitment, classification and compensation, and performance appraisal. It moved supervisors from classified to unclassified status and substituted "at-will" employment for "just cause job termination" on the assumption that effective and efficient government required business practices.[33]
- In 2000, Texas mandated at-will employment for civil service employees, with some exceptions, as part of a general movement toward decentralization and deregulation.[34]

The choice of criteria used to evaluate reform outcomes in state civil service systems is controversial because both practical and ideological objectives drive reform pressures for a range of actors with different objectives and perspectives.[35] It is probably necessary to assess reforms by considering the answers from a range of stakeholders (elected and appointed officials, personnel directors, supervisors, public employee unions, and affirmative action directors) along the operational criteria defined by the following questions:

- Have reforms made state agencies more responsive administratively to political leadership without significantly lowering their resistance to patronage pressures?
- Have reforms allowed managers greater flexibility and discretion without significantly eroding employee rights, affirmative action, and collective bargaining?
- Have reforms increased employee performance without significantly diminishing agencies' ability to attract and retain those motivated by public service values?[36]

Most published research differentiates incremental and radical **civil service reform**. It uniformly concludes that incremental reform is a normal and positive response to continued pressure to increase government performance. Furthermore, it generally concludes that radical civil service reforms have not significantly increased in agency responsiveness, managerial flexibility, and discretion or employee performance. Alternatively, based on both evidence and ideology, such research concludes that reforms have been done only at the cost of increased agency vulnerability to patronage pressures, eroding employee rights, affirmative action and collective bargaining, or diminishing agencies' ability to attract and retain highly qualified employees motivated by public service values.[37]

However, these are the conclusions of public administration scholars who uniformly support traditional civil service values and systems. Outside the university, there is broad ideological support for at-will employment because the public desires to keep government under the control of elected officials. Beyond occasional newspaper reports and anecdotal evidence, there is little statistical support for the hypothesis that at-will employment means a return to patronage politics. As public employment has changed to include alternative service delivery through private businesses and NGOs, it has become more efficient to maintain political responsiveness via contracts and privatization rather than individual patronage appointments. The sheer size and complexity of government agencies, combined with freedom of information and the Internet, makes coordinated efforts to politicize entire bureaucracies much less likely to succeed. Finally, as career employment and civil service protection become scarcer, public and private employment differences begin to blur so that at-will employment is no longer an issue. Younger workers may anticipate that their career paths will involve a number of different jobs with different organizations in different sectors.

Effects on Traditional Values and Systems

Increased reliance on third-party government and NSWA has implications not only for the delivery of government services, but also for the values that underlie traditional public HRM.

The new strategies diminish employee rights. It is likely that employees hired under NSWA will receive lower pay and benefits and will be unprotected by civil service regulations or collective bargaining agreements.[38] It seems logical to assume that as the criteria for success become more arbitrary or capricious, civil service employees—particularly those in mid-management positions—will begin to behave more like the political appointees whose jobs depend on political or personal loyalty to elected officials.[39]

The new strategies diminish social equity.[40] Recent research has shown that women and minorities experience lower rates of wage discrimination (another variation of equal pay for equal work) in the public sector when controlling for factors such as age and education. This is probably the result of equal pay for equal work, as well as promotional and advancement opportunities in the public sector. Managerial consultants are overwhelmingly white and male. Many part-time and temporary positions are exempt from laws prohibiting discrimination against persons with disabilities or family medical responsibilities.

These strategies have had a mixed impact on agency efficiency. On the plus side, the change in public agency culture toward identifying customers and providing market-based services increases productivity. In addition, the threat of privatization or layoffs has forced unions to agree to pay cuts, reduced employer-funded benefits, and changes in work rules.[41]

However, these emergent systems may actually increase some personnel costs, particularly those connected with employment of independent contractors, reemployed annuitants, and **temporary employees**.[42] **Downsizing** may eventually lead to higher recruitment, increased orientation and training costs, and loss of organizational memory and "core expertise" necessary to manage service contracting or privatization initiatives effectively.[43] Maintaining minimum staffing levels also results in increased payment of overtime and higher rates of accidents and injuries. As the civil service workforce shrinks, it is also aging. This means unforeseen increases in pension payouts, disability retirements, workers' compensation claims, and health-care costs. Outsourcing makes contract compliance, rather than traditional supervisory practices, the primary control mechanism over the quality of service. This creates a real possibility of fraud and abuse.[44]

Emerging then is an HRM framework that embraces both the management of control and collaboration, which is paradoxical, exposing the underlying tensions inherent in the values of monitoring (compliance) and empowerment (outcomes). Debates over the desire to maintain control mechanisms associated with traditional civil service systems (risk adversity) and the strategic attractiveness of responsiveness and managerial empowerment (stewardship) illustrate these tensions. Yet increasingly, research calls for understandings that move beyond either/or thinking.[45] Ambiguity and turbulence increase demands for a paradoxical approach to human resource management—one that embraces the simultaneous need for control and collaboration.

Opposing and interwoven elements are evident throughout government as citizens and public officials struggle with the coexistence of authority and democracy, efficiency and creativity, and freedom and control.[46] The new HR paradigm may be increasingly about the management of both control and collaboration and, more critically, about developing understandings and practices that accept, accommodate, and even encourage these tensions.[47] For example, state government agencies are increasingly using a model of collaborative social service provision and approaches for addressing social problems. These often involve overlapping partnerships with various public sector organizations and a recognition that the complexity of social issues is in part due to their residence within an interorganizational framework and that these problems cannot be tackled by any organization acting alone.[48] These new and often confusing organizational relationships suggest that HR managers will need to not only manage control and collaboration simultaneously but also become much more sophisticated in the competencies needed to work across organizational boundaries.[49] In the 1980s, the common mantra was "government must become more like business" by becoming more productive and efficient. Today, it is equally common to affirm, "Business must become more like government" in terms of accountability, transparency, and public sector ethics.[50]

The impact of third-party government on political responsiveness is problematic. The emergent values and systems place much less importance on the role of national government because the first value (**individual accountability**) reduces the role of government in society. If we view public problems as the results of individuals' personal choices, then the responsibility for dealing with the consequences of these problems is individual rather than societal. Downsizing and decentralization reduce the comparative importance of government in society and refocus governmental activity from a national to a state and local level. Continual budget cuts and pressure to "do more with less" result in agencies that are budget driven rather than mission driven. Moreover, budget-driven agencies that address public problems with short-term solutions designed to meet short-term legislative objectives are not likely to be effective. Long-range planning, or indeed any planning beyond the current budget cycle, is likely to become less important. Agencies will not be able to do effective capital budgeting or to adequately maintain capital assets (human or infrastructure).

CONFLICT AND COMPROMISE AMONG ALTERNATE PERSONNEL SYSTEMS

Historically, U.S. public HRM systems developed in evolutionary stages that are analytically separate but in practice overlapping. In the era of *privilege* (1789–1828), the small group of upper-class property owners who had won independence and established the national government held most public jobs. As this generation passed, an era of *patronage* emerged (1829–1882) during which public jobs were awarded according to political loyalty or party affiliation. Next, the increased size and complexity of public activities led to an era of *professionalism* (1883–1932) that defined public HRM as a neutral administrative function to emphasize modernization through efficiency and **democratization** by allocating public jobs, at least at the federal level, on merit. The unprecedented demands of a global depression and World War II led to the emergence of a hybrid *performance* model (1933–1964) that combined the political leadership of patronage systems and the merit principles of civil service systems. Next, social upheavals (1965–1980) presaged the emergence of the *people* era, in which collective bargaining emerged to represent collective employee rights, and affirmative action emerged to represent social equity. General dissatisfaction with government led to *privatization* and other business-based HRM solutions in the 1980s, followed by *partnerships* with NGOs and other contractors as third-party tools for public service delivery.

Because resources are limited, jobs allocated through one system cannot be allocated through others. Thus, advocates of each system strive to minimize the influence of others, often using defining events to increase pressure for change. For example, the assassination of President Garfield in 1881 directly related to the Pendleton Act in 1883. As another more contemporary example, the terrorist attacks on the World Trade Center and the Pentagon on September 11, 2001, dramatically increased the importance of safety (rather than cost or convenience) as the public's prime objective. This led to the amalgamation of many federal agencies into the U.S. Department of Homeland Security. It also led to the creation of many public jobs (in the Department of Defense and the Transportation Safety Agency) and to demands that these jobs be filled outside the traditional federal civil service system.[51]

However, carried to its extreme, each value creates distortions that limit the effectiveness of human resource management because other values are suppressed. The key here is that each value is fundamental to American political culture. The ascendancy of one at the expense of others distorts administrative processes. Responsiveness carried to extremes results in the hiring of employees solely based on patronage, without regard for other qualifications, or in the awarding of contracts based solely on political considerations (**kickbacks** and **corruption**). Efficiency, carried to extremes, results in over-rationalized personnel procedures—for example, going to decimal points on test scores to make selection or promotion decisions, or making the selection process rigid in the belief that systematic procedures will produce the "best" candidate. **Individual rights** carried to extremes result in overemphasis on seniority or on due process and rigid disciplinary procedures. Social equity carried to extremes results in personnel decisions being based solely on group membership, disregarding individual merit or the need for efficient and responsive government. Moreover, we might expect that antigovernment values carried to extremes would eventually result in the emergence of a society dominated by markets rather than communitarian values or the public policy-making process. The weaknesses of market models—primarily their inability to address distributive equity or indivisible public goods—act to limit reliance on service contracting, privatization, user fees, and other business mechanisms.

Under ideal circumstances, public personnel management would reflect a combination of values associated in complementary ways. In reality, attempts by each system or value to dominate lead inevitably to stabilizing reactions and value compromises. For example, it is often hard to distinguish between political appointments and those resulting from civil service or affirmative action systems because hiring authorities rarely would choose a manager or professional based solely on one value. Over time, personnel systems will reflect the dominant values in a particular jurisdiction. The more stable the values, the more permanent the personnel systems and practices will become and the more dominant the influence of that culture on the organization. Stable personnel systems reflect the political cultures they operate in. Table 1-3 below presents the six stages of evolution, the dominant values and systems at each stage, and the pressures leading to the next stage of evolution.

BUILDING GOVERNANCE CAPACITY[52]

Governance capacity is the ability of public, private, and nongovernmental organizations to work together toward economic development in the context of political, social, and environmental sustainability. Because the rule of law is essential to maintaining these governance coalitions, and because government alone exercises authoritative power through the rule of law, **government capacity** (making good policy decisions and using scarce resources effectively) is the key to development. Government capacity—or the lack thereof—is perhaps the most obvious factor affecting perceptions of governance. In developed countries, governance usually means *maintaining* government's ability to coordinate policy, gather information, deliver services through multiple (often nongovernmental) partners, and replace hierarchical bureaucracies with more flexible mechanisms for managing indirect government. In developing countries, it probably means *establishing* government's ability to deliver vital public services (through core administrative functions like budgeting, human resource management, and program evaluation), while simultaneously focusing on more fundamental changes (e.g., citizen participation, decentralization, innovation, and entrepreneurial leadership) necessary for effective political systems.

Building Public HRM Capacity

Public HRM systems are of course not unique to the United States. Other developed Western countries have merit systems that vary based on history and other conditions.[53] The process of building public HRM capacity in developing countries is relatively uniform because pressures for modernization and **democratization** tend to parallel though lag behind those in the Western world; administrative reforms are introduced by Western consultants or exposure to the West; and Western lenders often mandate administrative reforms as a condition of continued credit.[54]

TABLE 1-3 The Evolution of Public HRM Systems and Values in the United States

Stage of Evolution	Dominant Value(s)	Dominant System(s)	Pressures for Change
Privilege (1789–1828)	Responsiveness/Representation	"Government by founding fathers"	Political Parties + Patronage
Patronage (1829–1882)	Responsiveness/Representation	Patronage	Modernization + Democratization
Professionalism (1883–1932)	Efficiency + Individual Rights	Civil Service	Responsiveness + Effective Government
Performance (1933–1964)	Responsiveness/Representation + Efficiency + Individual Rights	Patronage + Civil Service	Individual Rights + Social Equity
People (1965–1979)	Responsiveness/Representation + Efficiency + Individual Rights + Social Equity	Patronage + Civil Service + Collective Bargaining + Affirmative Action	Dynamic equilibrium among four competing values and systems
Privatization (1980–now)	Responsiveness/Representation + Efficiency + Individual Accountability + Limited government + Community Responsibility	Patronage + Civil Service + Collective Bargaining + Affirmative Action + Alternative Mechanisms + Flexible Employment Relationships	Dynamic equilibrium among four progovernmental values and systems, and three antigovernmental values and systems
Partnerships (2002–now)	Responsiveness/Representation + Efficiency + Individual Accountability + Limited Government + Community Responsibility + Collaboration	Patronage + Civil Service + Collective Bargaining + Affirmative Action + Alternative Mechanisms + Flexible Employment Relationships	Dynamic equilibrium among four progovernmental values and systems, three antigovernmental values and systems

In the first stage, the *elite leaders* of successful independence movements establish new nations. The transition to a second stage (*patronage*) follows as these emergent nations strive to strengthen the conditions in civil society that underlie effective government (such as education, political participation, economic growth, and social justice) by refining their constitutions, developing political parties, and creating public agencies. This transition is often difficult.[55]

The third stage, if it occurs, is a transition from patronage to *merit systems* marked by passage of a civil service law, creation of a civil service agency, and development of personnel policies and procedures. It happens due to internal pressures for efficiency (modernization) and human rights (democratization). Often, international lenders and donor governments add external pressures that emphasize government capacity, transparency, and citizen participation.

If the transition to civil service occurs, developing countries then seek to balance conflicting values and personnel systems to achieve the contradictory objectives that characterize the fourth stage of public personnel management. They must establish an optimum level of public employment, maintain administrative efficiency and protect public employee rights, and achieve both uniformity and flexibility of personnel policies and procedures.

Table 1-4 shows the dominant values and systems at each stage of this evolutionary process, and the pressures for change that lead to evolution from one stage to the next.

The Impact of Contextual Variables on National Development

Adoption of innovations that improve government capacity is a complex process that is heavily influenced by contextual variables related to time orientation; sovereignty and capacity; empowerment and accountability; and adaptability, flexibility, and incrementalism.

- *Time orientation.* Successful innovation diffusion and adoption, even under favorable circumstances, usually takes years, and often decades. Thus, organizational commitment to policy objectives usually extends beyond the involvement of any one program director or elected official.
- *Sovereignty and capacity.* In many cases, innovation diffusion and adoption takes place in **fragile states** where either sovereignty or capacity may be problematic. Creating new national sovereignty is different from, and harder than, building government capacity.
- *Empowerment and accountability.* Successful organizational change relates to empowerment and accountability. Empowerment is the increased ability of the poor to make political, social, or economic choices, and to act on those choices. This ties with accountability because it relates to result-oriented and customer-focused applications of New Public Management to managing development programs. The key to both is to develop a multilateral development assistance plan and a multinational, multi-institutional framework for financing development over a long period of time all supported by a participative and client-centered development management process.

TABLE 1-4 Evolution of Public Personnel Systems and Values in Developing Countries

Stage of Evolution	Dominant Value(s)	Dominant System(s)	Pressures for Change
One	Responsiveness/Representation	"Government by elites"	Political Parties + Patronage
Two	Responsiveness/Representation	Patronage	Modernization + Democratization
Three	Efficiency + Individual Rights	Civil Service + Patronage	Responsiveness + Effective Government
Four	Responsiveness/Representation + Efficiency + Limited Government	Patronage + Civil Service + Collective Bargaining + Privatization	Dynamic equilibrium among pro- and antigovernmental values and systems

- *Adaptability, flexibility, and incrementalism.* The more a policy decision is imbued with values, the less applicable the rational method, where inputs cannot be quantified as accurately. While theoreticians look for an all-encompassing model, a practitioner might find other processes to be more efficacious.[56] Although problems seem similar across nations, types of solutions that are effective in one context may not succeed in another political, economic, or social setting. The composition of the critical mass of stakeholders is specific to the context and may not be generalized for application elsewhere beyond a few observations. "Smart practice" development program administration is not so much a toolkit of ideal practices as an operational guideline that emphasizes reducing mechanisms and factors that inhibit adaptation to contingency.[57]

"Wicked Problems": Culture, Circumstance, and Power

FAVORABLE POLITICAL CULTURE In the United States, the public HRM system developed through successive (and successful) fights against the excesses of patronage, and against social pressures to be the "employer of last resort," in a well-developed economy that provides ample jobs outside government. Although our conflicts with corruption, cronyism, and nepotism are not completely resolved, we do expect that government will provide services efficiently, using honest and qualified employees. Exceptions generate cynicism or indignation precisely because they *are* exceptions. If they were the norm, they would not be news. Nor would they generate reform pressures to make government more honest or efficient.

It took us over two centuries to develop an effective balance between patronage and civil service. It is not reasonable or appropriate to insist that developing countries make this transition easily or quickly. Patronage politics characterized public personnel management at all levels in the United States until at least 1900. It continues today in many governments. In some levels and sectors of government it may not be a major issue; but cynics would respond that patronage is less serious only because it has been replaced by corrupt contracts as a more effective means of exchanging campaign contributions for access to public officials.[58]

FAVORABLE HISTORICAL CIRCUMSTANCES The development of U.S. public personnel management has occurred within a context of almost two centuries of democratic government under a single Constitution and within a civil society widely considered controlled by laws rather than by individuals. Though our policy-making process is costly, complex, and tortuous, it results in outcomes that are generally considered to be transparent, effective at maintaining government authority, and politically responsive to the will of the electorate. Our tax system functions well, in spite of (or because of) its voluntary nature. While our society is deeply affected by conflicts based on race, ethnicity, and class, it provides great opportunity for personal growth and economic advancement. Our political and administrative processes are generally open to public scrutiny thanks to laws facilitating access to records by the press and public.

POWER By every meaningful economic, political, and military measure, the United States is the most powerful country in the world. This power largely exempts us from influence by other nations or international agencies. Indeed, our power is so great that we can either ignore these organizations (as we characteristically do with the United Nations) or use them as instruments to accomplish our own international economic and political objectives (as we do with the World Bank and the International Monetary Fund).

By contrast, factors beyond their control may make it difficult for less developed countries to establish conditions of statehood that we in the United States take for granted: a national identity, the rule of law, and a self-sufficient economy. Even the development of stable patronage systems may be hampered by societal conditions (e.g., nonfunctional justice systems, inability to meet even minimum standards of education and health care, political leadership based on "cults of personality" rather than on true pluralist political parties, and overly centralized and authoritarian political systems).[59] These conditions generally impede the evolution of rational administrative structures and systems.[60] For example, organizations in many less developed countries share common structural and managerial attributes that differ from those typically found in North America, Europe, and Japan: *low* levels of role specialization, formalism, and morale, and *high* levels of centralization, paternalism, authoritarian leadership, rigid stratification, and dysfunctional conflict.[61]

Clearly the most significant difference between the evolution of public personnel management in the United States and in developing countries today is that we in this country were able to first progress from patronage to civil service, second integrate them into an effectiveness model that combined efficiency and patronage, third integrate affirmative action and collective bargaining into the mix, and finally establish the boundaries between public personnel management and emergent market-based techniques like privatization and service contracting.[62] By contrast, fledgling personnel systems in less developed countries are likely to face obstacles—pressure for patronage; underpaid and poorly qualified civil servants; and inadequate public program planning, budgeting, management, and evaluation. A less developed country that has successfully moved from patronage to civil service still faces pressure from unions and the emergent middle class for high levels of public employment, *and* pressure from lenders to reduce public employment and favor export-oriented agriculture, mining, and logging activities over the domestic industries and services needed to achieve economic and social development. As hard as this evolution has been for us, think how much harder it is for developing countries to establish functional civil service systems, combat patronage, deal with politically powerful unions, and balance demands for contracting and divestiture from international lenders and corporations.[63] How well would we have done if we had had to develop in the same way, facing these conflicts simultaneously rather than sequentially?

Table 1-5 shows the factors that affect public personnel systems.

Building Governance Capacity through Reciprocal Technology Transfer

In a world focused on building networked governance capacity, it is best to act on the principle that **technology transfer**—the diffusion and adoption of innovations from their place of origin to other geographic areas and policy settings—is a reciprocal exchange between producers and consumers.[64] Therefore, a final lesson for us in the United States is that many public HRM innovations come from outside the country.[65] The U.S. experience with "reinventing government" owes much to the neoliberalism of Margaret Thatcher in England.[66] Many recent suggestions for Social Security reform are derived from the market-based public employee pension systems long used in Chile;[67] students of race relations in the United States are intrigued by South Africa's structural and behavioral transition from apartheid toward democratic pluralism;[68] and democratic theorists study the high rate of political participation in Costa Rica, achieved through political education in schools, youth elections, and literacy. As we seek to innovate, and to "do more with less," it is always wise to consider what we can learn from others as well as what they can learn from us.

TABLE 1-5 How Country Conditions Affect Public Personnel Systems

Negative Indicators	Positive Indicators
1. TRANSITION FROM INDEPENDENCE TO A FUNCTIONAL PATRONAGE SYSTEM	
Negative Indicators	**Positive Indicators**
• High reliance on charismatic leadership	• Stable political parties
• Restricted freedom of speech and press	• Open information and free media
• High emphasis on export of agricultural products and raw materials	• Balanced, domestically focused economic growth, including professional/technical
• Capital flight	• Domestic reinvestment of capital
• Repression based on race, ethnicity, or class	• Some social justice
• Inadequate electoral process	• Functioning electoral process
2. TRANSITION FROM PATRONAGE TO A FUNCTIONAL CIVIL SERVICE SYSTEM	
Negative Indicators	**Positive Indicators**
• Government process considered low on effectiveness, rationality, and transparency	• Government process considered high on effectiveness, rationality, and transparency
• Widespread patronage appointments, and job retention based on salary "kickbacks"	• Civil service law, public personnel agency, and policies and procedures
• High unemployment or underemployment	• Low unemployment or underemployment
• Public sector the "employer of last resort"	• Balanced economic growth/development
• Underpaid, underqualified employees	• Adequately paid, qualified civil service
• Widespread employment discrimination based on race, gender, or ethnicity	• Low level of employment discrimination based on race, gender, or ethnicity
• High degree of administrative formalism	• Low degree of administrative formalism
• High role of the military in civil society and government	• Reduced role of the military in civil society and government
• Reforms due mainly to international economic and political pressure	• Reforms due mainly to domestic political, social, and economic pressure
3. TRANSITION BEYOND CIVIL SERVICE TO A MATURE PUBLIC PERSONNEL SYSTEM	
Negative Indicators	**Positive Indicators**
• Overrigidity, uniformity, and centralization of HRM policies and practices	• Balance of flexibility/rigidity, centralization and decentralization, and uniformity and variation
• Overemphasis on employee rights or on managerial efficiency	• Balance between employee rights and managerial efficiency
• Over- or underemployment in the public sector	• Balanced public and private employment

Summary

We can view public HRM from several perspectives. First, it is the *functions* (planning, acquisition, development, and discipline) needed to manage human resources in public agencies. Second, it is the *process* for allocating public jobs as scarce resources. Third, it reflects the influence of seven symbiotic and competing *values* (political responsiveness/representation, efficiency, individual rights, and social equity under the traditional progovernmental paradigm; and individual accountability, downsizing and decentralization, and community responsibility under the emergent privatization and partnerships paradigms) over the criteria and process for allocating public jobs. Fourth, it is the *systems* (laws, rules, and procedures) used to express these abstract values—political appointments, civil service, collective bargaining, and affirmative action under the traditional model; and alternative mechanisms and flexible employment relationships under the emergent paradigms of privatization and partnerships.[69]

Conceptually, we can view U.S. public HRM as a historical process through which new systems emerge to champion emergent values, are integrated with the mix, and are in turn supplemented—neither supplanted nor replaced—by their own successors. From a practical perspective, this means that public HRM is laden with the contradictions in policy and practice resulting from these often unwieldy and unstable combinations of values and systems, and is fraught with the inherent difficulties of utilizing competitive and collaborative systems to achieve diverse goals. Civil service is the predominant public HRM system because it has articulated rules and procedures for performing the whole range of HRM functions. Other systems, though incomplete, are nonetheless legitimate and effective influences over one or more HRM functions.

The evolution of public personnel management in developing countries reflects a process similar and yet different from that we are familiar with in the United States. On the one hand, pressures for modernization and democratization tend to parallel though lag behind those in the Western world; Western consultants introduce administrative reforms; and Western lenders often mandate them as a condition of continued credit. On the other hand, each country's administrative systems and innovations reflect its own history, culture, and conditions. Yet beyond this, most developing countries face the difficult prospect of developing civil service systems to move past patronage, curbing the power of politically influential unions while maintaining employee rights, and achieving the benefits of privatization while avoiding its pitfalls.

Key Terms

administrative effectiveness *7*
affirmative action systems *8*
Civil Service Reform Act of (1978) *7*
civil service (merit) system *5*
civil service reform *13*
collective bargaining *5*
community responsibility *9*
corruption *15*
decentralized government *9*
democratization *15*
downsizing *14*
efficiency *15*
employee rights *4*
faith-based organizations (FBOs) *10*
fragile states *18*
franchise agreements *11*
governance capacity *16*
government capacity *16*
human resource management (HRM) *3*
individual accountability *14*
individual rights *7*
kickbacks *15*
merit system *5*
Merit Systems Protection Board (USMSPB) *7*
National Performance Review *9*
nongovernmental organizations (NGOs) *9*
nonstandard work arrangements (NSWA) *10*
Office of Personnel Management (USOPM) *7*
partnerships *10*
Pendleton Act (1883) *5*
personnel management *3*
planning, acquisition, development, sanction (PADS) *4*
Plum Book 5

political patronage system *7*
political responsiveness *4*
political representation *4*
privatization *8*
public personnel systems *10*
purchase-of-service agreements *10*
regulatory incentives *11*
representative bureaucracy *8*
scientific management *6*
Senior Executive Service (SES) *7*
social equity *4*
spoils system *5*
subsidy arrangements *11*
tax incentives *11*
temporary employees *14*
technology transfer *20*
third-party government *10*
values *4*
vouchers *11*

Discussion Questions

1. Identify and describe the four public personnel management functions (PADS).
2. Why are public jobs scarce resources? What is the significance of this observation?
3. What are the four competing values that have traditionally affected the allocation of public jobs? What three nongovernment values that have emerged recently conflict with them?
4. What is a personnel system?
5. Identify and describe the four traditional competing public personnel systems. What are the two emergent antigovernment personnel systems that have recently been added to them?
6. Why is it possible to trace the development of public personnel management as conflict and symbiosis among alternative personnel systems?
7. How would you evaluate state civil service reform efforts in Florida, Georgia, and Texas?
8. In what respects is the evolution of public personnel management in developing countries similar to and different from its evolution in the United States? Why?
9. What can we learn from other countries that might help us with our own HRM issues?
10. As responsible public administrators and public personnel managers, what can we do to promote the development of rational and transparent government, at home and abroad?

Exercise: Values and Functions in Public HRM

Identify the appropriate value(s), systems, and functions in these examples. Explain your choices.

1. A state is going to fill a vacancy in its community development agency. The state representative who controls the appropriations committee for all legislation involving the agency has suggested that an applicant from her district fill a high-level position in the civil service. A major contributor to the governor's reelection campaign contends that a prominent real estate developer should fill the job. Neither candidate has the education or experience specified as desirable in the job description.
2. A federal agency is considering a layoff. It anticipates a budget shortfall that is going to require cutbacks in personnel since the legislature has shown no indication that it is willing to raise taxes. The agency director has suggested that it compute a layoff score for each employee, based primarily on the person's performance appraisal. The Federation of Employees, which is the recognized bargaining agent for the agency's employees, strongly objects and proposes that the layoffs be based on seniority.
3. A county anticipates a request by surrounding cities to provide water services for all county residents. This will require upgrading the skills of a substantial number of county employees and will provide those employees with opportunities for advancement. The union insists that the training

slots be allocated to current employees on a seniority basis. The affirmative action officer, seeing this as an opportunity to increase the number of minorities in higher paying positions, proposes to set aside several of the openings for current minority employees.

4. A city government is looking for ways to reduce costs. The city commission amends its charter to remove the sanitation department from the civil service system. This in effect nullifies the collective bargaining agreement between the city and its unionized sanitation employees. The city lays off all these employees and instead contracts for solid waste services provided by an outside private contractor.
5. A state government closes many of its public parks and recreation areas because prison construction has taken an increasing share of state revenues and caused corresponding budget cuts in many other state agencies. It has increased user fees at others, in an effort to generate revenues sufficient to keep the parks open. The three results from this are all predictable. The number of visitors at state parks and recreation areas declines as higher user fees exclude many people. Those visitors that do come to the parks complain increasingly about inadequate facilities and maintenance. Finally, attendance and profits at private recreation theme parks (Disney World, Busch Gardens, etc.) increases dramatically.

Case Study: Political Clearance for "Buck" Pleake

Reaction against political patronage systems focused at the federal level in 1883 when the assassination of newly elected President Garfield by a disappointed job seeker caused an outpouring of criticism against the inefficiencies of the spoils system. Nevertheless, patronage remained a powerful force at the state and local levels, especially in agencies like corrections, public works, transportation, and county sheriff. During the 1970s and 1980s, newly elected officials routinely fired the patronage employees appointed by their predecessors and replaced them with their own appointees. They received their jobs for having supported the newly elected official's candidacy—and sometimes because of an informal commitment to "voluntarily" return a percentage of their salaries as a direct political contribution, or as a disguised contribution through the purchase of tickets to political dinners or other fund-raising events.

Although elected officials and other supporters of patronage systems defended the contributions as voluntary, in reality employees who quit contributing risked losing their jobs, because local party leaders declined to give them the political clearance they needed to certify their loyalty for the patronage position. This is what happened to "Buck" Pleake, a long-time Indiana State employee who had to reapply for political clearance to retain his job. In fact, the requirement was impossible to meet and was imposed deliberately because he had chosen to test the "voluntary" nature of the campaign contributions required of all employees by ceasing to contribute.

After reading the background information on the case, answer the following questions.

1. Was "Buck" Pleake's political contribution voluntary or involuntary?
2. Why did the Indiana State Employees Association raise the issue with the Governor?
3. What were the governor's conflicting responsibilities in the case? How did he resolve them?
4. What is the proper balance between competencies and political or personal loyalty in determining suitability for a government job? Why?
5. What has been the relationship between the political, social, and economic conditions in the United States and our evolution toward more diverse and elaborate public personnel systems?
6. To what extent is this U.S. experience comparable with that of the developing countries?

STATE of INDIANA

INDIANAPOLIS

INDIANA STATE HIGHWAY COMMISSION
100 North Senate Avenue
Indianapolis, Indiana 46204

Greencastle, Indiana
November 8, 1974

Jewell M. Pleake
RR #1
Stilesville, Indiana

Dear Sir,

In compliance with the Indiana employee's patronage system, requiring patronage clearance, I requested on October 4, 1974 and again on October 9, 1974, that you return to me a completed patronage form.

As you have not complied with my request, I am notifying you on instructions from John Harlan, District Administrative Officer, effective November 12, 1974, that your employment, as shop foreman, from the Greencastle sub-district garage, Crawfordsville district, Indiana State Highway Commission, has terminated.

Yours truly,

Harold Baire

Harold Baire, Superintendent
Sub-District Garage
Greencastle, Indiana

cc: Thomas Milligan
Judson Dutton
Paul Green
Kelsey McDaniels

POLITICAL ENDORSEMENT – INDIANA REPUBLICAN STATE COMMITTEE
(This is not an application for employment)

Dept. ____________________

Name ____
(Last) (First) (Middle Initial)

Address ____
(Street or Route) (City or Town) (Zip)

County __________ Twp. __________ Precinct __________ Cong. Dist. __________

Telephone __________ Birth Date __________ Political Party __________

Did you vote in the last Primary election? ______ If so, in what county? __________

Signature ______________________________ Date __________

Endorsements

(2) Precinct Comm. __________ (1) Vice Comm. __________

(4) Twp. or Ward Chr. __________ (3) Vice Chr. __________

(6) County Chr. __________ (5) Vice Chr. __________

(7) State Chr. __________

Jewell Venice Pleake
R. R. #1
Stilesville, Indiana

Your application for political clearance has been processed and approved by the Indiana Republican State Central Committee.

THIS CARD MAY BE USED AS PROOF OF POLITICAL CLEARANCE.

MAR 14 1973

INDIANA STATE EMPLOYEES ASSOCIATION, INC.

632 ILLINOIS BUILDING, 17 WEST MARKET STREET, INDIANAPOLIS, INDIANA 46204 • (317) 632-7254

November 13, 1974

Governor Otis R. Bowen, M.D.
State House
Indianapolis, Indiana 46204

Dear Governor Bowen:

I am taking this opportunity to correspond with you at some length because I believe we have a matter that deserves your personal attention. I am not sure in my own mind that this matter has been brought to your attention, although I have attempted to proceed through regular channels, including Mr. William Lloyd, your Executive Assistant.

While I could complain about the many instances of what we believe to be outright harassment of state highway employees, one particular case illustrates the problem very well and raises some profound questions. I am referring to the case of Jewell V. ("Buck") Pleake, formerly an employee of the Greencastle sub-district of the Crawfordsville District of the Indiana State Highway Commission.

Buck Pleake had been employed with the ISHC for some six years. Being promoted up to the position of Shop Foreman, Buck has proven himself to be a dependable, conscientious employee and one who is well-respected among his peers. We have encountered nothing in Highway Department records or in our discussions with Highway officials that would make us believe otherwise.

On October 4, 1974, Buck was suddenly given a new set of "Patronage Clearance" papers and told to have them completed by the following Monday--an action which requires no less than eight signatures be obtained. I will not attempt to detail all that occurred to Buck as he tried to comply. Perhaps I can illustrate how ludicrous the affair became if you can picture Buck waiting outside the Operating Room of a local hospital to get his county vice-chairperson, Mrs. Swisher, to sign. Mrs. Swisher, a nurse, was apparently very put out by the whole affair and would not sign the form and directed they be left for her to deal with later. The clearance papers did not surface again for almost two weeks. As he attempted to obtain the signatures, it became increasingly clear to Buck that he had been singled out because he was not paying "2%." Finally, Mr. Paul Green, the Sixth District Chairman, flatly refused to sign, saying that Mr. Pleake had already been replaced. On November 11, 1974, Buck received a letter notifying him he was officially terminated from his employment. His termination was solely based on his failure to complete these new clearance papers.

Lest I forget, Buck was "cleared" for his job when first employed six years ago and he also received a postcard from Republican State Central Committee in March, 1973, indicating he was "recleared" since the change to your Administration. The postcard said that it was proof of clearance. It has become very apparent to us that Buck's recent attempt at reclearance and subsequent discharge was directed by Tom Milligan, the Republican State Chairman. Mr. Milligan has been publicly quoted as saying that employees should be fired if they don't pay their "2%," job performance notwithstanding.

This situation frankly raises doubts in my mind as to who is the final authority in running the Highway Commission, a state governmental agency. The entire chain of events leads me to believe the political party runs the state Highway Commission, not the officials who were elected and appointed to do so. In these days of Watergate backlash, I am distressed to see such a situation allowed to persist. We have been told continually through this chain of events that the decisions were left in the hands of others and that even the District Engineer could not resolve the problem, but rested with the District and State Chairmen.

More important is the fact that your commitment has been that "job retention should be based on the ability to perform adequately and the quality of the work done." I quote from your letter to me dated September 27, 1974, at which time you also indicated that any employee political contributions should be strictly voluntary.

Mr. Pleake's job promotions and previous political clearance speak for themselves and would leave only this recent decision not to pay 2% as the sole reason behind this effort by the State Republican Chairman and may in fact alienate a dedicated Republican such as Mr. Pleake, and others as well. It also raises the question of integrity on the part of the Republican State Central Committee who issued a "proof of clearance" to Mr. Pleake in March 1973.

Governor, if the precedent is allowed to stand that an employee is at any time subject to sudden "reclearance" in order to keep his job, then we have both done a disservice to the employees. If the criterion upon which job retention is based is politics or contribution, I foresee morale dropping to an all-time low in state government. In the Highway Department, where the problem is particularly acute, many will begin to abandon their employment at the earliest possible opportunity, for they will know that even if they do their job well, they will never be secure. This is particularly disturbing to me, now that the important period of snow and ice removal is fast upon us.

I honestly believe the situation to be very critical. At the same time, I have considerable confidence in your ability to govern and I appreciate the many fine things that have been accomplished to better state service during your tenure. I request that you give this situation your personal and immediate attention.

Sincerely,

Charles F. Eble

Charles F. Eble
Executive Secretary, ISEA

P.S. - This situation also involves Mr. Pleake's son.

cc: Bose, McKinney & Evans

CFE:pvt

OFFICE OF THE GOVERNOR
INDIANAPOLIS, INDIANA 46204

OTIS R. BOWEN, M. D.
GOVERNOR

November 14, 1979

Mr. Charles F. Eble
Executive Secretary
Indiana State Employees Association, Inc.
417 Illinois Building
17 West Market Street
Indianapolis, Indiana 46204

Dear Mr. Eble:

Attached is a memo that I am sending out today to all department heads and to the Republican State Chairman.

Sincerely,

Otis R. Bowen, M.D.
Governor

ORB:vw

TO: All Department Heads
Mr. Thomas S. Milligan

FROM: Otis R. Bowen, M.D.
Governor

RE: 2% Contributions

DATE: November 14, 1974

Rumors and accusations are coming to my attention that threats of firing and replacements are being made to patronage employees.

I want to reiterate what I have said publicly several times:

> "Job retention should be based on the ability to perform adequately and the quality of work done."

ORB:vw

OFFICE OF THE GOVERNOR
INDIANAPOLIS, INDIANA 46204

OTIS R. BOWEN, M. D.
GOVERNOR

September 27, 1974

Charles F. Eble
Executive Secretary
Indiana State Employees Association, Inc.
417 Illinois Building
17 West Market Street
Indianapolis, Indiana 46204

Dear Mr. Eble:

Thank you very much for your recent letter and the resolution. Please express my thanks to the members of your association. I appreciate your kind remarks and hope that encouragement of voluntary contributions be continued. I feel that everyone has an obligation to support the political party and perhaps those who are employed by government directly or indirectly as a result of political activity have a little more obligation than others not so employed.

Once again, I emphasize that my remarks and my letter and my attitude are that it should be voluntary and that I make no threats whatsoever concerning job retention being dependent upon contributions. Job retention should be based on the ability to perform adequately and the quality of the work done.

Kindest personal regards,

Otis R. Bowen, M.D.
Governor

ORB:lkd

Notes

1. The General Accountability Office (GAO) (2008). *The Plum Book (United States Government Policy and Supporting Positions).* Available at: www.gpoaccess.gov/plumbook/index.html (accessed on April 13, 2009).
2. The White House (2009). *Appointments.* Available at: http://www.whitehouse.gov/appointments/ (accessed on April 13, 2009).
3. US-INFO (2006). A history of federal civil service. *Biography of an ideal.* Available at: http://www.opm.gov/BiographyofAnIdeal/ (accessed on February 23, 2008).
4. Civil Service Reform Act of 1978. P.L. 95-454, October 13, 1978.
5. Heclo, H. (1977). *A government of strangers.* Washington, DC: The Brookings Institution.
6. Sayre, W. (1948). The triumph of techniques over purpose. *Public Administration Review, 8*: 134–137; and Fisher, J. (1945). Let's go back to the spoils system. *Harper's, 191*: 362–368.
7. Jost, K. (June 22, 2007). Has the Justice Department become too politicized? *The CQ Researcher, 17* (24): 553–576.
8. West, William F., and Robert F. Durant (2000). Merit, management, and neutral competence: Lessons from the U.S. Merit Systems Protection Board, FY 1988-FY 1997. *Public Administration Review, 60* (2): 111–122.
9. Mosher, F. (1982). *Democracy and the public service* (2nd ed.). New York: Oxford University Press.
10. National Performance Review (1993). *From red tape to results: Creating a government that works better and costs less. Executive summary.* Washington, DC: US GPO; and National Performance Review (1993). *Reinventing human resource management: Accompanying report of the National Performance Review.* Washington, DC: US GPO.
11. Osborne, D., and T. Gaebler (1992). *Reinventing government: How the entrepreneurial spirit is transforming the public sector.* Reading, MA: Addison Wesley Longman.
12. Personal Responsibility and Work Opportunity Reconciliation Act of 1996, H.R. 3734, 104th Congress, 2nd Session.
13. Welfare-to-Work program, adopted in 1997 as an amendment to The Personal Responsibility and Work Opportunity Reconciliation Act of 1996 (PRWORA).
14. Community Services Block Grant Program, Reauthorization Act of 1998 (P.L. 105-285).
15. Community Services Block Grant Program for Mental Health and Drug Treatment Program. The Children's Health Act (2000). Substance Abuse and Mental Health Services Administration, Washington, DC.
16. Executive Order 13198. Agency Responsibilities With Respect to Faith-Based and Community Initiatives. *Federal Register* 66FR 8497 (1/31/01); Executive Order 13280. Responsibilities of the Department of Agriculture and the Agency for International Development With Respect to Faith-Based and Community Initiatives. *Federal Register* 67, 77145 (12/16/02).
17. Rockefeller Institute of Government (2003). *The public benefit of private faith: Religious organizations and the delivery of social services.* Albany, NY: Rockefeller IOG.
18. Frederickson, Patricia, and Rosanne London (May/June 2000). Disconnect in the hollow state: The pivotal role of organization capacity in community-based development organizations. *Public Administration Review, 60* (3): 230–239.
19. Eikenberry, Angela, and Jodie Kluver (2004). The marketization of the nonprofit sector: Civil society at risk? *Public Administration Review, 64* (2): 132–140.
20. Kosar, Devin (2006). *Privatization and the federal government: An introduction.* Washington, DC: Congressional Research service; O'Looney, John A. (1998). *Outsourcing state and local government services: Decision-making strategies and management methods.* Greenwood, CT: Greenwood Publishing Group; and Martin, Lawrence L. (2002). *Contracting for service delivery: Local government choices.* Washington, DC: International City/County Management Association.
21. Siegel, Gilbert B. (March 1999). Where are we on local government service contracting? *Public Productivity and Management Review, 22* (3): 365–388; O'Looney, John (1998). *Outsourcing state and local government services: Decision making strategies and management methods.* Westport, CT: Greenwood; and Martin, Lawrence L (1999). *Contracting for service delivery: Local government*

choices. Washington, DC: International City/County Management Association.

22. Mastracci, Sharon H., and James R. Thompson (2005). Nonstandard work arrangements in the public sector: Trends and issues. *Review of Public Personnel Administration, 25*: 299ff; and Brown, Judith (April 2005). Flexible working arrangements can be a legal landmine. *IPMA-HR News*, p. 1ff.
23. Light, Paul (1999). *The true size of government*. Washington, DC: The Brookings Institution.
24. Houseman, S. (2001). Why employers use flexible staffing arrangements: Evidence from an establishment survey. *Industrial and Labor Relations Review, 55*: 149–170.
25. Selden, Sally C. (2006). Classifying and exploring trends in state personnel systems. In J. E. Kellough and L. G. Nigro (Eds.). *Civil service reform in the states: Personnel policies and politics at the subnational level*. Albany, NY: State University of New York Press, pp. 59–76.
26. Hays, Stephen W., and Jessica E. Sowa (2006). A broader look at the "accountability" movement: Some grim realities in state civil service systems. *Review of Public Personnel Administration, 26* (2): 102–117.
27. Cayer, N. Joseph, and Charles Kime (2006). Human resources reform in Arizona—A mixed picture. In J. Edward Kellough and Lloyd Nigro (Eds.). *Civil service reform in the states: Personnel policies and politics at the subnational level*. Albany, NY: SUNY Press, pp. 239–257.
28. Naff, Katherine (2006). Prospects for civil service reform in California: A triumph of technique over purpose? In J. Edward Kellough and Lloyd Nigro (Eds.). *Civil service reform in the states: Personnel policies and politics at the subnational level*. Albany, NY: SUNY Press, pp. 259–278.
29. Riccucci, Norma (2006). Civil service reform in New York: A quiet revolution. In J. Edward Kellough and Lloyd Nigro (Eds.). *Civil service reform in the states: Personnel policies and politics at the subnational level*. Albany, NY: SUNY Press, pp. 303–313.
30. Hays, Stephen, Chris Byrd, and Samuel Wilkins (2006). South Carolina's human resource management system: The model for states with decentralized personnel systems. In J. Edward Kellough and Lloyd Nigro (Eds.). *Civil service reform in the states: Personnel policies and politics at the subnational level*. Albany, NY: SUNY Press, pp. 171–201.
31. Fox, Peter, and Robert Lavigna (2006). Wisconsin state government: Reforming human resources management while retaining merit principles and cooperative labor relations. In J. Edward Kellough and Lloyd Nigro (Eds.). *Civil service reform in the states: Personnel policies and politics at the subnational level*. Albany, NY: SUNY Press, pp. 279–302.
32. Nigro, Lloyd, and J. Edward Kellough (2006). Civil service reform in Georgia: A view from the trenches. In J. Edward Kellough and Lloyd Nigro (Eds.). *Civil service reform in the states: Personnel policies and politics at the subnational level*. Albany, NY: SUNY Press, pp. 117–144; and Nigro, Lloyd, and J. Edward Kellough (2006). The states and civil service reform: Lessons learned and future prospects. In J. Edward Kellough and Lloyd Nigro (Eds.). *Civil service reform in the states: Personnel policies and politics at the subnational level*. Albany, NY: SUNY Press, pp. 315–324.
33. Bowman, James, Jonathan P. West, and Sally Gertz (2006). Radical reform in the sunshine state. In J. Edward Kellough and Lloyd Nigro (Eds.). *Civil service reform in the states: Personnel policies and politics at the subnational level*. Albany, NY: SUNY Press, pp. 145–170.
34. Coggburn, Jerrel (2006). At-will employment in government: insights from the state of Texas. *Review of Public Personnel Administration, 26* (2): 158–177; and Coggburn, Jerrel (2006). The decentralized and deregulated approach to state human resources management in Texas. In J. Edward Kellough and Lloyd Nigro (Eds.). *Civil service reform in the states: Personnel policies and politics at the subnational level*. Albany, NY: SUNY Press, pp. 203–237.
35. Battaglio, R. Paul, and Stephen Condrey (2006). Civil service reform: Examining state and local government cases. *Review of Public Personnel Administration, 26* (2): 118–138; Kearney, Richard (2006). The labor perspective on civil service reform in the states. In J. Edward Kellough and Lloyd Nigro (Eds.). *Civil service reform in the states: Personnel policies and politics at the subnational level*. Albany, NY: SUNY Press, pp. 77–93; and Lindquist, Stephanie, and Stephen Condrey (2006). Public employment reforms and constitutional due

process. In J. Edward Kellough and Lloyd Nigro (Eds.). *Civil service reform in the states: Personnel policies and politics at the subnational level.* Albany, NY: SUNY Press, pp. 95–114.

36. Jackson, Oscar (May 2007). Public servants and public service. *IPMA-HR News*, pp. 1ff.
37. Kellough, Edward, and Lloyd Nigro (2006). Personnel policy and public management: The critical link. In J. Edward Kellough and Lloyd Nigro (Eds.). *Civil service reform in the states: Personnel policies and politics at the subnational level.* Albany, NY: SUNY Press, pp. 1–10.
38. Hsu, Spencer (September 4, 2000). Death of "big government" alters region: Less-skilled D.C. workers lose out as area prospers. *Washington Post*, p. A1+.
39. Brewer, Gene, and Robert A. Maranto (2000). Comparing the roles of political appointees and career executives in the U.S. Federal executive branch. *American Review of Public Administration, 30* (1): 69–86.
40. Wilson, George (2006). The rise of at-will employment and racial inequality in the public sector. *Review of Public Personnel Administration, 26* (2): 178–188.
41. Cohen, S., and W. Eimicke (1994). The overregulated civil service. *Review of Public Personnel Administration, 15* (1): 11–27.
42. Peters, B. Guy, and Donald J. Savoie (1994). Civil service reform: Misdiagnosing the patient. *Public Administration Review, 54*: 418–425.
43. Milward, H. Brinton (1996). Introduction: Symposium on the hollow state: Capacity, control, and performance in interorganizational settings. *Journal of Public Administration Research and Theory, 6* (4): 193–197.
44. Moe, Ronald C. (1987). Exploring the limits of privatization. *Public Administration Review, 47*: 453–460.
45. Drummond, H. (1998). Is escalation always irrational? *Organization Studies*, 19: 911–929; and Kisfalvi, V. (2000). The threat of failure, the perils of success and CEO character: Sources of strategic persistence. *Organization Studies, 21*: 611–639.
46. Lewis, M. (2000). Exploring paradox: Toward a more comprehensive guide. *Academy of Management Review, 25*: 760–776.
47. Soni, Vidu (2004). From crisis to opportunity: Human resource challenges for the public sector in the twenty-first century. *Review of Policy Research, 21* (2): 157–178.
48. Savas, Emanuel S. (2000). *Privatization and public–private partnerships.* New York: Chatham House.
49. Halley, A. (1997). Applications of boundary theory to the concept of service integration in the human services. *Administration in Social Work, 21* (3/4): 145–168.
50. Price, T. (August 3, 2007). Corporate social responsibility. *The CQ Researcher,* 17 (28): 649–672.
51. Underhill, Jack, and Ray Oman (2007). A critical review of the sweeping federal civil service changes: The case of the departments of Homeland Security and Defense. *Review of Public Personnel Administration, 27* (4): 401–420; Naff, Katherine, and Meredith Newman (2004). Symposium: Federal civil service reform: Another legacy of 9/11? *Review of Public Personnel Administration, 24* (3): 191–201.
52. Klingner, Donald (2006). Diffusion and adoption of innovations: A development perspective. In Guido Bertucci (Ed.). *Innovations in governance and public administration: Replicating what works.* New York: UN/DESA/DPADM, pp. 55–60.
53. Hirsch, Darryl (November 1999). *Merit systems in Western Democracies #1: An introduction to merit in Canada, the United States, Britain, Australia, and New Zealand.* Ottawa, ON: Research Directorate, the Public Service Commission of Canada.
54. Salgado, Rene (1997). *Public administration for results: Choice, design and sustainability in institutional development and civil service reform.* DPP Working Paper Series No. 106. Washington, DC: Interamerican Development Bank.
55. Collier, Paul (2007). *The bottom billion.* New York: Oxford University Press.
56. Hood, Christopher, and B. Guy Peters, with Grace O. M. Lee (Eds.) (2003). *Reward for high office: Asian and Pacific rim states.* London: Routledge.
57. Bardach, Eugene (2000). *Practical guide for policy analysis: The eightfold path to more effective problem solving.* New York: Chatham House; and Jones, Larry and Donald Kettl (2003). Assessing public management reform in an international context. *International Public Management Review, 4* (1): 1–16.
58. Darrough, Masako N. (2000). Privatization and corruption: Patronage vs. spoils. *International Public Management Journal, 2* (2): 273–298.

59. Klingner, Donald E. (December 2000). South of the border: Problems and progress in implementing new public management reforms in Mexico today. *American Review of Public Administration, 30* (4): 365–373.
60. Ruffing-Hilliard, Karen, in Ali Farazmand (1991). Merit reform in Latin America: A comparative perspective. *Handbook of comparative and development public administration.* New York: Marcel Dekker, pp. 301–312.
61. Kettl, Donald (1997). The global revolution in public management: Driving themes, missing links. *Journal of Policy Analysis and Management, 16* (3): 446–462.
62. Klingner, Donald E., and Mohamed G. Sabet (2006). Contemporary public human resource management: Patronage, civil service, privatization, and service contracting. In Krishna Tummala (Ed.). *Encyclopedia of life support systems.* New York: UNESCO.
63. Kearney, Richard C., and Steven W. Hays (Fall 1998). Reinventing government: The new public management and civil service systems in international perspective. *Review of Public Personnel Administration, 18* (4): 38–54.
64. Rogers, Everett (2003). *The diffusion of innovations* (5th ed.). Glencoe: The Free Press.
65. Klingner, Donald, and Charles W. Washington (January 2000). Through the looking glass: Realizing the advantages of an international and comparative approach for teaching public administration. *Journal of Public Affairs Education, 6* (1): 35–43.
66. Savoie, Donald J. (1990). Public management development: A comparative perspective. *International Journal of Public Sector Management,* 3: 40–52.
67. Mesa-Lago, Carmelo (1996). Pension reform in Latin America: Importance and evaluation of privatization approaches. In William Glade (Eds.). *Bigger economies, smaller governments: The role of privatization in Latin America.* Boulder, CO: Westview Press, pp. 89–134; and Gunter Nagel, S. (1997). Developments in social security systems: Reflections on the work of the Council of Europe in this field. *International Review of Administrative Sciences, 63* (2): 225-243.
68. Perkins, Edward J. (1990). New dimensions in foreign affairs: Public administration theory in practice. *Public Administration Review, 50* (4): 490–493; and Harrison-Rockey, Samantha (1999). What state has been reached in the reform and transformation of the structures and systems of government? The case of South Africa. *International Review of Administrative Sciences,* 65 (2): 169–182.
69. Klingner, Donald E. (2006). Societal values and civil service systems in the United States. In J. E. Kellough and L. G. Nigro (Eds.). *Civil service reform in the states: Personnel policies and politics at the subnational level.* Albany, NY: SUNY Press, pp. 11–32.

CHAPTER 2

Doing Public HRM in the United States

Because public HR management is conceptually similar around the world, researchers and administrators may try to develop and apply uniform "best practice" solutions to build global governance capacity.[1] However, these efforts are usually unsuccessful because local conditions (cultural, economic, political, and social) profoundly influence the sustainable adaptation of HR innovations from one context to another.[2] This means that while the first chapter could focus on conceptually uniform HRM functions, values, and systems, a practical textbook must focus more specifically on what HR is in context. Because those who study and practice public HRM in the United States comprise the primary audience of this book, that country will be the focus of our analysis.

Five issues dominate a contextual discussion of public HRM in the United States:

- Now and historically, how many public employees are there? Which agencies and which levels of government employ them? How has the increased use of third-party government and contingent workers affected public employment? What are the realities of public employment as opposed to the myths used to reinforce alternative values and systems?
- Personnel managers and the technical specialists they supervise do only a small part of HRM. Others share this responsibility: elected officials establish policies and fund systems; appointed officials design systems; and personnel managers develop policies and procedures. However, managers and supervisors utilizing HR policies, rules, and practices to accomplish organizational goals perform most human resources management daily. How do they work together in practice?
- Those performing the shared roles that comprise public HRM work in a variety of personnel systems. How do the patterns of law and policy that characterize each system affect HRM practice in a given organization?
- How do these shared HRM roles and functions translate into *structures and administrative behavior* in a given organization?
- How do the evolving values and systems described in Chapter 1 affect the *roles and competencies*, and therefore the experience and training, required of those who aspire to careers in public HRM as either specialists or general public administrators?

By the end of this chapter, you will be able to:

1. Discuss the myths and realities of public employment in the United States.
2. Explain how elected and appointed officials, managers and supervisors, and personnel directors and specialists share responsibility for public HRM functions.
3. Describe how systems affect public HRM functions in practice.
4. Describe some design dilemmas faced in public personnel systems.
5. Discuss contemporary HRM role expectations for elected and appointed officials, HR directors and specialists, and managers.
6. Understand the four key HRM roles: technician, professional, educator, and mediator.
7. Describe the technical, ethical, and professional competencies needed for a career in public HRM and tell how to get them.

PUBLIC EMPLOYMENT IN THE UNITED STATES: MYTHS AND REALITIES

While the national government predominates in many countries, state and local governments predominate (based on employment and spending) in the United States because of both state constitutional powers and a decentralized political culture. There are 3,033 counties in the United States—all states except two have county governments. In 2007, there were 36,011 subcounty, general-purpose governments in the United States, including cities, towns, and municipalities.[3] There are also 14,451 school districts and over 37,000 other special districts (e.g., hospitals, airports, and fire protection).

In the public's view, federal employees often symbolize government bureaucracy. However, in reality this level constitutes only about 13 percent of all public employees. Federal government employment peaked at 3.4 million during World War II, receded to 2.0 million in 1947, and rose again to 2.5 million in 1951. After fifteen years of minor fluctuations, federal employment gradually rose again to 3.1 million in 1987. It began to decline again in 1990, reaching a current level of 2.7 million in 2006,[4] about the same level as in 1966.[5] Both state and local government employment have grown steadily since World War II. In 2005, there were 5.1 million state and 13.9 million local employees.[6] Table 2-1 shows these trends.

TABLE 2-1 Government Civilian Employment, 1940–2005[7]

	EMPLOYEES (IN MILLIONS)[a]			
Year	**Total**	**Federal**	**State**	**Local**
1940	4.4	1.1	3.3	
1950	6.4	2.1	1.1	3.2
1960	8.8	2.4	1.5	4.9
1970	13.0	2.9	2.8	7.4
1980	16.2	2.9	3.8	9.6
1990	18.4	3.1	4.5	10.8
2000	20.9	2.9	4.9	13.1
2005	21.7	2.7	5.1	13.9

[a]Federal, state, and local number may not add to "Total" due to rounding.

TABLE 2-2 Government Employment by Function and Level of Government, 1997[8]

Function	Total	%	Federal	%	State, Local, Other	%
Total	19,540	100	2,807	14	16,733	86
Education	8,969	46	11		8,958	46
Hospitals	1,223	6	163	1	1,060	5
Health	548	3	136	1	412	2
Public Welfare	507	3	9		498	3
Social Insurance Administration	165	1	69		96	
National Defense	777	4	777	4	0	
Space Research & Technology	20		20		0	
Police	951	5	95	1	856	4
Fire Protection	356	2	0		356	2
Corrections	709	4	30		679	4
Postal Service	854	4	854	4	0	
Transportation	666	4	67		599	4
Natural Resources	397	2	191	1	206	1
Parks & Recreation	354	2	24		330	2
Housing & Community Development	141	1	18		123	1
Sewerage	129	1	0		129	1
Solid Waste Management	115	1	0		115	1
Financial Administration	533	3	139	1	394	2
Judicial and Legal Administration	419	2	53		366	2
Other Government Administration	406	2	22		384	2
Water Supply	318	2	0		318	2
Electric Power	158	1	0		158	1
Gas Supply	20		0		20	
Transit	388	2			388	2
All other	417	2	129	1	288	1

These 21.7 million public employees work in a variety of functions. The primary federal functions are national defense, postal service, and financial management. The primary state and local functions are education, police protection, highways, corrections, welfare, and utilities. Education is by far the predominant state and local government function, comprising more than half of state and local public employment (see Table 2-2).[9]

SHARED RESPONSIBILITY FOR PUBLIC HRM

Three groups share responsibility for public HRM: **elected and appointed officials**, personnel directors and specialists, and other managers and supervisors. Political leaders (legislators, executives, and their political appointees) are responsible for creating agencies, establishing their program priorities, and authorizing their funding levels. Because pay and benefits constitute the largest part of agency budgets, personnel departments cannot design jobs or fill positions until elected officials do their jobs. In addition, although the same general functions (PADS) are required regardless of which

TABLE 2-3 Shared Responsibility for Personnel Functions

FUNCTION	LEVEL		
	Elected and Appointed Officials	**Managers and Supervisors**	**Personnel Directors and Specialists**
Planning	Estimate revenues; set program priorities	Manage to mission within a budget	Develop job descriptions, implement pay and benefit plans
Acquisition	Influence values that guide the selection process	Hire and fire employees	Develop hiring rules and procedures
Development	Define agency and program goals and priorities	Make sure employees have clear goals, skills, feedback, and rewards	Develop training and evaluation systems
Sanction	Determine appropriate personnel systems	Counsel and discipline employees and policies	Develop policies and programs for drug testing, discipline

systems dominate HR policy and practice, political leaders must designate and authorize the personnel system. For example, Congress passed legislation, which the President approved, permitting the then newly created Department of Homeland Security to create its own personnel system, independent of the existing federal system.

Once this happens, **personnel directors and specialists** design and implement personnel systems or direct and help those who do. In civil service systems, they usually work within a personnel department that functions as an administrative staff support service for *managers and supervisors*. These are responsible for achieving agency goals within a prescribed budget and personnel ceilings. HR directors both help administrators use human resources effectively and constrain their personnel actions within limits imposed by political leaders, laws, and policies.

Administrators and supervisors (from first-level supervisors to senior directors) are responsible for the managerial activities most directly connected with goal accomplishment. Supervisors instruct and train employees, provide informal feedback on how they are doing, and recommend pay increases (or disciplinary action and dismissal) based on their assessment of employee job performance. Thus, they implement almost all the rules, policies, and procedures that constitute personnel systems on a day-to-day basis. This is critical because the relationship between employees and their supervisors is the key influence on how effectively employees are developed and used. Effective supervision and effective human resources management go hand in hand, setting the climate, or **organizational culture**, that embodies the organization's HRM policy. Table 2-3 shows how these three groups share HRM responsibilities.

SYSTEMS AFFECT HOW PUBLIC HRM IS DONE

While the basic HRM functions remain the same under all systems we have identified, system values dictate the relative emphasis among functions and how they are performed.

HRM under a Patronage System

Under a patronage system, HRM heavily emphasizes recruitment and selection of applicants based on personal or political loyalty. The other three functions are irrelevant or de-emphasized. The HR specialist is therefore not a personnel director, but instead a political advisor or even a political party official. This person identifies individuals who deserve or require a political position, screens them informally to make sure their personal and political background does not include activities or associations that might embarrass or discredit their boss politically, and then recommends who to hire for which position. The elected official makes the appointment (or nominates the individual, if legislative confirmation is required) based upon the candidate's competencies, political or personal loyalty, financial or campaign support for the elected official, or support by an influential interest group seeking access to the policy-making process. It may be important to nominate and appoint women or minorities as political symbolism, but affirmative action laws do not apply to judicial, legislative, or other patronage positions (**exempt appointments**). Once hired, political appointees are subject to the decisions of the elected official. Few rules govern their job duties, pay, or rights: they serve "at the pleasure of" the appointing authority. Nor is development a priority. They are hired for a current position, not for a career. In many cases, the person appointed may have little or no managerial experience relevant to the job he or she will be filling. Though they may end up serving in a series of progressively responsible political positions, there is no guarantee of that.

HRM in a Civil Service System

In a civil service system, HR is a department or office that supports the city manager, school superintendent, hospital director, or other chief administrator, and in the world of "strategic thinking" about human resources the person serves as a key advisor. Because civil service is a complete system, HRM has a balanced emphasis on each of the four major personnel functions (PADS). Contemporary HRM also means thinking strategically about how these functions fit together to support the objectives elected officials and other **stakeholders** (e.g., managers, employees, and interest groups) have for public agencies.

PLANNING Traditionally, HR maintains the system of position management. The total number of positions, the types of jobs, and their pay levels are established and restricted legislatively by pay and personnel ceilings. Pay is usually tied to the classification system, with jobs involving similar degrees of difficulty being compensated equally. HR completes yearly pay plan updates as budget planning exercises or in anticipation of collective bargaining negotiations. HR develops and updates the agency's retirement and benefits programs and negotiates with benefit providers. It keeps records like eligibility and use of sick leave and vacation time, enrollment and maintenance in various health insurance programs, and life insurance or savings bond purchases. It handles eligibility and processing of retirement requests (including calculation of authorized benefits), disability determinations, and monitors workers' compensation claims for job-related injuries and illnesses. Under more contemporary models that emphasize strategic thinking, the HR department moves beyond position management to productivity measurement and improvement through strategic alignment of human resources with organizational mission and programs. For this to occur, the HR department must focus less on control of personnel inputs and more on measurement and management of HR outputs and outcomes.

ACQUISITION HR schedules periodic tests for frequently available jobs, such as secretary and maintenance worker. It advertises vacant or new positions, reviews job applications for basic eligibility, and gives written tests. It might arrange interviews with applicants, conduct them, and evaluate test results. HR compiles a list of those eligible for employment, keeps it current as some applicants get other jobs, and gives ranked lists of eligible applicants to managers in units with vacancies. After the manager interviews and selects one applicant, HR processes the paperwork required to hire and pay the person. In addition, HR is responsible for establishing and maintaining the databases that enable online posting of positions and hosting of applications.

DEVELOPMENT HR orients new employees to the organization, its work rules and benefits. It tracks and distributes notices of training or transfer opportunities. In some organizations, HR may utilize competencies to establish training programs and to work with agency managers to help design an annual training menu. It may train supervisors and employees concerning newly developed or mandated HR policies and programs. HR also tracks and processes all **personnel actions**—changes in employee status such as hiring, transfer, promotion, retirement, or dismissal.

SANCTION HR establishes and staffs an employee grievance and appeals procedure. It tells supervisors the rules of employee conduct, establishes the steps used to discipline an employee for rule violations, and makes sure the organization follows its own procedures if an employee appeals this disciplinary action or files a grievance. Importantly, HR staff frequently serve as advisors to managers and supervisors considering disciplinary actions. Because merit systems are the only ones that incorporate all four functions, it is hard to imagine a contemporary agency or organization that does not utilize some form of this comprehensive system as its HR core around which other systems can relate.

HRM in Collective Bargaining and Affirmative Action Systems

If employees are covered by a collective bargaining agreement, the personnel department is usually responsible for negotiating the agreement (or hiring an outside negotiator who does this), bringing pay and benefit provisions into accord with contract provisions, training supervisors on how to comply with the contract, and representing the agency in internal grievance resolution or outside arbitration procedures. Because collective bargaining is a partial personnel system, civil service systems continue to provide most of the rules and procedures relating to acquisition and development.

The HR department implements rules emphasizing social equity for protected classes (minorities, women, and persons with disabilities) in recruitment, hiring, and promotion decisions. The affirmative action director shares responsibility with the personnel director in this area. Once members of the protected classes are hired, other personnel systems (civil service or collective bargaining) influence the way planning, development, and sanction functions occur.

Public HRM under Third-Party Government and NSWA

In general, reliance on privatization and contractors reduces public employment, thereby reducing the public HR department's direct workload. However, it increases the indirect work needed to develop, tender, and evaluate contracts. HR directors, staff, and managers work increasingly with citizen volunteers and community-based organizations, much as personnel directors for not-for-profit organizations (such as community recreation programs, hospitals, and schools) have traditionally used volunteers to supplement paid staff. In these cases, public managers need to become more skilled in recruiting, selecting, managing, and motivating volunteer workers.[10]

Use of contingent or contract workers hired under NSWA generally means less emphasis on planning and employee development, at least for these employees. The organization is typically staffed for minimum workload levels, and additional employees are recruited temporarily as needed based on fluctuations in workload. Employee development is largely irrelevant. Contingent workers are hired with the skills needed to perform the job immediately. Performance evaluation is unnecessary—if they do their jobs adequately, they are paid; if not, they are let go at the end of their contract and not called back when workload once again increases.

The sanction function is also less important with respect to these workers. Of course, employers are required to maintain a safe and healthy workplace; but compliance with the Americans with Disabilities Act, the Family and Medical Leave Act, and the Fair Labor Standards Act may not be required for temporary, part-time, or seasonal workers.[11] Nor is it hard, from the employer's perspective, to maintain the terms of the employment relationship. Like political appointees, at-will employees have no right to retain their jobs. They can be discharged for any reason, or no reason, without management having to give a reason or support it.

Hybrid Systems: The Real World of Public HRM

In the real world, political leaders often disagree about which personnel system should predominate. If competing systems have developed and implemented contradictory rules, the public personnel director usually responds to, initiates conflict among, or mediates among competing systems. We have little systematic knowledge about the dynamics of trying to manage multiple personnel systems, some of which exist in contract agencies outside the focal organization. There is a nice example in Chapter 3 of the challenge faced in attempting to integrate different systems—one inside and one outside the focal agency. Effective HR managers must not only be adept at using a range of techniques but also be sensitive to the competing values and systems that influence technical choices. Here are some examples:

- *Civil service.* Fill the position with one of the applicants who placed in the highest category of those qualified for the position.
- *Civil service/political patronage appointment.* Pick the candidate with the most political support from among those applicants at least minimally qualified for the position.
- *Civil service/affirmative action appointment.* Make sure the applicant pool has a sufficient number of women and minorities who meet the minimum qualifications for the position. Then pick either the most qualified applicant or the most qualified minority applicant, depending on the extent of pressure and legal authority to appoint a minority group member.
- *Civil service/collective bargaining appointment.* Fill a promotion or job assignment internally through a bidding process that emphasizes seniority, as specified by the collective bargaining agreement.
- *Civil service/contract appointment.* Reclassify large groups of clerical or technical positions as exempt. Fill them as needed with temporary and part-time workers hired as

independent contractors. Their pay stays the same or increases slightly. They no longer get benefits like sick leave or vacations. The employer no longer has to pay payroll taxes such as worker's compensation or Social Security because these are now the contractor's responsibility.

- *Civil service/contract professional appointment.* Reclassify a vacant position as exempt (outside civil service, filled through an annual employment contract). Offer civil service employees the opportunity to compete for it. The one who takes the job gets a significantly higher salary and an attractive benefit package but no longer qualifies for civil service protection or "bumping rights" back into a classified position in the event of a layoff. Civil servants often retire from their classified positions on Friday and resume work on Monday as contractors performing the same duties in a different type of employment relationship.

Staffing an organization would become agonizingly slow and inefficient if every hiring or promotion decision involved a basic decision about competing systems or rules. While these decision choices are theoretically present in any hiring decision, groups of positions in fact fall under specific personnel systems or decision rules. When the external political context changes, exerting pressure to alter hiring criteria, then the negotiation is over the rules that apply to groups of positions (though the "trigger" event may be a specific vacancy). For example, the George W. Bush administration, through the Office of Management and Budget, asked each federal office to submit an annual report on activities with potential for outsourcing and required "competitive sourcing" wherever possible. This gave the agency the opportunity to bid in competition with private contractors. While this review process was not unique to this administration, its emphasis on the process and its inclusion as one of the core components of his management agenda was.

DESIGN DILEMMAS IN HRM SYSTEMS

While personnel functions (PADS) are uniform, the system that dominates HRM functions has profound effects on their relative importance, organizational location, and method of implementation. Regardless of which system or combination of systems control policy and practice, laws establish and regulate the organizational structure and relationships within which each agency performs public HRM functions. These follow a pattern tied closely to the evolution of personnel systems described in Figures 1-3 and 1-4.

Another design dilemma is centralization versus decentralization. As central civil service agencies mature, they become larger and more specialized. This can lead to delays in providing services to other agencies if rules become more of a hindrance than of a help to service delivery. Because these agencies have developed their own internal personnel departments that assist agency managers and link with the central personnel agency on all requisite functions, these agencies tend to exert pressure for more autonomy. The argument goes, now that the civil service principles are firmly established within the political and administrative culture, it is more efficient and effective to decentralize operational control to these agencies. In addition, in periods of limited hiring where economies of scale do not apply, or tight recruitment markets where fast action on available and interested candidates is essential, pressures for decentralization increase. Under such conditions, the role of the central personnel agency tends to transform from direct responsibility for personnel functions to indirect responsibility and oversight of agencies' HR planning, management, and evaluation efforts. Size matters. In big agencies, HRM may be staffed by hundreds of employees in separate divisions. In small local governments, HR may be only a part of the responsibilities of the chief administrative officer or an assistant.

Public HRM also parallels private sector innovations, because both are responsive to the same changes in available technology, workforce characteristics, and other contextual variables.[12] Public agencies may handle activities like training, pay and benefits administration, or recruitment and selection through "headhunters" or employment services. Or, a jurisdiction may decide to outsource all HR functions and either abolishing the public personnel agency to a system oversight and legal compliance role.[13]

Transitional countries or "fragile states" face a different type of design dilemma. Their leaders may support modern HR systems and methods. However, if the country is culturally, economically, or socially unprepared to support them, matching form and substance in policy and practice can be challenging.[14]

ROLE EXPECTATIONS FOR HR MANAGERS

Just as changes in conditions, values, and systems influence the structure and practice of public HRM, so they affect the role expectations for the three groups who share organizational responsibility for HRM implementation.

Role Expectations for Elected and Appointed Officials

For elected and appointed officials, political responsiveness and representation are the ultimate values in HRM and other public policy areas. Voter discontent with high taxes or inefficient agencies generates political pressure for them to adopt policies that favor privatization, service contracting, and NSWA. This pressure also drives major civil service reforms that have reduced the number of permanent employees. Voter unease at reports of cost overruns at privatized prisons or sexual harassment of inmates by private contractors' employees are likely to make the pendulum swing the other way, resulting in increased political pressure in favor of retaining civil service standards and controls. Regardless, elected officials' decisions reflect public attitudes toward supporting public services or allowing taxpayers to keep their own money and make their own choices as individuals in the private market.

Elected officials therefore want managers and HR professionals to achieve the advantages of each competing system while avoiding their disadvantages. However, limited resources and divided legislative and executive policy responsibilities may lead to uncoordinated policy outcomes. A legislatively approved tuition remission program for all state employees may not be accompanied by sufficient funding for state universities to offer the public administration courses most employees want. An affirmative action plan for new minority employees may be approved at the same time a state budget crisis leads the governor to impose a hiring freeze. So it goes in a democracy.

Role Expectations for HRM Directors and Specialists

Public and political expectations of HRM directors and specialists have evolved over time.

WATCHDOGS During the transition from patronage to merit, public HR managers championed merit system principles because they generally viewed the field as a conflict between good and evil. They considered themselves **"watchdogs,"** responsible for guarding employees, applicants, and the public from the spoils system. This required knowledge of civil service policies and procedures, and the courage to apply them in the face of political pressure.

COLLABORATION During Stage Four (1933–1964), through such tools as personnel ceilings and average grade-level restrictions, public personnel managers helped legislators and chief executives maintain budgetary controls and position management. In effect, they became responsible for synthesizing two distinct values (bureaucratic compliance as the operational definition of organizational efficiency and civil service protection as the embodiment of employee rights).[15] Despite inherent tensions, in time of war, the values of employee rights and organizational effectiveness supported both bureaucratic neutrality and political responsiveness.

CONSULTATION During Stage Five (1964–1992), public managers and HRM specialists struggled to develop flexible and equitable reward allocation through such alterations to classification and pay systems as rank-in-person personnel systems, broad pay banding, and group performance evaluation and reward systems. The resultant work management system required integration of conflicting values and systems.[16] They had to work with managers to increase productivity, with elected officials to increase agencies' political responsiveness, and with employees to maintain their rights under civil service systems.

CONSULTATION AND CONTRACT COMPLIANCE Under the current constellation of values and systems, public HR managers must still work consultatively with agency managers and employees. Yet, the operational definition of "good management" is narrow by previous standards: They have fewer options and less discretion in balancing conflicting objectives.[17] First, more than ever, they must manage public employees and programs in compliance with legislative and public mandates for cost control. Given the common presumption that the public bureaucracy is an enemy to control rather than a tool to use to accomplish public policy objectives, they have less opportunity to exercise professional responsibilities in balancing conflicting values. Either legislative micromanagement or the predominant value of cost control may preclude concern for employee rights, organizational efficiency, or social equity.[18]

Second, while "people skills" will continue to be important, they will increasingly be defined as minimizing maximum loss through risk management and contract compliance, rather than as maximizing human development and organizational performance. While civil service and collective bargaining will continue to be important, public HR managers will increasingly be responsible for developing and managing a range of public employment systems for contract, temporary, and at-will employees, and for working with volunteers and community-based NGOs.[19] In this sense, a calculating perspective tends to supplant a uniform and idealistic view of public service motivations. This represents a narrowing of the public HR perspective.

Third, even with this minimalist view of personnel management, there are countervailing pressures to develop an employment relationship characterized by commitment, teamwork, and innovation.[20] HR will develop variable pay systems that reward individual and group performance. The key to this paradox is the emerging distinction between **core employees** (those regarded as essential assets) and **contingent workers** (those regarded as replaceable costs). Success will require human resources to develop two divergent personnel systems, one for each type of worker, and to maintain both at the same time despite their conflicting objectives and assumptions.

In the *Partnership Era* (2002–present), public human resource increasingly operates within the framework of collective structures, processes, and people. Shaping and managing collaborative agendas will become even more difficult as frequent changes in government policy and in the organizations involved in partnership impact the roles of and job changes for public sector employees. Mobilizing resources, managing conflict, and building network capacity will be the benchmarks of collaborative success.[21] Table 2-4 shows these changing values and systems.

Role Expectations for Managers and Supervisors

In a way, adapting to changing role expectations is hardest for managers and supervisors. First, value conflicts surrounding public administration have intensified. Elected officials understandably tend to pass the responsibility for achieving multiple and conflicting objectives on to managers and supervisors, without necessarily giving them the tools or resources needed to do this. When revenue shortfalls or other emergencies occur, cuts are disproportionately likely to fall on internal agency staff services—like HR, information systems, and budget management—but less likely to affect short-term productivity that cuts to direct services. All this leaves managers and supervisors responsible for achieving, or at least attempting to achieve, many activities formerly left to HRM professionals. Thus, individual managers must often choose between short-term productivity and long-term organizational effectiveness, between spending time with employee issues and letting employees fend for themselves while the manager focuses on planning, budget management, or crisis control.

KEY ROLES: TECHNICAL EXPERT, PROFESSIONAL, EDUCATOR, AND ENTREPRENEUR

The key HRM role is to be able to respond to events, be they routine or catastrophic. HR managers must play a variety of roles as they seek to help the organization remain effective and learn from its own experiences. These are technical expert, professional, management educator, and organizational entrepreneurs.[22]

Technical Expert

Entry-level specialists (in large HR departments) or generalists (in small ones) are the **technical experts** responsible for HR planning, acquiring, developing, and sanctioning.

- *Benefits administrators* enroll new employees in benefit programs, advise employees of changes in benefit programs, and ensure compliance with federal pay and benefit laws. This job requires knowledge of federal laws with respect to health, life, and disability insurance; and of pay and benefits; employment contracts; and pension systems.
- *Contract specialists* develop background information to support management's positions during contract negotiations or administer contracts to ensure that labor and management comply with negotiated agreements. Under third-party government models, they develop and negotiate service contracts with vendors, or employment contracts. This requires experience with business law, policy analysis, contract negotiation, or contract compliance.

TABLE 2-4 The Role of the Public HR Manager in the United States

Stage	Dominant Value(s)	Dominant System(s)	HRM Role
Privilege (1789–1828)	Responsiveness	"Government by elites"	None
Patronage (1829–1882)	Responsiveness/ Representation	Patronage	Recruitment and Political clearance
Professionalism (1883–1932)	Efficiency + Individual Rights	Civil Service	"Watchdog" over agency managers and elected officials to ensure merit system compliance
Performance (1933–1964)	Responsiveness/ Representation + Efficiency + Individual Rights	Patronage + Civil Service	Collaboration with Legislative limits
People (1965–1979)	Responsiveness/ Representation + Efficiency + Individual Rights + Social Equity	Patronage + Civil Service + Collective Bargaining + Affirmative Action	Compliance + Policy implementation + Consultation
Privatization (1980–now)	Responsiveness/ Representation + Efficiency + Individual Accountability + Limited government + Community Responsibility	Patronage + Civil Service + Collective Bargaining + Affirmative Action + Alternative mechanisms+ Flexible employment relationships	Compliance + Policy implementation + Consultation + Contract compliance + Strategic thinking about HRM
Partnerships (2002–now)	Responsiveness/ Representation + Efficiency + Individual accountability + Limited government + Community responsibility + Collaboration	Patronage + Civil Service + Collective bargaining + Affirmative action + Alternative mechanisms+ Flexible employment relationships	Compliance + Policy implementation + Consultation + Contract compliance + Strategic thinking about HRM + Tension Management + Boundary Spanning

- *Diversity experts* interpret and enforce laws protecting different groups in a diverse workforce. This requires knowledge of equal employment opportunity and affirmative action laws and compliance agencies, and of related personnel functions like strategic HRM, recruitment and selection, performance management, training and development, and organizational justice.
- *Employee assistance program specialists* coordinate programs offered by the organization or by contract providers, as a response to personal problems that affect work performance: alcohol and drug abuse, debt, domestic and workplace violence, life-threatening diseases, legal problems, and so on. They interpret federal laws protecting the rights of employees with disabilities, informally counsel supervisors and employees, and orient employees to the agency's health benefits.
- *Human resource information systems specialists* design the systems needed to manage human resources strategically by integrating data about organizational needs and individuals' competencies.
- *Job analysts* determine jobs' appropriate competencies and minimum qualifications, respond to managers' requests for reclassification, and determine whether employees can perform the essential functions of a position under the Americans with Disabilities Act. This job requires the ability to determine competencies and write job descriptions.
- *Payroll specialists* or *compensation specialists* administer the payroll system. This requires knowledge of job design, pay equity, strategic HRM, and federal and state laws concerning wages, hours, and employment contacts.
- *Risk managers* develop and enforce personnel policies that limit the organization's exposure to legal or financial liability. In particular, personnel managers who function as risk managers are responsible for reducing employer liability for workers' compensation; disability retirement; and negligent hiring, retention, or referral claims. They may share this function with an attorney and budget officer. Risk managers must know law and regulations related to occupational safety and health, workers' compensation, and disabilities.
- *Staffing specialists* administer examinations, establish lists of eligible applicants, and refer eligible applicants to managers for interviews and selection. This requires knowledge of personnel law, affirmative action, and recruitment and selection procedures.
- *Testing Specialists* develop exams for positions and defend the reliability and validity of current tests. This job requires knowledge of testing, measurement, and validation procedures.
- *Training and development specialists* determine training needs, develop programs, train, and evaluate their effectiveness. They have training or experience as adult educators.

Professional

Conceptually, the issue of whether HR managers are **administrative professionals** seems to focus on whether an identifiable body of competencies defines the occupation, an accepted process of education and training exists for acquiring these competencies, and a standard of 4 that guides their application. Given the conflicting values and competing systems that can guide public HRM, good job performance will require that they recognize inherent role conflicts yet continue to make sound professional decisions in a climate of political and economic uncertainty.[23]

Management Educator

In addition to professional and technical responsibilities, HR managers and specialists educate other managers by encouraging them to see HRM as a set of strategically interrelated activities that taken together give employees the ability and willingness to work together effectively. The HR director must see the "big picture" and work as a member of the management team to educate other managers to think about human resources strategically. This person is responsible for experimentation—testing personnel policies or procedures such as a new benefit or performance-evaluation method on employee turnover or productivity. However, personnel directors rarely innovate. Instead, they transfer technology by learning about, adapting, and adopting ideas that have worked elsewhere. This is **organizational learning** and **knowledge management**: passing along improved HRM policies and procedures—formally and informally—to employees and other managers.[24]

Organizational Entrepreneurs

Over the last ten years, there probably has been more emphasis than ever on HR strategic thinking, workforce planning, and management as keys to organizational success. Clearly, in the past, there were incredible investments in civil service systems as antidotes to the inefficiencies and inequities associated with patronage. However, today's thinking is different. What drives contemporary strategic HRM is not moral imperatives, but the broader global imperative of administrative modernization.

In that sense, one should expect a reaction and, indeed, leadership from HR specialists and professionals. That is exactly what is happening. Traditional personnel managers have viewed the field as narrow and static. They picture it as a collection of administrative techniques applied within a structure of rules, policies, and laws that clearly define the limits of acceptable professional behavior, designed to promote both efficiency and fairness. They see themselves as continually acting within a consensus on one system—rather than many—and its underlying values. They tend to define themselves, and others tend to define them, as technical specialists working within a staff agency.

More contemporary public personnel managers view the field as emergent and dynamic. They tend to define themselves, and others define them, as interpreters or mediators among competing systems, stakeholders, and values. They see themselves as professionals whose role involves a blend of technical skills and ethical decision making, and as key players in developing corporate HRM strategy. The federal Office of Personnel Management has made a similar observation. "While HR professionals will need the traditional HR competencies that have served them well in the past they will also need new competencies to support changing roles."[25] This Office of Personnel Management report cites a survey showing the doubling in emphasis on human resources professionals as strategic business partners (p. 8). The essence of this emergent professional public personnel management role is synergy; the exploitation of pressure points where conflicting systems compete and converge; and the reconciliation of conflicting values, changing conditions, competing stakeholders, and a diverse workforce into a coherent and dynamic whole.

The movement to identify HR professionals' competencies and certify HR professionals symbolizes the evolution of the human resources professional's role. Both are important elements associated with the evolving strategic role for HR professionals. The International Personnel Management Association for Human Resources sponsors a **certification** program for human resources professionals. Certification programs are associated with the movement of occupations to professions. An essential precursor of certification is the belief that there are unique and not readily available knowledge, skills, and abilities and an ethical approach to practice that should characterize those who call themselves human resources professionals. Specialized knowledge, not easily acquired, is the key. Moreover, as the practice of human resources moves into the strategic realm—strategic partner to agency leadership—certification signifies that there is specialized knowledge needed to make this move more than a rhetorical claim. The International Public Management Association for Human Resources (IPMA-HR) model reflects this view.[26] Among the competencies are:

- Assesses and balances competing values
- Knows business system thinking
- Links human resources to the organization's mission and service outcome.

Other agencies, associations, consulting firms, and governments are also working to define HR competencies.[27]

BUILDING A CAREER IN HRM

Historical traditions emphasize the technical side of personnel management, with less emphasis on policy-related analytical work, relationships with outside organizations, and conflicting values. These traditions view both employees and management as clients served through the merit system. A more contemporary view emphasizes different activities and relationships. Modern HR professionals work closely with other officials within their own agency (budget directors, attorneys, collective bargaining negotiators, affirmative action compliance officers, and supervisors) and outside it (legislative staff, union officials, affirmative action agencies, civil service boards, health and life insurance benefit representatives, pension boards, ethics commissions, and employee assistance programs). By performing effectively in a climate of change and uncertainty, they assert their central role in agency management, developing not only their own professional status but also that of their profession.[28] Because of this conflict and instability, there is a high demand for HRM professionals in public and private organizations, whether they work as HR directors or as managers with specific HRM competencies. Three issues are relevant: (1) what competencies do HRM professionals need, (2) how can they get them, and (3) how can they maintain their skills in a complex and changing environment?[29]

What Competencies Do HR Managers Need?

Traditional public HRM requires *technical* competencies. Personnel specialists must know the extensive body of techniques needed to recruit, select, train, evaluate, and motivate employees under a range of personnel systems. For managers, this means learning how to work within the limits of law and policy to reward good employees and get rid of bad ones: rewriting job descriptions to increase an employee's pay level, reaching quality applicants on a list of eligibles, or giving outstanding performance evaluations to high-quality employees.

Public managers in general and HR directors in particular must apply the *professional* standards and judgment needed to responded adequately to the conflicting demands and expectations of advocates for competing values and systems. They must be sensitive to the need for administrative systems to be responsive to legitimate political values and public participation, especially in local government. These amorphous expectations challenge the shield that the rhetoric of merit has provided the traditional manager. Trends such as privatization and service contracting blur distinctions between public and private. Given complex and conflicting laws (e.g., affirmative action, labor relations, professional liability, employee privacy, due process, and pay equity), "merit" can mean different things under different circumstances. HR professionals should welcome the opportunity to move from a traditional, technical view of the field to a modern, professional view involving interpretation of and mediation among conflicting interests.

This transition includes *ethical* competencies: the ability to balance conflicting expectations like employee rights and organizational effectiveness, to reconcile competing systems and values, to make complex decisions quickly, and to communicate them effectively. Today's public HR professional must have a humanistic orientation toward employees, a positive orientation to managerial objectives, and close working relationships with other professionals inside and outside the organization. No one manager can possess expertise in all these areas, but no complex public agency can overlook them in their complement of competencies.

How Do HR Professionals Get These Competencies?

While all public managers need to know something about HRM because it is an important part of the field, many students have a more specific interest—they want a job. Their interest leads to two questions: As a student, what courses should I be taking to qualify myself for an HR position? As applicant, how do I get a job?

People enter HRM through varied career paths. Some start as entry-level specialists. University training (a BPA, a master's degree, or even a graduate professional certificate) can impart added knowledge that can enhance their performance and career options. Because public personnel functions also involve others besides personnel specialists (such as managers, supervisors, and appointed officials), many human resource management courses have more general usefulness for anyone considering a career in public policy or management. The National Association for Schools of Public Affairs and Administration (NASPAA) is the accrediting agency for schools offering graduate-level public HRM and public administration programs.[30] In addition, many degree programs also offer related specialization courses:

- *Administrative law*: impact of rules and regulations on public administration, including HRM.
- *Collective bargaining*: impact of unions on public personnel management, legal and political antecedents, contract negotiation, and administration procedures.
- *Test development*: development and validation of devices for selection, promotion, and placement (sometimes offered by the psychology department).
- *Pay and benefits*: job analysis, classification, and evaluation; setting wages and salaries through job evaluation and/or market surveys; mandatory employee benefits (workers' compensation and Social Security), and optional ones (health insurance, pensions, etc.).
- *Training and employee development*: design, implementation, and evaluation of orientation, and training and development programs (sometimes taught in an adult education department)
- *Affirmative action compliance*: work force diversity; equal employment opportunity; affirmative action; and employment equity without respect to gender, race, national origin, age, religion, disability, or other nonmerit factors.

- *Organizational development and change*: assessing organizational performance and changing structure and culture to make it more effective.
- *Role of women and minorities*: changing organizational culture to make it more equitable for women and minorities.
- *Vocational rehabilitation*: career counseling and placement, particularly in response to issues involving disability, ADA accommodation, and other medical conditions (sometimes offered through a program in health services or public health).
- *Productivity improvement*: How to make organizations more efficient and effective through the application of policy-analytic techniques.
- *Comparative or development administration*: offered through public administration, business administration, economics, or international relations programs.
- *Third-party government*: Use of alternative mechanisms such as privatization and service contracting to accomplish public program objectives.

Those without significant HRM experience may have a harder time breaking into the field. Worldwide changes in labor markets, plus the changing political conditions under which public administrators work today, mean that there is more competition for professional jobs in many fields, including public personnel management. Often, recent college graduates without significant public personnel management experience are competing against experienced professionals. How do you "get your foot in the door" under these conditions?

- Take courses that offer the competencies HR managers need. Earn a minor, a concentration, or even a professional certificate.
- Include an **internship** as part of your university curriculum. Make sure it is with an organization that is looking for employees—one that uses internship programs as a recruitment mechanism rather than just a source of temporary, free labor. Your best gauge of this is by asking your university's internship placement coordinator, your professors, or current employees who started work there as interns. While a formal internship option may not be feasible for a mid-career student, expressing interest and aptitude on-the-job may help with a lateral transfer into personnel work. With some creative thinking and job design, it may be possible to share some time in the personnel office or to gain experience by seeking out personnel-related tasks in your own office.
- Tailor your résumé so it highlights the education, experience, skills, and knowledge needed for a job in personnel management. Identify related courses in management, computer sciences, statistics, psychology, law or other fields.
- Practice applying and interviewing so you can respond to questions interviewers ask. Why do you want this job? What work experience have you had that shows your aptitude or ability for personnel work? If you lack related experience, what skills and abilities do you have that would make it easy to learn? Why are you the best candidate for the position? Good luck!

How to Keep Your Competencies Current

Training begins to become obsolete the moment the course is over. Clearly, HR professionals—whether specialists or supervisors—need to take charge of their own career development. Suggested methods are professional associations, research libraries, and the Internet.

Professional associations offer the opportunity to network with other professionals locally, to attend national and regional conferences, and to receive member services such as newsletters or professional journals. All offer continued education and career advancement options for working professionals.

- The American Management Association (AMA)[31]
- The American Society for Public Administration (ASPA)[32]
- The American Planning Association (APA)[33]
- The Association for Public Policy and Management (APPAM)[34]
- The American Political Science Association (APSA)[35]
- The Association for Research in Non-Profit and Volunteer Associations (ARNOVA)[36]
- The International City/County Management Association (ICMA)[37]
- The International Public Management Association for Human Resources (IPMA-HR)[38]
- The Society for Human Resource Management (SHRM)[39]

Research libraries are indispensable for keeping your competencies current. They do still as repositories for paper books and periodicals, including **reference books**[40] and **loose-leaf services** (serial publications providing current information on specific areas of personnel practice and procedure).[41] While it is possible to do research in the library using paper-based materials, they are in fact gateways to electronic information available on the **Internet** using a computer, an **internet service provider** (**ISP**), and communications software. Individuals, organizations, or agencies create a **home page**, a website identified with their Internet address (**URL**). These include:

- **Periodical indexes**. Electronic compilations of professional and popular periodical literature, arranged so that author, publication, key word, and so on may locate references[42]
- **Professional journals**. Generally, periodicals in the human resource management area are found in the HF5549.5 area (Library of Congress cataloging system).[43]
- **State and local Web resources**. Many professional associations and other organizations maintain websites with useful information about state, local, and regional governments.[44]
- **Federal and comprehensive Web resources**. The federal government and other institutions maintain websites with information about the federal government, or U.S. jurisdictions in general.[45]
- **Legal research**. If you wish to research specific legislation, check publicly accessible sources for information on federal and state laws.[46] Private companies also provide this service—for a fee—to law firms.[47]
- **Other publications and public documents**. Available online or in paper from general sources,[48] or from individual agencies.[49]

Internet browsers like Google.com are automated retrieval services used to locate materials on a particular subject, using branching logic trees and keyword addresses. Many government agencies, the Library of Congress, and universities maintain browsers to help scholars find their way around the Web.[50] However, while trained librarians have carefully chosen journals and books for library purchase, Internet-based information has no hierarchical quality control or editorial process. Just because information is available "on the Web" does not mean it is current or accurate. Use only library-recommended sites if you want to find documented information for academic or professional research purposes.

How to Develop Ethical Competencies

Initially, civil service reformers sought to establish public HRM's professional credibility by emphasizing its political neutrality and contributions to administrative efficiency. Ironically, however, this emphasis on nonpartisan and "scientific" rationality isolated public personnel managers from the value conflicts that characterized other professions, minimized ethical dilemmas, and created the illusion among public officials (and among personnel directors and specialists themselves) that the field was value-free. By focusing personnel management on administrative techniques instead of broad human resource policy questions, it had exactly the opposite effect desired—devaluing the status of the profession rather than affirming it. As a vestige of this tradition, many public personnel managers are either impatient or complacent with ethical choices. They view civil service as a moral ideal superior to other systems, whose competing claims to legitimacy are always suspect.[51] They are inclined to consider **ethics** unnecessary, because it is easier to think of administrative actions as purely technical, rational, and morally superior; or impractical because competing claims require pragmatic compromise.

However, contemporary HR managers are more likely to find ethical dilemmas challenging and inevitable. They arise out of the scarcity of public jobs and legitimate, conflicting expectations over how to fill them. To succeed, HRM professionals must not only do things right, they must do the right things.[52] They are fated to wrestle with choices imposed by external conflicts among competing systems and to derive from these choices the existential satisfaction of each day coming closer to unattainable objectives under conditions of ethical uncertainty.[53]

Summary

There are about 21 million public employees in the United States. While it is widely believed that most work for the national government in social welfare programs, the fact is that most work for state and local governments, primarily in education.

Political leaders, managers and supervisors, and personnel directors and specialists share the functions needed to manage human resources in public agencies. Civil service systems are the predominant public personnel system because they have articulated rules and procedures for performing the whole range of personnel functions. Other systems, though incomplete, are nonetheless legitimate and effective influences over one or more personnel functions. While personnel functions remain the same across different systems, their organizational location and method of performance differ depending upon the system and on the values that underlie it.

Public personnel managers have distinct role expectations as technicians, professionals, educators, and ethical mediators. Traditional HR managers and specialists (those who operate within a consensus on one system and its underlying values) tend to see themselves as technical specialists. Contemporary HR managers (those who work as educators and mediators among competing systems and values) tend to see themselves as professionals whose role involves a blend of technical, professional, and ethical competencies.

HR managers normally receive specialized undergraduate or graduate training. It may take a combination of specialized experience and education to advance into the profession. Rapid changes in the field require lifelong learning and career development through such mechanisms as professional associations, research libraries, and the Internet.

Key Terms

administrative professional *50*
contingent workers *47*
core employees *47*
elected and appointed officials *40*
ethics *56*
exempt appointments *42*
home page *55*
HRM directors and specialists *46*
Internet *55*
Internet browser *55*
internship *54*
knowledge management *51*
loose-leaf services *55*
management educator *51*
managers and supervisors *48*
organizational culture *41*
organizational learning *51*
personnel actions *43*
professional associations *55*
professional journals *55*
reference books *55*
stakeholders *42*
technician *56*
URL *55*
"watchdogs" *46*

Discussion Questions

1. How many public employees are there? How many work for each level of government (national, state, and local)? What functions does each level of government specialize in?
2. What does each of these three groups (elected and appointed officials, managers and supervisors, and HR directors and specialists) contribute to public personnel management?
3. Describe similarities and differences in the way HR managers and specialists function in different public HR systems.
4. What are the six stages in the development of the role of the public HR manager? What different expectations have people had for them in each stage?
5. What are some examples of ethical dilemmas HR professionals face?
6. What competencies do HR managers need, and where can they get them?
7. What suggestions would you offer persons who want to enter the HR field? How might they use professional associations, university courses, libraries, and the Internet for career development?

Case Study: Choosing a Municipal Personnel Director

A south Florida city needed a new HR director. It advertised in the local newspaper and in the *Recruiter* section of the *IPMA Newsletter*

DIRECTOR OF HUMAN RESOURCES
CITY OF SUNNY SKIES

The city of Sunny Skies is a city of 60,000 with 650 employees. It has a mayor-council form of government. It is primarily residential, with population shifting from older Anglo retirees to a broader mix of working-class families from a range of racial and ethnic groups. The city police department's officers are covered by a collective bargaining agreement with the PBA; a three-year contract was negotiated last year. The city's civil service system covers 400 employees. Others, including all managers, are in exempt positions filled through performance contracts.

The City seeks an HR director with proven ability to manage the department responsible for testing, selection, affirmative action, job analysis, salary and benefits, performance evaluation, and collective bargaining. Excellent benefits, including an employer-funded 457 pension program. Salary range $95,000–$145,000, dependent upon qualifications. Proof of citizenship required. We are a drug-free workplace and an AA/EEO employer.

Two hundred persons applied from all over the United States. An outside consultant firm, looking for the following minimum qualifications, conducted initial screening based on the following criteria:

- *Experience*: Ten to fifteen years of progressively responsible personnel experience, including at least three years as a personnel director. Public sector and municipal experience preferred.
- *Education*: BA/BS degree in human resource management or a related field (public administration, business administration, organizational psychology). MA/MS in public administration, human resource administration, or related field preferred.

An interview panel was formed, headed by the assistant city manager. It included the assistant director of the public works department, a police epartment major, two personnel managers from other nearby cities, and an outside expert. The panel was representative of the City's employees and labor market, with respect to gender, ethnicity, and race. After the outside consultant firm had selected the 12 most qualified applicants, the interview panel scheduled appointments with eight of them. Four were interviewed in their local communities through videotape. The interview panel (or the videotape operator) asked the following questions of each applicant:

First, tell us something about your career:

1. What is your most innovative accomplishment in your present position? Why is it so significant?
2. Describe the most difficult personnel problem you have encountered in recent years. How did it arise? How did you resolve it? How did you communicate your decision to employees and/or other managers? How did they respond? If you encountered the problem now, how would you handle it differently?
3. What has been your greatest professional disappointment or setback? How did you respond to it? What did you learn from the experience?
4. Where do you see yourself working in five years?
Next, please tell us something about your human resource management style:
5. What kinds of supervisors do you like, and why?
6. What factors are most important in evaluating the performance of your subordinates?
7. What methods do you use to keep informed of personnel issues or problems coming up in your organization? How have these methods worked for you?
8. What do you perceive affirmative action to be? What general policies do you establish to achieve it?
Briefly describe your work experience with each of these specific personnel issues:
9. collective bargaining contract negotiations
10. workers' compensation issues or claims
11. termination of civil service employees
12. sexual harassment issues and policies
13. disciplinary action and grievances
If you were personnel director, how would you deal with each of the following issues?
14. What is your understanding of the drug and alcohol testing and related requirements of the Omnibus Transportation Employee Testing Act of 1991?
15. What is the best balance between flexibility and uniformity of personnel policies and procedures? If you had to, how would you increase uniformity and structure? How would you "sell" these changes to the city manager, the department directors, and employees?
16. The City hires contract attorneys to handle some personnel-related legal issues and handles others in-house through the city attorney. In your view, which issues should be handled which way? If it is determined that the City's reliance on contract attorneys' services is excessive, what would you do to reduce this reliance? What in-house resources (financial and personnel) would you need to do this? How long would it take?
17. As a representative of the City in contract negotiations, you may be required to conduct collective bargaining negotiations when you do not have authorization to offer a COLA increase or any other increase in benefits to the union. Have you ever been in such a situation? How would you conduct the negotiation?
18. The city manager has asked you to evaluate the City's classification and pay plan. It appears that the shrinking tax base could result in civil service layoffs due to possible budget shortfalls. If cuts could not be met through attrition or by not filling vacant positions, what alternatives to layoffs are there? If layoffs were unavoidable, how would you do them?
19. Bringing employees on the job after their interviews sometimes takes several months. What timetable is reasonable? What possible methods would you consider to expedite the hiring process?

20. A promotional exam was administered, and an eligibility list established and published, for a contractually covered position. A person on that list approaches you and claims that the employee at the top of the list is believed to have been given answers to the questions by the department head of the unit in which the promotional position exists. What would you do?
21. A female employee tells you in confidence that she feels a male co-worker is sexually harassing her. The harassment involves unwanted and unsolicited sexual remarks, and some nonsexual touching. She has not mentioned this problem to anyone else. She insists that she wants no action taken against the offending employee and that she can handle the situation on her own. What do you do?
22. Same as above, except now the offending party is her immediate supervisor. Would you handle the issue any differently?
23. The City has several different types of employees (civil service, contract, no benefits, etc.). Performance evaluation and reward systems differ for each group, which causes frustration for employees and equity issues for the personnel department. What would you do about this, if anything?

In closing:

24. What knowledge, skills, and abilities make you the most qualified candidate for this position?
25. If you were offered the job today, when would you be able to start?
26. What questions, if any, do you want to ask us about the job or the City?

Discussion Questions

After reading this case study, answer the following questions:

1. Why did 200 people apply for this job? How qualified are the top applicants likely to be?
2. What do you think the primary duties of the HR director will be?
3. Based on the background information and interview questions, what are the shared HR roles of the personnel director, managers, and the city manager in this City? Who does what?
4. What specific competencies are important in doing this job well? What would be most important to you if you were the city manager? if you were a department director? an employee? a taxpayer?
5. Which of these skills, knowledge, or abilities is likely to be gained through formal education and degrees? Which through experience?
6. This case study is an example of how public HRM has changed recently. What changes can you identify with respect to each of the following variables?
   - Required competencies
   - Required education and experience
   - Selection methods
   - Environmental change and uncertainty
7. Assume you were interested in applying for this position. Which aspects of your own education or experience might you emphasize in proposing your qualifications for the job? What additional competencies do you need to become a competitive applicant for this job?

Notes

1. Kettl, D. (1997). The global revolution in public management: Driving themes, missing links. *Journal of Policy Analysis and Management, 16* (3): 446–462.
2. Klingner, D., and L. Jones (April 2004). Smart practice development administration in Iraq and other high security risk nations: Lessons from colonial experience. *International Public Management Review*, 5 (1): 41–57.
3. U.S. Census Bureau (March 2007). 2007 *Census of Governments*. Washington, DC: U.S. Department of Commerce. Available at: http://www.census.gov/govs/www/cog2007.html. Retrieved on April 22, 2009.

4. U.S. Census Bureau (2008). *The 2008 Statistical Abstract,* Table 482. Available at: http://www.census.gov/compendia/statab/cats/federal_govt_finances_employment.html. Retrieved on April 22, 2009.
5. U.S. Census Bureau (September 2004). *Compendium of Public Employment: 2002*. Series GC02 (3)-2. Washington, DC: U.S. Department of Commerce, p. 2. Available at: http://www.census.gov/prod/2004pubs/gc023x2.pdf. Retrieved on December 2, 2007.
6. *Ibid*., Table 447.
7. Bowman, J., J. West, E. Berman, and M. Van Wart (2004). *The professional edge: Competencies in public service*. Armonk, NY: M. E. Sharpe. p. 2; and U.S. Census Bureau (2008), Table 447.
8. U.S. Census Bureau (2000). *Compendium of Public Employment: 1997*. Series GC97 (3)–2. Washington, DC: U.S. Department of Commerce, p. 2.
9. U.S. Census Bureau (March 2007). 2007 *Census of Governments*. Washington, DC: U.S. Department of Commerce. Available at: http://www.census.gov/govs/www/cog2007.html. Retrieved on April 22, 2009.
10. Pynes, J. (1997). *Personnel administration in nonprofit agencies*. San Francisco, CA: Jossey-Bass.
11. Brown, J. (June 2004). Contingent workers: Employing nontraditional workers requires strategy. *IPMA-HR News*, p. 9ff.
12. Sampson, C. (1998). New manifestations of open systems: Can they survive in the public sector? *Public Personnel Management*, 27 (3): 361–383.
13. Coggburn, J. (2007). Outsourcing human resources: The case of the Texas Health and Human Services Commission. *Review of Public Personnel Administration 27* (4): 315–335; and Pennington, A. (October 2004). Outsourcing: Is it right for labor relations? *IPMA-HR News*, p. 27.
14. Widner, R. (2008). *Institutions for fragile states*. Washington, DC: The National Academy of Public Administration and Princeton University, unpublished monograph.
15. Moynihan, D. P. (2004). Protection versus flexibility: The Civil Service Reform Act, competing administrative doctrines, and the roots of contemporary public management debate. *The Journal of Policy History*, 16 (1): 1–33.
16. National Performance Review (1993). *Reinventing human resource management*. Washington, DC: Office of the Vice President.
17. Ingraham, P. (2006).Building bridges over troubled waters: Merit as a guide. *Public Administration Review*, 66 (4): 486–495.
18. Woodard, C. (2006). Merit by any other name—reframing the civil service first principle. *Public Administration Review,* 65 (1): 109–116.
19. Warner, M., and A. Hefetz (2004). Pragmatism over politics: Alternative service delivery in local government, 1992–2004. *The Municipal Year Book 2004*. Washington, DC. International City/County Management Association, pp. 8–16.
20. Kellough, E., and L. Nigro (2006). Dramatic reform in the public service: At-will employment and the creation of a new public workforce. *Journal of Public Administration Research and Theory,* 16: 447–467.
21. Milward, H. B. (1996). Symposium on the hollow state: Capacity, control, and performance in interorganizational settings. *Journal of Public Administration Research and Theory, 6* (2): 193–195; and Peters, B. G., and J. Pierre (1998). Governance without government? Rethinking public administration. *Journal of Public Administration Research and Theory, 8* (2): 223–243.
22. This choice of roles is arbitrary. Others are possible. See: National Academy of Public Administration (1996), *A competency model for hr professionals,* as cited in Steve Nelson (September 2004), The state of federal civil service today, *Review of Public Personnel Administration, 24:* 202–215.
23. Office of Personnel Management (2005). *Modernizing merit: OPM's guiding principles for civil service transformation*. Available at: http://www.opm.gov/Strategic_Management_of_Human_Capital/documents/merit/. Retrieved on January 5, 2008.
24. Stehr, S. D., and T. M. Jone (April 1999). Continuity and change in public personnel administration. *Review of Public Personnel Administration, 19*: 32–49; Klingner, D., and G. Sabet (December 2005). Knowledge management, organizational learning, innovation diffusion and adoption, and technology transfer: What they mean and why they matter. *Comparative Technology Transfer and Society, 3* (3): 199–210.
25. Office of Personnel Management (September 1999). *Looking to the future: Human resources competencies*. Washington, DC: Office of Personnel

Management, p. 7. www.opm.gov/studies/Trans2.pdf

26. International Personnel Management Association for Human Resources. www.ipma-hr.org/content.cfm?pageid=194
27. See National Institutes of Health (http://hr.od.nih.gov/competencies/occupation-specific/201.htm); the University of Michigan (www.hr.umich.edu/hra/HRA.pdf); Society for Human Resource Management (http://www.elearning.shrm.org/hrCompetencies.aspx); The Learning Portal (https://utcess.utc.com/prv8/lpauth.splash_page_prc).
28. Klingner, D. (September 1979). The changing role of public personnel management in the 1980s. *The Personnel Administrator, 24*: 41-48; and Nalbandian, J. (Spring 1981). From compliance to consultation: The role of the public personnel manager. *Review of Public Personnel Administration 1* (1): 37–51.
29. Wilson, C. (February 2005). Professional development: Taking control of your own destiny. *IPMA-HR News*, pp. 9, 11.
30. National Association for Schools of Public Affairs and Administration (2006). [Online]. Available at: www.naspaa.org. Retrieved on October 29, 2006.
31. American Management Association (2006). *Public and nonprofit sector division*. [Online]. Available at: http://apps.aomonline.org. Retrieved on October 22, 2006.
32. American Society for Public Administration (2006). Available at: http://www.aspanet.org. Retrieved on October 22, 2006.
33. American Planning Association (2006). *About us*. [Online]. Available at: http://www.planning.org. Retrieved on October 22, 2006.
34. Association for Public Policy and Management (2006). [Online]. Available at: www.appam.org. Retrieved on October 22, 2006.
35. American Political Science Association (2006). *Public administration division*. [Online]. Available at: www.h-net.msu.edu/~pubadmin. Retrieved on October 23, 2006.
36. Association for Research in Nonprofit and Volunteer Agencies (2006). [Online]. Available at: www.arnova.org. Retrieved on October 23, 2006.
37. International City/County Management Association (2006). *Who we are*. [Online]. Available at: www.icma.org. Retrieved on October 22, 2006.
38. International Public Management Association for Human Resources (2006). *Mission statement*. [Online]. Available at: www.ipma-hr.org. Retrieved on October 22, 2006.
39. The Society for Human Resource Management (2007). [Online]. Available at: http://www.shrm.org/hrlinks/. Retrieved on December 5, 2007.
40. Some good HRM reference books are: *American salaries and wages survey* HD4973.A67 (9th 2007) American Chamber of Commerce Researchers Association (ACCRA) *Cost of living index Employment Discrimination Law*. BNA Books. KF3464.S34 2007 U.S. Department of Labor (2002-2003). *Occupational outlook handbook occupational outlook quarterly* HF5382.5.U5 03 *State Compensation Laws: Minimum wage/overtime, prevailing wage, wage payment*. CCH KF 3490. Z95 S73.
41. Loose-leaf services. Current employment law; published by West, Bureau of National Affairs (BNA), Prentice Hall (PH) and Commerce Clearing House (CCH). Examples: *Americans with disabilities*, BNA Vol. 1-present BUS KF3469.A5A45 *Collective bargaining negotiation & contracts*, BNA BUS HD6500.B8 *EEOC Compliance manual*, CCH BUS KF3464.A6C6 *EEOC decisions*, CCH BUS KF3464.A56E65 *Employment practices decisions*, CCH Vol. I-present BUS KF3464.A6E46 *Employment practices guide*, CCH BUS KF3464.A5C65 *Fair employment practice cases*, BNA Vol. 1-present 3 BUS KF3464.A6E46 *Human resources management*, CCH HF5549.H865 *Individual employment rights cases*, BNA Vol. 1-present BUS HD6971.8.I5 *Individual retirement plans*, CCH BUS KF3510.A6I5 *Labor arbitration reports*, BNA Vol. 56-present *Labor relations reference manual*, BNA Vol. 61-present BUS HD5503.A7224 *Labor relations reporter*, BNA BUS KF3385.L3 *Occupational safety & health cases*, BNA Vol. 1-present BUS KF3568.A2B87 *Occupational safety & health reporter*, BNA 1973-present BUS KF3570.Z9B9 *Payroll management guide*, CCH BUS KF6436.A6C6 *Pension plan guide*, CCH BUS HD7106.U5C6 *Wage and hour cases*, BNA Vol. 19-present BUS HD4974.W3
42. Examples: Academic Search Premier, Business Source Premier, CQ Researcher, Lexis/Nexis.
43. Core professional journals: *Academy of Management Journal, American Review of Public*

Administration (ARPA), Compensation and Benefits Review, Congressional Quarterly, Government Executive Magazine (GovExec.com), Harvard Business Review, HR News (formerly The IPMA Newsletter), Journal of Public Administration Research and Theory (J-PART), Nonprofit and Voluntary Sector Quarterly, Personnel Journal, Public Administration and Development, Public Administration Review (PAR), Public Personnel Management, Public Productivity Review, Review of Public Personnel Administration (ROPPA), and Training and Development Journal.

44. Center for Governmental Research: http://www.cgr.org, Council of State Governments: http://www.csg.org, National Association of Counties: http://www.naco.org, National City Government Resource Center: http://www.geocities.com/CapitolHill/1389, National Conference of State Legislatures: http://www.ncsl.org, National League of Cities: http://www.nlc.org, State and Local Government on the Net: http://www.statelocalgov.net, State and Local Governments: http://www.loc.gov/rr/news/stategov/stategov.html, URISA (Urban and Regional Information Systems Association): http://www.urisa.org, and U.S. State and Local Gateway:http://www.usa.gov/Government/State_Local.shtml.
45. FedWorld: http://www.fedworld.gov, Harvard Business School Human Resources Management Cases: http://harvardbusinessonline.hbsp.harvard.edu/b02/en/cases/cases_home.jhtml, Thomas: http://thomas.loc.gov [Library of Congress], U.S. Census Bureau: www.census.gov, Best of Practices: www.gol.org/bestof/html, and First Gov: http://www.firstgov.gov/Citizen/Citizen_Gateway.shtml.
46. Law Librarians Society of Washington, DC, Legislative Sourcebook: http://www.llsdc.org/sourcebook/fed-leg-hist.htm, Cornell University: http://supct.law.cornell.edu, http://www.findlaw.com/casecode, http://www.supremecourtus.gov. Full text state statutes and legislation: http://www.prairienet.org/~scruffy/ f.htm.
47. Congressional Information Service: CIS/Annual [year], Legislative Histories of U.S. Public Laws.
48. *Catalog of U.S. Government Publications* [Online]. Available at: http://catalog.gpo.gov. Retrieved on December 5, 2007; Government Periodicals Index [Online]. Available at: http://academic.lexisnexis.com/online-services/government-periodicals-index-content.aspx; and *Library Resources for Administrative History.* [Online]. Available at: http://www.archives.gov/research/alic/reference/admin-history/congressional-hearings.html. Retrieved on December 5, 2007.
49. Suggested agencies are: The U.S. Office of Personnel Management (OPM): http://www.opm.gov; U.S. Merit Systems Protection Board (MSPB): http://www.mspb.gov; U.S. Equal Employment Opportunity Commission (EEOC): http://www.eeoc.gov
50. Examples of open-access Web sites containing information on public management: www.loc.gov (U.S. Library of Congress); www.gpoaccess.gov (U.S. Government Printing Office); and www.usa.gov/Agencies/State_and_Territories.shtml (U.S. state and local governments). Information is also available from government agencies, universities, professional associations, and other proprietary organizations: International Public Management Association Human Resources: www.ipma-hr.org; U.S. Office of Personnel Management: http://www.opm.gov; U.S. Merit Systems Protection Board: http://www.mspb.gov; Government Accounting Office: www.gao.gov; National Academy of Public Administration: www.napawash.org; and Work Index: http:// www.workindex.com.
51. Mosher, F. (1982). *Democracy and the public service* (2nd ed.). New York: Oxford University Press.
52. Bennis, W., and B. Nanus (1985). *Leaders: The strategies for taking charge.* New York: Harper & Row.
53. Bowman, J., J. West, E. Berman, and M. Van Wart (2004). *The professional edge: Competencies in public service.* Armonk, NY: M. E. Sharpe.

PART TWO

Planning

CHAPTER 3

Thinking Strategically about HRM

Just a decade ago, the primary focus of personnel systems and human resources professionals shifted from defending merit system principles to a concern for maximizing productivity. Theoretically and historically, merit system principles were seen as instruments of productivity, but implementing merit principles required both a regulatory as well as a facilitative mindset. In actuality, the emphasis on regulation often won out, and personnel departments largely were seen as regulating the discretion of management in human resources areas rather than facilitating human resources practices.

In part, this shift signifies that merit systems are no longer framed exclusively as antidotes to patronage systems. Civil service systems—the instruments of merit values—now are evaluated as a means to an end rather than the ends in themselves they had become. This emphasis is part of a growing realization that organizations must continually align their administrative systems in ways that allow employees to complete their work effectively. This requires designing and managing administrative systems in response to changes in external environments that affect organizational mission and objectives. Effective human resource management is defined by how well employees are completing work that (1) advances existing agency goals, (2) positions the organization to respond to present and future external environmental changes, and (3) protects employees from inappropriate political influences. The third piece of the definition has become far less prominent than it has been historically.

The new focus is seen in many ways: for example, attempts to exempt the recently created Department of Homeland Security from the traditional federal personnel system, creating a Chief Human Capital Officer in federal agencies at least symbolically on par with Chief Financial Officers, and the increasing emphasis on workforce planning at all levels of government and in larger nonprofits as well as private firms. In short, this human resources management renewal emphasizes strategic thinking about human resources issues, highlighting the human resources responsibility of executive level leadership and managerial cadres as well as the evolution in roles of personnel specialists.

For many organizations with civil service systems, the changes have required increased flexibility and experimentation in many areas: with privatization, contracting out, and utilization of part-time and temporary workers; decentralization of the personnel function and rethinking of the role of central personnel offices; rank-in-person versus rank-in-job personnel systems with more flexibility in managing pay; team as well as individual performance evaluation; and experimentation with variable pay based on performance.

Managers find themselves buffeted by demographic statistics that fundamentally alter the supply of labor at the same time they are experiencing the clash between traditional values of civil service systems and the market-based values.

By the end of this chapter, you will be able to:

1. Identify traditional civil service system assumptions.
2. Describe the challenges to these assumptions posed by contemporary work and organizations, demographic trends, market-based values, and new concepts of governance.
3. Identify the consequences of these challenges for twenty-first-century public service systems.
4. Describe the contemporary model of HRM that links these challenges with values, functions, organizational mission, and multiple perspectives.
5. Identify four key recommendations for improving public sector HRM.
6. Relate the concept and practice of workforce planning to strategic HRM.
7. Connect indicators and standards to evaluation of HRM systems and to effective management of human resources.
8. Discuss how a strategic human resource management information system can drive databased human resource management.

THE ASSUMPTIONS OF TRADITIONAL CIVIL SERVICE SYSTEMS

Civil service systems grew up in response to patronage challenges and associated needs for greater efficiency and effectiveness in carrying out government missions. Civil service systems balance the values of efficiency and individual rights and rest on a foundation of assumptions about work that were developed when the roots of these systems were planted decades ago—not coincidentally at a time when the profession of mechanical engineering and its rational/analytical approach to problem solving was finding itself in great demand. Note in the following assumptions about traditional human resources management the influence of the engineer's thinking:

- Public sector work is organized around the role of government as a deliverer of services.
- This work can be divided into individual packets of duties and responsibilities called jobs.
- Duties and responsibilities remain stable over time because government work is performed in bureaucratic organizations designed to promote stability and routine.
- Worker competencies are valued and assessed in relationship to particular jobs, and personnel functions are oriented around positions rather than the people who occupy those positions.
- The analytical focus on individual jobs and the relationship of one job to another provide a rational system for pay, recruitment, and selection, and appraisal of employee performance.

These **assumptions about civil service systems** were essential to successful transition from the era of patronage, and they have provided sound guidance for the design and implementation of civil service systems for years. However, many argue strenuously that they seem less appropriate for today's work environment.

Challenges fall into four categories: **the nature of contemporary work and organizations**, **demographic trends**, **market-based values**, and a new concept of **governance**.

CHALLENGES TO THESE TRADITIONAL ASSUMPTIONS

Contemporary Work and Organizations

Increasing specialization of work and the rapidity of change characterize *contemporary work and organizations*. While the knowledge needed to address today's problems becomes more specialized, the problems themselves remain broad, requiring teams of specialists. The practice of medicine and the continuous development of specializations is a familiar example. Other examples are plentiful. Public responses to gangs involve families, social service agencies, the courts, the police, recreation specialists, teachers and school district personnel, as well as the employment of both volunteers and professional workers. This complexity and specialization requires teams of people working together, often in temporary arrangements with nongovernmental actors, until the particular problem they are dealing with changes and the composition of the team and partners must be revised.

The concept of working in teams of specialists and organizations is very different from the idea that work can be divided discretely into manageable packets of duties and responsibilities. Rather than managing individual workers, many of today's managers are responsible for teams of workers, where the focus is on the group, and on networks of groups, as well as the members. Effective managers today must be equally adept at working in hierarchy and in teams. In teams, the interpersonal skills that used to be less relevant to individual work become crucial. Good citizenship behaviors and personal attributes like courtesy, friendliness, conflict resolution, effective listening, persuasiveness, and speaking ability become assets to teams even if they are often absent from traditional job descriptions and appraisal instruments. Rather than a job description determining what the employee does, increasingly, the person with specialized knowledge, working in concert with others, heavily influences his or her actual work by helping define what the duties and responsibilities ought to be or at least how the job ought to be carried out.

The rapidity of change largely corresponds to the rate of innovation in the technological software and hardware utilized for work, the degree of dynamism in the marketplace, and the relationship between markets and governing actions. The more competitive the marketplace, the more responsiveness business expects from government. For example, when developers put all the pieces into place: the land, the tenants, the architects and planners, the financing, and so on, they want a responsive city hall that will process a rezoning application and site plan and issue building permits in a timely fashion; and they want the city's work oriented toward the developers' needs, not vice versa, so the project can be built on schedule and the developer can get on to the next project. Public personnel systems dominated by procedures focused on fairness rather than timeliness can drive the development community crazy when vacancies in the planning department, for example, cause delays in application reviews and issuance of permits as the hiring process continues at a different pace—focused on a wider range of values than human resources management in the private sector.

The pace of change also influences the degree to which today's knowledge, skills, and abilities are suitable for tomorrow's work. As we will see in Chapters 5 and 7, recruiting based on a standard job description may secure talent for today but might limit the organization's ability to respond for tomorrow. A worker's character, willingness, ability, and aptitude to learn what he or she does not know may be more important than the knowledge, skills, and abilities that person brings to the present job.

Demographic Trends

While the current fiscal crisis challenges longer-term trends, those trends will reassert themselves once the economy resets itself. The single biggest influence on human resources management will be the scarcity of labor, all kinds, but particularly those with specialized knowledge. Whether public or private, the need for labor dominates strategic thinking as well as the day-to-day pressure to fill vacancies and retain valued employees.

The results of an ambitious research project involving thirty major public and private organizations in North America and Europe led to the following observations:

> Three powerful forces—increasing longevity, declining fertility, and the disproportionate size of the 'Baby Boom' generation—together drive an unprecedented and relentless shift in the age distribution of the population and workforce in industrialized countries. As workforce growth slows, there are not enough young workers to replace the population and skills of Baby Boomers as they reach retirement age, and labor and skills shortages will become chronic.[1]

While layoffs and furloughs dominate today's thinking, recruitment, training, and retention of employees will resurface as the ratio of retirees to new workers, reflected in Table 3-1, adds to the scarcity of labor.

The fact that virtually all adults, whether married or not, are working outside the home has made balancing work and family obligations a critical challenge for today's worker, manager, and employer. Today's **demographic trends** show that super pop has joined super mom. Women have become all too familiar with the stressful responsibilities for nurturing a family and working outside of the home, and now their husbands are experiencing similar demands and the stress associated with balancing family needs, work responsibilities, and personal interests. Working too hard in organizations that are downsizing or understaffed, perhaps holding a part-time job as well, shuffling kids around day care, soccer matches, and music lessons change one's expectations about work and one's perspective on what it means to be an employee. Increasingly, family responsibilities include taking care of parents. This means giving medical care while they are alive and settling their legal and financial affairs once they pass away. This is complicated by geographic mobility—the one who lives closest to a parent who needs care often ends up in the caregiver role. While these family-friendly organizational characteristics may at one time have been "fringe benefits," in today's world, where workers not jobs are the scarce resources, these organizations are now increasingly focusing on recruiting and retaining workers.

Market-Based Values

Now familiar antigovernmental rhetoric is matched by a resurgence of political support for *market-based values*. If government cannot solve certain problems, then let the marketplace try, advocates argue. Privatization, contracting out, and temporary staffing result from this kind of sentiment, accompanied by and encouraged in an environment where raising taxes is difficult. In this kind of environment, where organizations cannot be depended upon to foster

TABLE 3-1 Full-Time Permanent Age Distributions Federal Government Civilian Workforce, 1985–2006

	1985		2006	
Age	**Count**	**Percent**	**Count**	**Percent**
<20	4,501	.25	593	.00
20–24	74,036	4.04	28,072	1.7
25–29	175,458	9.58	91,465	5.6
30–34	267,219	14.59	116,102	7.1
35–39	326,345	17.81	170,402	10.4
40–44	257,809	14.07	238,027	14.6
45–49	228,517	12.47	286,140	17.5
50–54	225,745	12.32	311,237	19.1
55–59	161,926	8.84	251,750	15.4
60–64	84,731	4.63	102,763	6.3
65–69	20,461	1.12	26,932	1.6
70>	5,164	.28	9,515	.6
Total	1,831,912	100	1,631,000	100
Average age	42.3		47	

U.S. Office of Personnel Management, Office of Workforce Information, Central Personnel Data File (CPDF) at www.opm.gov/feddata/html/Age_Dist.asp (2008).

long-term employment, once economic opportunities are plentiful, employees become career entrepreneurs, responsible for managing their own successes, failures, and future.

At no time in recent memory have the distinctions between public and private sectors seemed less understood or important—a surging economy in the 1990s where fewer and fewer people depended upon government is important in this trend. Moreover, the role the federal government took a decade later during the most recent recession has highlighted the interdependencies. The role of government as a deliverer of services at state and federal levels is yielding to the concept of government as "guarantor" of services, as services are contracted out. Agency managers have had to adjust their thinking from the management of people and services to the management of contracts, knowing that they still are going to be held politically accountable for the quality of service delivery.

The blending of public, private, and nonprofit work is reflected in expectations of citizens who receive public services, regardless of who delivers them. No amount of explanation will satisfy a citizen who has to stand in line at the county treasurer's office or the department of motor vehicles office and then goes to the bank and receives instant service or better yet, to an ATM. Similarly, the popularity of FedEx or UPS has challenged the Postal Service. These expectations require more funding for personnel and better wages to attract better people, but they also require more delegation of authority to those actually serving the public. At the same time that expectations for rapid, customized responses have increased, the traditional role of government, as arbiter of political values, has not decreased. Working through questions of values takes time, and developing managers who can understand "customer service" values with traditional "community building" values is a challenge for ways an agency thinks about its human resources needs.

New Concepts of Governance

Associated with the emphasis on markets versus government and the employment of private firms and nonprofit organizations in public services delivery, we encounter the term *governance*. *Governance* is a concept that broadly encompasses how public values are allocated and services provided. In the past, it was hard to distinguish between governance and government because the legislative, executive, and judicial institutions of government fulfilled "governance" functions. Now, everything is up for grabs. The IRS employs private firms to collect late taxes; prisons are constructed and operated by private firms; private security firms are employed by the defense department in war zones; and nonprofits have become essential partners in the delivery of social services. While these changes importantly affect traditional issues regarding accountability and the values these networks incorporate, they also have an impact on contemporary human resources management.[2] For example, it is now widely accepted that government merit systems have incorporated the value of social equity into their HR principles. Can the same be said for the partners in the governance networks designed around service delivery? Can one expect a private company to value social equity and individual rights as much as a government agency? Should one expect it of a company that must compete in the market place where timeliness, risk, and financial imperatives create far more pressure on administrative practices than in government? In short, while the value of networked systems in delivering public services has become more popular in part because of the antigovernment value movement and the need for specialized approaches and skills to specific public problems, have we underplayed the challenges and costs encountered when trying to mesh administrative systems from different sectors, including HR?

THE CHALLENGES OF COORDINATING HRM SYSTEMS-AN EXAMPLE

For several years a local government human services department has provided a grant to a nonprofit organization for an academic program for youth expelled from school. The grant award document includes all the standard government contractual language; some might call it the fine print. Included in the standard language is the requirement for the contracting party to certify staff working under the grant have not been convicted of certain serious criminal offenses. Government staff felt they had a good working relationship with the organization. As part of annual monitoring procedures, the nonprofit staff had verbally indicated they had a process for conducting criminal background checks on all staff and volunteers.

One evening the local news featured a story on an individual who had robbed a bank and led police on a chase through the downtown area during the lunch hour before crashing his car into a building. A key feature of the story was that the individual arrested was a youth worker for the academic program funded by the local government. The news reporter went on to disclose that the individual was on parole for a murder conviction at the time the robbery occurred. When contacted about the incident, the nonprofit indicated it was aware of the individual's past criminal history but it: (1) did not personally believe the individual had committed the crime, (2) had a mission-driven commitment to giving people a second chance; and (3) felt staff persons with imperfect histories offered youth the opportunity to learn from the mistakes of others. Local government staff, on the other hand, viewed the nonprofit's stance as untenable and fraught with liability concerns, both for the nonprofit and the local government as the primary provider of funds for the program.

Faced with loss of the grant, the nonprofit implemented new personnel policies requiring criminal background checks and disallowing employment of individuals convicted of certain offenses within a set timeframe.[3]

CONSEQUENCES OF THESE CHALLENGES FOR THE TWENTY-FIRST-CENTURY PUBLIC SERVICE SYSTEMS

Table 3-2 summarizes the shifts taking place in human resources management as organizations move from traditional civil service to merit systems built for the twenty-first century. We have included an exercise at the end of the chapter based on this illustrative chart.

One can see that the shifts noted in the table illustrate the trend away from human resources management as a regulatory function and toward the view that human

TABLE 3-2 Shifting from a Traditional Public Sector System to a System for the Twenty-first Century

Traditional Public Service Systems	Public Service Systems for the Twenty-first Century
1. Single system in theory; in reality multiple systems not developed strategically	1. Recognize multiple systems; be strategic about system development; define and inculcate core values
2. Merit definition that had the outcome of protecting people and equated fairness as sameness	2. Merit definition that has the outcome of encouraging better performance and allows differentiation between different talent
3. Emphasis on process and rules	3. Emphasis on performance and results
4. Hiring/promotion of talent based on technical expertise	4. Hire, nurture, and promote talent to the right places
5. Treating personnel as a cost	5. Treating human resources as an asset and an investment
6. Job for life/lifelong commitment	6. Inners and outers who share core values
7. Protection justifies tenure	7. Employee performance and employer need justifies retention
8. Performance appraisal based on individual activities	8. Performance appraisal based on demonstrated individual contribution to organizational goals
9. Labor–management relationship based on conflicting goals, antagonistic relationship, and ex-post disputes and arbitration on individual cases	9. Labor–management partnership based on mutual goals of successful organization and employee satisfaction, ex-ante involvement in work-design
10. Central agency that fulfilled the personnel functions for agencies	10. Central agency that enables agencies, especially managers, to fulfill the personnel function for themselves

Abramson, Mark A. (ed.). *Towards a 21st Century Public Service: Reports from Four Forums.* The Pricewaterhouse Coopers Endowment for the Business of Government. January 2001, p. 29.

resources management is a strategic element of organizational goal fulfillment. Of the differences noted in Table 3-2, in this chapter we want to focus on the first—thinking strategically about human resources management.

THE CONTEMPORARY MODEL OF HUMAN RESOURCES MANAGEMENT

Clearly, we need to replace the traditional function- and values-based closed systems model of public service HRM with one that responds to the four fundamental challenges confronting contemporary HRM. This model must incorporate values, functions, organizational mission, and the perspectives of multiple stakeholders. But, it must do so in a manner that reflects organizational learning in response to a changing and uncertain environment. Figure 3-1 describes this model of how contemporary human resources management works when viewed from a strategic perspective.[4]

The model shows that at the core are environmental forces like workforce demographics and reductions in staffing and outsourcing of services, the political values we described in the first chapter, and the four perspectives we will describe in the next few paragraphs. Agency mission provides an important overall filter through which the environment, values, and perspectives are understood and engaged. In our case, the human resources functions are the targets for the strategic thinking. The model also shows that consequences—both good and bad—of detail issues at the technical core of human resources management can trigger environmental forces, values, and perspectives.

According to Wilson,[5] an organization's hierarchy is divided into **operators** (employees), **managers**, and **executives**. Operators are those responsible for completing the core work of the agency. In a small police department, these would be the officers on the street and the

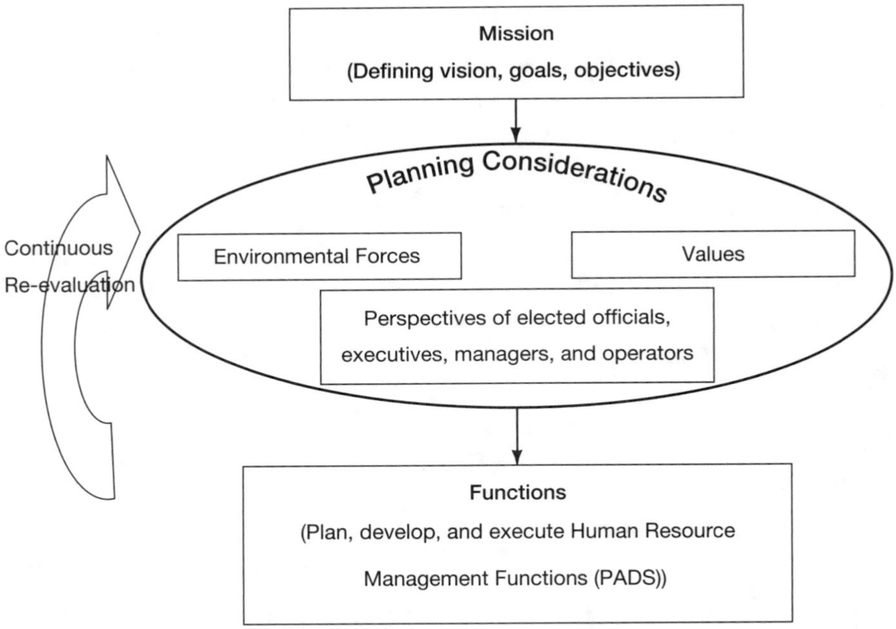

FIGURE 3-1 Strategic Thinking about Human Resources

detectives and those that support them; in a hospital, these would be the nurses and the physicians and support personnel primarily responsible for treating and caring for patients; in a drug rehabilitation facility, the counselors would fall into this category; for the park service, these would be the rangers and personnel that help with and support the ranger's work. From the operator's perspective, wages, working conditions and benefits are important; but operators also are concerned with having the opportunity to do their work well.

But employees are not uniform in their perspective which depends upon their status as full time or part time, permanent or temporary, civil service or contract, unionized or not. The terms of the employment contract—expectations and obligations of employee and employer—changes, depending upon ones' status. Managers bring a different perspective, according to Wilson. They find themselves positioned between the operators and the executives of an agency. They are responsible for conveying the needs of operators to executives and for translating the policy interests of executives to the operators. Wilson sums up the manager's perspective by saying that they are responsible for dealing with the constraints that operators have to work under: the sometimes vague or conflicting directives; procurement, personnel, accounting, and budgeting processes that do not always facilitate the operator's work but make sense from other perspectives.

Agency executives are primarily responsible for maintaining the agency's legitimacy. This means that they are continually alert for external forces—like legislatures and interest groups—that might place the agency under undue scrutiny and limit its autonomy to do its work. Autonomy is crucial to an agency, enabling it to adapt to changing conditions. For example, it is much different working under a procurement policy that requires hierarchical approval for all purchases over $1,000 than under one that delegates this authority to line departments. Tight procurement rules often result from scrutiny from critics outside the agency. In short, the work of the executive is to build and maintain credibility for the work the operators are performing. The more credibility, the more flexibility the agency will be allowed, which theoretically will promote productivity.

Elected officials bring yet another *perspective*. Their concerns may or may not be directed at a specific agency or policy area. Inevitably, they will reflect the interests and concerns of their constituents. Political accountability is very important to them; and in addition to their policymaking or legislative role, most take their oversight role very seriously. In the human resources arena, elected officials are largely responsible for the creation of position management through their focus on external control of agency resources (e.g., through line-item budgets, control over appropriations, and control over number of positions and average grade level). Elected officials are responsible for setting agency missions and objectives legislatively and for engaging administrative officials, hopefully in a partnership, to achieve those objectives, and for expecting agency leadership to develop and implement administratively sound and politically sensitive human resources plans that reflect strategic thinking.

How the Model Works

Even though we like to depict strategic thinking in a linear fashion, in actuality it rarely is as rational or orderly a process as the model would have us believe. Mostly, strategic considerations start with the problems an agency faces in the short term. Let's say that the legislature has voted low wage increases for several years, and agency managers are having difficulty accomplishing their work because they cannot retain quality employees who are moving to lucrative jobs. This would be noticed in the human resources core.

The inability to complete work at an acceptable standard is what causes an agency to react, that is, to focus its time and energy. Often, this draws the attention of those outside the agency, including interest groups. Then, the analysis begins, the problem is defined based on the perspectives of those who see the problem as important, alternatives are sought, and larger issues may be recognized and the environmental forces identified as having a more or less direct effect on an agency.

Here is a real example. Some time ago, a gap in revenue needed to provide public transportation in Los Angeles became a collective bargaining issue.[6] The Transit authority's position is to reduce overtime, hire more part-time drivers, and to create more transit districts, which will have the effect of creating a partially nonunionized work force. The efficiency and rights issues abound here, affecting both the sanction and planning functions. Driving some of this is the profound emphasis that the embrace of the marketplace has given to the Transit Authority's alternatives. In the midst of this struggle are found people of lower socio-economic status who rely on public transportation to get to work. The political pressures to settle the strike are immense, but financial implications of alternative settlements are significant, and the struggle for power between the union and the Transit Authority underlies it all.

As these immediate issues are faced and dealt with, the environmental forces behind them become more apparent and salient, and they are more likely to enter into broad human resources planning. The key is whether the agency is able to engage in noncrisis strategic planning that in its broadest sense will incorporate environmental forces into the agency's thinking about its mission. The strategic thinking will link the two—environmental forces and agency mission—through the identification of problems and possible solutions. The problems will reflect more than a short-term reactive perspective; they will be future oriented. The greater potential impact these broad forces have on the core personnel functions of the agency—planning, acquisition, development, and sanction—the more important thinking strategically about human resources issues is.

In summary, **strategic human resources management** is the purposeful resolution of human resource administration and policy issues to enhance a public agency's ability to accomplish its mission in an efficient and equitable way. The key to strategic thinking is connecting human resources management with agency goals, cognizant of environmental forces, and without losing sight of public service values like individual rights and social equity. This is not simple! It highlights an age-old debate about the role of staff functions like personnel administration. How independent should personnel administrators be in order to enhance the quality of personnel services? How subservient should they be in order to aid agency managers? Strategic thinking requires an *understanding* of how organizational human resource management functions relate to one another, to their environmental context, and to agency goals; a *vision* of the importance of human resources in goal accomplishment and in building a workforce committed to public service values; and a *commitment* on the part of elected officials, personnel administrators, managers, and employees to work for the kinds of changes that will enhance concern for human resources issues.

FOUR KEY RECOMMENDATIONS FOR IMPROVING STRATEGIC THINKING ABOUT PUBLIC SECTOR HRM

The President's Management Agenda, announced in 2002 as a comprehensive initiative to improve management and performance of the federal government, recognized the importance of strategic human resources planning. One of the five governmentwide initiatives is "Strategic management of human capital."[7] Annually, agencies are required to submit data assessing progress toward the plans they have development to advance the initiatives. The Office of Management and Budget reviews and grades each department on each initiative.[8] Similarly, reflecting on agency transformation, Comptroller General Walker of the Government Accountability Office concluded, "GAO believes that strategic human capital management must be the centerpiece of any serious change management initiative and effort to transform the culture and operations of any large organization, including government organizations."[9]

At its fall 2000 meeting, the National Academy of Public Administration (NAPA) set out to establish strategic guidelines for a new presidential administration. Its recommendations illustrate how strategic thinking can be applied to human resources management. We believe that the issues and recommendations are just as relevant today as when they were published. Even though they are targeted to human resource policy and administration in the federal government, there are many recommendations that are applicable at all levels.

According to NAPA, in order to improve fundamentally the future of human resources for the federal government, presidential leadership in cooperation with key stakeholders such as federal employee unions, managers, executives, senior political appointees is essential. The four key recommendations for reforming the people side of government follow along with our comments:

Human Capital Needs to Be a Top Priority: Not Just an HR Issue, but an Executive Priority of the White House and Every Agency

This recommendation conveys the importance of human resources and human resources planning for organizational performance in two ways. First, it includes "capital," referring to people who work in an agency or organization. Earlier they were called "employees," then "human resources," and now we use the term "human capital." The evolution of the term itself conveys increasing importance of human resources, symbolically elevating human resources to the level of "financial capital." Second, it places responsibility for human capital planning at the highest government or agency, or organizational levels. The message here is that within the function of human resources planning are found fundamental issues—like those resulting from an analysis of the demand and availability of labor in light of agency mission—that affect an agency's future effectiveness. This first theme is very consistent with Comptroller General Walker's lessons learned from the Government Accountability Office's transformation and with the President's Management Agenda. This recommendation squarely accentuates the PADS function of planning.

Recruit, Retain, and Develop a Skilled and Diverse Workforce, Including Redefining Public Service Careers and Promoting Public Service

This recommendation focuses directly on workforce planning. What will this agency need from its workforce of the future? What can we count on from today's workforce? Where are the gaps? We will have more to say about workforce planning later in this chapter. Further, the recommendation emphasizes the need to look at potential employees rather than jobs as scarce resources. Recognizing this, it seeks to promote public service work, not only implying the importance of showing how "government jobs" can tap into a person's public service motivation, but also suggesting the need for employee and family friendly workplace polices. Note the inclusion of diversity in this recommendation—the absence of the term "social equity" or "affirmative action"—recognizing that in a country with an increasingly diverse citizenship, legitimacy of governing institutions—in part—depends upon how well those serving the public understand them. The recommendation suggests that the traditional path of entering an agency or organization at the bottom level and working one's way up the career ladder will probably involve moving from one agency to another and/or one sector to another. We see this recommendation primarily encompassing the PADS functions of acquisition and development.

Modernize Performance Management and Training/Development Systems

In part, this recommendation comes closest to looking at human resources management as an internally focused administrative system. There are real nuts and bolts implied in this recommendation from the need for updated Human Resources Management Information Systems, pay systems tied to performance, establishing goals and objectives for employees and positions, and then evaluating based on those guides. Also, and importantly, this recommendation carries through on the human capital theme by focusing on the need for developing human resources through investments in training and development.

Decide How much Standardization is Necessary in the Human Capital System

Of all the recommendations, this may be the most challenging because clearly it raises values questions as well as fundamental questions of organizational design "integration versus differentiation" and "centralization versus decentralization." The key to successfully providing agency discretion is to be clear about fundamental values, values that then form the framework within which discretion can be exercised. Police departments run into this challenge every day—trying to instill in patrol officers the fundamental values that will guide them as they exercise discretion in the street even in the absence of close supervision.

In the case of human resources management, the fundamental issue regards the importance of equity and rights—fairness in human resources management AND even more importantly how that importance is going to be insured. Decentralizing gives discretion to tailor human resources policies and practices to different environments and needs, but it also runs the risk—just as in the police example, though probably not as serious in potential consequences—that the need for flexibility, speed, and tailoring of practices will strain the fairness value which is more easily captured in uniform rules. Of course, uniform rules that fail to acknowledge different environments and contexts result in a gap between the formal rules and practices that evolve out of necessity. There is no easy response to this recommendation, which is one element of the sanction function in the PADS quartet.

WORKFORCE PLANNING AS A KEY TO STRATEGIC HRM

Throughout this and the following chapters, we refer to *workforce planning*, providing brief references to its importance. It is a key tool in human resources strategic thinking, and we will describe it in some detail in this section. As we suggest in our model, usually something immediate needs to trigger a strategic view. In the case of workforce planning, recruiting top-notch specialists and managers has become increasingly difficult. This observation draws more attention to demographics of the workforce—demographics that have been around for some time. It is not as if the profile of today's workforce could not have been predicted—at least in broad brush—twenty years ago. The combination of difficulty in hiring and retaining top-quality employees with demographic analysis suggests a trend that is not going away once the current fiscal crisis is over, leading to the desire to plan and try to anticipate, react, and even control the trend. Workforce planning is one of these deliberate responses.

"DEMOGRAPHY IS DESTINY: MANAGEMENT SUMMARY"[10]

In a Nutshell

Situation:

- Three powerful forces—increasing longevity, declining fertility, and the disproportionate size of the "Baby Boom" generation—together drive an unprecedented and relentless shift in the age distribution of the population and the workforce in industrialized countries.
- As workforce growth slows, there are not enough young workers to replace the population and skills of Baby Boomers as they reach retirement age, and labor and skills shortages will become chronic. The fasted growing source of "new labor" will be older people, including those already retired.
- The workforce is growing increasingly diverse, in terms of not only age, but also gender, ethnicity, background, education, lifestyle, and other variables.

Challenges:

- Maintain an adequate supply of labor and skills to sustain business operations and growth despite upheavals in the workplace.
- Redefine the terms of "employment" and "retirement" to attract, retain, motivate, and leverage workers of all ages and various backgrounds.
- Act now to adjust workforce management practices before a labor and skills crisis builds. Those who act early will be prepared for a demographically inevitable future and enjoy short-term workforce productivity benefits along the way.

Key techniques:

- Recruiting and retaining young workers.
- Avoiding a brain drain by meeting mid-career challenges.
- Transcending age bias to leverage mature workers.
- Embracing flexible work arrangements.
- Filling skills gaps and mastering training challenges.
- Aligning compensation, benefits, and other attractors.
- Anticipating demographically driven labor shortages.

Googling "workforce planning" turns up so many sites that one would think that every organization everywhere is engaged in this activity. The International Public Management Association for Human Resources permits us to narrow our view. In winter 2004, the Association published a special issue of *Public Personnel Management* on Workforce and Succession Planning.[11] That issue describes the changing workforce, the metrics of workforce planning, and it provides article-length case studies from the City of Virginia Beach, the state of Pennsylvania, and Henrico County in Virginia. Furthermore, in 2002, IPMA-HR published a Workforce Planning Resource Guide.[12]

Another very credible case is provided by the work of the National Aeronautics and Space Administration (NASA).[13] The NASA report is very useful as a learning tool because it shows the place of workforce planning within a greater workforce strategy. Clearly, workforce planning is a key, but the report shows how important it is to be able to project changes in mission and goals as an integrated feature of the planning. In NASA's case, that analysis reveals areas where the agency would have excess capability and areas where it would have needs. Then, the report addresses management actions necessary to achieve optimal balances between the supply of and demand for labor.

Here are the key elements of NASA's workforce planning strategy: (p. 8 of the report)

- Guidance from and coordination among management at all levels of the Agency regarding the identification of each Center's core capabilities and its current and anticipated work demand.
- Coordinated assessment and planning effort at each Center to identify specific workforce requirements based on work demand and funding.
- Identification of workforce requirements for strong, healthy Center capabilities.
- Assessment of how to utilize both internal and external workforce to meet work requirements.
- Assessment of optimal internal workforce to meet work requirements and sustain a healthy Center.
- Identification of management actions necessary to achieve optimal near-term balance between demand and supply and long-term balance between potential demand and projected supply.

Hennepin County, Minnesota's workforce planning processes is similar to NASA's, suggesting that the methodology of workforce planning is becoming well known and agreed upon. Their steps are outlined below:

- Review of the current workforce profile of each department within the county.
- Identify key department issues and trends and relate the priorities of each department to its present structure.
- Estimate the workforce needed to provide core services.
- Develop a workforce plan.[14]

Ann Daly's summary of the workforce planning effort in Hennepin County reveals that it fits into a broader HRM plan. She writes:

> The workforce planning documents and diversity development plans tie to the Hennepin County Balanced Scorecard (BSC) which is a management and measurement tool used to support ongoing results-based decision making, planning and budgeting at all levels of the county. The BSC is an organizing framework that helps us to align our efforts and resources with the county's overarching goals. We have used customer satisfaction surveys, program progress reviews and placement and development inventories when measuring

how workforce planning and demographic data contributes to departmental results. Workforce planning in Hennepin County has supported the overall mission of the county to provide superior service and improve efficiency by maximizing workforce potential. (p. 9)

THE ROLE OF INDICATORS AND STANDARDS IN HRM SYSTEM EVALUATION

These examples of workforce planning and the role it plays in a broader strategy focus on human resources lend credence to the extent to which workforce planning is occurring in innovative organizations and agencies that would endorse Comptroller General Walker's observation that human capital is at the center of organizational success. Another factor-reinforcing this emphasis is contained in a 2007 report of the Partnership for Public Service issued on the "State of the Public Service."[15] The Partnership is a nonprofit organization whose focus is the revitalization of the federal government and public service. The report calls for a **comprehensive indicator system** for our federal workforce. It uses a car's gas gauge to make its point. "Basically, much of the federal government is a car heading out on a long road trip without a working gas gauge. So what does the federal government need to do? That's easy. Get a gas gauge that works." (p. 4).

1. **The right talent**—Is government getting not only the best people, but also the right talent with the skills and abilities to help agencies achieve their goals?
2. **An engaged workforce**—Is the federal workforce engaged and using its abilities to deliver results?
3. **Strong leadership**—Are senior government leaders inspiring and empowering workers to perform at their best?
4. **Public support**—Do the public support our government and do top job candidates view the federal government as an employer of choice?
5. **Systems and structures**—Is the federal government's infrastructure enabling or inhibiting workers from doing their jobs well?
6. **High performance**—How well are federal workers doing their job of delivering services to the American people and promoting and implementing policies that strengthen our nation?

In other words, we might argue that recognition of strategic human resources thinking and planning as a key element in organizational planning is contained not only with notable examples of workforce planning, but also with the realization that "what is measured is important." In other words, the emphasis on developing indicators that can be used to help assess the condition of HRM in an organization, agency, or level of government suggests that the phrase "people are our most important asset" is becoming more than a platitude. With indicators, we begin to develop systematically gathered information that permits us to assess whether or not people really are an important asset.

Continuing along the line of reasoning that strategic thinking in human resources management is on a noticeable developmental path is a breakthrough model of human resources systems assessment that the National Academy of Public Administration prepared at the invitation and for the use of the University of California.[16] The resultant robust **assessment model** (CAHRS) was developed in response to the sentiment at the university that "A world class educational and scientific institution deserves a world class human resources program to support the acquisition, retention and development of its human talent." (p. iii)

The cornerstone of the model is validated HR standards—the line of reasoning here parallels the logic of the call from the Partnership for Public Service for "indicators of performance." These standards were derived from the HR model that the team developed and validated with a group of experts and in several pilot locations. The standards strive to balance both strategic and operational dimensions, and the report states that the model and standards are transferable to organizations other than the University of California. The process of evaluation is set up very much like an accreditation review. The seven standards are derived from the proposed HR model:

- Standard for HR systemwide management
- Standard for HR strategic management
- Standard for HR operations and program assurance
- Standard for employment and talent management
- Standard for total compensation and benefits
- Standard for training and development
- Standard for work environment and employee/labor relations

Each standard is defined with several key contributing elements identified. Success attributes are then attached to each contributing element, and specific indicators of success are developed for each attribute. There are "essential" success indicators that must be met in order for an agency to meet the standard, and there are other supporting indicators. For example, the standard of "employment and talent management" includes "talent acquisition" as one of four contributing elements. There are two success attributes associated with talent acquisition. One of them is, "Acquires a sufficient number of highly skilled, diverse and competent employees when needed to meet priority mission goals." There are five success indicators associated with this attribute. The essential success indicator for this attribute is, "Recruits talented and diverse candidates based on identified needs and recruitment plans." The standards with associated contributing elements, attributes, and success indicators provide a systematic framework within which a jurisdiction can assess the results of its HRM commitment.

So far in this chapter, we have seen a significant investment and maturity in the field of human resources management. This is reflected in the evidence that strategic thinking is employed as necessary for human resources to truly been seen as the core of organizational success. Strategic thinking has moved well beyond the idea that "it would be nice to think strategically about human resources management" to the point that we now have models to assess both the strategic and operational success of human resources systems.

THE STRATEGIC HR FUNCTION

In the past, the U.S. Office of Personnel Management (OPM) operated as a centralized personnel agency, primarily responsible for the recruitment and assessment of federal employees and the oversight of agency-level personnel operations. However, in the past decade many of OPM's prior responsibilities have been decentralized, and, as a result, OPM has been pushed to take on the role of a strategic partner with other federal agencies. One example of OPM's efforts to be more strategic is the agency's operation of a reimbursable consulting branch targeted toward other federal agencies in need of assistance due to emerging management challenges, reorganizations, or new agency initiatives. Much like private sector management consulting firms, this branch advertises its services to other federal agencies and relies on fees earned from its services to meet its operating budget.[17]

ACHIEVING DATA-DRIVEN HRM THROUGH A STRATEGIC HUMAN RESOURCE MANAGEMENT INFORMATION SYSTEM

The ability to think and plan strategically depends in part on access to reliable information about the past, present, and future and the ability to integrate information produced in the past by separate administrative processes and possibly maintained in separate databases. As a simple example, knowing the age breakdown of an organization's workforce will alert managers to staffing issues associated with retirements and anticipated personnel outlays. The ability to break that information down by skill level and an understanding of the market value of those skills and their availability will enhance human resource planning. Similarly, the movement to develop indicators of success requires a **human resources management information systems (HRMIS)**. Of course, none of this makes any difference if the organization itself does not know where it is headed, which makes a connection with legislative or political intent crucial.

It is possible to design, purchase, or contract out for a management information system that routinely collects information on various factors contributing to organizational effectiveness and to present this information to managers in the form of reports they can use to make necessary changes in policies or procedures. An agency might routinely produce information on equipment costs, personnel costs, overtime, and productivity. HRMIS are routinely integrated with accounting, purchasing, and budgeting software.

Electronic "data marts" are common repositories for information extracted from large databases within an organization but prepared for a single department or group of workers to follow a single HR subject like retirement schedules and workforce planning. Data marts are useful because users can take advantage of available knowledge without having to worry about issues involved with data base construction and management. In addition, "electronic dashboards" can give a visual and timely portrayal of performance indicators—like progress toward workforce diversity goals.[18] In addition, they can be constructed to provide personally tailored information for common transactions like applying for jobs, updating, personal profiles, benefits changes, and compensation viewing.

With the portability and accessibility of electronic data and security concerns, human resources managers must be aware of regulations and statutes that govern the privacy and confidentiality of electronic data storage and transmission. With the number of software products that interface with an HRMIS, the human resources manager also is challenged to identify technology options and make choices. Proper planning to align the requirements with the needs and strategic direction of the HR department and the organization will enhance the value of the investment in an HRMIS. Therefore, involvement with the "project management office" and the "information technology department" early in the process will assist in the ultimate success of the system.

Summary

Strategic human resource management requires the purposeful resolution of human resource program and policy issues within agencies and with agency partners, including nonprofit and private sector firms—to enhance legislative and administrative visions and goals and in the process to promote equity and fairness in human resources management. Contemporary work and organizations, demographic trends, and market-based values, and evolving understanding of governance models and practices challenge traditional views of public personnel management.

The most important message in this chapter is that human resources management issues are strategic in nature as long as labor is considered an asset in addition to a cost. However, strategic thinking must go beyond simple workforce planning. It must incorporate as well a critical view to what human resources managers can add to an organization, what personnel functions can be outsourced or decentralized, and how public service values can be reflected in human resources planning. Once seen in this way, human resource concerns transcend what a personnel department can accomplish on its own. The strategic issues outlined in this chapter require top management attention.

Key Terms

assessment model *79*
assumptions about civil service systems *66*
comprehensive indicator system *79*
contemporary work and organizations *67*
demographic trends *68*
elected officials' perspective *73*
executive perspective *73*
governance *67*
human capital *75*
human resources management information systems (HRMIS) *81*
managerial perspective *73*
market-based values *68*
operator (employee) perspective *72*
strategic human resources management *74*
workforce planning *76*

Discussion Questions

1. What are the assumptions that underpin traditional public personnel management systems?
2. How do contemporary work and organizations, demographic trends, market-based values, and new concepts of governance challenge the assumptions of traditional public personnel systems? Give examples from your own experience.
3. Identify three shifts noted in Table 3-2 that in general you think are most important to effective human resources practices today.
4. Identify the components of the human resources model and how the components interact. After reviewing the examples in the book of how the model works, give an example of your own, either real or hypothetical.
5. Describe and discuss the operator, manager, executive, and political perspectives on human resources management. If you are now working outside of school, which perspective best describes your position? Give one example of how two of the perspectives might coincide and an example of how they might clash.
6. Go online and find the "President's Management Agenda." Then, view the scorecard. What do you think about the idea of a scorecard that reports assessments of progress toward administrative goals? Using the four issue areas in the NAPA (2000) report, how would your agency rate itself in these areas?

7. Describe the key elements in workforce planning. For each element, discuss how much progress your agency has made in workforce planning.
8. Using the six elements of the proposed "comprehensive indicator system," where would your agency score highest and where do you see the need for improvement.
9. If strategic thinking and workforce planning are key elements in achieving organizational transformation and goal accomplishment, why do you think the importance in strategic human resources management was less important in the past than it is today?
10. Put yourself in the place of a public employee, either hypothetical or real. As a public employee or a future public employee, how do you wish to be categorized, as an "asset" or a "cost"? Are you the equivalent of an appreciating piece of property or are you a liability to be minimized? Do you like these categories: assets and costs? The key question is where the heart and soul of employees fits into a picture of strategic human "capital" management—if at all.

Exercise: Evaluating your Human Resources Management System

As an individual or in a team of students, pick an organization with which you are familiar, from your experience as an employee, a community volunteer, or a relative of one of these. Assess that organization.

For each element in the table below, place a circle around the number that best characterizes your organization's Human Management Resource System. Discuss where your agency is doing well and what area needs improvement. If there was one step your agency could take to improve human resource management (excluding hiring, firing, or transferring someone!), what should it be?

1. Single system in theory; in reality multiple systems not developed strategically — Recognize multiple systems, be strategic about system development, define and inculcate core values development, define and inculcate core values

1 2 3 4 5 6 7 8 9 10

2. Merit definition that has the outcome of protecting people and equates fairness with sameness — Merit definition that has the outcome of encouraging better performance and allows differentiation between different talents

1 2 3 4 5 6 7 8 9 10

3. Emphasis on process and rules — Emphasis on performance and results

1 2 3 4 5 6 7 8 9 10

4. Hiring/promoting of talent based on technical expertise — Hiring, nurturing, and promoting of talent to the right places

1 2 3 4 5 6 7 8 9 10

5. Treating personnel as a cost — Treating human resources as an asset and as an investment

1 2 3 4 5 6 7 8 9 10

6. Providing job for life/lifelong commitment — Involving both inners and outers who share core values

1 2 3 4 5 6 7 8 9 10

7. Protection from political influence and unfair treatment justifies tenure — Employee performance and employer need justifies retention

1 2 3 4 5 6 7 8 9 10

8. Performance appraisal based on individual activities					Performance appraisal based on demonstrated contributions to organizational goals				
1	2	3	4	5	6	7	8	9	10
9. Labor–management relationship based on conflicting goals, antagonistic relationship, and ex-post disputes and arbitration of individual cases					Labor–management partnership based on mutual goals of successful organization and employee satisfaction, ex-ante involvement in work design				
1	2	3	4	5	6	7	8	9	10
10. Central agency that fulfills the personnel functions for agencies					Central agency that enables agencies, especially managers, to fulfill the personnel function for themselves				
1	2	3	4	5	6	7	8	9	10

Notes

1. Concours Group (now nGenera) in partnership with Ken Dychtwalk and Age Wave (2003). *Demography is destiny*. www.concoursgroup.com/Demography/DD_MgmtSumm.pdf
2. National Academy of Public Administration (Fall 2006). *Forum: Managing the Workforce of the Future*. GOV.
3. Personal correspondence with John Nalbandian (Summer 2008).
4. The model differs from the previous edition. Created by U.S. Army Major Terence Ray in fall 2006 when he was an MPA graduate student at the University of Kansas.
5. Wilson, J. Q. (1989). *Bureaucracy*. New York: Basic Books.
6. Rabin, J. L., and N. Riccardi. (October 18, 2000). Strike settled: Bus service to resume today. *Los Angeles Times*. www.latimes.com.
7. The President's Management Agenda (2002). www.whitehouse.gov/omb/budget/fy2002/mgmt.pdf
8. http://www.whitehouse.gov/omb/budget/fy2005/managing.html
9. Reported in Walters, J., and C. Thompson (2005). The transformation of the government accountability office: Using human capital to drive change. Washington, DC: IBM Center for the Business of Government, p. 19.
10. Concours Group (now nGenera) in partnership with Ken Dychtwalk and Age Wave (2003). *Demography is destiny*. www.concoursgroup.com/Demography/DD_MgmtSumm.pdf
11. Kiyonaga, Nancy B., ed. (Winter 2004). *Special Issue: Workforce and Succession Planning*, 33, No. 4. Public Personnel Management.
12. International Personnel Management Association for Human Resources (2002). *Workforce planning resource guide for public sector Human resource professionals*. www.ipma-hr.org.
13. National Aeronautics and Space Administration (2006). *Workforce strategy*. www.nasapeople.nasa.gov/HCM/WorkforceStrategy.pdf
14. Daly, A. (August 2006). Workforce Planning: Maximizing Workforce Potential. *International Public Management Association for Human Resources*, p. 7–9.
15. Partnership for Public Service (2007). *State of the public service conference: Report of proceedings*. http://www.ourpublicservice.org/OPS/publications/viewcontentdetails.php?id=116
16. National Academy of Public Administration (July 2007). *A model and process for the certified assessment of human resources systems: A pathway to assurance*. NAPA: Washington, DC.
17. http://www.leadership.opm.gov/Custom/index.aspx
18. See examples of electronic dashboards from San Jose State University at http://www.oir.sjsu.edu/Reports/dashboards/

The HR Role in Policy, Budget, Performance Management, and Program Evaluation

The conceptual model in Chapter 3 explains how an organization can remain relevant by responding appropriately to environmental change and uncertainty in ways that reflect strategic thinking about human resources. However, here, as elsewhere, analytical integration comes at the price of operational clarity. Chapter 4 links this conceptual model to the real world by describing the sequential processes by which ideas become programs. These are policy making, budgeting, performance management, and program evaluation.

Issues become part of a public agenda through the policy process. This process is chaotic and unpredictable, for it involves the serendipitous convergence or "coupling" of agendas, alternative solutions, and politics, all leading to government action.[1] During this process, problems become public policy issues; these issues are framed by competing political agendas; legislatures authorize and chief executives approve policy solutions as law and fund them through a budgeting process. These policy and budget processes are the headwaters of public personnel management because they all lead eventually to paying people to do things.

Human resource planning (HRP) is that aspect of public HRM that mediates between the political environment and managerial implementation of public programs through core HRM activities such as workforce planning, job analysis, job classification, job evaluation, and compensation. In brief, HRP matches agency managers' "wish lists" with political realities generated by projected revenues and political philosophies and goals within a much broader context of factors like the supply and demand for labor. For the line manager, the process begins with a request from the budget office: "What kind and how many positions do you need in order to meet program objectives?" In many cases, this request is preceded by some kind of strategic planning process that helps establish priorities and goals. It ends with legislative authorization of programs and appropriation of funds required to implement them.

Program implementation leads to performance management and program evaluation. Many interests—political, administrative, and clients are but a few—influence how an agency's performance is measured, and how those measurements affect program evaluation. While decisions about a program's continued funding are based on both political and administrative criteria, data-driven decisions are only possible if the agency has a **management information system** that can provide valid and timely information about program performance. Because pay and benefits typically comprise about 70 percent of an agency's budget, an HR manager who can provide valued information about the costs and benefits of alternative methods of public service delivery can be a valued member of the leadership team responsible for making these decisions.

By the end of this chapter, you will be able to:

1. Explain how policy making, budgeting, performance management, and program evaluation are critical to managing public agencies.
2. Describe the HR manager's role in supporting these processes.
3. Explore the difficulties of defining and managing organizational performance in contemporary public service delivery options such as contracting and privatization, public–private partnerships, and organizational networks.
4. Tell how to enhance the role of public HRM management by using data-driven performance management and program evaluation to resolve issues of productivity and privatization.

POLICY MAKING, BUDGETING, PERFORMANCE MANAGEMENT, AND PROGRAM EVALUATION

These core management functions are how organizations develop programs, allocate resources to them, and benchmark their effectiveness.

Policy Making

The American democratic system of government has a constitutional structure that guides and constrains policy design. **Policy making** is the process by which all levels of government make and implement policies. Many experts use a six-stage model to describe the process: initiation, estimation, selection, implementation, evaluation, and termination. Under this model, policy issues initiate with elected officials and the general political environment comprising interest groups, issue networks, and the media. Initiation and estimation both involve how issues are framed (defined or perceived). Once approved through a legislative and executive process, agencies implement them as legal responsibilities, within appropriated funding limits. Periodic evaluations are the basis for future funding. Either the legislative or the executive branch can terminate a program by refusing to renew the enabling legislation, or by not appropriating funds for it.

Being able to analyze policy making as a six-stage process may make it easier to study, but it does not make it easier to understand in practice. Rational, linear models simply cannot include all the imponderable pressures and events that enable issues to advance to the top of politicians' agendas, or to become important to voters.[2] In the pharmaceutical industry, researchers sometimes develop drugs and then accidentally learn what diseases they can cure. The serendipitous discovery that penicillin kills infectious bacteria was actually a solution in search of a problem. Viagra and similar drugs were originally developed to treat high blood pressure. Their marketing and use changed dramatically once male users reported the drug's unanticipated side effect. In similar fashion, policy solutions often languish until they match with an appropriate problem. For example, victim restitution and community-based treatment of nonviolent offenders have always been possible solutions to crime. However, they become politically feasible only after politicians and the public confront the high cost and low effectiveness of lengthy prison sentences. Thus, policy making incorporates both rational and nonrational elements. It relies on defining events like 9/11, tipping points at which people will favor small hybrids instead of large SUVs, changes in available technology, and other unpredictable factors.[3]

Budgeting

A **budget** is a document that attempts to reconcile program priorities with projected revenues. It combines a statement of organizational activities or objectives for a given time period with information about the funds required to engage in these activities or reach these objectives. Historically, the most important purpose has been external control. A **ceiling budget** controls an agency directly by specifying limits to expenditures through appropriations, legislation, or indirectly by limiting agency revenues.

Other types of budgets have different purposes. A line-item budget, which classifies expenditures by type, is useful for controlling types of expenditures as well as their total amount. Performance and program budgets are useful for specifying the activities or programs on which funds are spent, and thereby assist in their evaluation. By separating expenditures on the basis of function (such as health or public safety) or type of expenditure (such as personnel and equipment) or by source of revenue (such as property tax, sales tax, or user fees), administrators and legislators can keep accurate records of an agency's financial transactions for the maintenance of efficiency and control.

Because program approval and appropriations are related, policy making and budgeting involve many of the same participants. Interest groups exert pressure on administrators and legislators to propose or expand favorable programs. Department administrators use these pressures and their own sense of their department's mission, goals, and capabilities to develop proposals and specify the resources (money, time, and people) needed to accomplish them. Chief executives coordinate and balance the requests of various departments. After all, resources are limited and departmental objectives should be congruent with the overall objectives of the city, nonprofit agency, or state or national government. In many cases, the chief executive has a staff agency responsible for informing departments or agencies of planning limitations, objectives, and resource limits. In smaller jurisdictions, the chief administrative officer individually may perform this coordinating function. In addition, in other cases, there may be a budget task group or department representatives that cooperatively seek to align budget requests with revenue forecasts. The chief executive or chief administrative officer presents the combined budget request of all departments within the executive arm to a legislature or board (city council, county commission, nonprofit board, state legislature, or Congress).

Legislative action on appropriations requests varies depending on the legislature's size and the staff's capabilities. At the national and state levels, committees consider funding requests from various agencies. These committees examine funding requests in the light of prior expenditures, testimony from department heads and lobbyists, and the committee members' own feelings about the comparative importance of the agency's programs and objectives. Appropriations requests are approved when the committee agrees on which programs should be funded and on the overall level of funding.

In an elementary view, after new programs are authorized, funded, and signed into law, the executive branch is responsible for executing them. The chief executive is responsible for administering the expenditure of funds to accomplish the objectives intended by the legislature; department administrators are responsible for managing their budgets and programs accordingly. **Financial management** is the process of developing and using systems to ensure that funds are spent for the purposes for which they have been appropriated. Through an accounting system, each agency keeps records of financial transactions and compares budgets with actual expenditures. Agency managers engage in financial management when they take steps to limit expenditures, transfer funds from one budget category to another to meet program priorities, or borrow or invest idle funds.

Audit, the last step in the budget cycle, is the process of ensuring that funds were actually spent for the intended purpose and in the prescribed manner. Controller's offices inside the organization, and auditors outside, review expenditures for compliance with legislative mandates and prescribed procedures. In the case of waste, fraud, and abuse, agencies may be required to return funds and responsible officials may be subject to organizational reprimand and criminal prosecution by state authorities.

Figure 4-1 shows the process of budget preparation, approval, and management. This process is a recurrent ritual whose frequency depends on the length of the appropriations cycle. Most governments budget annually, although the problems associated with continually developing and evaluating programs have led some states to develop biennial budgets (every two years). In the typical annual budget cycle, an agency or a department is normally developing the next year's budget a year in advance of the period for which it is requesting funds. At the same time, it is also evaluating programs from the prior year. Although most governments follow an annual cycle, their budget years begin and end on different dates. For most state governments their fiscal year begins on July 1 and ends on June 30, while the federal government's fiscal year begins October 1 and ends September 30. Other governments follow the calendar year, January 1 to December 31.

Budgeting can be viewed politically as a contest among opposing agencies for scarce resources, organizationally as the formal set of policies and procedures that govern the approval process, or informally as a ritualized interaction among the conflicting expectations of program managers, political executives, legislators, and lobbyists. The less revenue available, the more contentious the budgeting process, with access to legislators and legislative committees—a scarce resource. Furthermore, where antigovernment emotion infuses legislative sessions, the stakes are high for agency administrators who see their agency's programs threatened with reduction, elimination, or transfer to the private/nonprofit sectors. Budgeting then becomes much more "political," in that decisions are made more on philosophical inclination or particularized interests than on rational and analytic planning that administrators are more comfortable with.

Performance Management and Program Evaluation

Because decisions on future funding for programs and agencies are likely to involve an evaluation of past performance, **performance management** becomes a critical part of the planning process. It is complex because the criteria used for **program evaluation** differ

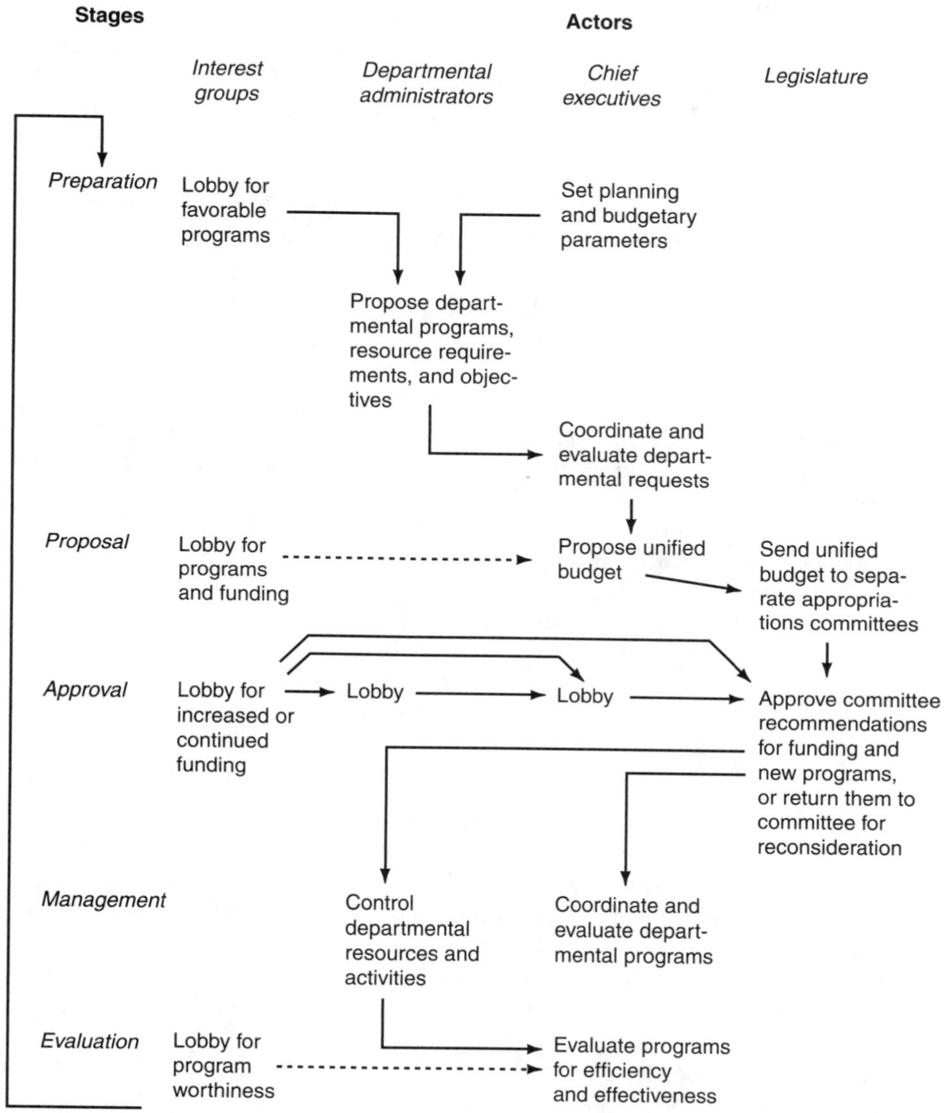

FIGURE 4-1 The Budget Process (*Source*: Donald E. Klingner, *Public Administration: A Management Approach* © 1983 by Houghton Miffin, Boston, Mass All rights reserved)

across different users, and the measures vary with the interests involved. The important thing to remember is that performance measure generally shifted from evaluation of inputs (expenses) by means of audits to evaluation of program **outcomes** by **performance measures**. That is, regardless of whether an agency spent its money in accordance with the appropriations law, or whether the program achieved its predicted results, and if those results contributed toward solving the policy issue at hand.

Various terms like *output*, *performance*, *efficiency*, *effectiveness*, and *bang for the buck* are commonly associated with productivity. Technically, **productivity** concerns two specific assessments of performance. First, **efficiency** is a ratio of outputs to inputs. Measuring efficiency requires identifying a performance outcome (such as the number of lunches served in a school cafeteria or the number of arrests made by a police department), and identifying the resources used to produce the outcome such as employee hours worked or funds allocated. The efficiency ratio then becomes:

$$\frac{\text{Number of meals served}}{\text{Number of cafeteria employee hours worked}} \quad \text{or}$$

$$\frac{\text{Number of arrests}}{\text{Police department personnel costs}}$$

Efficiency can increase either by increasing the number of meals served with the same number of employees, or by serving the same number of meals with fewer employees. However, what if we served more meals, yet the meals were unappetizing and not fully consumed? What if arrests failed to lead to convictions and instead crowded the courts? Could we say that productivity had improved? Probably not.

Productivity, then, also implies **effectiveness**, a concern with the quality of the output measured against some standard. Thus, a more valid productivity measure would incorporate a performance quality issue, such as:

$$\frac{\text{Number of meals consumed}}{\text{Number of cafeteria hours worked}} \quad \text{or}$$

$$\frac{\text{Number of arrests leading to convictions}}{\text{Police department personnel costs}}$$

Thus, concerns for efficiency focus attention on input–output ratios and answer the question, "Are we getting the most for our money?" Implied in this question is the effectiveness concern, "Are we accomplishing the goal we set out to accomplish?"

On top of this pyramid of questions is a **responsiveness** question, "Is the goal we set out to accomplish worthwhile in light of the other goals we might have chosen?" In the cafeteria example, the responsiveness question might have been, "Do we want to invest public money in school lunches or library books?" Once this question is answered, the school district can attend to the effectiveness and efficiency questions. The responsiveness question is difficult to answer because it requires stakeholders to explicitly clarify their outcome preferences and the values that underlie them. In many cases, an agency will not implement programs based on efficient or effective solutions to a problem because those programs run counter to the assumptions and values of key stakeholders. For example, preventing the spread of AIDS and other sexually transmitted diseases is a significant objective of many state and county public health systems. Two efficient and effective solutions are distributing condoms in prisons and providing intravenous (IV) drug users with clean needles or teaching them to use bleach to clean their own "works." However, implementing either solution is not possible in the current political environment because key stakeholders—elected officials and the interests they represent—consider that publicly accepting that sexual activity does occur in prisons or use of IV drug does occur among the general population means that they implicitly condone these practices, or at least that political opponents may effectively accuse them of this.

In practice, resolving political responsiveness issues means recognizing the differences between rational/economic and political/social perspectives on policy making. From a **rational/economic perspective**, an effective solution is one that **cost-benefit analysis (CBA)** shows has financial benefits greater than its costs. For example, investments in prenatal and newborn medical care produce benefits many times greater than their costs. Based on **risk assessment**, it is economically irrational to spend money to mitigate air pollution if the costs of mitigation programs are greater than the calculated value of the human lives lost by premature death or disability caused by air pollution. Yet, actual policy may run counter to these recommendations because a **political/social perspective** controls outcome assessment. For example, our current health-care system is based on third-party benefit policies that encourage relatively high investments in health care at the end of life and relatively low ones at the beginning. In addition, air pollution control policies are often based on the absolute value of human life rather than the relative risk of death from pollutants.

Because the responsiveness question requires explicit value judgments resulting in winners and losers, governments frequently focus on efficiency questions aimed at saving money. It is easier and more popular to ask why the school superintendent is making $180,000 a year than it is to determine whether the school district should be hiring more teachers or buying more computers. Critical responsiveness questions are often avoided until losses in service become so obvious that explicit discussions of political priorities must take place.

HOW THE HR MANAGER SUPPORTS THESE PROCESSES

The primary role public personnel managers play in the **policy-making** process combines their staff responsibility of assisting other department heads and their line responsibility of directing their own departments. Their staff responsibility is to work with department heads so they can realistically predict the human resource needs of various program options. In this role, they function as neutral experts. Their second role in the policy-making process is to provide input—again as neutral experts—on the positive and negative consequences of alternative policy options for staffing needs in their own departments. For example, a decision to contract out a particular service may result in reduced staffing needs for the agency responsible for that program, but increased contract negotiation and compliance responsibilities for the HR department.

Public HR managers play a similar staff role in the budget process. First, their staff responsibility is to work with department heads so they can realistically predict the pay and benefit costs associated with alternative program delivery options. In addition, they ensure that requests will conform to personnel policy and practices and will reflect the hiring or downsizing needs of agencies. For example, a city police chief may have received a mandate from the city council to "cut crime." Translated into budget terms, this may mean that the council is willing to allocate additional money to hire more police officers. Working with the chief executive officer and the personnel and budget departments, the police department will analyze staffing; examine the classification scheme to determine the salary associated with each new position; and determine total costs including wages, benefits, uniform allowances, recruitment, training, and equipment. Then the department will develop a request reflecting the combined analysis and possibly the political realities of the budget process in order to anticipate the city council's reaction. The police chief will submit the request to the city manager (or mayor), who then reviews it against other council priorities and revenue projections and forwards it to the council, or appropriate council committee, as part of a total proposed budget. The HR director's second budget preparation function is to develop and defend the budget needed to provide personnel support services (such as recruitment and selection, job analysis and classification, operation of the payroll and benefits system, training and orientation, performance evaluation, grievances and disciplinary action, and collective bargaining) to other departments.

Because pay and benefits constitute such a large proportion of an agency's budget, both HR managers and budget officers are heavily involved in budget management throughout the year. Agency managers and supervisors play the primary role because they are responsible for controlling and reallocating human resources to meet program priorities within budget constraints. Agency personnel managers respond to the priorities set by managers by filling positions, paying employees, and otherwise implementing their decisions. However, they also monitor accident rates that affect worker compensation premiums and use of health-care benefits for their impact on future insurance premiums. In a cutback situation, agency personnel managers may have to help prepare plans to reduce personnel expenditures. These plans commonly include freezes on hiring and promotions and cutbacks on hours worked, proposed reductions in benefits, and the replacement of permanent workers with part-time or temporary employees.

Public HR managers also play a critical role in **productivity improvement** by monitoring the efficiency or effectiveness of program **outputs** compared with personnel costs, or departmental compliance with legal requirements. Table 4-1 shows examples of using an HRMIS for data-driven strategic performance measurement.

Here again, their role is secondary to that of program managers and supervisors, who are directly responsible.[4] Effective HR oversight over performance management is indirect. It means making sure that managers and supervisors apply valid effectiveness measures and reduce agency exposure to financial and legal liability. This means that the HR manager's focus should be strategic rather than operational.[5] However, in reality, it is extraordinarily difficult for HR directors to avoid being drawn into departmental personnel issues because individual personnel actions, when considered together, comprise the conflict between competing values, objectives, and demands.[6] Their understandable tendency is to react immediately and concretely to requests for individual personnel actions from agency directors or other elected and appointed officials, rather than by viewing and responding to these requests in a way that more adequately reflects their strategic oversight responsibilities. The HR department may also engage in "firefighting" because its existing management information system does not allow more strategic and data-driven decision making.

An example of the linkages between budgeting, productivity, and a human resource information system might focus on whether cost reductions can beneficially occur through an early retirement program. The pension costs, lump-sum payouts, payouts for sick leave, and loss of valued competencies have to be weighed against the lower salaries and benefits of younger workers who might need to be added.[7] Recruitment, selection, and training costs of newer workers have to be calculated as well, along with the newer knowledge that they might bring to the workplace.

TABLE 4–1 HRMIS Applications to Program Evaluation

Activity	HRMIS Applications
PLANNING	
Human resource planning	Compile inventory of current employees' skills; determine whether these meet forecast future needs
Job analysis and classification	How many employees are in different occupations?
Compensation	Determine current pay and benefit costs for all employees; project the cost of alternative proposed pay and benefit packages, online benefits enrollment, and monitoring
ACQUISITION	
Affirmative action	Compare actual utilization of particular groups with their representation in the labor market; assess organizational affirmative action plan compliance
Recruitment	Compile new hire estimates based on anticipated staffing needs; Are current recruitment efforts sufficient to meet them?
Selection	Do an applicant's qualifications meet minimum standards for a given position? Do selected applicants meet performance standards for their positions?
DEVELOPMENT	
Productivity	Record performance of organizational units; compare to other units or previous time periods
Performance appraisal	Record employee performance; compare to other employees, performance standards, or previous time periods
Training and development	Summarize training activities and costs; assess training needs by comparing skills; assess OD needs by measuring organizational climate
Employee motivation and job design	Measure employee productivity, turnover, absenteeism, and internal motivation; assess effect of changes in job design on productivity and motivation
Safety	Record injuries, accidents, and illnesses; use these data to change safety regulations, selection critiera, or employee orientation
SANCTION	
Labor–management relations	Collect and compare salary and benefit data against that of other positions or jurisdictions; compute the cost of proposed changes in pay and benefits
Discipline and grievances	Compile reports on the number and type of grievances and disciplinary actions; use these data to recommend changes in work rules, employee orientation, or supervisory training
Constitutional rights of employees	Record cases of sexual harassment or civil rights violations; use these to improve affirmative action compliance, employee orientation, or supervisory training
CONTROL AND ADAPTATION	
Evaluation	Collect data through HRMIS to evaluate all public personnel management activities

MANAGING CONTEMPORARY ORGANIZATIONAL PERFORMANCE

The governmental response to revenue shortfalls draws attention more broadly to the productivity of public agencies.

Broadly speaking, programs that offer productivity programs seem to cluster into three areas. The first area includes those programs that traditional HR directors commonly propose and manage:

- Job simplification
- Job enrichment, employee empowerment, and use of teams where appropriate
- Incentive awards
- Increased sophistication in training
- Competency-based hiring, training, and appraisal methods
- Specification of work standards
- Increased office communication, team building, and organizational development
- Total quality management
- Alternative work schedules

The second area is predicated on increased use of technology. Its implementation thus requires the HR director to work cooperatively with other members of a management team (e.g., capital budget directors, financial managers, cost-benefit analysts, and **information and communications technologies** (**ICTs**) specialists):

- Labor-saving capital equipment shifting from three- and two-person sanitation crews to a one-person side-loaded truck
- More sophisticated software in areas like record keeping, payroll, and billing along with an integration of financial and human resource information databases.
- Electronic tools for scheduling, tracking of projects, and early warning of problems

The third set of projects and innovations involve changes in organizational structure, processes, and operating procedures. Their implementation requires not only the cooperation of other members of a management team, but also the support of elected and appointed officials whose policy and budget decisions reflect basic choices among interacting public HRM systems and their underlying values:

- Privatization
- Contracting out
- Substituting temporary and part-time employees for career employees
- Reduction-in-force
- Flexibility in civil service procedures
- Selective decentralization or reorganization into homogeneous units
- Increased use of performance measures and work standards to monitor productivity
- Consolidation of services
- Use of economic-rational decision models for scheduling and other problems

Thus far, we have been discussing productivity from the perspective of a single agency. This perspective is natural because classical organization theory and definitions of effectiveness were defined from the perspective of a single focal organization.[8] Yet **public–private partnerships** that involve the use of contractors or privatization means an increase in the number of organizations involved with service delivery and complicate traditional notions of accountability between elected officials and administrators. For example, the contracting out of foster-care services in Kansas illustrates how market-based challenges to traditional political and administrative perspectives complicated expectations of accountability. The result was a situation where the challenge of accommodating three crosscutting expectations of accountability (derived from the three competing perspectives of politics, administration, and markets) made the already-complex job of public management even more difficult.[9] For another example, the use of private contractors (e.g., Blackwater or Halliburton in Iraq) to supplement uniformed military and civilian government employees raises similar issues of Congressional oversight and accountability.[10]

Today, the context of performance management is likely to comprise networked transorganizational systems.[11] The activities defined as boundary spanning from the perspective of a single organization relating to its environment are more likely to be viewed as internal communication and information exchange from a network perspective. Effective public policy responses require coordinated flows of information, decision making, and program implementation within a **network** of organizations representing different levels of government (local, state, national, and international) and different sectors (business, government, and community-based organizations.[12] It was the lack of network effectiveness as much as the lack of individual organizational effectiveness that led to ineffective responses to Hurricane Katrina. In sum, the locus for evaluating effectiveness has shifted from the individual organization to the network, and the criteria for outcome evaluation have shifted from organizational effectiveness to network performance.[13] Public administrators in general, and public HR managers in particular, must focus on issues like interagency effectiveness, multilateral accountability, organizational culture, and personal ethics generated by conflict and collaboration across sectors and levels of government.[14]

ENHANCING THE HR MANAGER'S ROLE IN PRODUCTIVITY AND PRIVATIZATION DECISIONS

Because they enable an agency to measure performance accurately and to rationally predict the costs and benefits of alternative methods of delivering public services, HRMIS is crucial to managerial and political decisions about what services the government should provide and who should deliver them. Why should a city government collect trash when a private vendor could do the same? Why should the government manage lodging and concessions in public parks when private businesses could do the same? In fact, in the federal government, each agency or department is required annually to provide an analysis of which HR activities could be outsourced and which are inherently governmental.

These examples highlight the most popular form of privatization—contracting with private business to deliver the services that governments have been providing.[15] It may result in the abolition of the agency (at times an intended ideological goal). Privatization offers all the advantages of service purchase agreements but holds down labor and construction costs on a larger scale. It has become commonplace in areas like solid waste disposal where there is an easily identifiable "**benchmark**" (standard cost and service comparison with the private sector), and where public agency costs tend to be higher because of higher pay and benefits.[16]

Governments have contracted with private business for services like street construction and repair, tree trimming and planting, ambulance service, vehicle towing and storage, building and grounds maintenance, data processing, legal services, and tax bill processing.[17] HR directors are not the primary decision makers on this issue. Elected officials, agency heads and staff, chief administrative officers, and department heads lead the discussion. Yet in their role as mediators and experts, HR directors are often asked to assess the pros and cons of privatization, especially as it affects the workforce. How should they respond to such requests? Fortunately, they can do so as neutral experts, based on a wealth of available research on privatization's parameters, pros, and cons.[18]

Other, more sweeping examples of privatization abound. For example, the new city of Sandy Springs, Georgia, has virtually no permanent employees. It contracts with an engineering firm to provide nearly all services except police and fire which it contracts with the county. The city manager reports that administration is easier than will an array of full- and part-time employees. If there is a serious personnel problem, the manager or department head simply tells the contract manager from the engineering firm, and that person takes care of it.[19] Similarly, some years ago in Santa Clarita, California, the city manager told one of the authors how much easier it was to contract with the L.A. County Sheriff's department for public safety services than to administer the city's own police force. The big issue for him was "no union negotiations." Moreover, virtually all the officers knew the city because they lived in the San Fernando Valley. The police chief was treated and acted like a permanent department head.

Chandler and Feuille identify four characteristics of the services most frequently contracted for by local governments: (1) there is no compelling reason that government deliver the service, (2) a number of private-sector firms could usually supply the service, (3) the service usually requires low levels of skilled labor, and (4) outputs are usually easy to monitor.[20] Siegel, summarizing twenty years of state and local governments' experience, concludes that privatization and service contracting outcomes are most likely to be successful when governments:

- Pick a service with clear objectives that can be measured and monitored.
- Use in-house or external competition and avoid sole-source contracting.
- Develop adequate cost accounting systems to compare service alternatives and monitor contractor performance.
- Consider negative externalities such as impacts on an existing workforce, impacts on the local economy, other governments or functions, governmental policies, or certain societal groups.[21]

Privatization's impact on productivity has been mixed. Advocates claim that contracting out frequently saves public dollars because competing firms are more likely to provide services more efficiently than government monopolies. They highlight the savings that can be achieved through economies of scale. For example, while one city may be unable to purchase an expensive piece of equipment to repave streets, a private company with contracts to several cities could. They also point out that private companies have more flexible personnel practices, allowing them to hire and lay off employees easily and save money with less generous wages and benefit packages and with more temporary and part-time employees. Moreover, they attribute productivity increases to a change in public agency culture toward identifying customers and providing market-based services.[22]

Critics assert that privatization may result in cutting corners to maximize profits, provide incentives to deal only with clients who are easy to serve, increase the risk of graft and corruption, and reduce the capacity to deliver the service if privatization does not work.[23] Another concern is that the flexibility accompanying privatization may release the private firm from obligations to follow open meetings laws and open records acts. Further, privatization creates collaborative networks that diffuse accountability. Whom do citizens hold accountable when they are dissatisfied with a service the government outsources?[24] Moreover, the personnel techniques that have become more common under these emergent systems may actually increase some personnel costs, particularly those connected with employment of independent contractors, reemployed annuitants, and temporary employees.[25] Downsizing may eventually lead to higher recruitment, orientation and training costs, and loss of the organizational memory and "core expertise" necessary to effectively manage contracting or privatization initiatives.[26] Minimum staffing usually results in increased payment of overtime and higher rates of employee accidents and injuries. As the civil service workforce shrinks, it is also aging. This means increases in pension payouts, disability retirements, workers' compensation claims, and health-care costs.

In addition to its impact on productivity, productivity remains controversial because it involves the reallocation of jobs from the public to the private sector. This brings values and personnel systems into conflict and highlights the inherently political underpinnings of public HR policy and administration. For example, those responsible for finances may favor contracting out as a way of averting a costly union contract and work rules. However, the loss of public jobs invites the political displeasure of employee unions. Even though the private contractor would hire many public employees, unions object strenuously to contracting out because their members will usually find themselves with lower wages and benefits even if they keep their jobs.[27] Social equity may suffer as women and minorities who benefit from gains in government employment find themselves at a disadvantage with employers less commitment to affirmative action and merit.[28] Moreover, private employers are under no obligation to provide constitutional protections to their employees or to the clients they serve.[29]

Enthusiasm for productivity improvement in government opens opportunities for an expanded role for the HR manager. The price for entering this decision-making arena is expertise that those involved in productivity projects will value and subsequently search out. This involves knowledge of technical operations and service delivery options and the ability to apply knowledge of the applied behavioral sciences to issues of performance management, productivity improvement, and privatization.[30] Knowledge of the applied behavioral sciences is becoming increasingly valuable considering the impact that productivity decisions have, especially those involving privatization and downsizing, on workforce morale and commitment. Understanding organizational change processes; the conditions that ease adaptation to change; the conditions that produce resistance to change; and the competence to deal with uncertainty, conflict, and anxiety are qualities of the effective HR manager as case study three at the end of the chapter shows. Academically, this knowledge is found in the social sciences: psychology, sociology, anthropology, social psychology, communication studies, and political science. The application of social science knowledge to real-life problems often is referred to as **applied behavioral science (ABS)**. In the federal government, the extensive research by the Office of Personnel Management and the Merit Systems Protection Board into federal employee attitudes and the effectiveness of pay for performance fall into this category of expertise.

April 5, 2008
To: John Nalbandian
Fr: Department Head
Re: Downsizing

As organizations "thin" and the competition for scarce public jobs increase, the process of filling vacancies that are retained in the budget becomes a war within the organization. If the position is actually re-budgeted and advertised, the competition for this public job now creates a large number of applications. Many times, individuals with real qualifications for the position are at a premium due to private-sector competition. Other applicants will cite that local residency, community knowledge, and even friendship with staff or local officials should outweigh required job skills. Thus, often we are confronted with a selection process with many wrong solutions and few win-win outcomes. The result will often be a political or legal challenge to the selection decision. In addition, many public organizations are losing the "in-house generalists" in the middle management ranks of the organization through the thinning of the organization. These individuals began their careers in very technical areas. However, due to tenure, career advancement, and program needs, they have grown into positions of mid-management and effectively operate the organization day-to-day. These positions are exactly those that are at risk in each budget cycle. In an attempt to reduce personnel costs, we quickly rule out department heads, technical staff, and lower-level operating staff from serious consideration for a reduction-in-force. This leaves the middle management supervisors and operational generalists or program operators as the moving targets of the budget process. Each time a person like this is cut, it becomes more difficult for program staff to negotiate needed compromises within the organization.

The result is a decline in staff who share a public-sector philosophy of providing service in an equitable manner for the community. Instead, the hard-core technical staff remain and find themselves unable to communicate with other parts of the agency. The greatest challenge from this conflict is that many of the day-to-day decisions on operations are now made at the highest level of the organization, where they may become politicized. They are brokered on the top floor of city hall or among the department heads of the city. The remaining energy and time of the administrative team after these in-house wars provides little opportunity for creative solutions or ideas leading to better public services.

Summary

There is a close relationship between policy making, budgeting, performance management, and program evaluation. Because these involve both political and technical decisions, the HR manager—supervisor, line manager, or personnel specialist—is centrally involved.

Once approved, a policy represents compromises over political and technical issues concerning governmental programs and objectives. A budget is the allocation of resources to agencies to initiate or continue a program. Performance management focuses on how to implement government programs and services as effectively and efficiently as possible. Frequently, the focus is on how to scale back on programs and service levels without damaging the quality of public services unacceptably. Program evaluation is the application of political and economic criteria—developed through techniques such as risk analysis and cost-benefit analysis—to asses an operational program's efficiency, effectiveness, or political responsiveness.

In the current environment, performance management is likely to occur in public–private partnerships or networked organizations that complicate issues of authority and accountability. One area that continues to attract advocates of administrative efficiency is the privatization of public services. Nevertheless, the hope that the private sector can deliver public services at lower cost is tempered by concerns that employee and client rights will be eroded, that social equity claims will receive less attention, and that accountability mechanisms like open meeting laws and open records requirements will be diminished.

These increased options for performance improvement potentially offer HR managers an expanded role in strategic workforce planning. To actually assume this role, they must be informed and effective members of a team of managers, elected, and appointed officials who understand technical operations and service delivery options and who can apply this knowledge as internal consultants to issues of performance management, program evaluation, and productivity improvement.

Key Terms

applied behavioral science (ABS) *97*
audit *88*
benchmark *95*
budget *87*
ceiling budget *87*
cost-benefit analysis (CBA) *91*
effectiveness *90*
efficiency *90*
financial management *88*
human resource planning (HRP) *85*
information and communications technologies (ICTs) *94*
management information system (MIS) *86*
network (organizations) *95*
outcomes *89*
outputs *92*
performance management *88*
performance measures *89*
policy making *86*
political/social perspective *91*
productivity *89*
productivity improvement *92*
program evaluation *88*
public–private partnerships *94*
rational/economic perspective *91*
responsiveness *90*
risk assessment *91*

Discussion Questions

1. How do policy making, budgeting, and performance management epitomize the impact of the value of political responsiveness on public personnel management?
2. How are HRP and forecasting in public agencies related to the budgetary process?
3. Define and then describe the relationship among the three alternative definitions of productivity (efficiency, effectiveness, and responsiveness).
4. Describe the elements in a HRMIS and the role such a system plays in an organization's ability to meet its goals? If you are familiar with such a system, what information does it produce that is helpful to agency managers? What are the drawbacks?
5. What are the pros and cons of contracting out? If you have experience with contracting out, what challenges did you face in writing the contract specifications and what challenges did you face in administering the contract?
6. Describe the HR manager's enhanced role in seeking productivity improvements.

Case Study #1: A Day in the Life of a City Manager

One year ago, in April, Cityville (population 80,000), a suburban city, hired you, Arlene Mayberry, as the new city manager. You brought a reputation for sound financial management and were chosen unanimously by the council. Cityville has experienced revenue shortfalls in the past two years due to a revenue decline in sales tax. The shortfall resulted in modest increases in the mill levy during these two years. The school board's mill levy increased substantially a year ago due to a cutback in state aid to school districts. The county's levy is scheduled to rise modestly for the next three years due to commitments previous commissions have made to a significant capital improvements program.

In April, Save Our City, a group dedicated to holding the line on taxes, surprised everyone, including you, by electing two of its slate of three candidates to the city council. The council now consists of these two members, Robert Pipes and Caroline Nixon, both elected to four-year terms; Jane Scott, a very politically astute middle-of-the-road council member who has two years remaining on her term; Max Laney, an ex-police officer supported by the Fraternal Order of Police, with two years remaining on the council; and Ron Reaume, who ran on a platform expressing concern for rebuilding a sense of community and respect for diversity and was elected to a two-year term. Reaume has already said he will not run for reelection. Scott and Laney have not indicated their plans.

You view this group as very diverse politically and potentially difficult to work with. You expect that a number of issues will be decided on split votes. In the summer following the election, after considerable debate and political maneuvering, the new council accepted the budget you had proposed on a 3-2 vote. The fiscal year runs from January 1 to December 31. None of the council members wanted to raise taxes, and the two-mill increase you reluctantly proposed was reduced to one mill with the two Save Our City council members voting against adoption; they favored no tax increase under anything other than financial exigency.

After adoption, Pipes and Nixon jointly issued a press release calling for tightening the belt, increased productivity, and sacrifices just like those made by private-sector small businesses and ordinary citizens. The newspaper carried a front-page story without editorial comment, even though the publisher is known to be sympathetic to their cause.

After the budget was adopted, during the fall and winter it became obvious that police-community relations were showing signs of strain. A self-appointed task force representing a coalition of culturally diverse groups met and held a number of forums to gather information about how citizens felt the police were treating them. The forums were not well attended, but it was clear from those who did attend that individual members of minority populations in Cityville felt the police had treated them inequitably. For example, one African-American youth said he was walking home from a late-night job carrying a bag of groceries when he was stopped by the police and told to empty the contents of the bag.

In the spring, responding to a 911 family disturbance call, the police shot and killed a young Asian wielding a knife. The police claimed self-defense; the family, speaking little English, was distraught and suggested that the police had acted too quickly and more out of concern for their own safety than for the victim or family.

The event heightened tension in the community, even though the vast majority of Cityville supported the police. The council was aware of this majority, but Reaume in particular believed something ought to be done and urged city staff to make some suggestions. He became an occasional visitor to the meetings of the task force on police-community relations—now heavily attended—and pledged to introduce their anticipated report to the council. Laney defended the police at the next council meeting, noting that police work had become more dangerous in Cityville, and that these events, tragic as they are, happen in today's violent world.

The next week, Pipes and Nixon declared that it might be worthwhile to look into a possible contract with the sheriff's department for law enforcement. They contended that the sheriff's department was larger, had better training, and could provide law enforcement more cheaply than Cityville could on its own. Laney became extremely angry! The leadership of the police union quickly set up appointments with each of the council members. Reaume backtracked a bit, suggesting that rebuilding the sense of community in Cityville required maintaining an independent police force.

As this political maneuvering was going on, the budget process was beginning. The police chief, Jack "Buck" Fishbach, requested a meeting with you. Buck is a no-nonsense law enforcement officer, professionally trained and tolerant of city managers at best. He had been one of the original founders of the Fraternal Order of Police in Cityville when he was just a corporal, years ago. He reminded the city manager that ten years ago the city had passed a half-cent sales tax to hire new police officers. You knew this. The chief added that since that time, in order to show fiscal restraint, the city had not hired a single officer, despite the addition of some 10,000 citizens. This was news to you, and you kicked yourself for not knowing it already. Further, the chief claimed that the police had become exasperated and very angry because lack of staffing had required them to cut back on the very community-oriented activities they were now being criticized for not having performed. He said he was going to develop and present to you a budget proposal designed to augment staff over a five-year period. You knew that the only way to hire more police would be to raise the mill levy.

After the chief leaves, you get a call from the newspaper publisher wanting to know how things are going.

Questions

1. What are you going to tell the publisher?
2. How are you going to approach the budget?
3. How are you going to deal with the chief of police?
4. How are you going to deal with the council?

Case Study #2: Privatization

A majority of the governing body has pledged to the voters that it would explore all avenues available to privatize city services. It has directed the chief administrative officer to present council with some options. After discussion with department heads, the CAO has suggested the following: The city can save some $500,000 annually if it privatizes its sanitation service. This savings could translate into a reduction in the property tax of some 5 percent.

Council member Rodriguez asks how this savings can be achieved and whether the present sanitation workers will lose their jobs. The CAO responds that based on conversations with him, the contractor would hire all of the displaced employees who apply. "However," she adds, "a large amount of the savings probably would be achieved by reducing employee benefits, including health-care coverage. There will be no pension benefit."

Council member Johnston indicates that 70 percent of the employees who will have to change jobs are racial minorities. He noted that the skill level of the sanitation workers is such that they will not have any choice but to accept the reduced standard of living.

Council member Reyes acknowledges Johnstón's concern but indicates that the savings will be reflected in a property tax reduction that should benefit the poorest landowners the most than those on fixed incomes in modest homes.

Council member Richardson suggests that the city's economic development strategy is aimed at developing good-paying jobs. He asks if the privatization of sanitation services will advance that goal for minorities as well as other citizens and taxpayers.

Prior to the evening that the city council will discuss this item, the council members report that a number of taxpayers have called urging privatization and following through on campaign pledges. It appears to the council members that the majority of voters would favor the privatization.

At the evening the item is on the council's agenda, and the room is packed. On one side are members of a taxpayer's group in favor of the privatization. On the other side are about half the city's sanitation employees, and a group of African-American and Hispanic clergy and community activists who are against privatization.

Questions

1. What makes this case so difficult?
2. What expressions of different values can you find?
3. Who should make the decision whether or not to privatize? Defend your choice.

Case Study #3: Between a Rock and a Hard Place

To: John Nalbandian and Donald Klingner
Fr: Under-Secretary, State Department of Human Resources
Date: April 15, 1996
Subj: Downsizing

The Department of Human Resources administers Workers' Compensation Insurance, Unemployment Insurance, and a variety of Employment and Training programs. We do it with 150 fewer employees than we did 16 months ago. Real dollar reductions in federal funding have harshly cut into our ability to support our operations. Unlike most other cabinet-level agencies, the Department of Human Resources is 99 percent federal funded or employer-fee funded. Like most state agencies, personnel salaries and benefits are more than 80 percent of our total cost. When the federal budget takes a bite out of our budget, the only recourse is to reduce staffing. That is a polite euphemism for firing real people. It's a hard thing to do.

In January 1995, the department had 1,079 full-time equivalent positions and about 1,000 people actually on the payroll. The new administration inherited a funding problem that had been building for five years. Shifting personnel and costs between programs and funds had prevented layoffs during that time. The bill came due with the change of administrations. Unemployment insurance funds declined about 10 percent this year. Employment and training funds took a bigger hit. In total, the department received about $6 million less this year than last year. That was a 15 percent decrease. Again, I point out that this was a real dollar decrease, not a typical inside-the-beltway decrease in the increase.

Our programs are on staggered fiscal years, so the budget reality came home in July and then was reinforced with further funding cuts in October. In July, we instituted a hiring freeze to take the most advantage of attrition. About fifty people left the payroll and were not replaced. By October, it was clear that a layoff would occur, and we spent the next three months going through all the hoops and barrels at the division of personnel services in the department of administration. This was a learning experience for us as well. The most senior worker there could not remember when the state had last had a layoff. We were rewriting the book. The "bureaucracy myth" is not always fair, but in this case, it took us until the day of the scheduled layoff announcement before all the process was approved and paperwork cleared. We struggled with holdups, delays, and paper shuffling to no end. Every time we thought we were good-to-go, another person had to bless everything.

We were in constant communication with employees, talking about budgets, revenues, expenses. Layoffs were discussed at length. Positions for abolishment were identified based on the requirement to get the job done. All local offices were run through a staffing formula and nine were identified as too small to function at the soon-to-be reduced staffing levels. Those offices were announced for closing the same day as the layoff letters were mailed and layoff announcements made.

Despite our efforts to be open and clear, many employees were shocked and in disbelief that layoffs actually occurred and that offices were actually locked and shuttered. The culture of governmental/bureaucratic invincibility that has developed over the last thirty years made it impossible for the employees to believe what they were being told. The paradigm of government growth shifted, and they were blinded by their old ways of thinking about government employment.

We established contact teams to assist laid-off workers with unemployment benefits and job placement. The Secretary and I made special contacts on behalf of many workers to gain placement at other state agencies. We wrote many letters of reference. Some laid-off workers were rehired within our department on a temporary basis due to the unexpected arrival of a special grant. All these efforts helped ease the situation.

However, after all the bumping rights were exercised, the layoff affected more than 300 of the 1,000 employees in the department, either through demotion, reduction in pay, or termination. With one third of our department family dysfunctional, performing even daily operations was difficult. It took excessive and redundant planning to ensure that the public still received services during this time. It is a credit to all our public employees that little disruption occurred.

Due to civil service regulations and policies, seniority still rules in our state government. Among the saddest tasks of management is to tell highly skilled, fresh, gung-ho, young public employees and administrators that they will be laid off while older, less effective workers remain. The questions of equity, individual rights, and efficiency cut in many directions.

Now, with Congress locked-up, government shutdown, block-grant proposals, devolution to the states, and election-year posturing, we are preparing for additional cuts and taking steps to plan for future layoffs. It is naive to assume that our department and others are through with downsizing. I think it is only beginning.

Questions

1. The authors raise a number of concerns about the functioning of the agency. After identifying the problems the author states, try and separate them into those which can be addressed (if at all) by (a) elected and appointed officials, (b) managers and supervisors, (c) the personnel director, (d) employees.
2. What are the solutions to those problems that you identified as resolvable in your response to question 1? For each solution, specify the person or group responsible for implementing it, and how you would recommend they work to overcome any implementation barriers.
3. For those problems that are not resolvable under current conditions, specify the changes that would have to occur for the problem to be solved? How bad would things have to get? How would that make the problem resolvable?
4. If you were a manager in this organization, how would you deal with employee anxiety and the performance issues it can create?

Notes

1. Kingdon, J. (2002). *Agendas, alternatives, and public policies.* New York: Longman.
2. Kingdon, J. (2002). *Agendas, alternatives, and public policies* (2nd ed.). Longman; and Peters, B. G. (2006). *American public policy: Promise and performance* (7th ed.). Washington, DC: CQ Press.
3. Gladwell, M. (2002). *The tipping point: How little things can make a big difference.* New York: Back Bay; and Gladwell, M. (2005). *Blink: The power of thinking without thinking.* New York: Little, Brown.
4. Moynihan, D., and S. Pandey (2005). Testing how management matters in an era of government by performance management. *Journal of Public Administration Research and Theory, 15* (3): 421–439.
5. Walker, D. (2002). *Managing for results using strategic human capital management to drive transformational change.* [On-line]. Available at: http://eric.ed.gov/ERICWebPortal/custom/portlets/recordDetails/detailmini.jsp?_nfpb=true&_&ERICExtSearch_SearchValue_0=ED467532&ERICExtSearch_SearchType_0=no&accno=ED467532
6. Elling, R., and T. Lyke Thompson (2006). Human resource problems and state management performance across two decades. *Review of Public Personnel Administration, 26* (4): 302–334.
7. Mason, J., K. Brainard, L. Langer, P. Young, and A. Ross (2004). Pensions and other retirement costs: A ticking time bomb. *Municipal Finance Journal, 25* (1): 47–70.
8. Rainey, H. (2003). *Understanding and Managing Public Organizations* (3rd ed.). San Francisco, CA: Jossey-Bass.
9. Klingner, D., J. Nalbandian, and B. Romzek (June 2002). Politics, administration and markets: Competing expectations and accountability. *American Review of Public Administration, 32* (2): 117–144.
10. Cooper, M. (June 25, 2004). Privatizing the military. *The CQ Researcher, 14–24.*
11. Halley, A. (1997). Applications of boundary theory to the concept of service integration in the human services. *Administration in Social Work 21* (3/4): 145–168.

12. Brudney, J., L. O'Toole, Jr., and H. Rainey (2000). *Advancing public management: New developments in theory, methods, and practice.* Washington, DC: Georgetown University Press.
13. Kettl, D., and J. Fesler (2005). *The politics of the administrative process* (3rd ed.). Washington, DC: CQ Press.
14. Milward, H. B. (1996) Symposium of the hollow state: Capacity, control and performance in interorganizational settings. *Journal of Public Administration Research and Theory 6* (2): 193–195; Cohen, S. (2001). A strategic framework for devolving responsibility and functions from government to the private sector. *Public Administration Review 61*: 432–440; and Hatry, H. (2007). A challenging performance. Book review of David G. Frederickson and H. George Frederickson (2006). *Measuring the Performance of the Hollow State* (Washington, DC: Georgetown University Press), *Journal of Public Administration Research and Theory, 17*: 673–682.
15. Kosar, K. (2006). *Privatization and the Federal Government: An Introduction.* Washington, DC: Congressional Research Service.
16. O'Looney, J. (1998). *Outsourcing state and local government services: Decision making strategies and management methods.* Westport, CT: Greenwood; Martin, L. (1999). *Contracting for service delivery: Local government choices.* Washington, DC: International City County Management Association; and Scott, R. (June 2004). Talking trash with the private sector. *Public Management*, 12–16.
17. Savas, E. S. (2005). *Privatization in the city: Successes, failures, lessons.* Washington, DC: CQ Press; Warner, M., and A. Hefetz (2004). Pragmatism over politics: Alternative service delivery in local government, 1992–2002. *The Municipal Year Book 2004.* Washington, DC: International City/County Management Association, pp. 8–16; and Morgan, D., R. England, and J. Pelissero (2007). *Managing Urban America* (6th ed.). Washington, DC: CQ Press, p. 205.
18. Johnston, V., and P. Seidenstat (2007). Contracting out government services: Privatization at the millennium. *International Journal of Public Administration, 30*: 231–247.
19. Fn to Sandy Springs, GA
20. Chandler, T., and P. Feuille (1991). Municipal unions and privatization. *Public Administration Review, 51*: 15–22; see also, United States General Accounting Office. (March 1997). *Privatization: Lessons learned by state and local governments.* Washington, DC: United States General Accounting Office. GGD-97-48.
21. Siegel, G. (1999). Where are we on local government service contracting? *Public Productivity and Management Review, 22* (3): 365–388.
22. Savas, E. S. (1987). *Privatization: The key to better government.* Chatham, NJ: Chatham House.
23. Sclar, E. (2000). *You don't always get what you pay for: The economics of privatization.* Ithaca, NY: Cornell University Press; Warner, M. with M. Ballard and A. Hefetz (2003). Contracting back in—when privatization fails, in *The Municipal Yearbook.* Washington, DC: International City County Management Association, Chapter 4, pp. 30–36; and Hefetz, A., and M. Warner (2004). Privatization and its reverse: Explaining the dynamics of the government contracting process. *Journal of Public Administration Research and Theory, 14* (2): 171–190.
24. Page, S. (2004). Measuring accountability for results in interagency collaboratives. *Public Administration Review, 64* (5): 591–606; and Romzek, B., and J. Johnson (2005). State social services contracting: Exploring the determinants of effective contract accountability. *Public Administration Review, 64*: 436–449.
25. Peters, B., and D. Savoie (1994). Civil service reform: Misdiagnosing the patient. *Public Administration Review, 54* (6): 418–425.
26. Milward, H. B., and K. Provan (April 2000). Governing the hollow state. *Journal of Public Administration Research and Theory, 10*: 359–377.
27. Chandler and Feuille. Municipal unions and privatization; Walters, J. (November 1995). The Whitman squeeze. *Governing Magazine, 8*: 22.
28. Wilson, G. (2006). The rise of at-will employment and racial inequality in the public sector. *Review of Public Personnel Administration, 26* (2): 178–188.
29. Lindquist, S. A., and S. E. Condrey (2006). Public employment reforms and constitutional Due process. In J. E. Kellough & L. G. Nigro (eds.), *Civil service reform in the states: Personnel policies and politics at the subnational level.* Albany, NY: State University of New York Press, pp. 95–114.
30. Moffett, S., R. McAdam, and S. Parkinson (2003). Technology and people factors in knowledge management: An empirical analysis. *Total Quality Management, 14* (2): 215–224.

Defining and Organizing Work

The ways in which work is defined and organized tend to separate those responsible for public HRM into two camps—HR specialists and everybody else. In that respect, these functions generate responses like those that accompany topics such as rotating your car's tires or flossing your teeth. Experts consider them essential, but many of us do not spend enough time on them, and certainly do not want to spend more time talking about them.

For HR specialists, writing a **job description**—a **position's** duties and the minimum qualifications required to perform them—is the key to position management. And **position management** (classifying positions by job type and level of responsibility, and limiting total agency payroll to sum of the salaries authorized for all classified positions) is the cornerstone of personnel management from which all other activities derive. Others do not see it that way. Legislators and elected officials may concede that budget management and program evaluation are legislative oversight tools designed to limit the number of employees and the operating budget of agencies within budget guidelines, but the actual process of writing job descriptions and classifying positions is an administrative detail they are not concerned with. Managers and supervisors tend to consider job descriptions and position management undesirable and unnecessary restrictions on their ability to manage human resources flexibly and autonomously. Understandably, their main objective is to be able to freely shift employees from one job to another as circumstances dictate, without reference to formal job descriptions. And position management puts an additional type of restriction on a manager's budget autonomy—and therefore on their ability to meet program goals flexibly by preventing them from hiring additional employees or paying them more, even if they have money in their budget to cover these expenses.

Therefore, this chapter starts with that dilemma. How do we reconcile these competing perspectives on job analysis and classification within the context of contemporary public HRM? As indicated in Chapter 3, the objectives of public HRM have changed over time with the competition among traditional and alternative systems and values. Moreover, the focus of job analysis and classification is shifting from management of *positions* to management of *work* or of *careers*. This chapter will explore how these changes affect the way public agencies define work today.

By the end of this chapter, you will be able to:

1. Tell why different groups responsible for public agency HRM have different views of job analysis; and relate the historical development of the field to the conflict and interaction among underlying values and objectives: patronage jobs for elected officials, merit systems for civil service reformers, position management for HR directors and specialists, **work management** for managers and supervisors, and career management for employees and applicants.
2. Summarize why **traditional job descriptions** (those oriented toward position management) may not be suitable for supporting public personnel management as its focus has changed to work management and **employee management**.
3. Analyze work using a performance-oriented description, which incorporates work management and career management into the traditional job description.
4. Understand why job descriptions are important for jobs filled through other systems besides civil service, including the alternative mechanisms and flexible employment relationships that characterize nongovernmental personnel systems.

JOB DESCRIPTIONS: DIFFERENT GROUPS HAVE DIFFERENT OBJECTIVES

A job description is a brief statement that describes a job by listing major duties and specifying the minimum qualifications needed to do it. Exactly how job descriptions are prepared and used is a complicated story that has its origins in the creation of civil service systems and merit system principles. Because different groups have been involved, and because these groups have different perspectives, it is not surprising that attitudes toward job descriptions differ. Fundamentally, each of the important groups involved in HRM policy or implementation has a different perspective on job descriptions and position management based on the historical evolution of the field and their respective roles in it.

- *Elected and appointed officials* have three contradictory attitudes toward job descriptions. If they are in charge of an agency, they may consider job descriptions and position management an intrusion on patronage (their ability to hire who they want for policy making or other positions where personal or political loyalty are the most important selection criteria). Nowhere was this view of job descriptions more apparent than in the summer of 2008 when political appointees in the U.S. Department of Justice were caught dismissing job applicants for their political affiliation when the descriptions of the jobs they were applying for clearly stated that they were nonpolitical.[1] If they are more interested in oversight, they may consider position management essential to control the size and direction of agency staff as an important aspect of budget management and program evaluation. Finally, most elected officials may consider job descriptions and classification systems to be simply irrelevant unless their primary focus is budget cutting.
- *Merit system reformers* consider analyzing and classifying positions as the key to a successful transition from the evils of the spoils system to the greater effectiveness and equity of a civil service system as the basis for responsive and professional public administration.
- *Public HRM specialists* consider job descriptions and classification systems as the key to effective *position management*, which includes compliance with legislatively mandated controls over the number of positions and salary levels as part of the total budget

management process. In addition, they are the key to other functions like recruitment, selection, pay equity, and performance evaluation.

- *Managers and supervisors* have an ambivalent viewpoint on job descriptions. They may consider them a necessary first step to recruitment, performance evaluation, setting equitable pay, or disciplinary action. At other times, they may be an unwelcome intrusion on *work management*—their ability to creatively and flexibly use human resources to achieve program objectives.
- *Employees* may view job descriptions ambivalently. A current and accurate **position description** (**PD**) may clarify what they need to do to succeed on their job. On the other hand, criteria established in a job description (like specific types of experience or education) may seem unfair and artificial barriers to *career management*—personal mobility and advancement based on competencies. In some cases, job descriptions are also used as the basis for formal complaints in those instances where employees are asked to perform duties outside of their job descriptions but are not compensated accordingly.

Elected and Appointed Officials Focus on Politically Appointed (Patronage) Positions

Jobs are not defined, analyzed, or classified at all under political patronage systems. Employees simply are awarded a job and the salary that goes with it because they supported a successful candidate for elected office. Indeed, originally the justification for patronage jobs was that "no public job should be so complicated that any citizen could not complete it." Therefore, many advocates of the spoils system felt that any individual could perform any public job, without the necessity of setting minimum qualifications. Not only were minimum qualifications considered unnecessary, they also tended to interfere with elected officials' freedom to allocate jobs to their supporters. While some minimally acceptable level of performance might be required to avoid political embarrassment for the elected official, in some cases employees did not even have to show up to get paid. Moreover, today two changes in the nature of work—the proliferation of independent contractors and electronic communication—make political patronage even easier. For example, at the time of this writing, there were sixty one investigations being conducted into contracting associated with waging the war in Iraq. Independent contractors can be hired to temporary or part-time positions not subject to classification; and the reality of remote ("virtual") offices allow political appointees to work with little direct oversight.

Merit System Reformers Focus on Civil Service Systems

For merit system reformers fighting to increase government effectiveness in the face of patronage politics, job analysis epitomizes the principles of scientific management and budget transparency that enable them to control the spoils system. Founded on the Classification Act of 1923, which formalized job analysis and classification in the federal government, merit system reformers support job analysis because it is the essential first step to ensure that employees are hired and promoted based on ability and performance, and that jobs of equivalent difficulty are paid the same salaries. Without this, it is simply not possible to hire or pay employees to support the values of individual rights or administrative efficiency. Again, anyone who assumes that objective and fair pay systems are inevitable, or that they are easy to achieve, has only to look at the chronic and interrelated economic, political, and social problems that plague governments in developing countries—corruption, incompetence, and "brain drain."

Operationally, creating a civil service system means identifying how many employees work for each agency by job type, geographic location, and salary. This enables personnel specialists to develop a **staffing (manning) table**, a roster of all authorized positions in an agency. Hopefully, as personnel actions result in employees being hired, transferred, or discharged, the position management information system will keep this information current. While the need to develop an adequate position management information system may seem self-evident, and the steps involved in doing so may seem childishly simple to complete, the political culture of patronage politics can make it difficult to achieve this basic administrative reform. The important thing to realize here is that merit systems do not simply arise out of general societal pressures for modernization. Instead, they develop because reformers first win political approval for specific administrative reforms designed to make it more difficult for patronage systems to operate openly or secretly. Once these reforms are enacted as law, they must still become routinized administrative procedures.[2] Under patronage systems, it is actually quite difficult to determine how many employees actually work for an agency because there are three possible answers, all different: (1) all persons on the payroll (whether or not they are expected to show up for work), (2) all persons who actually show up for work on a regular basis, and (3) the authorized positions in an agency (whether or not they are filled and whether or not those individuals actually show up for work).

Each of these answers is the result of different pressures on patronage systems. The first option, a payroll "padded" with persons who get paid but never show up for work, results from allowing elected officials to place nonemployees on the public payroll as a reward for political or personal loyalty (and perhaps to pocket a percentage of salary as a "kickback" from the nonworking "employee"). The second option, a valid payroll matching the number of actual employees, is the objective of civil service reformers. The third option, a payroll inflated by showing as filled positions those that are actually vacant, allows senior managers to pocket the salaries of "ghost" employees as a reward for their own political loyalty. It is widely accepted that the first and third options are corrupt and wasteful. But given that the primary function of public employment under a patronage system is to buy political support, this waste and corruption are irrelevant, or at least less important than maintaining a leader or party in power. This tension between patronage and merit systems is by no means limited to the past or to underdeveloped countries. Occasionally, local governments in the United States will cut civil service positions to save money at the same time they are adding political employees to the payroll. These may be legitimate excepted appointments (outside the merit system), or they may simply be positions created because a powerful elected official wants a friend to have a job and happens to control the budget of the agency in which the new job is to be created.

HR Specialists and Position Management

Once a transition from patronage to civil service has taken place, merit system reformers have sought to restrict patronage by entrusting HR directors and specialists implementing civil service through **position management**. This means ensuring that public agencies limit pressure by elected officials to create patronage positions by limiting the number of employees an agency can hire and requiring agencies to account for these positions by identifying which ones are filled or vacant, what the salary attached to each position is, and (therefore) what is the total agency payroll. As part of public administration, position management supports rational budgeting by limiting the total amount that can be spent on salaries and benefits. In addition, it fosters rational policy making and implementation by making the staffing of agencies consistent with the intent of the law and the objectives of public programs.

The underlying assumption of position management is that public agencies, left unprotected, will be unable to resist pressure from elected officials to add patronage positions or to fill vacant civil service positions with patronage employees. The way personnel specialists seek to protect the merit system is by working inside the agency to implement legislatively imposed **personnel ceilings**—These are budget limits on the agency **payroll** and position management limits on the number and type of personnel they can employ. Frequently, position and budgetary controls are combined through the imposition of **average grade-level restrictions**, which limit the number of positions that can be created and filled at each level of the agency hierarchy. A low average grade level means that most positions are low-level positions.

Theoretically, at least, these position management techniques are analogous to line-item budgets in that they focus on *inputs* to the governmental process (number and type of employees). Together, line-item budgeting and position management have historically been successful at forcing compliance and accountability because the first controls the budget and policies of the executive branch, and the second controls the allocation of personnel and money to implement programs in executive agencies.

HR specialists (personnel directors and technicians) have long considered job analysis the heart of personnel management because for them the ability to specify a job's duties and the **minimum qualifications ("quals")** needed to perform them satisfactorily (in terms of the type, level, and length of education and experience) is an essential prerequisite to other personnel functions like recruitment, selection, training, performance evaluation, and workforce planning. They regard setting minimum qualifications as essential to establishing an equitable pay range for the position and encouraging **career development** by creating **career ladders** (vertically linked positions within the same occupational field) by which employees could advance to positions of increasing responsibility as they met the **minimum quals** (minimum qualifications) for the next higher position on the ladder.

So, historically during the period of transition from patronage to merit, and even today among specialists, the ability to conduct a job analysis and write a good job description is considered an essential HRM competency. Two of the authors began their careers as management interns in the federal civil service agency (the U.S. Office of Personnel Management, formerly the U.S. Civil Service Commission). This program involved one to two years of rotational assignments, with the authors assisting such memorable accomplishments as a nationwide computerized testing and score reporting system for all entry-level jobs and drafting what later became the law implementing technical assistance programs among federal, state, and local personnel agencies. Nevertheless, many disgruntled HR specialists had worked their way up "through the ranks" rather than through an internship program that offered what they considered an unfair promotional advantage to recent college graduates who were not nearly as smart as they thought they were. For these specialists, the success of the entire internship boiled down to the answer the graduate of the internship program could give to a single question: "Can you write a good job description?" Other skills and experiences might be useful, but unless an HR trainee had learned this, he or she could not be considered qualified as a technician or a professional in the field.

Managers and Supervisors Focus on Work Management

As might be expected, however, the control over program inputs that is achieved by line-item budgets and position management is less critical for managers and supervisors whose primary objective is managerial effectiveness, not legislative compliance. This is because budgets and personnel ceilings function well to control the size and direction of inputs to an agency; they are quite ineffective at making the agencies more productive, as measured by program outputs. Public managers have policy objectives to accomplish and limited resources with which to do so. For the work to be done with the most efficient use of human resources, the agency must hire the right number of people, with the right qualifications, for the right jobs, in the right locations. It must pay people enough money to be competitive with other employers, but not more. This is true regardless of which type of public personnel system predominates, especially for agencies that focus on mission and consider themselves bound to definite performance standards and clear paths of political accountability. Under these conditions, managers need to be rewarded for flexible and responsible stewardship of personnel and financial resources. As such, they are likely to resent job descriptions and classification systems, commonly viewed as legislative "micromanagement," because it restricts their flexibility and autonomy. Alternatively, they may be unable or unwilling to function as managers because they have for too long been accustomed to citing legislative controls as the reason for not managing resources creatively or effectively. Overall, some of the primary reasons public managers dislike job descriptions and position classification include the narrow divisions created between positions, the limited ability of descriptions and classifications to adapt to changing technologies, and the associated demand for standardization.[3]

Employees Focus on Career Management

Employees have a different perspective than either managers or elected and appointed officials. They want to be treated as individuals, through a continual process of supervision, feedback, and reward. They want to know what their job duties are and how performance will be measured. They want to be paid fairly, based on their contributions to productivity and compared with the salaries of other employees. They want their individual skills and abilities to be fully utilized in ways that contribute to a productive agency and to their own personal career development.

Today, the current emphasis on flexible employment relationships makes us forget that civil service systems were originally created to prevent elected and appointed officials from hiring and firing public employees at will. This stability was designed to make government more efficient and to increase public confidence in the quality of public service. Moreover, today, the widely accepted notion that civil service systems provide a safe haven for lazy and incompetent employees makes us forget that civil service systems were originally created to protect employee rights by establishing clear criteria and procedures for selection, reassignment, promotion, or discharge. This is based on the assumption that people work most productively when they have adequate skills, clear objectives, adequate resources and organizational conditions to do their jobs, and clear feedback and consequences. They work not only as individuals but also as members of groups that collectively shape the culture of the agency and the ways in which employees work together to meet objectives.

In summary, these five different perspectives on job analysis frequently come into conflict because they embody different values and objectives about public HRM. Elected and appointed officials emphasize either the internal discretion to make political appointments or the external authority to control agency activities by controlling personnel inputs. Merit system reformers view job analysis as the key to effective and transparent budget management and personnel management. HR directors and specialists have traditionally allied themselves with civil service reformers to emphasize external control over patronage through position management. Managers and supervisors consider job descriptions increasingly irrelevant to flexible use of human resources, and employees are more concerned with how minimum qualifications and classification systems impede their personal career development. Much of the trend toward professional (rather than technical) personnel management is connected to the movement toward seeing HRM in strategic terms and can be seen as the transition of public personnel managers from a policing role (control over employees and managers through position management) to an enabling role (facilitation of employee productivity and satisfaction, or of managerial autonomy and responsibility) through more enlightened job analysis techniques. Moreover, this change in roles affects the way all personnel functions are performed.

JOB ANALYSIS AND JOB DESCRIPTIONS: MOVING TOWARD A BETTER MODEL

So where does all this lead us? It means that any discussion of how to define and organize work depends on the context and the participants. Job descriptions began with civil service reformers and HR directors and specialists. They evolved toward greater emphasis on managerial effectiveness (work management) and employee aspirations (career management). In addition, they now incorporate the flexibility and focus on efficiency appropriate to market-based values and systems.

Traditional Job Analysis is a Tool for Position Management

Job analysis is the process of recording information about each employee's job. It is done by watching the employee work, talking with the employee about the job, and corroborating this information by checking it with other employees and the supervisor. It results in a product. The product could be a set of job specifications that are general to a set of positions (e.g., Admin Assistant I) and that job descriptions themselves grow out of or it could be the **job description** itself—a written statement of the employee's responsibilities, duties, and qualifications. It may also include a **qualifications standard ("qual standard")** that specifies the minimum competencies and qualifications (education, experience, or others) an employee needs to perform the position's duties at a satisfactory level.

Traditionally, job descriptions have been used as the "building blocks" of position management. By requiring that a legislatively authorized position be identified before an employee could be hired or promoted into it, job descriptions controlled the size of the bureaucracy and its occupational diversity. They have functioned well in this capacity because they specify the job title, occupation classification, level of responsibility, salary, and location of the job in the organizational hierarchy. Similar jobs (positions) can be classified into an occupational series, along with other jobs involving similar job duties. Jobs in different occupations but of comparable difficulty (requiring similar skill, effort, or responsibility, and performed under similar working conditions) can be classified into a common **grade level**. Each position can be identified by an occupational and grade-level code, much as a point on a graph can be located by measuring its distance from the vertical and horizontal axes.

Because each job (position) can be classified into a common occupational series as one of a number of identical positions in the agency, its grade level served to fix salary and relationship to other positions above and below it in the agency's bureaucratic hierarchy. This has had the additional benefit of identifying, in a manner similar to military rank, the power of the individual in the organization. To emphasize the power of classification systems, consider that federal government employees in Washington, DC, have long been accustomed to identifying themselves and evaluating others based on classification system shorthand. A federal employee might describe a coworker by saying, "She's an 11 at Agriculture, a program analyst." Both of them would immediately understand that the employee in question was a GS-343-11: that is, a classified civil service employee, pay grade 11, in the occupational specialty of program analyst. She would outrank a GS-343-9, but be subordinate to a GS-343-12.

While not all classification systems are as complex as that used by the federal government, all traditional job descriptions contain common elements, as shown in Figure 5-1: an occupational code and/or title, a pay grade, an organizational locator, a position in the hierarchy, job duties, and required minimum qualifications.

Traditional Job Descriptions Do Not Help Supervisors Manage Work

The traditional job description is designed to limit patronage appointments by classifying positions by job type, skill level, and agency and to promote efficiency and employee rights by ensuring that employees are qualified to perform their jobs and paid equitably based on their qualifications. It minimizes patronage by facilitating external control over patronage hiring. The use of standardized job descriptions for a range of positions, with

Job Title: Secretary
Position No: 827301-2
Pay Grade: GS-322-4

Responsibilities	Works under the direction of the Supervisor, Operations Support Division
Duties	Performs a variety of clerical functions in support of the Supervisor and the mission of the Division: types correspondence and reports compiles reports maintains inventory of supplies arranges meetings and conferences answers the phone handles routine correspondence performs other duties as assigned
Qualifications	High school degree or equivalent Typing speed of 40 wpm At least six months experience as a Secretary at grade GS-322-3, or equivalent

FIGURE 5-1 Traditional Job Description

each one identified by a different position number and organizational location, is useful for reducing paperwork and providing position management (external control over the total number of positions and their salary level).

However, the characteristics that make the traditional job description effective against patronage also work against its usefulness as a work management tool for managers and supervisors. Conceptually, traditional job descriptions promote an artificially static view of work and organizations. Jobs change over time as an organization's goals shift; and if the goal of the personnel system is to promote rational management of work or employees, it does not make sense to "freeze" a job or an organization at one point in time. Nor does it make sense to unduly restrict the ability of the organization to move people from one job to another, as work needs change. In addition, with increasing emphasis on working in teams, the whole concept of an individual job may be questioned.

The traditional job description promotes a hierarchical and control-oriented relationship between the organization and its employees that works against employee involvement and "ownership" of the organization or its mission. The job description in Figure 5-1 lists the general duties performed by any number of administrative assistants. Because it applies to a range of positions, it is necessarily vague concerning the nature of the tasks (job elements) involved. The employee may be working in a foundry, a personnel office, or a chemical supply house. In each case, specific duties will differ. The entry "other duties as assigned" leaves the job description open to any additions the supervisor may assign but does not leave room for changes in the work caused by the employee's particular skills or abilities. Thus, this traditional job description is flexible, but only unilaterally, and in a way that assumes hierarchical and downward control over work performance by the agency.

Traditional job descriptions are ill suited to work management because they assume that work can be divided into individual units called jobs and that these jobs can be differentiated by occupational type and arranged into hierarchies of increasing responsibility. This eventually impedes the rational allocation of employees to work or the flexible assignment of employees to jobs as the mission of the agency changes. As job analysis becomes more detailed, classification and pay systems become more complex to keep pace. After a while, this results in the creation of so many occupational categories and skill levels that people become frozen into a job. In addition, supervisors are frequently impeded from moving employees from one type of work to another, in that their tasks are "frozen" by their original job description.

Traditional job descriptions focus on the type of work to be done, not productivity or **performance standards**. They do discuss duties, but they do so for purposes of task analysis and **job classification**, not employee performance. From a manager's perspective, traditional job descriptions are deficient because they do not spell out the performance expected of the employee. Nor do they specify the linking or enabling relationship among competencies, performance standards, and minimum qualifications that in reality both supervisors and employees need to work productively in an organization.

Employees and supervisors both know that a general statement of job duties must at some point be augmented by more specific information about the conditions under which the job is performed. For example, is the work done individually or in a team setting? That fact, in combination with the skills and motivation of a range of applicants, will make a real difference in how work is performed, and it calls into question the relevance of the concept of individual productivity. Is the filing system a database or a manual system using paper documents? What types of correspondence are considered "routine"? Do all duties occur continuously, or do some require more work at certain times? Are all duties equally important, or are some more important than others? What written guidelines or supervisory instructions are available to aid the employee? What conditions make task performance easier or harder?

Thus, the traditional job description does not contain enough useful information to orient applicants or employees. Therefore, the supervisor must use orientation or an initial on-the-job adjustment period to teach employees how the work they do *really* fits into the organization's mission.

More critically, there are no standards for minimally acceptable employee performance of job duties. This omission causes basic problems for the supervisor, who is the person responsible for arranging the conditions of work to make the employee productive. How can this be done if the quantity, quality, or timeliness of service required is not specified? Moreover, it is hard to establish or evaluate performance standards unless these take into account fluctuating conditions. For example, it is easier for a salesperson to increase sales 10 percent annually in an industry growing by 20 percent annually than to achieve the same rate of increase in a declining market.

Moreover, traditional job descriptions specify a general set of minimum qualifications for each position. If jobs have been classified according to the type of skill required, these minimum qualifications may also be based on the competencies needed to perform duties. In general, however, traditional methods blur the following logical sequence of relationships among **tasks**, standards, **competencies**, and minimum qualifications:

1. Each task must be performed at a certain minimum standard for the organization to function well.
2. Certain competencies are required to perform each task up to standard.
3. Certain minimum qualifications ensure that the employee will have the requisite competencies.

Executives are handicapped because such traditional job descriptions describe only the personnel inputs into a job and not the resultant outputs in terms of organizational productivity. That is, they do not specify how many employees would be needed to produce outputs at a given level of quantity, quality, or timeliness. Because traditional job descriptions do not lend themselves to output analysis, they are not as useful a part of the human resource planning, management, or evaluation process.

Managers are responsible for carrying out most HR functions, even in traditional organizations. They, not the personnel director or personnel specialists, are the ones responsible for interviewing applicants, deciding whom to hire, orienting new employees, giving them feedback on performance, and evaluating their performance formally so as to provide either discipline or positive reinforcement depending on the outcomes.

Managers are handicapped because they cannot readily use such job descriptions for recruitment, orientation, goal setting, or performance evaluation. If new employees are recruited based on the brief description of duties and qualifications given in the traditional job description, extensive interviewing by managers may be needed to select the applicants most qualified for a particular job. Orientation will require clarification of the job description to fit the particular organizational context, but this may be incomplete because of other demands on the manager's time. If the organization uses management by objectives (MBO) goal setting and evaluation procedures, these will be unrelated to the job descriptions used only by the personnel department for position management and recruitment.

For these purposes, individual jobs should each have a separate job description, in recognition of the variability of tasks, conditions, standards, and competencies they require. They should help the manager and the employee by serving as links among personnel functions such as selection, orientation, training, and performance appraisal. These two problems—the lack of evident relationship among tasks, standards, competencies, and qualifications, and the lack of clear information about the nature of the job—reduce the usefulness of job descriptions for executives, managers, and employees.

Traditional Job Descriptions Do Not Help Employees Manage their Careers

Because traditional job descriptions give only a brief outline of duties, employees must wait to find out about working conditions and performance standards until after they have been hired. Yet this may be too late; unclear or inequitable psychological contracts are a cause of much unrest between employees and organizations. Evaluating employees without giving them clear performance standards is a sure way to increase anxiety and frustration. Traditional job descriptions generally do not help employees answer the most important questions they have about their jobs. Such questions include:

- Which job duties are most important, and why?
- What makes the job easy or hard to accomplish?
- What competencies (skills, knowledge, and abilities) are needed for the job, and why?
- What performance standards will be applied to judge their work? How will their job performance be measured and evaluated?
- What performance standards will they need to meet to keep their jobs?
- How will this job prepare them for other progressively more responsible positions?

Moreover, employees cannot use traditional job descriptions for career development because they do not specify how increases in minimum qualifications are related to increases in skills required for satisfactory task performance. It is easiest for employees to accept the qualifications for a position and to strive to meet them through upward mobility programs if these linkages are more apparent.

Traditional Job Descriptions Limit and Stereotype the HRM Profession

Personnel managers, and the HRM function itself, are most seriously affected by traditional job descriptions' focus on position management rather than on the primary concerns of managers or employees. Because traditional job descriptions are unsuitable to work management, managers and employees consider them a waste of time. Inevitably, job descriptions tend to be regarded in the same light as inventories of office equipment or the updating of workplace safety regulations—something that must be done yet does not add value or help the bottom line. Therefore, if personnel managers consider job descriptions to be one of the most important personnel tools, and if managers and employees know from their own experience that job descriptions are irrelevant to their needs, then the impression may be created that other personnel activities are equally unimportant. This logic is frequently used to belittle performance evaluation, job analysis, training needs, surveys, and other items from the personnel manager's stock in trade.

Consequently, the traditional job description's focus on position management makes it more difficult for contemporary HR managers to effectively establish their own professional credentials. The traditional job description has been largely responsible for the traditional view of personnel management as a series of low-level operational techniques used mainly for external control or system maintenance purposes. Position management and legislative compliance are historically respected roles for public personnel managers, but they are less important today, in a world of strategic planning, than many other objectives and values, including management efficiency and effectiveness, or employee rights.

How to Improve Traditional Job Descriptions

Job descriptions continue to be useful under a range of personnel systems, but their reputation has been tarnished. This is because, in their present form, they are more effective at position management than management of work or employees. What changes would make them more relevant to managers' and employees' needs?

Job descriptions would be more useful if they clarified the organization's expectations of employees and the links among tasks, standards, competencies, and minimum qualifications. These improved job descriptions would contain the following information:

1. *Tasks*. What work duties are important to the job?
2. *Conditions*. What things make the job easy (such as close supervision or written guidelines explaining how to do the work) or hard (such as angry clients or difficult physical conditions)?
3. *Standards*. What objective performance levels (related to organizational objectives) can reasonably be set for each task, measured in terms of objectives such as quantity, quality, or timeliness of service?
4. *Competencies*. What knowledge, skills, and abilities are required to perform each task at the minimum standard under the above conditions?
5. *Qualifications*. What education, experience, and other qualifications are needed to ensure that employees have the necessary competencies?

These changes are all related because they clarify the enabling relationship among tasks, conditions, standards, competencies, and qualifications. In other words, they specify the qualifications needed to demonstrate that an employee has the competencies required to perform essential job functions at acceptable performance standards under a given set of conditions. Taken together, these refinements emphasize the relationship of jobs to management of work and employees, rather than of positions. They do so by focusing on outputs (what is actually produced by a job) rather than inputs (which positions are allocated to the agency).

Two examples of performance-oriented job descriptions are shown in Figures 5-2 and 5-3. These examples show why **performance-oriented job descriptions** are superior for management of work and employees. They provide clearer organizational expectations to employees. They encourage supervisors and employees to recognize that both standards and competencies can be contingent upon conditions. For example, an administrative support specialist can type neater copy more quickly with a word processor than with a manual typewriter, and the skills required are different. In the second example, an increase in each probation officer's caseload from 60 to 100 clients would inevitably affect the quantity, quality, or timeliness of visits with probationers. A probation officer preparing pre-sentence investigation reports for a new judge might be expected to have a lower level of accepted recommendations.

Adiministrative Assistant/Receptionist
Operations Support Division
Position No.: 827301-2
Pay Grade: GS-322-4

TASKS	CONDITIONS	STANDARDS
Type letters	Use PC, MS Office Suite, and agency style manual	Letter completed in 2 hours, error-free
Greet visitors	Use appointment log provided by supervisor about waiting, provided supervisor is on time	No complaints from scheduled visitors
Maintain files	Use Access database management software and instructions provided by supervisor	Update files weekly, with accuracy and completeness

REQUIRED COMPETENCIES

Able to type 40 wpm
Courtesy
Microsoft Office Suite (Word, Excel, Powerpoint, and Access)

MINIMUM QUALIFICATIONS

High school degree or equivalent
Two years word processing, especially MS Word
One year database management, especially MS Excel

FIGURE 5-2 Performance-Oriented Job Descriptions

Thus, job descriptions can do more than just establish a link between tasks, conditions, and standards, which is useful to employees and supervisors. This link is the logical connection between duties and qualifications required for content validation of qualifications standards under affirmative action programs or civil service systems, and for employee productivity under personal service contracts and other alternative/flexible employment relationships.

THE ROLE OF JOB DESCRIPTIONS IN ALTERNATE PUBLIC PERSONNEL SYSTEMS

All personnel systems are responsible for accomplishing common functions (PADS). Because work must be defined before employees or independent contractors can be selected, job descriptions are important under affirmative action, collective bargaining, and alternative mechanisms and flexible employment relationships.

Juvenile Probation Officer
State Department of Corrections

TASKS	CONDITIONS	STANDARDS
Meet clients to record their behavior	Caseload of not more than 60; supervisor will help with hard cases; use departmental rules and regulations	See each probationer weekly; keep accurate and complete records per DOC rules and regulations
Report criminal activity to supervisor		
Prepare pre-sentence investigation reports	Average of five per week; supervisor will review cases per court instructions;	Reports complete and accurate per judge; judge will accept recommendation in 75 percent of cases

REQUIRED COMPETENCIES

Knowledge of the factors contributing to criminal behavior
Ability to counsel probationers
Ability to write clear and concise probation reports
Knowledge of different judges' sentencing preferences for particular types of offenders and offenses
Knowledge of law and DOC regulations concerning pre-sentencing investigations and probation

MINIMUM QUALIFICATIONS

High school degree or equivalent plus four years of experience working with juvenile offenders, or a BS degree in criminal justice, psychology, or counseling
Possess a valid driver's license

FIGURE 5-3 Performance-Oriented Job Descriptions

Affirmative Action

By specifying the minimum qualifications for a position and by logically relating minimum quals to job tasks, job descriptions are the most critical element of equitable personnel practice. That is, they act affirmatively to ensure that applicants and employees are not discriminated against based on nonmerit factors. Moreover, they reduce the impact of favoritism by requiring that vacancies be identified and posted, that all qualified applicants have the opportunity to apply, and that applicants not hired be informed as to the reason for their nonselection. Of course, there are widespread abuses in recruitment and selection procedures, and the folklore of public personnel management is filled with fables confirming every suspicion: highly qualified white male applicants who were not hired because they were the "wrong gender" or the "wrong color" and highly qualified minority or female applicants who were included in the interview pool only to demonstrate a "good-faith effort" at recruiting a diverse workforce, yet who never had a real chance of being fairly considered for the position. Nevertheless, job analysis and job descriptions are at the heart of test validation, affirmative action compliance, and reasonable accommodation of persons with handicaps under the Americans with Disabilities Act.

Collective Bargaining

Job analysis and classification are also central to collective bargaining. First, collective bargaining starts with the identification of an appropriate bargaining unit, either occupation based or agency based. In either case, the number and identity of positions eligible for inclusion in the bargaining unit presumes that all positions, those included as well as those excluded, have been analyzed and classified in advance.

Once a union has been selected as a bargaining agent, it begins to negotiate with management. Frequently, contract negotiators justify requested pay and benefits by comparing pay and benefit levels with similar jobs in other jurisdictions. Contracts stipulate pay, benefits, and working conditions applicable to covered employees or to employees in specified occupations. Contracts may prohibit management from assigning employees work outside their classification or above their grade level. They will certainly specify that disciplinary action can only be taken against employees who do not perform their jobs satisfactorily, for tasks assigned in their job descriptions, as measured against previously defined performance standards.

Third-Party Service Delivery Mechanisms

In one sense, job descriptions hinder productivity because they tie up resources without adding value. That is, they require work to write and review, without directly contributing to the outputs by which the effectiveness of the organization is measured. However, in another sense, they create value by specifying the nature of the work to be done, and the rewards the organization is prepared to pay to have it done. For those public administrators contemplating the use of alternative means of service delivery, it takes but a moment's reflection to realize that clarity with respect to performance expectations and rewards is at the heart of establishing most third-party mechanisms for delivering public services without the use of government agencies, employees, or appropriated funds.

If a public agency decides to outsource a public service or use a private sector contractor or a volunteer-based organization to deliver a public service, no meaningful contract can be written or enforced unless outputs or outcomes are specified; nor can the performance of public agencies, private contractors, and volunteers be compared unless the performance standards and pay and benefits are clearly specified. For example, a City considering contracting out security services at public housing or transit facilities will have to define what level of service, and what level of employee qualifications, will be needed to do the job—whether it is eventually done in-house or contracted out.

Nonstandard Work Arrangements (NSWA)

Flexible employment relationships make it easier for management to hire, fire, and reassign workers. They also tend to remove agencies somewhat from legislative controls based on position management. However, job descriptions are more important than ever under these alternative and flexible employment systems because their objective is work management and their function is to define jobs. Consider that management needs some criteria to separate "core" and "contingent" positions. These criteria can include occupation, level of difficulty, or geographic location. Nevertheless, whatever criteria are used, jobs need to be defined and classified based on the nature of the work. Moreover, consider employment of workers on short-term performance contracts. These need to clearly specify the terms and conditions of employment, lest the rewards offered are not proportionate to the skills and responsibilities.

Summary

Many current controversies in public personnel management center around the appropriateness of a focus on positions, work, or employees. Traditional job analysis defines the position as the unit of analysis and develops classification systems based on the type of work and its level of responsibility in the organizational hierarchy. More contemporary approaches focus on work management—flexible use of human resources to accomplish the mission of the agency. In addition, employees have yet a third perspective—career development. Performance-oriented job descriptions offer a way of bridging between traditional and contemporary HRM and, therefore, of linking the professional status of HR to the organizational productivity and career development that are considered more important to mature civil service systems than using position management to control patronage and enforce legislative priorities. There is no doubt that job analysis will continue to be an important personnel activity, because it is required not only for civil services systems but also for alternatives to them. One of the key points of conflict within public personnel management is the extent to which the system should be driven by market models or by broader concerns of social equity and individual rights.

Key Terms

average grade-level restrictions *109*
career development *109*
career ladders *109*
competencies *114*
employee management *106*
grade level *111*
job analysis *111*
job classification *113*
job (position) description *105*
minimum qualifications ("quals") *109*
payroll *109*
performance standards *113*
performance-oriented job descriptions *116*
personnel ceilings *109*
position *105*
position description (PD) *107*
position management *105*
qualifications standard ("qual standard") *111*
staffing (manning) table *108*
traditional job descriptions *106*
work management *106*

Discussion Questions

1. How does the historical development of job analysis relate to the differing objectives of elected and appointed officials, merit system reformers, HR directors and specialists, supervisors and managers, and employees? How are these reflected in the concepts of position management, human resource management, and career development?
2. Why are traditional job descriptions unsuitable for supporting personnel management as its focus has changed to human resource management and career management?
3. How do performance-oriented descriptions differ from traditional job descriptions? Why are they more effective from the supervisor's viewpoint? From the employee's viewpoint?
4. How can performance-oriented job descriptions be combined with traditional (position management-based) job analysis and classification systems?

Case Study: Who'S Most Qualified to be Minority Recruitment Director?

Background

You have recently been appointed Personnel Director of the state police. The organization consists of about 1,000 uniformed officers and 200 civilian employees. Its primary mission is to promote highway safety through enforcement of traffic laws and assistance to motorists. In recent years, the state police agency has come under increasing public criticism. The major complaint: too much attention is being paid to writing traffic tickets; a more appropriate focus would be on attacking the organized crime and drug trafficking that increasingly overwhelm urban police departments. In addition, many community activists believe that the state police routinely discriminate against African Americans and Hispanics in both employment and enforcement of traffic laws, and in antidrug and antigang operations.

Morale is low among younger officers, who see themselves as victims of societal conflicts. Turnover among recruits averages 25 percent during the first year after they complete a three-month training course required of all state-certified law enforcement officers. Reasons most often given for leaving the state police are working conditions, lack of immediate promotion opportunities, and the feeling the advancement is based on "whom you know, not what you know." Many observers consider the state police to be a highly political organization because the governor appoints its top administrative positions. Some observers believe that, as a result, top management lacks experience in law enforcement or management, and that this reduces the organization's morale and effectiveness.

As Director of Personnel, your task is to select an assistant who will be responsible for developing, administering, and evaluating a minority recruitment program for the agency. An outside consulting firm has selected three candidates as being the most qualified of several hundred applicants who responded to nationwide advertising for the position. You and your panel have interviewed each applicant. Now it is time to pick the one most qualified for the position.

Process

Divide into discussion groups with four or five people in each group. The instructor should designate the groups as A, B, C, etc. Within twenty-five minutes, place all three candidates in rank order, based on their relative qualifications for the position. The résumés of the candidates are given in Figures 5-5, 5-6, and 5-7. Before you do so, be prepared to defend your selection by writing a brief performance-oriented job description for the position. This means you will need to answer each of the following questions:

1. What job duties are most important to the position?
2. What competencies will successful applicants need to perform these essential job duties?
3. What objective performance standards could you use to assess whether the minority recruitment director is doing a good job?
4. What conditions make the job particularly easy or hard to perform? (Hint: think of laws, resources, organizational conditions, etc.) How do these conditions affect the performance standards that should be established, or the competencies that should be required?
5. What minimum qualifications will successful applicants need to ensure that they have these competencies? Specify education (type, level, and length), experience (type, level, and length), and any other qualifications you consider essential
6. In what rank order should the three candidates be placed? In your group's column, write a "1," "2," or "3" opposite each candidate's name. (See Figure 5-4.)

CANDIDATE	GROUP A	GROUP B	GROUP C	GROUP D	GROUP E
Harold Murphy					
John Lewis					
Norma Sikorsky					

FIGURE 5-4 Rank the Applicants

7. Why is the applicant you chose the most qualified for the job?
8. What selection criterion was most important in making the choice? Place a check beside it.
9. Which value (political responsiveness, efficiency, or social equity) is most enhanced by your selection decision and criteria?
10. How confident are you that your selection criteria are job related?
11. How would you validate the criteria if asked to do so by a federal court or by an affirmative action compliance agency?
12. What is the appropriate definition of *merit* in this situation?
13. Was your group ever tempted to pick the "best" candidate first, and then identify the desired competencies and minimum qualifications based on that candidate's resume (rather than identifying the desired competencies and qualifications first, and then ranking the candidates against them)? If so, what does this show about merit-based selection procedures?

Postscript

The State Police Agency hired John Lewis for the position of minority recruitment director. The selection panel comprised several senior state police officers and one of the book's authors as an outside observer. There were no women or racial minorities on the selection panel, but they were unanimously in favor of hiring Jones because his military background and demeanor led them to view him as the most likely candidate. Moreover, he was an African American, and recruitment of African American male police officers was considered a higher priority than recruitment of women or other minority groups.

For almost two years after his appointment, John Lewis gained nationwide attention for his ability to recruit African American state police officers. As the only one of the three candidates with first-hand recruitment experience, he did an excellent job recruiting through schools, community organizations, and minority newspapers and radio stations. State police agencies throughout the region studied his methods and results as the example they were trying to emulate in their own agencies.

Nevertheless, as strong and successful as his recruitment efforts were, within two years of his appointment it became evident that there were problems with his overall job performance. First, turnover among new recruits and trainees continued to be high. The personnel director concluded that it was because the John Lewis lacked experience with other key personnel functions (like orientation and training, performance evaluation, and career development) that related to retention. Once out of the academy, new recruits were still being assigned as trainee troopers with senior officers who were quite likely to be white males. Their view of the organization, and of the role of minorities in it, was not always consistent with the John Lewis' mission and vision for minority recruitment. Therefore, the state police personnel director ended up hiring someone with a background similar to Harold Murphy who could help John Lewis institutionalize his successful minority recruitment program by designing and evaluating similar changes in other functions. These included diversity training for all officers, development of mentoring programs for new minority recruits, and increased attention to racial harassment or informal discrimination in the agency. In addition, police supervisors received training in performance appraisal, promotional assessment, and other functions needed to advance minorities along a career trajectory once they had joined the state police.

Second, John Lewis was a good minority recruitment program director, well liked and respected by state police officers regardless of race. He communicated forcefully and effectively with recruits, state police officers, and the hierarchy of uniformed command. However, he was not a politically adept speaker who could be trusted to deal smoothly or comfortably with the media or with federal compliance agencies. He was not an accomplished report writer or program evaluator. Therefore, the state police personnel director and media relations representative needed to cover many of these aspects of the job.

In short, the ideal candidate would have had the composite competencies of all three finalists: John Lewis' minority recruitment experience, Harold Murphy's overall HRM expertise, and Norma Sikorsky's media relations, program evaluation, and political networking skills. In fact, the nature of the job, and the requisite competencies, did evolve over time. Initially, the critical need was to hire someone with John Lewis' background to plan and manage a successful minority recruitment effort. Next, to prevent minority recruitment problems from continuing as minority retention problems, the state police needed to hire someone with Harold Murphy's background. As the program matured, it needed continual positive communication with compliance agencies, the state legislature, and the Governor's office to maintain good political relations.

Questions

After reviewing the outcome of the case, please answer the following discussion questions.

1. How does the outcome show that jobs and organizations change over time?
2. How does the outcome show that definitions of "merit" change over time, even for the same job?
3. How would you recommend that job descriptions be revised to accommodate these changes? How would you "sell" these recommendations to managers and employees, given their varied concerns and priorities?

John Lewis
1327 W. Addison Street
Minneapolis, MN

Job Objective: A responsible professional position in minority recruitment, higher education administration, or personnel management.

Employment History:

2006–Present Assistant Director of Admissions, Northern Minnesota State College. Responsible for minority recruitment, minority financial aid, and internship programs for a 25,000 student state university system institution. Since 2006, the percentage of minority students has increased from 7% to 11%, despite cuts in Federal loans and other financial aid programs.

2000–2006 1st Lieutenant to Captain, U.S. Army. Responsible for a variety of combat assignments in the United States and overseas. Rifle Platoon Leader responsible for the health, morale, welfare and safety of 43 men (2000–2004). Company executive officer (2004–2005). Battalion Air Operations Officer (2005–2006).

Awards and Decorations:

2007: "Who's Who" (Outstanding Young Men in America)

2000–2006: Silver Star, Bronze Star Medal with "V" Device for Valor (Two Oak Leaf Clusters), Air Medal, Army Commendation Medal with "V" Device for Valor, and Purple Heart (Two Oak Leaf Clusters)

1997–1998: Medgar Evers Memorial Scholarship, Jackson State University

Education:

1999: BA in Psychology, Jackson State University, Mississippi.

FIGURE 5-5 John Lewis' Résumé (African American Male)

Harold Murphy
3732 18th Street
Arlington, VA

Job Objective: A responsible professional job as a human resource manager.

Employment History:

2005–Present Personnel Director, Northern Virginia Community College. Responsible for management of labor relations, recruitment and selection, training, and affirmative action compliance. Represents NVCC in negotiating session with staff union.

2001–2008: Assistant Personnel Director, Manassas Crossroads Bank, Manassas, VA. Responsible for selection, payroll and benefits administration and staff development.

Education:

2005: M.S. in Government (Personnel Management), the George Washington University, Washington, D.C. Master's Thesis: "Minority Recruitment Problems in Virginia State Government."

2001: B.A. in Business Administration, George Mason University. Senior Honors thesis: "Politically Incorrect: Conflicts between Union Seniority Systems and Affirmative Action Compliance."

Honors and Awards:

2001: Phi Beta Kappa, Pi Sigma Alpha, cum laude.

Professional Activities:

"Managing Privatization and Labor Relations Issues in State University Systems," National Association of University Personnel Administrators Conference, New Orleans, 2008.

Personal Information: married, good health

FIGURE 5-6 Harold Murphy's Résumé (White Male)

Notes

1. U.S. Department of Justice (2008). *An investigation of allegations of politicized hiring in the Department of Justice Honors Program and Summer Law Intern Program*. Report prepared by the U.S. Department of Justice Office of the Inspector General and the U.S. Department of Justice Office of Professional Responsibility.
2. Klingner, D. E. (1996). Public personnel management and democratization: A view from three Central American Republics. *Public Administration Review, 56* (4): 390–399.
3. Naff, K. C. (2003). Why public managers hate position classification. In S. W. Hays and R. C. Kearney (eds.), *Public personnel administration: Problems and prospects* (4th ed.). New Jersey: Prentice Hall

Norma Sikorsky
P.O. Box 6597
Salem, OR

Job Objective: A responsible position in management, media relations, or affirmative action compliance.

Employment History:

2007–Present Assistant to the Chief of Staff of the Governor of Oregon, responsible for the coordination of statewide affirmative action plans for state agencies. Made recommendations on affirmative action programs to state agency affirmative action program directors. Responsible for media relations and legislative relations between the Governor's office and affirmative action compliance agencies. Represented the state at numerous state and national affirmative action compliance conferences and news conferences.

2003–2007 Assistant Coordinator of Title IX Planning. Principal staff assistant to the Deputy Director of Education, State Board of Education. Responsible for advising the Deputy Director on design and implementation of statewide funding and curriculum changes required for compliance with federal funding guidelines for women's athletic programs under Title IX.

Education:

2007: M.A., Education, University of Oregon
2002: B.A., Education, University of Oregon

Honors and Awards:

2006: "Golden Tongue Award," Oregon Media Relations Association
2001: NCAA Finalist, Track and Field, State of Oregon

References:

The Hon. Slade Gordon
U.S. Senate Office Building
Washington, D.C.

William Groves
Director, Affirmative Action Programs
State of Oregon

FIGURE 5-7 Norma Sikorsky's Résumé (White Female)

CHAPTER 6

Rewarding Work

Pay and Benefits

Traditionally, potential employees were attracted to the public sector jobs because civil service jobs were thought to be stable and secure when compared to jobs in the private sector. Though salaries might have been lower than in the private sector, benefits were good and the promise of career employment meant that they would be able to stay long enough to collect them. But as public agencies have moved toward alternative mechanisms and flexible employment relationships typical of more market-based models, both public agencies and their employees find that they need to rethink their reward systems. To be effective, the **total compensation** package—pay and benefits—must meet the needs of employee and employer under current employment conditions:

- For employees, economic rewards are the measure of their worth to their employer. Pay and benefits must be fair compared to other employees and to the job market.
- For employers, economic rewards must be competitive enough to attract and retain employees with valued competencies. Because organizations and jobs are increasingly unstable, and because work is increasingly team based and client centered, pay and benefits must be flexible and easy to administer.

Along with pay, benefits are a critical component of total compensation. The high cost of employee benefits, the importance and expense of health care, and the need to combine flexibility and ease of administration to meet employer productivity needs and employee equity concerns mean that compensation and benefits managers occupy an increasingly important role in human resource management.

By the end of this chapter, you will be able to:

1. Describe the contemporary pay and benefits environment.
2. Identify the elements included in a total compensation package.
3. Understand the laws governing compensation policy and practices.
4. Describe the comparative advantages and disadvantages of competing systems used to determine pay—point-factor job evaluation, rank-in person, and broad-banding.
5. Discuss how pay-for-performance systems work, and how they differ from traditional civil service seniority and cost-of-living adjustments.

6. Identify the issues involved in pay disparity based on race and gender.
7. Discuss how pay is set in alternative personnel systems.
8. Describe the benefits to which all employees in the United States are legally entitled.
9. Discuss discretionary benefits like pensions, health insurance, and paid vacations.
10. Discuss other emergent benefit issues and their relationship to work/family conflicts.

THE CONTEMPORARY PAY AND BENEFITS ENVIRONMENT

Traditionally, civil service compensation systems were designed with the assumption that an individual job was a basic unit of measurement and that the relationship of one job to another could be determined and its value assessed apart from the job incumbent. Seniority and equity were valued as products of a stable working environment. Today, the basic assumption of stability has been replaced by dynamism and change. Even if not fully experiencing the tumultuous changes occurring in the private sector, public employers and employees are not shielded entirely.

Siegel[1] emphasizes the trend away from traditional civil service systems, based on their negative image, the increasing focus on public sector accountability, and increased emphasis on flexibility and contract management. Within civil service systems, he identifies three elements as characterizing the future of compensation policy and practices:

1. Turn away from long-term (seniority) toward shorter-term perspective
2. Performance orientation in compensation
3. Retrenchment in level and types of benefits

The impact these elements have on public sector compensation policy and practices can be captured with the term **new pay**. Compensation consultant Howard Risher has written extensively about this topic and characterizes new pay in the following manner:[2]

1. Responsibility for day-to-day salary management shifts from the human resources staff to managers and supervisors.
2. Broad banded ranges and wide salary ranges replace traditional classification and pay systems.
3. "Paying the job" gives way to "paying the person."
4. Performance appraisal emphasizes a wider range of raters, including peers, subordinates, and clients/customers.
5. Team and group incentives replace conventional merit pay for individuals.
6. Pay plans are increasingly tailored to specific work situations, not "one size fits all."

Each of these changes is predicated upon the changing work environment this book describes. In the contemporary labor market, the concept of stable job content no longer applies, and traditional pay plans based on predictability are perceived as a competitive disadvantage. Along with instability in the labor market, there has been an increasing emphasis on accountability and shaping individual and team performance toward specific organizational goals and objectives. As such, pay associated with performance is seen as a crucial, if not proven, incentive in this regard.

THE ELEMENTS OF A TOTAL COMPENSATION PACKAGE

Even as we move into an era where many positions may not include traditional benefits like sick leave, holidays, or pensions, the amount employers spend on total compensation (pay and benefits) is substantial. In 2006, state and local governments spent approximately 60.7 billion dollars on total payroll costs, and in 2008, for public and private employers combined, the cost of employee benefits alone equaled about 30 percent of total employer costs, 23 percent when excluding paid time off.[3,4] For state and local government employers, this portion was higher, 34 percent of total costs and 26 percent when excluding paid time off, than that for private sector employers, 29 percent of total costs.[5]

Usually, when employees think about their salary, they think of take-home pay, and employees usually never even see a record of some benefits such as the employer's contribution to Social Security, workers' compensation, and unemployment insurance. Thus, most employees are unaware of their total compensation. Figure 6-1 shows the basic components of a total compensation package and identifies some of the indirect, or nonsalary, "benefits" included in compensation.

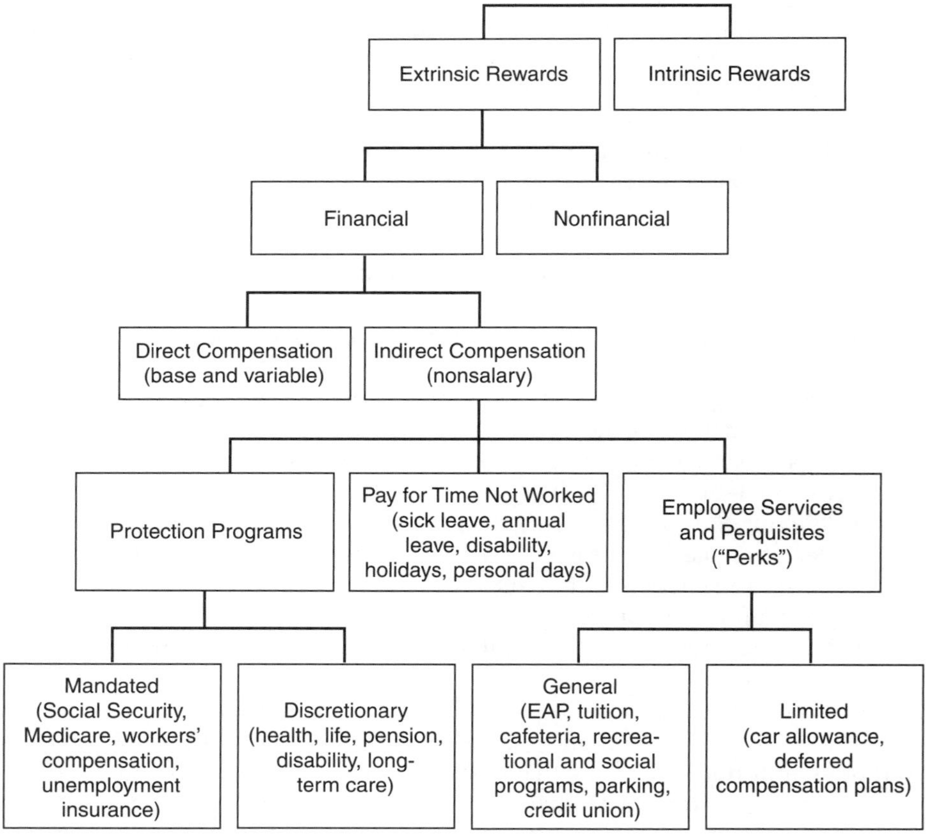

FIGURE 6-1 Total Compensation Package (Adapted with permission from T1—Total Compensation Management, American Compensation Association (ACA), 14040 N. Northsight Blvd., Scottsdale, AZ 85260; 602–951–9191.)

LAWS AFFECTING COMPENSATION POLICY AND PRACTICE

Pay setting in public agencies is governed by legal constraints, historical practice, and the relative power of stakeholders. Along with various state statutes, four primary federal laws apply: the **Fair Labor Standards Act (FLSA)** of 1938, the Equal Pay Act of 1963, the 1964 Civil Rights Act (Title VII), and the Age Discrimination in Employment Act of 1967. This section discusses the provisions of the laws that apply to public agencies, the outcome of these laws' interaction with historical practice, and the impact of these outcomes on the pay-setting process under alternative personnel systems.

The Fair Labor Standards Act (FLSA) was originally passed in 1938 to regulate minimum wages, overtime pay, and record-keeping requirements for private employers. In 1985, the U.S. Supreme Court's decision in **Garcia v. San Antonio Metropolitan Transit Authority** made state and local governments subject to its wage, hour, and record-keeping requirements. Garcia has profoundly affected public personnel practices in state and local government. Employees must be paid the **minimum wage** (currently $5.85 per hour). Employees (with the exception of executives, administrative employees, and professionals) must be paid time-and-a-half for overtime, defined as more than forty hours per workweek (or given "**comp time**" during the same pay period). Employers are required to keep records going back two to three years of all employees' wages and hours, and to provide these records to the Department of Labor upon request.

Because it is not always clear whether employees are exempt from or covered by the FLSA, and because covered employees require more complex staffing patterns or considerably higher personnel costs, keeping up with FLSA provisions is critical to state and local governments. Many local government employees (particularly police officers and firefighters) have irregular work schedules that pose particular problems for compensation specialists.[6]

The Equal Pay Act of 1963 requires employers to provide men and women with equal pay for equal work. In order to win relief under this law, the plaintiff must demonstrate that jobs requiring equal skill, effort, and responsibility that are performed under similar working conditions are paid differentially on the basis of sex. But "equal work" is narrowly defined under the terms of this Act—it does not include dissimilar jobs, and it exempts pay differentials resulting from the impact of seniority or merit systems.

The Civil Rights Act of 1964 (Title VII) forbids discrimination with respect to pay and benefits on the basis of nonmerit factors. While it does not prohibit any sex-based pay differentials that are legal under the Equal Pay Act of 1963, subsequent court cases have held that it goes beyond the equal pay provisions of the EPA by allowing equal pay for comparable jobs—those not identical, but requiring equivalent skill, effort, and responsibility, and performed under similar working conditions.

The Age Discrimination in Employment Act prohibits employers from paying older workers less than younger ones for equal work. And as the workforce gets grayer, it has another important provision—prohibiting employers from using pension plan provisions to force older employees to take early retirement.

ALTERNATIVE WAYS OF SETTING PAY IN PUBLIC AGENCIES

Setting pay in the public sector has traditionally focused on maintaining internal equity within organizations and ensuring external equity with alternate employment sectors. However, meeting both needs has often been challenging for public sector organizations. The point-factor job evaluation system, the long-standing norm in setting public sector pay, is primarily focused on ensuring internal equity between jobs within an organization but has been characterized as highly standardized, inflexible, slow to respond to changing market conditions, and inadequately linked to employee performance. In response to growing disenchantment with this system and the desire to be more competitive with the private sector, many public sector organizations have implemented more flexible pay setting systems; the most common of which are rank-in-person, broad-banding, and pay-for-performance systems.

Point-Factor Job Evaluation

Point-factor methods of job evaluation are popular in many businesses and civil service systems because of their objectivity, stability, and reliability for pay-setting purposes.[7] Despite their complexity and high development costs, they have largely supplanted other evaluation methods because of their perceived internal validity (within the agency) and the ease with which objective factors can be used to validate the system in the face of attacks by employees, unions, and affirmative action compliance agencies.[8]

The data used in analyzing a job for purposes of developing a job description also form the basis for **job evaluation**. The purpose of job evaluation is to determine the worth of the a job or position (rather than the value of the work or quality of the person's performance). Although several methods of job evaluation have been used, the most prominent today is the **point-factor method**. It compares jobs on an absolute scale of difficulty, using several predetermined job-worth factors that are quantified to make numerical comparisons easier. This is how it is done:

1. Analyze all jobs in the organization.
2. Select factors that measure job worth across all positions. Common factors include supervisory responsibility, difficulty of duties, working conditions, and budgetary discretion. It may be necessary to break jobs into broad occupational classes first and to develop separate **compensable factors** for each class.
3. Weigh job factors so that the maximum possible value is 100. (e.g., there could be five factors worth 20 points each, or two worth 20 each and one worth 60).
4. Develop and define **quality levels** for each job-worth factor, and apportion points within that factor to each quality level. For example, if "working conditions" is selected as a job-worth factor with a total value of 20 points out of 100, then the following quality levels might be established for this job-worth factor:
   a. 0 points: office work
   b. 10 points: occasional outside work, some walking or standing required
   c. 20 points: constant outside work in bad weather; heavy lifting required.
5. Evaluate each job along each job-worth factor and compute the point total.
6. Establish realistic pay ranges for benchmark positions based on market comparisons with similar jobs elsewhere.
7. Pay benchmark jobs the market rate, and pay other jobs in proportion to their comparative point totals.

Figure 6-2 shows a simplified example of the point-factor method. It compares the worth of five jobs within a hypothetical city's government, each based on three job-worth factors and defined by three or more quality levels. It can immediately be seen that this initial attempt to create an equitable job evaluation system results in some obvious pay

JOB-WORTH FACTORS

- competencies (30 points),
- working conditions (30 points), and
- responsibility (40 points) = 100 points total

QUALITY LEVELS

Competencies	30—professional knowledge and independent judgment
	20—technical knowledge under supervision
	10—some technical skill under close supervision
Working Conditions	30—constantly unpleasant and dangerous
	20—occasionally unpleasant or dangerous
	0—office work
Responsibility	40—makes decisions affecting a major program area
	25—makes decisions affecting a department
	15—makes decisions affecting a division
	10—makes decisions affecting individual clients

POINT-FACTOR EVALUATION AND PAY

Job	Competency	Conditions	Responsibility	Total	Salary
Mayor	30	0	40	70	$80,000
Police Chief	30	0	25	55	$66,500
Lieutenant	30	10	15	55	$66,500
Sergeant	20	10	10	40	$53,000
Police Officer	10	30	10	50	$62,000

FIGURE 6-2 Example of Point-Factor Job Evaluation

inequities: police lieutenants would make the same as the police chief, and police officers would make more than the sergeants who supervise them! Note, however, that this is entirely due to the choice of job-worth factors and quality levels, and their relative weights. Each of these four choices is based on the professional judgment of the job analyst. When the results defy reality or common sense, the job analyst will usually alter the choice or relative weight of the job-worth factors, or the definition and relative weight of the quality levels for each factor.

These changes would probably result in alterations of the method to the example shown in Figure 6-3. In this case, the relative value of the five jobs has been altered by changing the value of the job-worth factor "responsibility" from 40 to 60 points, and by reducing the value of the other two factors to 20 points each. And the quality factors' point values have been readjusted based on the change in point allocation to the three job-worth factors. The result has more internal equity, meaning that it results in total job evaluation scores for various departments that make more sense when compared to each other within the organization. The point is that once ratings are initially established by the job analyst, they should be reviewed by an internal committee of managers from evaluation

JOB WORTH FACTORS

- competencies (20 points),
- working conditions (20 points), and
- responsibility (60 points) = 100 points total

QUALITY LEVELS

Competencies	20—professional knowledge and independent judgment
	14—technical knowledge under supervision
	7—some technical skill under close supervision
Working Conditions	20—constantly unpleasant and dangerous
	10—occasionally unpleasant or dangerous
	0—office work
Responsibility	60—in charge of a large organization
	45—in charge of a major department
	30—supervises more than ten employees
	15—supervises fewer than ten employees
	0—no supervisory responsibilities

POINT-FACTOR EVALUATION AND PAY

Job	Competency	Conditions	Responsibility	Total	Salary
Mayor	20	0	60	80	$92,000
Police Chief	20	0	45	65	$78,500
Lieutenant	20	10	30	60	$74,000
Sergeant	14	20	15	49	$64,100
Police Officer	7	20	0	27	$44,300

FIGURE 6-3 Revised Example of Point-Factor Job Evaluation

scores for various positions that make more sense when compared to each other within the organization. The point is that once ratings are initially established by various departments, including personnel and budget. This committee should reach consensus on adjustments to the point values and relative salaries for the various positions, reflecting both market information and their true worth to the organization.

Despite its strength in establishing internal equity, one of the main challenges of maintaining a competitive pay structure under a point-factor system is ensuring pay rates are adequately linked to an appropriate labor market. Adjusting pay on the basis of comparable local market pay rates is referred to as a **locality pay adjustment**; however, the process of doing so requires human resources professionals to decide how often to survey wage rates offered in corresponding markets as well as which markets to make comparisons to. Inevitably, this process can become politically charged in those cases where employees perceive that inappropriate or untimely comparisons are being made. For instance, in a rapidly changing labor market, employees may feel that **benchmark positions** should be compared to those on the private sector labor market every year, but this would generally be too expensive for most jurisdictions to carry out. Additionally, employees may feel cheated if salary surveys include labor markets with low average wage rates. For example, federal employees in Washington D.C. have long complained that their salaries should not be benchmarked against those offered in neighboring Baltimore, MD, because doing so has the inevitable effect of lowering their wage rates. Instead, some have argued that New York, NY, or Boston, MA, might be more appropriate comparison markets. Last, this process becomes even more complicated when the ability of governments to offer competitive pay rates is taken into account. Although salary surveys may uncover the presence of below market public sector wage rates, this does not mean that government jurisdictions will possess the fiscal means of raising wage rates to competitive levels.

Another fundamental weakness of job evaluation methods was highlighted in the introduction to this chapter—they focus on the relative worth of jobs or positions, rather than the importance of the work to the mission of the agency or the quality of employee's performance. Thus, in an era where the focus of human resource management is shifting from inputs to outputs and outcomes, and where work is allocated flexibly rather than hierarchically, job evaluation has increasingly come under attack as outmoded and off target.[9] Critics charge that it reinforces bureaucratic hierarchy and lack of initiative and discourages innovation, development of internal and external relationships, and mission orientation among employees. Employees tend to focus on internal competition for upward classification and pay increases rather than on customers and mission. And classification and evaluation systems tend to stifle organizational change by tying any alteration in work duties or relationships to potential changes in internal status and pay. Creative managers soon learn that jobs can be "upgraded" by rewriting job descriptions to gain more job evaluation points. Thus, job evaluation creates incentives to create additional supervisory positions and waste resources, because supervisors can gain higher grades based on the number of resources they use and the number of employees they supervise.

Rank-in Person

Rank-in-person systems are an alternative to point evaluation systems and are traditionally found in the military, in paramilitary organizations such as police and fire departments and the U.S. Public Health service, in the U.S. Foreign Service, and in university faculties. Rank-in-person systems differ from traditional job classification and evaluation (**rank-in-job** systems) because their focus is not on the duties of a particular position, but on the competencies of the employee. Under a rank-in-job system, all employees are classified by type of occupation and level of responsibility, and these factors are tied to a job analysis, classification, and evaluation system. In other words, the employee accepts a job and the rank is in the job, not the person who occupies it. Under this system, employees qualify for promotion from one rank to another based on competencies and education (assuming promotions are available).[10] And the rank is carried with the employee who moves from one job to another.

Since the rank attaches to the person rather than to the position, employees can be freely assigned or reassigned within the organization without its affecting their pay or status. This has the advantage of reducing the immobility and status concerns generated by traditional job evaluation. It also enables the matching of employees to work based on the specific skills or abilities required. This feature offers organizations that use rank-in-person systems tremendous flexibility, and it is much more effective at utilizing workforce diversity to match employee talents with agency needs. For example, assume the U.S. Public Health Service needs to respond to an increased incidence of hepatitis among hospital workers in Phoenix. Since the agency uses a rank-in-person system, it can search its employee data banks to come up with a list of specialists who are experienced in hepatitis-B research and education, bilingual, and living in or able to relocate to Phoenix. Once identified, individuals can quickly be put to work without worrying about whether they are in the "right" grade level or occupational specialty.

There are obviously major disadvantages to both alternatives. Rank-in-person systems still must control total budget allocations for personnel by personnel ceilings and average grade levels. And employees will continue to focus on assignments perceived as developmental or as required for advancement to the next highest rank ("ticket punching"). The agency must develop relatively sophisticated human resource management information systems if it is to effectively match work with employees. A traditional rank-in-job system requires only a match of the occupational code and grade level of the vacant position with a roster of employees who meet the minimum qualifications for that grade level. A rank-in-person system requires cataloging (and confidentiality) of a range of employee data, detailed analysis of required competencies, and rapid matching of skills with needs through a user-friendly information system. Further, it requires a set of standards and procedures to decide how a person moves from one rank to another. These systems tend to be very career oriented with employees starting at entry level and progressing through ranks rather than moving laterally from one organization to another.

One additional variation of rank-in-person pay is competency-based pay, a system in which individuals are compensated based upon their competencies, formal educational attainment, or professional certifications. For instance, employers might compensate professional employees for attaining advanced graduate degrees or certifications, even though the competencies acquired may not be directly applicable to the employee's current position. According to the IPMA-HR, "competency-based pay has proved to be more successful when used in a wide cross section of non-exempt, professional, and managerial positions."[11]

Broad-Banding

Broad-banding (also referred to as **Pay-banding or Grade-banding**) has emerged as an attractive compromise that retains job evaluation yet allows more flexible and performance-based management of people and work.[12] In place of complex systems with dozens of **pay grades** and hundreds of occupational classifications, grade-banding systems arrange jobs into broad occupational classes and a few pay bands (such as "training level," "full performance level," and "expert performance level"). Managers are authorized to adjust salaries within ranges without having to gain approval from personnel for endless reclassification requests, and employees have clearer and less restrictive career mobility ladders.[13] In theory, this also allows for greater managerial flexibility in offering pay rates more in line with those offered in the private sector labor market.

Grade-banding originated in the 1980s in the private sector in the United States, where it was adopted by Citicorp, General Electric, Xerox, and AT&T. It was introduced on an experimental basis in the federal government in 1981 as a research innovation authorized by the Civil Service Reform Act of 1978.[14] Early demonstration projects were developed for the Pacer Share project, Naval Laboratories, and the National Institute of Standards, among others. Although efforts to gain Congressional approval for the governmentwide adoption of grade-banding within the federal government have been thus far unsuccessful, a number of agencies have since implemented comprehensive pay bands, including the Government Accountability Office and Internal Revenue Service (IRS), and both the Departments of Defense and Homeland Security have plans to implement comprehensive pay-banding systems as well.[15]

In general, broad-banding has produced favorable results: less wasted time in job analysis for reclassification purposes, a diminished importance of hierarchical levels inside the organization, improved managerial ability to use salary increases to stimulate productivity, and more flexible employee mobility. But there is one negative outcome—most examples report a tendency for average salaries to "creep" upward toward the top of whatever pay ranges are authorized. So it remains to be seen whether managers can resist this pressure and manage effectively within their budgets.

PAY FOR PERFORMANCE

One of the most politically charged and attractive alternatives to traditional pay systems in the public sector is **pay-for-performance**, also referred to as merit pay, and given its importance it is discussed in greater detail in the following sections. In the 1980s, skepticism of the government's ability to solve public problems contributed to government cutbacks and demands that government become more businesslike. These led to development of pay-for-performance systems based on the fundamental belief that a person's pay ought to reflect his or her contribution to the organization.[16] And "best practice" examples from the private and public sector suggest that flexible, performance-based incentives allow management—and employees—to use **merit pay** or **gain sharing** to work more closely together toward the maximization of both productivity *and* productivity-based pay increases.

Public sector experiments with performance-based compensation systems grew out of this movement, with the federal government leading the way. The Civil Service Reform Act of 1978 required federal agencies to develop job-related and objective performance appraisal systems that could be used for training, promotion, and disciplinary personnel actions. The Act also mandated performance-based compensation systems for senior- and middle-level federal managers, but these systems were later eliminated due to a perceived lack of effectiveness.[17] However, despite this lack of early success, pay-for-performance systems have experienced a resurgence in the past decade with states such as Georgia and Florida implementing comprehensive pay-for-performance systems and large federal agencies like the Department of Defense seeking to do so as well.[18]

Traditional Merit Pay, Seniority Pay, and Cost-of-Living Adjustments

In theory, traditional civil service pay systems maintain a separation between merit pay, pay for seniority, and cost-of-living increases. First, merit pay is given to reward superior performance on the assumption that once rewarded the performance will be repeated. Second, **seniority pay** increments (also known as **time-in-grade** increases) are given on the assumption that seniority increases an employee's skills, and hence value to the agency. Third, **cost-of-living allowances (COLA)** or market adjustments are given to employees to maintain external pay equity in the face of a competitive labor market.

But in reality, there is no clearer example of the confusion between intent and effect of pay systems than the practical relationships that exist among these three factors. First, the total amount of payroll budget allocated to merit increases is usually quite small (1–2 percent at most) because of budget constraints and uneasiness among elected officials about voter reactions to "paying employees bonuses to do what they ought to be doing anyway," or unwillingness to trust managers to allocate bonuses fairly. This means that personnel managers and supervisors are faced with the unpalatable alternatives of allocating relatively large bonuses to a few employees (thereby heightening conflict over the distribution of a relatively small merit pool), or spreading the merit money in small, symbolic increments among a larger group of employees and thereby diluting its effectiveness as a reward. Second, merit pay is usually permanent, in that it becomes part of the **base pay** upon which future increments are computed. It is never reduced, thus mitigating its motivating potential. Further, it is usually given for satisfactory performance (which almost every employee attains as a matter of attendance not performance). Finally, despite the impact of work groups on organizational performance, merit pay is usually allocated to individuals. Thus it tends to undermine an organizational culture of teamwork regardless of how it is allocated. Under these circumstances, it is easy to see why many employees, supervisors, and managers consider merit pay not to be worth the trouble (see Figure 6-4). Last, seniority pay has also been named as a culprit in discouraging performance, turnover, and risk taking in agencies. Just because employees have done things longer is no guarantee they do them better. Indeed, given the need for innovation in the face of technological change, it is equally likely that experience is an impediment to efficiency.

ONE SUPERVISOR's VIEW

March 2001

TO: John Nalbandian

RE: Reactions to the state's merit pay system:

1. The state never funded it the way it was supposed to be funded when it was first implemented. Employees received ratings of STANDARD, ABOVE STANDARD, and EXCEPTIONAL. If employees received a STANDARD evaluation, they moved up one step on the pay scale. If they received ABOVE STANDARD, they moved up two steps, and three steps for EXCEPTIONAL. Unfortunately, the state could never fund the plan, so as long as an employee received a STANDARD or above rating, they moved only one step. There is no incentive for employees to do anything above STANDARD work. Classified workers say, "Pays the same!"

2. My second complaint is that since the state is not funding it, then they should not be requiring supervisors to justify the ABOVE STANDARD and EXCEPTIONAL ratings. For example, if an employee receives STANDARD, the supervisor is not required to make any comments. If an employee receives ABOVE STANDARD or EXCEPTIONAL, then the supervisor has to write comments under each of the critical elements being evaluated. Many supervisors are not going to take the time to rate employees accurately; it's easier to rate everyone STANDARD. I'm sure you can imagine how that affects morale!

Performance evaluations are important and have a purpose. However, I feel like I can make a much better connection with the employee if I sit down and talk with him/her about the job. So, for myself, I would rather spend more time talking with the employee than jumping through hoops to complete paperwork.

FIGURE 6-4 A Supervisor's View of Merit Pay and Pay for Performance

Taken together, these three types of adjustments have a questionable impact on agency efficiency and employee performance in civil service systems. If pay increases fail to keep pace with inflation or a competitive labor market, managers and personnel directors out of necessity seek to retain competent employees by inappropriately using combinations of COLA, time-in-grade increments, and merit increases. In the end, the distinctions between the purposes of these systems and their effects tend to disappear.

Different Types of Performance-Based Pay

While base pay and indirect pay influence attraction and retention of quality employees, **variable pay** is believed to affect an employee's motivation and the channeling of work toward organizational goals and objectives. Essentially, variable pay is a one-time payment to an employee for accomplishment of preset goals or objectives. These rewards can be given individually or to teams of employees, but the critical feature is that they are contingent upon organizationally valued performance and they do not become part of base pay in contrast to traditional merit pay. Figure 6-5 shows various types of pay for performance. Individual incentives, such as piece-rate pay plans, continue to be effective where output can be quantified.[19]

Under all pay-for-performance systems, a critical variable is whether merit pay is added to the base or excluded from it. The appropriate answer to this question depends on the organization's intent. If the purpose of merit pay is to reward long-term performance over several years, it may be useful to add it to base pay, particularly when working with a rank-in-person job evaluation system. But if the primary purpose is to make the annual performance review more meaningful by establishing pay differentials based on employees' relative success (or lack thereof) at meeting performance targets, then it may be better to keep merit pay separate from base pay. In this way, an employee's current pay is, in fact, based on current performance. Similarly, an organization may wish to consider the relative advantages of individual and group incentive pay systems. Traditionally, merit pay systems have focused on individuals because individual jobs are the historical focus of performance evaluation and pay. But as performance in teams becomes more important, managers and personnel departments may wish to focus more on the performance of individuals as members of a work team.[20] Under these circumstances, gain sharing (team-based pay)

CONTRIBUTION TO BASE SALARY		LEVEL OF PERFORMANCE: Individual	LEVEL OF PERFORMANCE: Group
	Added to base	(a) Merit plans	(d) Small group incentives
	Not added to base	(b) Piece rates commissions bonuses	(c) Profit sharing gainsharing bonuses

FIGURE 6-5 Pay-for-Performance Classes (*Source*: Reprinted with permission from *Pay for Performance*, © 1991 by the National Academy of Sciences. Published by National Academy Press, Washington, DC.)

becomes an innovative solution that everyone may find attractive—taxpayers, managers, and employees (even when they are unionized). The basis of gain sharing is team-based bonuses.[21] Implementation problems include issues defining who is to be a member of the gain-sharing team, measuring baseline productivity and productivity increases, and determining the size of the gain-sharing pool. For gain sharing to work, public sector employees and managers must be allowed the same freedom from "red tape" that characterizes the private sector—the ability to purchase goods or services on the open market without reference to a list of approved suppliers or purchasing department procedures, or exemption from specific provisions of collective bargaining agreements that may regulate employees' ability to work out of classification or at a different geographic location. Ironically, those most opposed to gain sharing are often those who gain the most from traditional adversarial collective bargaining (labor attorneys) and traditional civil service "red tape"—classification specialists, personnel directors, purchasing directors, and comptrollers!

Problems and Prospects in Implementing Pay For Performance

Although the push for pay-for-performance systems continues at all levels of government, scholarly research demonstrating the broad success of these systems is limited.[22] However, despite this lack of recorded success, many public sector employers have continued to move forward with pay-for-performance systems, the most recent example being the adoption of a pay-for-performance system by the State of Kansas in 2008.[23] If the continued implementation of pay-for-performance systems is inevitable, then one must ask, "Why have performance-based compensation systems' expectations not been realized?" and "Why do employees, managers, legislators, and taxpayers continue to believe in them in spite of this?"

First, not all work lends itself to pay for performance. For example, where goals are difficult to identify or quantify and when discreet individual contributions are hard to distinguish, such plans face severe obstacles. Second, some organizational cultures and structures do not lend themselves to performance-based compensation. For example, organizations that pride themselves on teamwork and cooperation often find the competitive and individualistic norms underlying many pay-for-performance plans contrary to their organizational culture. Third, as is the case with the system proposed for the Department of Homeland Security, external factors like the presence of a union or legal constraints or political forces may block successful implementation.[24]

Given these many preconditions, it is not surprising that existing performance-based compensation systems—whether found in public or in private sectors—do not accomplish very well the several goals set out for them.[25] Milkovich and Wigdor found that less than one-third of the employees in the various surveys they reviewed rated their performance-appraisal plan effective in tying pay to performance or communicating organizational expectations about work.[26] And Risher indicates that despite the predominance of merit pay policies in the private sector, there is little confidence that anyone has figured out how to make them work effectively.[27]

At the federal level, where pay for performance has been researched thoroughly, it has been found that not enough money is set aside to establish a motivating effect, that performance appraisals are inflated, and that employees suspect the equitable distribution of the monetary rewards. Gabris and Mitchell summarize the pay-for-performance experience by writing: "So much do we want to think that extrinsic incentives will, under proper conditions, motivate employees, that we somehow refuse to accept the overwhelming evidence suggesting that this theory does not work well in an applied and general sense. The theory may be internally elegant and logical, but not practical."[28] However, for those agencies still seeking to implement pay-for-performance systems, the U.S. Merit Systems Protection Board finds that optimal conditions for successful implementation include "a culture that supports pay for performance; effective and fair supervisors; a rigorous performance evaluation system; adequate funding; a system of checks and balances to ensure fairness; appropriate training for supervisors and employees; and ongoing system evaluation."[29]

Given the overwhelming evidence suggesting at best only cautious optimism for performance-based compensation systems other than piece-rate incentive plans, why do they continue to attract advocates? Perry suggests that pay-for-performance systems have become ingrained in the institutional order of our society.[30] They are "part of the ritual and myth that help to retain the legitimacy of the governance system." Bureaucracies are established as rational instruments of public policy, and nothing appears more rational than rewarding employees monetarily on the basis of their performance. According to Kellough and Lu, the professed link between performance and pay suggests control by politicians, administrators, and the public over bureaucrats and conveys to the public that government is both responsive and efficient.[31] In addition, in a typical governmental setting where equity concerns permeate public policy making and service delivery, it should not be surprising that attempting to measure, differentiate, and reward performance would find an unwelcome home. Without the discipline and driving force of a competitive, market-oriented environment, internal equity is likely to drive out the underlying rationale for variable pay.

ISSUES INVOLVED IN PAY DISPARITY BASED ON RACE AND GENDER

Judging by its laws related to pay equity, the United States is an egalitarian society—discrimination in pay and benefits on the basis of age, sex, race, or other nonmerit factors is prohibited. But judging by its history of personnel practice with respect to pay equity, ample evidence justifies the conclusion that our society has unfairly discriminated against women and minorities in particular. There are, however, two sides to this question, and one should not reach even tentative conclusions on so important an issue without examining both.[32]

Proponents of labor market mechanisms for pay setting admit that women and minorities earn less than men and nonminorities, and that pay rates for male-dominated jobs are higher than those for female-dominated jobs. But they deny that these differences are based on sex or race discrimination as such. They attribute the difference in men's and women's salaries to traditional labor market explanations: Women have lower seniority than men because they leave the labor market to have children or move from one job to another to accompany their husbands (without commensurate increases in pay or status). Minorities, on the other hand, earn less because they tend to be clustered in low-paying, low-status service jobs.

Proponents of pay equity, on the other hand, charge that women and minorities find themselves concentrated in these occupations and employment situations because of social values and conditions.[33] As justification for this view, they compare salaries for different groups in the public and private sectors. In the private sector, where antidiscrimination laws apply but "employment at will" laws limit the power of women and minorities to protest employment conditions, the disparity between salaries of white males and other groups remains. However, in the public sector, where similar laws apply but are more enforceable because of merit systems and collective bargaining rights, researchers have found that the pay differential between white males and other groups is almost nil at entry level and varies only marginally while moving up the pay scale.

At the heart of this controversy is a fundamental dilemma that must be recognized and addressed, but can never be resolved. For advocates of government efficiency, it simply makes no sense to pay women and minorities more than one would have to pay them under a market model (unless required to by specific laws such as minimum wage provisions of the **FLSA**). The fact that women and minorities receive lower wages may be socially and ethically unfortunate, but it is the primary responsibility of the employer to provide services while meeting a payroll at the lowest possible cost, not to be an instrument for solving social problems. Advocates of wage equity and **comparable worth** (equal pay for work of equal value to the organization, regardless of status) hold exactly the opposite view. For them, balancing the budgets of public agencies by maintaining lower salaries for women and minorities is morally indefensible. It violates Title VII for private employee and denies public employees the rights to equal protection and due process under the Fourteenth Amendment. At present, the judicial status of comparable worth is unclear, but the decisions of the Supreme Court in the 1990s suggest that this issue is more likely to be dealt with in legislatures and through labor relations than in the courts.[34]

SETTING PAY IN ALTERNATE PERSONNEL SYSTEMS

The manner in which pay is set under alternative public personnel systems reflects the conflict among the values of efficiency and equity, and the historical practice within which these values and systems have evolved.

The appointing official sets political appointees' pay, though always within general limits established legislatively. Adjustments to pay are set the same way, based both on statutory limits and external and internal market comparisons. In local governments, frequent trade-offs occur between salaries and benefits, so that it is (some would say this is deliberate) hard to determine the actual rate of pay increase or to compare it meaningfully with pay paid for similar work in other jurisdictions.

Civil service employees' pay is usually established by the chief executive but authorized by the legislature. While civil service pay increases are usually justified or opposed on the basis of market comparisons, market factors are only indirectly used as the basis of setting pay. And the greater job security of civil service employees represents an intangible financial benefit that is difficult to factor into the market equation. This model applies most directly to federal civilian employees, whose pay and benefits are set directly by Congress rather than through collective bargaining.

Under a collective bargaining process pay, benefits and working conditions are set by direct negotiations between agency management and employee union representatives. But there are critical differences between collective bargaining in the public and private sectors. Public employees are usually prohibited from going on strike to influence the outcome of salary negotiations; and the appropriate legislative body must ratify policies with budgetary implications (such as pay and benefit increases) before they take effect. This is because state and local governments are prohibited from deficit financing of operating budgets, and because state legislatures may not legally delegate their appropriations authority to management negotiators in the collective bargaining process. In practice, this means that collective bargaining systems set wages through direct negotiations and indirect political influence on the legislature. For example, teachers' and police officers' unions frequently support local school board or city council candidates in exchange for support for pay and benefit increases when collective bargaining agreements are ratified.

Privatization, contracting out, exempt appointments, and the use of temporary workers to reduce full-time equivalent staffing levels, which are now increasing, have proven powerful alternatives to unions' political influence over the contract negotiation and ratification process. Union supporters call it a threat. It offers managers and elected officials the option of approving a negotiated contract, or of deciding to provide the same services through privatization or by replacing public employees and hiring contract workers instead. Usually contract employees without sought-after technical knowledge and skills have much lower pay and benefits than their unionized or public counterparts (because these salaries and benefits are set by a market model rather than through legislative deliberations and collective bargaining). Elected officials usually regard employees as voters and constituents and as people who can help or hinder their efforts to respond to citizen requests. Finally, they see them as employees with needs.

Affirmative action initially developed out of minority concerns over job access. But as access has increased, minorities and women have shifted their focus to pay and benefits. The impact of seniority systems on minority access to employment or promotions has been a prime target of affirmative action proponents. In most cases, courts have held that seniority systems developed with a race- or sex-neutral intent are legitimate, even if their effect is to give preference to white males. In some cases, however, courts have ordered modification of seniority systems, primarily by establishing dual seniority lists and requiring quota-based promotions until workforce comparability is achieved. This extreme solution is invoked only in cases where historical patterns of racism or sexism exist, where voluntary affirmative action compliance is ineffective, and where the resultant quota system is a temporary expedient that does not entirely bar qualified white males from consideration.

REQUIRED EMPLOYEE BENEFITS

Part of a total compensation package includes benefits. Employee benefit programs may be separated for analytical purposes into two categories: **entitlement** or mandated benefits, and **discretionary benefits**. Entitlement benefits are those to which employees are entitled by law (Social Security, workers' compensation, and unemployment insurance). Law does not mandate discretionary benefits, but the employer may provide them as part of a benefit package to attract or retain employees. There is considerable range in the discretionary benefits offered to employees, depending not only upon the employer's budget but also upon the type of personnel system.

Social Security

Social Security is a federally administered, defined benefit plan intended to supplement employer-sponsored discretionary retirement systems.[35] While coverage is compulsory for most types of employment, members of state and local retirement systems may or may not participate in the Social Security system depending upon the nature of their specific retirement plan. Currently (2006), employees pay 7.65 percent of wages up to a maximum of $94,200. Employers are required to match this contribution. The Social Security system also provides disability, death, survivor, and senior citizens' health benefits (Medicare). Although federal employees were exempted from participating in Social Security at one time under the Civil Service Retirement System (CSRS), all federal employees hired after January 1, 1984, must now participate in the system under the Federal Employee Retirement System (FERS).

Workers' Compensation

Worker's compensation is an employer-financed program that provides a percentage of lost wages and some medical and rehabilitation benefits to employees who are unable to work because of a job-related injury or illness. Employers pay a percentage of payrolls into a state-operated insurance pool, or a jurisdiction self-insures or can buy a private insurance contract. Because the percentage paid is based on the history of claims against the fund, employers seek to avoid payment of benefits for claims they consider fraudulent, and to adopt workforce health and safety policies to reduce the incidence of job-related injuries and accidents. Workers' compensation administration is a complex topic, and those who wish to focus on it should consult more specific references.[36]

Unemployment Compensation

In 1976, state and local government employees became eligible for **unemployment compensation**. This benefit provides a portion of regular wages to employees who have been separated without misconduct and who are actively looking for work and unable to find it. There is wide variation from state to state concerning waiting periods for eligibility, length of time benefits are paid, and level of benefits provided. States establish unemployment compensation funds through enabling legislation, and the system is funded through a federal tax on employers based on size of payroll.

OPTIONAL EMPLOYEE BENEFITS

It comes as a shock to many workers newly arrived in the United States to learn that many benefits taken for granted in Europe or Latin America are not necessarily provided to employees in the United States, particularly those working outside of traditional civil service systems.[37] These include pensions, health insurance, and paid leave.

Pensions

Retirement benefits, usually mandated by law for federal, state, and local government public employees, nevertheless largely remain as an important discretionary element in many other employee benefit systems.[38] Obviously, the magnitude of public pension funds and the value of their benefits to the individual employee mean that there are many managerial and policy issues associated with their development and administration. From the viewpoint of the individual employee, some primary issues are vesting, portability, defined benefit versus defined contribution plans, disability retirement, continuation of benefits after retirement, and the relationship between pension plan requirements and age discrimination. From the viewpoint of pension fund management policy, key issues are disclosure requirements, actuarial standards, and strategic investment potential.

Normally, employers require employees to have worked a minimum number of years (usually five) prior to vesting. **Vesting** simply means that an employee is entitled to that portion of accrued retirement benefits contributed by the employer (naturally, any employee contributions can be reclaimed by the employee upon withdrawal from the system and termination of employment. Vesting discourages turnover. This may be an advantage or a disadvantage to the agency. Employees and some employers favor **portability**, which means that benefits earned in one agency may be transferred to another. Many state systems are already portable, in that employees working in one state agency or local government are eligible to transfer benefits if they work for any other agency that is a member of that state system. For example, a recent survey by the Public Retirement Institute indicated that many state employees can transfer in or purchase retirement credits for previous service with military, in-state state and local governments, and other state governments.[39] True portability involves transferring assets from one plan to another or from one jurisdiction to another (such as the Teachers Insurance and Annuity Association – College Retirement Equities Fund system, the International City/County Management Retirement Corporation, or employer-sponsored tax-sheltered annuities authorized by the IRS).

State and local systems have traditionally been **defined benefit** plans. That is, employees and employers contribute a portion of salary, but the benefits are predictable based on the number of years of service and salary level and some multiplier. As of 2007, 83 percent of state and local employees had access to defined benefit plans and 96 percent of those employees chose to participate in their employer's plan.[40] Private pension funds are more likely to work on a defined contribution basis. That is, employees or employers contribute and thereby invest a fixed percentage of tax-deferred salary, and benefits upon retirement or withdrawal from the system will vary depending on the success of investments by the fund. In a **defined contribution** plan, like a private sector 401(K), individual employees are able to make choices about how their tax-deferred contributions are invested, as opposed to defined benefit systems where financial managers make these decisions for them. But employers need to provide flexibility and employee education for these plans to work well.[41]

Defined contribution plans are gaining popularity because they place more responsibility on employees, are more suited to employees who expect to work for several employers over their work life, are easier to administer, and often cost less because an employer's contribution completely ceases once the employee leaves or retires. But defined contribution plans require more education of employees regarding their retirement needs, investment opportunities, and risk. Many employers offer some combination of a defined benefit plan along with a defined contribution plan that employees may utilize if they wish. Under the so-called "cash balance" plans, many private employers seek to encourage portability and reward younger workers by decreasing pension benefits for older, long-term workers.[42] Whether employees favor defined contribution or defined benefit plans depend on their age and mobility. Older employees who plan on spending many years with one employer will favor defined benefit programs. Younger workers, or those who plan on career switches, are more apt to favor a front-loaded (defined contribution) system where issues of vesting and portability do not arise.

Increasingly, employees elect flexible retirement options as an alternative to either full-time employment or sitting at home in retirement. Phased retirement and deferred retirement options continue to offer employees the chance to balance work and family demands or health concerns.[43] Deferred Retirement Option Programs (DROP) offer employees otherwise entitled to retirement under a defined benefit program to continue working.[44] Instead of having the continued compensation and additional years of service taken into account for purposes of the defined benefit plan formula, the employee has a sum of money credited during each year of the continued employment in a separate account under the employer's retirement. The account earns interest and is paid to the employee, in addition to whatever benefit the employee has acquired under the defined benefit plan based on earlier years of service, when the employee eventually retires.

At its best, **disability retirement** allows employees who are unable to work because of illness or injury and not normally eligible to retire (in terms of age or years of service) to retire with benefits. At its worst, it is a device used by employees to retire early at the employer's expense, or by employers to induce an unwanted employee to retire early. Personnel directors can fulfill the intent of disability retirement programs and minimize fraud by considering alternatives such as light duty positions or early retirement programs. Long-term disability benefits are provided either by insured or self-insured long-term disability plans or with a disability retirement benefit through the pension plan.

One additional issue faced by public pension systems is the relationship between benefit accrual provisions and age discrimination in employment. Traditionally, pension systems interlocked with mandatory retirement policies in that employees were forced to retire by a certain age (sixty-five or seventy, earlier for public safety employees) because the employer stopped paying benefits into the pension plan when the employee reached that age. However, recent court decisions have held that such provisions represent disparate treatment of older workers, and thereby violate the Age Discrimination in Employment Act of 1967.[45]

This logic was enacted into law in 1990 by the Older Workers Benefit Protection Act (PL 101-43). This law permits early retirement programs provided that they do not result in age discrimination. Early retirement incentives that provide a flat dollar amount, service-based benefits, and a percentage of salary to all employees above a certain age, or give employees who retire credit for additional years of service will be lawful. In addition, many agency managers favor the flexibility that such programs offer, as opposed to involuntary layoffs based on reduction-in-force criteria. This law was applied to state and local governments beginning in 1992. In those states where state law denies disability retirement to an individual after a certain age, modifications have to be made in the plan.[46]

In the private sector, pension systems are regulated by **Employee Retirement Income Security Act of 1974 (ERISA)**. There is no public sector counterpart to this law. This means that public sector pension plans, such as collective bargaining activities, are regulated by a hodgepodge of state laws. There are no uniform standards for informing beneficiaries, taxpayers, or elected officials concerning their financial condition. In some cases, public pension funds have been managed by private investment firms whose speculative investments during the junk bond era of the 1980s have placed them at risk and have given rise to issues of disclosure and accountability for fund management.[47]

Much confusion also exists about the actuarial standards to which public pension systems should conform. These standards are assumptions about the rates of employment, death, inflation, and so on that are used to calculate the relationship between payments into the system and benefits drawn from it. Two types of systems are used—fully funded and pay-as-you-go. In a fully funded system, contributions of current employees are adjusted to meet the demands on the system by retirees, so that the system always remains solvent. Under a pay-as-you-go plan, employee contributions bear no necessary relation to payments, and funds are appropriated from general revenues to pay retirees' pensions. However, there is no federal requirement that public pension funds be operated in conjunction with generally accepted accounting principles applicable to private pension plans as set forth in ERISA.

Perhaps the most neglected aspect of defined benefit public pensions is their strategic investment effect. Traditionally, the administration of state and local pension systems restricted pension fund investments to low-interest, low-risk assets. During the 1980s, some pension fund managers were able to obtain higher rates of return by investing more speculatively (unsecured government bonds, real estate). While the excesses of the 1980s have put a halt to much of this activity, it is still necessary for states to establish some reasonable balance between security and rate of return. This is particularly true given the potential of public pension funds, because of the sheer size of their investment activity, for stimulating and directing economic growth in specified geographic areas or industries. For example, in Minnesota the Minneapolis Employee Retirement Fund (MERF) has formed an investment corporation that lends money to high-tech industries wishing to relocate to the area.

Health Insurance

There is widespread agreement today that serious problems exit with the system of health-care delivery in the United States. According to the U.S. Department of Health and Human Services, expenditures on health care were estimated to have reached $2.1 trillion in 2006, up from $1.6 trillion in 2002.[48] Despite this high cost, there are tremendous inequities in the distribution of health-care benefits. Many Americans are denied health care because they cannot afford it. According to a survey conducted by the Centers for Disease Control in 2006, an estimated 43.6 million persons were without health insurance at the time of the survey, 54.5 million had been without insurance in the twelve months leading up to the survey, and 30.7 million of those surveyed had been without insurance for more than twelve months.[49]

The greater cost of medical technology and increased longevity are primarily responsible for the increase in health costs. Our present system is geared toward the development of high-technology advances that provide a longer life span for the elderly at a high price; it is driven by a third-party reimbursement system that discourages cost control or cost-benefit analysis. As a result, retirees are creating a staggering liability for employers. In the absence of sweeping public policy reforms needed to overhaul our health system, employers have adopted what for them are reasonable strategies to contain health-care costs. These are (1) providing "permanent" employees (those with job security through civil service or collective bargaining systems) with education, early detection, and treatment programs; (2) using temporary or contract employees to meet fluctuating employment needs; and (3) working vigorously to encourage managed care programs and competitive bidding for health-care-benefit contracts.

Two important federal laws affect employers who choose to provide health benefits for employees. Under **the Consolidated Omnibus Budget Reconciliation Act (COBRA)**, employees under some circumstances have the right to continued health coverage for a limited time period following retirement or termination. And under **Health Insurance Portability and Accountability Act of 1996 (HIPAA)**, the Department of Labor requires that employers and health insurers coordinate changes in benefit coverage resulting from personnel actions, and at the same time maintain confidentiality of employee records.

Sick Leave, Vacations, Holiday Pay, and Discretionary Days

Employers provide sick leave so employees are not forced to work sick, and so they may accrue enough sick leave to last them through a major illness or injury without loss of pay. In this respect, sick leave is an employer investment in employee health. Unused sick days are usually computed for pension purposes as part of time worked when the employee retires, but are not credited to the employee if he or she leaves the organization prior to retirement eligibility.

Vacation days are a traditional benefit. Some jurisdictions provide discretionary days or personal days as well, and all provide some holiday leave for full-time employees. In contrast to sick leave, vacation and discretionary days are perceived to be the property of the employee (since employees are usually compensated for some unused vacation days upon termination of employment). Since the number of days provided usually increases with seniority, they may also provide an incentive against turnover.

Two elements of sick leave and vacation policy are worth examining here because of their implications for employee cost and performance. First, regardless of their differing purposes for the employer, many employees tend to treat sick leave and vacation indistinguishably, taking either type of leave whenever they want to be away from work. Employers can discourage this practice by clarifying the difference between the two types of leave during employee orientation, and by enforcing this distinction through disciplinary action against sick leave abuse. Employers should recognize that changing family roles have resulted in numerous single-parent households. Under these conditions, sick leave policies must reflect parental responsibilities to care not only for themselves but also for their children and parents.

Accrued sick leave and vacation time represent an unfunded liability for the agency. Leave may be accrued at one salary rate and used at another. While this liability is acceptable in the case of sick leave, agencies should prohibit employees from accruing large amounts of annual leave. In addition, employees not choosing to take vacations may burn out. If supervisors are not allowing them to take leave because of heavy workload, this indicates more fundamental HRM problems. Although there is no evidence of its widespread use in the public sector, some agencies may also choose to combine sick leave and vacation time into one discretionary leave allotment. However, doing so eliminates the traditional distinction between sick leave and vacation days, thus requiring more advance planning by supervisors and HRM professionals.

EMERGENT EMPLOYEE BENEFIT ISSUES

To all these items must be added some other employee benefit issues that are either continually in ferment or newly emergent.[50] These include parental leave, **child care** and **elder care**, flexible spending accounts, tuition remission, and flexible benefit plans.

Family and Medical Leave Act of 1993 (FMLA)

The increasing number of single parents and dual-income families has focused attention on work/family conflicts.[51] Situations traditionally taken care of by "mom," such as attending sick children or an elderly parent, become family challenges. The **Family and Medical Leave Act (FMLA) of 1993** recognizes the importance of this conflict by providing twelve weeks a year of unpaid leave to an employee to cope with taking care of a sick family member, elder care, childbirth, or adoption. The leave may be taken all at once but need not be: There are provisions for intermittent leave. The law applies to employers with fifty or more employees and is estimated to cover some 50 million American workers. For some employers the FMLA represents a major departure from past practice, but for others it simply reinforces existing policy.[52]

Research assessing the impact of the Act generally shows positive results. According to estimates provided by the U.S. Department of Labor in 2005, 2.4 million to 13 million workers have taken leave under provisions of the Act.[53] The majority of respondents to a three-year study of states that implemented parental leave legislation in the 1980 reported no increase in the percentage of women who took unpaid leave after childbirth, and no increase in the length of leave. There was also no increase in the cost of training administration or unemployment insurance as a result of the state laws.[54] Smaller companies have experienced problems adjusting work schedules and replacing workers with specialty skills.

Experts suggest the FMLA be implemented uniformly within an agency, based on coordination with existing absenteeism and leave policies, workers' compensation programs, and annual leave. Employees eligible and ineligible for FMLA should be identified in advance. Specific policies should be developed for requesting leave (including intermittent or reduced leave), along with procedures for medical certification. The personnel department should establish formal procedures for maintaining contact and monitoring the status of leave and scheduled return to work for employees who are granted FMLA leave. The agency should plan ways to cover the workload of an employee on leave, such as temporary replacement or distribution of workload. Policies and procedures should be clearly communicated to employees through orientation and training.[55]

Child Care, Elder Care, and Long-Term Care

While the FMLA provides some relief from intermittent work/family conflicts, the continuing problem of daily care for children and the elderly is not addressed in this law.[56] The decrease in parents staying at home during the workday has led to increases in employer-operated day-care centers, flexible spending accounts for child care, child-care referral services, and flexible scheduling for employees. At first, these actions were seen primarily as an employee benefit. But as agencies began to face shortages of qualified employees, child care has been demonstrated to be a necessity primarily to recruit or retain qualified female employees or dual-income families. In an era of increased workforce diversity, employees' ability to find satisfactory child-care arrangements will substantially reduce a major work/family conflict.[57]

The issues with employer-subsidized child care include cost, fee setting, and liability risks. But these are technical concerns rather than major impediments to the adoption of child-care policies and programs. And the fundamental value orientation of child care remains unassailable. If employees are assets, so are their children.

As the population of the elderly increases, care for elderly family members has become a crucial work/family issue and will continue to be a greater challenge in the near future. Elder care involves time off, flextime, or subsidized adult care in an attempt to minimize this conflict. According to a survey conducted by the International Public Management Association (IPMA) and National Association of State Personnel Executives (NASPE) in 2001, fewer than 10 percent of the surveyed public sector agencies offered elder-care assistance for their employees.[58] One way of dealing with work/family conflicts is to give employees more flexibility in scheduling their work.[59] Compressed workweeks, flexible scheduling of the workday, and negotiating the location of work are all possible ways to permit employees to deal with family issues that affect their work.

In addition, some employers are using the concepts of buying and selling vacation days and moving to the concept of "paid days off" instead of vacation days, holidays, sick days, and personal days. Trading vacation days actually involves the employee buying time from the employer or selling it to the employer. There are tax implications and administrative costs, but it does give employees flexibility over time. Providing "paid days off" gives employees more flexibility as well, and it does not require employees to "call in sick" when they have a child-care problem.

With a longer life span, workers face the problem of long-term care for themselves and spouses as well as their parents. According to the U.S. Department of Health and Human Services, approximately 70 percent of persons over the age of sixty-five will need long-term care, and by 2020 it is estimated that 12 million people will need such services.[60] Long-term care has become a key part in retirement planning, and some employers provide the opportunity for employees to purchase **long-term care insurance**. A recent IPMA/NASPE survey showed that 66 percent of respondents offered long-term care insurance as a benefit.[61]

Educational Benefits

In today's marketplace, public and private employers are increasingly finding it necessary to provide competitive educational benefits to employees. One such benefit is tuition remission. Many employers find that tuition remission rewards performance and helps retain desirable employees, and a recent survey conducted by IPMA found that 82 percent of respondents offered some form of tuition reimbursement to their employees.[62] Additionally, employers are finding that new hires are coming into the workforce with considerable student loan debt, and some more proactive public employers are beginning to offer student loan repayments as an added educational benefit. These benefits vary greatly in the amount of loans eligible for repayment and many also require service agreements prior to repayments. One example of such programs is the federal government's Student Loan Repayment Program.[63]

Flexible Benefit Programs

Flexible benefit programs are sometimes called cafeteria plans because they offer employees a menu of benefits. A full-fledged plan is developed by costing the employer's contribution to each of a variety of employer-sponsored benefit programs, and allowing employees to select alternative mixes of benefit packages depending on their needs. This has the major advantage, for the employee, of full utilization of benefits without duplication or gaps. This makes the employer's benefit package of greater value to the employee and is a tool for recruitment and retention.[64]

There are administrative and financial barriers to flexible benefit programs. First, given the wildly fluctuating cost of alternative benefits, it may be difficult for the employer to constantly calculate (and recalculate) the comparative costs of all options. Second, reconfiguring alternative benefit packages on a constant cost basis may be difficult for employees, who are unable to project benefit usage or the relative utility of alternative benefits accurately. Third, full employee utilization of benefits may increase benefit costs for the employer (who may have been able to reduce costs by relying on such overlaps as duplicate health insurance for two employees in a family). Fourth, increased benefit costs tend to force health and life insurance providers toward uniform defined benefit programs to reduce "shopping" from one program to another. In this environment, the advantages of flexible benefit programs may tend to diminish.

Rather than this full-service cafeteria approach, more typically, flexible benefit programs are isolated to a pretax premium plan for group health insurance and various flexible spending accounts. A medical flexible spending account might permit workers to direct a pretax payroll deduction that can be used for medical expenses not covered by health insurance. In another version, the worker could authorize a pretax payroll deduction for child care. These medical flexible benefit programs give workers a tax break without great administrative cost. The flexible benefits employers may choose to provide and the conditions under which they may be considered taxable income by employees are closely regulated by the IRS (**Section 125 Cafeteria Plans**).

One interesting development is that employers are increasing the flexibility and managerial discretion attached to work/life benefit programs by making them contingent upon employee performance. In March 1999, a study conducted by the American Compensation Association indicated that 18 percent of respondents currently use some form of work/life program to reward employee performance.[65] The rewards most likely to be tied to productivity are eligibility for flexible work, tuition reimbursement, or paid time off.

PAY, BENEFITS, AND CONFLICT AMONG PERSONNEL SYSTEMS

From this discussion of benefits, a conflict emerges between individual rights (pay and benefits for employees) and agency efficiency (reduced pay and benefit costs). And the outcome of this issue directly affects the conflict among competing personnel systems. For in the short term, at least, the systems that offer the lowest costs are those that provide employees with the lowest pay and least benefits—temporary and contract employment. Furthermore, the attractiveness of temporary and contract employees who are granted few, if any, benefits by the purchasing employer is the fact that a number of benefits like vacation, holiday pay, and sick leave are pegged to an employee's salary, which usually reflects longevity.

It should be noted that despite their relatively short expected tenure in office, political appointees have frequently been able to include themselves in the benefit provisions offered to public employees. The justification for this is that the relatively low salaries paid to political appointees (compared with their private-sector counterparts) necessitate attracting top candidates with a benefit package as well. Cynics would say that because legislators have the authority to approve pay and benefits for public employees, they have often also used their authority to approve pay and benefit increases for themselves.

Summary

Pay and benefits are fundamental ways that employers attract, reward, and retain employees. Pay setting takes place on the basis of job evaluation and market comparisons, through different processes depending on the personnel system involved and the philosophy of the public employer. New pay advocates seek to attract individuals with valued competencies by paying a competitive market wage and benefits, but their retention strategy is to reward performance through variable pay. This does not reward longevity nor does it add to benefit costs associated with pay rates inflated by merit or time-in-grade increases or cost-of-living adjustments.

Depending on the personnel system, employee benefits are regarded as an important motivator of employee retention as well as an increasing cost to employers. Some benefits are mandated by law in the United States: Social Security (or its equivalent), workers' compensation, and unemployment compensation. At least for civil service systems that define employees as a public resource, the emphasis is on providing a range of flexible and "family friendly" benefits that enhance the performance of an increasingly diverse workforce.[66]

Key Terms

base pay *136*
benchmark positions *132*
broad-banding *134*
child care *146*
comparable worth *140*
Consolidated Omnibus Budget Reconciliation Act (COBRA) *145*
compensable factors *130*
"comp time" *129*
cost-of-living allowances (COLA) *135*
defined benefit *143*
defined contribution *143*
disability retirement *144*
discretionary benefits *141*
elder care *147*
Employee Retirement Income Security Act (ERISA) *144*
entitlement benefits *141*
Fair Labor Standards Act (FLSA) *129*
Family and Medical Leave Act (FMLA) *146*
Flexible benefit Programs *148*
gain sharing *135*
Garcia v. San Antonio Metropolitan Transit Authority *129*
Health Insurance Portability and Accountability Act of 1996 (HIPAA) *145*
locality pay adjustment *132*
long-term care insurance *148*
merit pay *135*
minimum wage *129*
new pay *127*
pay for performance *135*
pay grade *134*
portability *143*
Section 125 Cafeteria Plans *149*
seniority pay *135*
time-in-grade *135*
total compensation *126*
unemployment compensation *142*
variable pay *137*
vesting *143*
workers' compensation *142*

Discussion Questions

1. What are the characteristics of the contemporary pay and benefits environment?
2. What is new about "new pay"? How does it reflect a departure from the way pay has traditionally been viewed in civil service systems?
3. What elements are included in a total compensation package?
4. What are the three laws governing public agency compensation policy and practices?
5. Describe the two competing systems—job evaluation and market models—used to determine pay, and discuss their comparative advantages and disadvantages.
6. What are the differences between merit pay, pay based on seniority, and cost-of-living allowances?
7. Identify the conditions necessary for a pay-for-performance system to work.
8. Describe the benefits to which employees in the United States are legally entitled.
9. What are some of the managerial and public policy issues associated with public pension and health benefits? If you were a benefits

manager and saw the costs of these benefits rising, what kind of recommendations might you make to account for employer and employee needs and interests?

10. If you were arguing pros and cons of wage discrimination based on race/gender, what kind of arguments would you develop?

11. Discuss other emergent benefit issues and their relationship to work/family conflicts.

12. What is the general relationship between pay and benefit systems and the conflict among public personnel systems and values?

Case Study: Reducing Unscheduled Absenteeism

Unscheduled absenteeism is a problem for many employers. Employers affected by it can design flexible work/life programs that allow employees to meet goals as well as manage their time away from work to meet personal needs. They can:

- Examine if their sick leave policy encourages unscheduled absences
- Train supervisors to be sensitive to lifestyle issues and signs of stress.
- Give employees the tools to deal with personal needs.
- Examine company workflows and culture to increase flexibility, and
- Get families involved in the workplace.[67]

But before employers choose to become involved with this issue, they need to become aware that it is a problem, and they need to accurately estimate its cost. The following case study shows how one city might do this.

The municipality of Cityville employs 500 people. Last year, excluding vacation time, which averages two weeks per employee per year, the rate of absenteeism was calculated at 3 percent. This 3 percent loss in scheduled work time is attributed to clerical workers (55 percent), blue-collar workers (30 percent), and professional staff (15 percent). The average hourly wage for clerical workers is $8.76 with an additional 30 percent in fringe benefits; for blue-collar workers $12.62 with an additional 35 percent fringe benefits; and for professional employees $17.42 with 33 percent fringe benefits.

Twenty-five supervisors, whose average wage and fringe benefits total $15.50 per hour, handle most of the absentee worker problems and estimate they spent about 30 minutes a day rearranging schedules and trying to organize work to compensate for the unscheduled absences. Cityville's finance director indicates that some $30,000 in incidental costs is associated with absenteeism. These include items like overtime, temporary help, and even an educated guess as to the costs attributed to lower quality of work done by the replacement workers. Problem: Using these amounts and the guide in Figure 6-6, estimate the total cost of absenteeism to the taxpayers of Cityville.

Answers to Case Study Questions

After several years, we and our students have reached reasonable consensus on the answers to these questions:

1. 30,000 hours
2. $11.22/hour
3. $3.63/hour
4. (a) $14.58/hour
   (b) $3.63/hour
5. $437,400
6. 3,125 hours
7. $15.50/hour
8. $48,437.50
9. $30,000
10. $515,837.50
11. $1,031.68

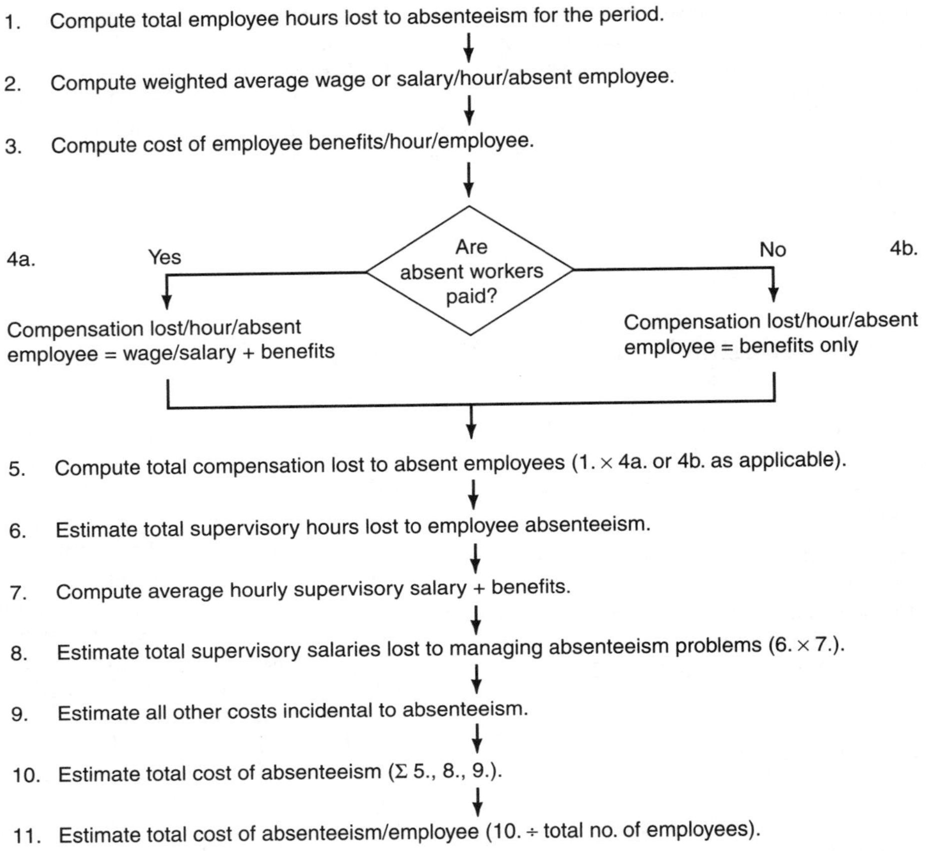
1. Compute total employee hours lost to absenteeism for the period.
2. Compute weighted average wage or salary/hour/absent employee.
3. Compute cost of employee benefits/hour/employee.
Are absent workers paid?
4a.
Yes
Compensation lost/hour/absent employee = wage/salary + benefits
No
4b.
Compensation lost/hour/absent employee = benefits only
5. Compute total compensation lost to absent employees (1. × 4a. or 4b. as applicable).
6. Estimate total supervisory hours lost to employee absenteeism.
7. Compute average hourly supervisory salary + benefits.
8. Estimate total supervisory salaries lost to managing absenteeism problems (6. × 7.).
9. Estimate all other costs incidental to absenteeism.
10. Estimate total cost of absenteeism (Σ 5., 8., 9.).
11. Estimate total cost of absenteeism/employee (10. ÷ total no. of employees).

FIGURE 6-6 Total Estimated Cost of Employee Absenteeism. (*Source:* Wayne F. Cascio, *Costing Human Resources: The Financial Impact of Behavior in Organizations*, 3rd ed. Boston PWS-Kent Publishing Company, 1991, p. 61.)

Notes

1. Siegel, G. B. (1992). *Public employee compensation and its role in public sector strategic management*. New York: Quorum, p. 161; and Siegel, G. B. (1998). Designing and creating an effective compensation plan. In Stephen Condrey (eds.). *Handbook of human resource management in government*. San Francisco, CA: Jossey-Bass, pp. 608–626.
2. Risher, H. (Winter 1994). The emerging model for salary management in the private sector: Is it relevant to government? *Public Personnel Management, 23*: 649–665. Risher, H. (2002). Bridging the chasm to a new pay system. *Public Management, 84* (9): 16–20. Risher, H. (2008). Planning and managing tomorrow's pay programs: Demographic shifts may trigger deep changes in traditional pay plans. *Compensation Benefits Review, 40* (4): 30–36.
3. U.S. Census Bureau (March 2006). *State and local government employment and payroll data*. http://www.census.gov/govs/www/apesstl.html
4. U.S. Bureau of Labor Statistics (March 2008). *Employer costs for employee compensation—March 2008*. http://www.bls.gov/news.release/pdf/ecec.pdf.
5. Ibid.

6. A detailed discussion of the impact of the FLSA on state and local governments is beyond the scope of this text. For more information, see the U.S. Department of Labor's Wage and Hour Division guidance for state and local government employers at www.dol.gov/esa/whd/
7. Plachy, R. (April 1987). The case for effective point-factor job evaluation. *Personnel, 64*: 30–32.
8. Barrett, G. V., and D. Doverspike (March 1989). Another defense of point-factor job evaluation. *Personnel, 66*: 33–36; Biondi, C., and J. MacMillian (November 1986). Job evaluation: Generate the numbers. *Personnel Journal, 65*: 56–63; and Sahl, R. (March 1989). How to install a job evaluation. *Personnel, 66*: 38–42.
9. U.S. Office of Personnel Management (2002). A White Paper. A fresh start for federal pay: the case for modernization. http://opm.gov/strategiccomp/whtpaper.pdf
10. Shareef, R. (Summer 1994). Skill-based pay in the public sector. *Review of Public Personnel Administration, 14*: 60–74; Ingraham, P. (1993). Flexible pay systems in the United States federal government. In *Pay flexibility in the public sector*. Paris: OECD; and Risher, H., and C. Fay (1997). *New strategies for public pay.* San Francisco, CA: Jossey-Bass.
11. International Public Management Association for Human Resources (2008). Competency Based Pay. http://www.ipma-hr.org/content.cfm?pageid=52
12. Risher, H., and B. Schay (1994). Grade banding: The model for future salary programs. *Public Personnel Management, 23*: 187–199.
13. For a thorough review of broad banding (history, strengths and weaknesses, implementation issues, and controlling costs) see: *Broadbanding: CPR Series* (1998). Washington, DC: IPMA.
14. Risher, H., and B. W. Schay. (1994). Grade banding: The model for future salary programs? *Public Personnel Management, 23*: 487–500.
15. National Academy of Public Administration (2003). *Broadband pay experience in the public sector*.
16. Flannery, T., D. Hofrichter, and P. Platten (1996). *People, performance and pay: A dynamic compensation for changing organizations*. New York: The Free Press.
17. Kellough, J. E., and S. C. Selden (1997). Pay for performance in state government. *Review of Public Personnel Administration, 17* (1): 5–21.
18. Nigro, L. G., and J. E. Kellough (2000). Civil service reform in Georgia: Going to the edge? *Review of Public Personnel Administration, 20* (4): 41–54; Condrey, S. E. (2002). Reinventing state civil service systems: The Georgia experience. *Review of Public Personnel Administration, 22* (2): 114–124. Bowman, J. S., M. G. Gertz, S. C. Gertz, and R. L. Williams (2003). Civil service reform in Florida: State employee attitudes one year later. *Review of Public Personnel Administration, 23* (4): 286–304.
19. Huish, G. (August 1997). Piece-rate pay plan in Clerk's office motivates quantum leap in quality production. *IPMA news*, pp. 22–23.
20. U.S. Merit Systems Protection Board (2006). Designing an Effective Pay for Performance Compensation System. http://www.mspb.gov/netsearch/viewdocs.aspx?docnumber=224104&version=224323&application=ACROBAT
21. Thompson, M. (1995). *Teamworking and pay.* Washington, DC: The Institute for Employment Studies, No. 281.
22. For a review of challenges within the U.S. Department of Defense, see the Government Accountability Office's 2008 report titled "Human Capital: DOD Needs to Improve Implementation of and Address Employee Concerns about Its National Security Personnel System." GAO-08-773.
23. State of Kansas (2008). A Brighter Future: Pay Plans. http://www.da.ks.gov/newpayplans/indivplans.htm
24. American Federation of Government Employees (AFGE) (October 2, 2008). DHS personnel system derailed, thanks to AFGE push to cut funding. AFGE press release.
25. Kellough, J. E., and H. Lu, (Spring 1993). The paradox of merit pay in the public sector. *Review of Public Personnel Administration, 13*: 46; Milkovich, G. T., and A. K. Wigdor (eds.). (1991). *Pay for performance: Evaluating performance appraisaland merit pay.* Washington, DC: National Academies Press; Risher, H. (Winter 1994). The emerging model for salary management in the private sector: Is it relevant to government? *Public Personnel Management, 23*: 651.
26. Milkovich and Wigdor. *Pay for performance*, p. 106.
27. Risher. The emerging model for salary management in the private sector, pp. 650–651.
28. Gabris, G. G., and K. Mitchell (Winter 1988). The impact of merit raise scores on employee

attitudes: The Matthew effect of performance appraisal. *Public Personnel Management, 17*: 375.
29. U.S. Merit Systems Protection Board (2006). Designing an effective pay for performance compensation system. p. xii.
30. Perry, J. L. (1991). Linking pay to performance: The controversy continues. In C. Ban and N. M. Riccucci (eds.). *Public personnel management: Current concerns—Future challenges.* New York: Longman, p. 80.
31. Kellough and Lu, The paradox of merit pay in the public sector, p. 55.
32. Abraham, Y. T., and M. T. Moore (Fall 1995). Comparable worth: Is it a moot issue? *Public Personnel Management, 24*: 291–314.
33. Joshi, H., and P. Padi (1998). *Unequal pay for women and men.* Cambridge: The MIT Press. See also: National Committee on Pay Equity (www.feminist.com/fairpay.htm); and the National Partnership for Women and Families (www.nationalpartnership.org/workandfamily/workplace/paydiscrim/payact.htm).
34. Gardner, S., and C. Daniel (Winter 1998). Implementing comparable worth/pay equity: Experiences in cutting-edge states. *Public Personnel Management, 27* (4): 475–489.
35. See: www.gov.ssa
36. Little, J., T. Eaton, and G. Smith (2000). *Workers' compensation* (4th ed.). St. Paul, MN: Westgroup; and Thomason, T., T. Schmidle, and J. Burton, Jr. (2001). *Workers' compensation: Benefits, costs and safety under alternative insurance arrangements.* Kalamazoo, MI: The W. E. Upjohn Institute for Employment Research.
37. Bergmann, T. J., M. A. Bergmann, and J. L. Grahn (Fall 1994). How important are employee benefits to public sector employees? *Public Personnel Management, 23*: 397–406.
38. For more information about pension and other benefits for retirees, see: American Association of Retired Persons (www.aarp.org); Employee Benefits Research Institute (www.ebri.org); International Foundation of Employee Benefit Plans (www.ifebp.org); and The Employee Benefits Security Administration, U.S. Department of Labor (http://www.dol.gov/ebsa/).
39. Harris, J. (February 2000). Purchase of service credit: portability for public sector employees. *IPMA news*, pp. 18–19.
40. U.S. Bureau of Labor Statistics (2008). *National compensation survey: Employee benefits in state and local governments in the United States, September 2007.* http://www.bls.gov/ncs/ebs/sp/ebsm0007.pdf
41. Employers add benefits to meet boomers' retirement needs (January 2000). *IPMA news*, p. 14.
42. Oppel, R. (August 20, 1999). Companies cash in on new pension plan. *The New York Times*, pp. C-1, 16.
43. Phased retirement gradually makes its way into the workplace (June 1997). *IPMA news*, pp. 18–19.
44. Calhoun, C., and A. H. Tepfer (August 1999). Deferred retirement option plans. *IPMA news*, pp. 13, 15; and Calhoun, C., and A. H. Tepfer (September 1999). Deferred retirement option plans. *IPMA news*, pp. 13, 15.
45. Equal Employment Opportunity Commission v. Commonwealth of Massachusetts. November 1, 1990. Docket Nos. 90-10640-H and 90-10150-Z.
46. Reichenberg, N. (December 1990). President signs ADEA bill. *IPMA news*, pp. 10–11.
47. County government sues financial advisors. Out-of-court settlement reached (April 1991). *PA Times, 14* (4), p. 1.
48. U.S. Department of Health and Human Services (HHS). *National Health Expenditure Fact Sheet.* http://www.cms.hhs.gov/NationalHealthExpendData/downloads/tables.pdf
49. U.S. Centers for Disease Control and Prevention (CDC). *Health insurance coverage: Early Release of estimates from the National Health Interview Survey, 2006.* http://www.cdc.gov/nchs/data/nhis/earlyrelease/insur200706.pdf
50. Champion-Hughes, R. (January 2000). Family friendly benefits. *IPMA news*, pp. 12–13.
51. Reed, C., and W. M. Bruch. (1993). Dual-career couples in the public sector: A survey of personnel policies and practices. *Public Personnel Management, 22*: 187–200.
52. Allred, S. (1995). An overview of the Family and Medical Leave Act. *Public Personnel Management, 24*: 67–73; Crampton, S. M., and J. M. Mishra (Fall 1995). Family and medical leave legislation: Organizational policies and structure. *Public Personnel Management, 24*: 271–290.
53. U.S. Department of Labor (2007). *Family and Medical Leave Act Regulations (A Report on the Department of Labor's Request for Information*

2007 Update). http://www.dol.gov/esa/whd/Fmla2007Report.htm

54. Reported in Buchanan, C. N. (July 1996). Oversight hearing on the Family and Medical Leave Act. *IPMA news*, pp. 7–8.
55. Fortney, D., and B. Nuterangelo (December 1998). An FMLA checklist: What can (and can't) an employer do with a returning employee? *IPMA news*, p. 10; and Kalk, J. (September 2000). What every employer should know about the Family and Medical Leave Act. *IPMA news*, pp. 7–8.
56. Kossek, E. E., B. J. DeMarr, K. Backman, and M. Kollar (1993). Assessing employees' emerging elder care needs and reactions to dependent care. *Public Personnel Management, 22*: 617–638; and Healy, M (June 17, 1996). Souix Falls May Represent the Future of Motherhood. *Los Angeles Times*, pp. A-1, 12.
57. Information on childcare options, laws and resources is available through: www.planetgov.com
58. International Personnel Management Association & National Association of State Personnel Executives (2001). *IPMA/NASPE 2000/2001 Benchmarking Survey: Total Compensation*.
59. Ezra, M., and M. Deckman (1996). Balancing work and family responsibilities: Flextime and childcare in the federal government. *Public Administration Review, 56*: 174–179.
60. U.S. Department of Health and Human Services (2008). National Clearinghouse for Long-Term Care Information. http://www.longtermcare.gov/LTC/Main_Site/Understanding_Long_Term_Care/Basics/Basics.aspx#needs
61. International Personnel Management Association & National Association of State Personnel Executives (2001). *IPMA/NASPE 2000/2001 Benchmarking Survey: Total Compensation*.
62. Ibid.
63. U.S. Office of Personnel Management (2008). *Student Loan Repayment Program*. http://opm.gov/oca/pay/StudentLoan/
64. Perry, R., and N. J. Cayer (Spring 1999). Cafeteria style health plans in municipal government. *Public Personnel Management, 28* (1): 107–117.
65. 1999 survey of performance-based work/life programs (January 2000). *IPMA news*, pp. 19, 22.
66. Durst, S. (Summer 1999). Assessing the effect of family friendly programs on public organizations. *Review of Public Personnel Administration, 19* (3): 19–48.
67. Checklist to reduce unscheduled absenteeism. *IPMA news*, December 1999, p. 18; and Browser, R. O., and S. Kane (August 2000). A successful sick leave incentive program: St. Louis County. *IPMA news*, pp. 12–13.

PART THREE

Acquisition

CHAPTER 7

Social Equity and Diversity Management

The United States can easily be considered one of the most diverse nations in the world; recent estimates show that one in three U.S. residents is a member of an ethnic minority.[1] In 2006, the U.S. population was approximately 12.4 percent African American, 14.8 percent Hispanic, and 4.5 percent Asian American or Pacific Islander, and by 2007, Hispanic representation grew to 15.1 percent of the total U.S. population.[2] However, along with this diversity comes the challenge of ensuring fair and equitable treatment of men and women from all ethnic and cultural backgrounds. This challenge lies at the heart of the topic of social equity, and meeting this challenge has and will continue to be one of the primary goals of human resources specialists and public managers at all levels of government. The means of achieving social equity in the workplace, however, has served as one of the most politically charged and complex issues of the past fifty years. This chapter provides an overview of the three major strategies or policies utilized to achieve social equity: equal employment opportunity (EEO), affirmative action (AA), and diversity management.

By the end of this chapter, you will be able to:

1. Discuss EEO and AA laws and compliance agencies.
2. Describe voluntary and involuntary AA compliance.
3. Describe the impact of legal decisions in interpreting and enforcing AA laws.
4. Discuss how increased contracting has shifted the focus of AA compliance from employment preference to minority contractor "set-asides."
5. Discuss how diversity management differs from both EEO and AA and describe how workforce diversification leads organizations to actively manage diversity by making changes in the organization's structure and processes.
6. Discuss how conflicts over the fairness of EEO, AA, and diversity management programs have affected the role of the public HR manager in achieving both productivity and fairness.

THE CONTEXT FOR EQUAL EMPLOYMENT OPPORTUNITY, AFFIRMATIVE ACTION, AND DIVERSITY MANAGEMENT

Given that EEO and AA are often referred to in the same breath and are almost invariably enforced by the same agencies, it is understandable that people confuse them. It may help to remember that both are designed to promote social equity, though through different methods. **Equal employment opportunity** refers to the policy of treating all individuals in the employment process fair and equitably, regardless of race or gender. In many instances, employers communicate their commitment to EEO to prospective applicants in the form of an EEO policy statement. For example, the State of Kansas posts the following statement on all applicable employment literature, "The State of Kansas is an Equal Opportunity Employer." The key point to take from this statement is that the employer does not discriminate against applicants and employees. **Affirmative action**, on the other hand, is distinct from EEO in that it refers to proactive efforts on the part of an employer to address the effects of past discrimination when EEO efforts alone will not suffice. As expected, these efforts have received the most attention in the debate over social equity because they force employers to temporarily abandon race/gender-neutral policies and to think in terms of group characteristics rather than individual attributes. **Diversity Management**, the most recent development in the challenge to achieve social equity, is distinct from EEO and AA in that its primary goal is to ensure that individuals of all backgrounds work harmoniously in the workplace and to take advantage of diverse points of view. It expands the concept of equity to include issues like religion, ethnicity, socio-economic background and is enabled in large measure by immigration, which has increased the likelihood that applicant pools have become more diverse over the years, especially in larger regional areas. In addition, it has moved the discussion in this broad area from the value of equity to one that incorporates the value of efficiency.

Although there are a myriad of laws and policies concerning social equity in the United States, see Table 7-1, the most important law is the **Civil Rights Act of 1964**.[3] Title VII of the Act prohibits employers and employment agencies from making employee or applicant personnel decisions based on race, color, religion, gender, or national origin and tasks the **Equal Employment Opportunity Commission (EEOC)** with enforcing the provisions of the Act.[4] Originally, the Act did not apply to the public sector, but the **Equal Employment Opportunity Act of 1972** mandated that state, local, and federal agencies adhere to the Act. Additionally, federal agencies and state and local governments are required to provide the EEOC with data on the employment of women and minorities within their organizations to ensure that they are meeting the spirit of the Act.

As previously stated, AA policies are those that take proactive steps to reduce underrepresentation through the preparation and implementation of **affirmative action plans (AAPs)**. Underrepresentation is generally said to exist when a particular group's employment levels within an organization are not on par with that group's presence in the relevant labor force. For example, Hispanics represented approximately 7.8 percent of the federal labor force in 2007 while representing 13.3 percent of the civilian labor force.[5] Given this disparity, the federal government has recognized that it needs to take "affirmative action" to recruit Hispanics into the federal labor force. The first government AA efforts were authorized by President John F. Kennedy, when he directed federal agencies to target their recruitment efforts in minority communities to address their low representation rates within the federal workforce. Among the efforts advocated by this approach to increasing diversity were visits by federal recruiters to colleges and universities with substantial

TABLE 7-1 Federal AA/EEO Laws and Compliance Agencies[6]

Law	Practice Covered	Agencies Covered	Compliance Agency
Civil Rights Act of 1964 as amended by the Equal Employment Opportunity Act of 1972 (40 U.S.C. Sec. 2000e) as amended by the Civil Rights Act of 1991 (P.L. 102–166)	Discrimination based on race, color, religion, gender, or national origin	Employers with fifteen or more employees	EEOC
Age Discrimination in Employment Act of 1967 as amended in 1974 (29.U.S.C. Sec. 631 and 630B)	Age discrimination against employees over thirty-nine years	Virtually all employers	EEOC
Americans with Disabilities Act of 1990 (P.L. 101–336)	Discrimination against qualified individuals with handicaps	Employers with fifteen or more employees	EEOC
Equal Pay Act of 1963 (29 U.S.C. Sec. 206d)	Discrimination in pay based on gender	Employees covered by the Fair Labor Standards Act	EEOC
Executive Order 11246	Discrimination based on race, color, religion, gender, or national origin	Employers with federal contracts and their subcontractors	U.S. Department of Labor
14th Amendment to the U.S. Constitution	Prohibits application of law unequally	All public employers	Various federal courts
Vietnam Era Veterans' Readjustment Act of 1974 (38 U.S.C. Sec. 2012, 2014)	Promotion of employment opportunity for disabled and other Vietnam-era veterans	Federal government and employers with federal contracts and their subcontractors	U.S. Department of Labor
Vocational Rehabilitation Act of 1973 (29 U.S.C. Sec. 701)	Prohibits discrimination against qualified individuals with handicaps	Federal agencies, grant recipients, and contractors	U.S. Department of Labor

minority student populations and advertisements in mainstream minority press outlets.[7] However, it is important to note that these original efforts did not include any numerical goals or hiring quotas for women and minorities.

In 1965, President Lyndon Johnson issued **Executive Order 11246**, which gave the Department of Labor the authority to enforce antidiscrimination policies among federal contractors under the Department's **Office of Federal Contract Compliance Programs (OFCCP)**. The Executive Order specifically prohibited **discrimination** by most employers providing goods or services to the federal government. Furthermore, it required those with fifty or more employees and government contracts of $10,000 or more annually to prepare a written plan identifying any **underutilization** (**underrepresentation**) of women and minorities and establishing goals and timetables to correct it. The OFCCP's use of numerical goals and timetables expanded during the Nixon administration, and in 1971, the federal government decided to apply the same strategy to federal agencies.

AFFIRMATIVE ACTION COMPLIANCE

Despite the rhetoric about "forced" compliance and "mandatory hiring quotas," it is important to remember that most affirmative action compliance is voluntary, and mandatory measures are only used as a last resort when agencies will not otherwise comply with the law.

Voluntary

Voluntary AA compliance occurs when a public employer recognizes a compensatory need to diversify its workforce and complies through the preparation of an AA plan that (1) identifies underrepresentation of qualified women and minorities compared to their presence in a relevant labor market; (2) establishes full representation as a goal; (3) develops concrete plans for achieving full utilization; and (4) makes reasonable progress toward full utilization.

Involuntary

Involuntary AA compliance occurs when an employer alters its personnel practices, as the result of investigation by a compliance agency that ends in a negotiated settlement, consent decree, or court order. Understanding these three involuntary compliance mechanisms requires some background knowledge of the process by which compliance agencies investigate employers. An applicant or employee who believes he or she has been discriminated against usually seeks redress through administrative channels within the organization where the alleged discrimination occurred. This may involve an appeal, informal and then formal, to the personnel office, affirmative action officer, or through union channels if available. The vast majority of concerns are settled in this way. If dissatisfied, the employee may file a formal complaint with the appropriate compliance agency.

Filing a complaint results in a formal investigation in which the investigating officer contacts the employer asking for a written response to the applicant or employee's charge of discrimination. The investigation may result in the complaint being rejected or the compliance agency filing a formal complaint against the employer.

Once a complaint is filed by the compliance agency, the employer may agree to the changes in its employment practices and whatever specific remedies will "make whole" the injury to the aggrieved employee or applicant. This acknowledgement is called a **conciliation agreement**. The employer usually enters into it primarily to avoid costly litigation.

A **consent decree** results when an employer and a compliance agency negotiate an agreement subject to the approval of a court and judicial oversight. It is usually entered into by an employer in litigation who "smells" defeat. In such cases, the employer may consider it beneficial not to admit guilt, but to agree to terms that may be more advantageous than those resulting from a guilty verdict may.

In situations where a compliance agency or individual has taken an employer to court over alleged AA violations and neither a conciliation agreement nor a consent decree can be agreed upon, a guilty verdict against the employer will result in remedies being imposed by a **court order**. Cases involving "egregious" and "pervasive" discrimination may result in mandatory hiring quotas, changes in personnel policies, and back pay for the victims of discrimination. Public officials will generally do their best to avoid this outcome because of the cost and unfavorable publicity associated with it.

With declining budgets and increased workloads, it is understandable that compliance agencies such as the OFCCP and the EEOC are under continual pressure to resolve cases administratively rather than resorting to court action. Additionally, they are also tasked with targeting complaints of multiple abuses by large employers.

IMPACT OF CASE LAW ON EEO AND AA COMPLIANCE

Given the confusion and conflict over whether EEO or AA is the best way to achieve social equity, the federal court system, and particularly the Supreme Court, has played a major role in interpreting and enforcing social equity through case law. The earliest opinions strongly endorsed EEO and traditional merit system values. Nevertheless, as the Court encountered systemic and pervasive employment discrimination, it became more sympathetic to social equity, reinforcing AA programs and race-based remedies in the 1980s. Now, it has swung back toward EEO principles.

The Court's initial approach in interpreting the Civil Rights Act of 1964 was contained in its unanimous opinion in ***Griggs v. Duke Power Company***.[8] Willie Griggs was a laborer at the Duke Power Company in North Carolina, where for years the workforce was segregated, with African Americans doing manual labor. In the early 1960s, Duke Power Company acknowledged that it had discriminated in the past but argued that it had recently instituted objective testing of applicants for selection and promotion. Griggs sued because the tests unfairly discriminated against African Americans and were unrelated to job performance. In a unanimous opinion, the Court established several points that prevailed until 1989. First, regarding Congress's intent, the Act was interpreted to have remedial as well as prospective intent.[9] That is, an employer could not simply say, "We discriminated in the past, but no longer do so." Second, the Court said that if an employer's personnel practices resulted in discrimination, lack of intent to discriminate would not constitute a valid defense. In other words, the consequences of employment practices were more important than their intent. Third, the Court said that once an inference of discrimination could be drawn, the burden of proof shifted to the employer to show that the personnel practices that had the discriminatory effect were in fact job related. Each of these findings sent a significant message to employers, and the case is viewed as a landmark employment discrimination decision.

The Court's opinion in *Griggs* emphasized traditional merit system values of individual rights and efficiency. The Court would protect *individuals* from discrimination and would allow them to compete based on competencies. It would not sacrifice job qualifications in favor of minority origins. In fact, writing for a unanimous court in 1971, Chief Justice Burger observed:

> Congress has not commanded that the less qualified be preferred over the better qualified simply because of minority origins. Far from disparaging job qualifications as such, Congress has made such qualifications the controlling factor, so that race, religion, nationality and sex become irrelevant. What Congress has commanded is that any tests used must measure the person for the job and not the person in the abstract.[10]

However, from 1971 to 1987 the Court faced challenges of systemic or institutionalized discrimination that Congress had not anticipated when it passed the Civil Rights Act of 1964 and the Equal Employment Opportunity Act of 1972:

- What should the Court do about pervasive racism or gender discrimination?
- What should the Court do in cases where employers voluntarily showed racial preference to resolve a discrimination problem that had not been litigated or formally alleged?
- How should the Court evaluate seniority systems that routinely discriminated against minorities, but that were not originally conceived with that purpose?
- What balance should it draw between compensation for those discriminated against and inadvertent injury to innocent nonminorities who might have to bear some of the cost in delayed promotions or loss of training or advancement opportunities for minorities who had historically been discriminated against?

Answers to these questions could not be found in the wording of civil rights legislation or the Constitution. Further, the legislative debates leading up to the Civil Rights Act of 1964 and the EEO Act of 1972 were so entangled that *any* answer to these questions could be justified with reference to legislative intent. The Court had to use the letter of the law, its intent as interpreted by the Court, and its own precedents in deliberating and reaching answers to these and other questions. *Griggs* was the last unanimous vote the Court recorded on an affirmative action case. By 1987, the Court had moved away from its colorblind interpretation in *Griggs* and embraced the value of social equity, struggling to find a balance between social equity, individual rights, and to a lesser extent, efficiency.

Sixteen years after *Griggs*, the Court confronted two very different cases. Litigation leading to a Supreme Court review in ***United States v. Paradise***[11] began in 1972 when a district court found pervasive, systemic, and obstinate exclusion of African Americans from employment with the Alabama Department of Public Safety. Continued failure to comply with consent decrees led the district court in 1983 to order the state to promote to the rank of corporal African American troopers at a 1:1 ratio with Caucasian troopers. This order would be enforced until at least 25 percent of the corporals were black or the department could produce a valid promotional examination—that is, one that had no adverse effect on qualified minority candidates. Supporting the state of Alabama, the federal government appealed to the Supreme Court, claiming it violated the individual rights of innocent nonminorities (the Anglo troopers who may have benefited from the discrimination but could not be shown to be party to it).

Also in 1987, the Court reviewed the **reverse discrimination** case of ***Johnson v. Transportation Agency***.[12] The transportation agency in Santa Clara County, California, noting a substantial underutilization of women working in the agency, voluntarily developed an AA plan that considered gender as one factor in employment decisions. After adopting the plan, the agency promoted Diane Joyce to the position of road dispatcher over Paul Johnson, who had achieved a nominally higher score than Joyce in a promotional interview. Johnson claimed reverse discrimination based on Title VII of the Civil Rights Act and the case eventually reached the Supreme Court. Joyce's promotion was upheld.

To decide whether the use of race and gender preference were lawful in *Paradise* and *Johnson*, the Court employed a two-pronged analytical framework it had developed since *Griggs* in 1971. First, employing the **strict scrutiny** standard for evaluating the use of AA, the Court asked, "Is there a compelling justification for the employer to take race into consideration in its AA program?" In *Paradise*, all the justices answered this question in the affirmative, agreeing that the "Alabama Department of Public Safety had undertaken a course of action that amounted to 'pervasive, systematic, and obstinate discriminatory conduct.' "[13] Therefore, the use of race to remedy the effect of this conduct was justified. In *Johnson*, a majority of the Court answered in the affirmative as well. The majority inferred discrimination based on gender from a comparison of the number of women working in several of the transportation agency's job classifications compared to their numbers in the county's total labor pool. Thus, they found justification for the use of gender in the county's AA plan.

In both cases, the Court then turned to the second and usually more important question involved in the strict scrutiny standard: Is the AA plan narrowly tailored to solve the discrimination problem, or does it create additional, unacceptable problems? In *Paradise*, a majority noted that the order was "narrowly tailored" and minimally intrusive because the promotion quota was limited in scope and duration. The remedy imposed a *diffuse* burden on the Caucasian troopers, and no individual nonminority employee must bear the entire cost of the remedy. In *Johnson*, a majority of the Court found the county's plan was narrowly tailored, and it did not "trammel" the rights of male employees. The plan did not set aside any positions for women; it did authorize consideration of gender as one factor in promotion decisions. The Court found that the county's plan was intended to "attain" a racial balance, not "maintain" one, which would have been illegal.

In both *Paradise* and *Johnson*, the Court showed its willingness to support social equity with remedies benefiting those who had not been the specific or identifiable victims of discrimination. None of the troopers who might benefit from the court's order in *Paradise* claimed to have been specifically discriminated against; and Diane Joyce did not claim gender discrimination. Nevertheless, they were members of a class who had been discriminated against. However, in both the 1987 cases, the Court was unwilling to dismiss the value of individual rights, as it considered the effects the AA in both cases would have on the lives of the innocent nonminorities. Further, the Court acknowledged the value of efficiency by requiring that the minority troopers in Alabama be qualified and by noting that Diane Joyce was qualified.

The ***Gratz v. Bollinger***[14] and ***Grutter v. Bollinger***[15] decisions (2003) represent the most recent Supreme Court decisions concerning the legality of affirmative action. In both cases, the University of Michigan was sued by white applicants who were denied admission to its undergraduate program (*Gratz*) and its law school (*Grutter*). In the case of undergraduate admissions, the University had maintained a system of granting a numerical preference points to minority applicants, solely based on race, to increase their presence in the undergraduate student body. In the case of law school admissions, the University used race as one factor among many in the admissions process, but did not utilize a numerical procedure, like the undergraduate program, for doing so. In a mixed decision issued simultaneously, the Supreme Court ultimately ruled against the numerical procedures used in undergraduate admissions because they did not treat applicants as individuals but in favor of the more individualized approach used by the University's law school, thus implying that the court would look favorably upon broader, more tailored affirmative action programs.

Interestingly, the law school admissions case was accompanied by many supporting briefs advocating for the University's continued use of race as a factor in admissions decisions. One of these briefs was submitted by an extraordinary group of former military officials and former executive level civilian officials from the Department of Defense. This seems contrary to expectations. Why would a generally conservative military support affirmative action? The reason falls into the realm of diversity management more than EEO or

AA and suggests that the value of efficiency has become increasingly linked to diversity because diversity is related to competencies. Reading the brief, one is taken with the racial conflict that existed within the armed forces during the Vietnam War. Seeking a diverse officer corps that could match the diversity of enlisted personnel became an important goal in developing effective armed forces, and each branch of the military now has a prep school for high school graduates with potential to attend U.S. military academies in preparation for careers in the officer corps. If the court would have struck down the law school case, the brief suggests that the prep schools, which are populated with a very diverse student body, would have been jeopardized.[16]

CONTRACT "SET-ASIDES"

As governments increasingly implement programs through contracts for goods and services, AA advocates—and opponents—recognize that the focus of compliance efforts has shifted from government employment to the personnel policies and practices of government contractors and subcontractors. Initially, efforts to improve the "mix" of contractors were thwarted because contractors were overwhelmingly white males. This led to the elaboration of procedures making it easier for **minority business enterprises (MBEs)** to qualify as bidders, to post performance bonds, and to respond to **requests for proposals (RFPs)** issued by government agencies. In some cases, this included formal or informal quotas—minimum percentages of contract funds (or **minority set-asides**, as they are sometimes called) that had to be awarded to minority contractors or subcontractors.

Naturally, these revised criteria led to abuses, such as the creation of so-called MBEs that showed minorities or females as corporate directors but were actually covertly created and financed by white-owned firms as a mechanism for winning set-aside contracts. Awarding contracts to MBEs that in some cases were not the lowest or best-qualified bidders provoked opposition among white-owned contractors and advocates of efficiency or cost reduction as the dominant criterion for awarding contracts.

In resolving conflicts between EEO and preferential (AA) treatment of contractors, the Supreme Court faced the same issues underlying similar conflicts for employees and tended to resolve these conflicts based on prevailing political weight of the two opposing values. By 1989, with the inclusion of President Reagan's appointees, the value of individual rights grew and the value of social equity declined. This reversal was seen in *Richmond v. Croson* in 1989 and then reinforced in *Adarand v. Peña* in 1995. In ***Richmond v. Croson***,[17] the Court ruled 6 to 3 against the city of Richmond's voluntary plan that required at least 30 percent of each city contract to be sublet to minority contractors. While recognizing that the city's population was 50 percent black and less than 1 percent of the city's prime contracts had gone to MBEs, and despite substantial anecdotal evidence of widespread discrimination against minority contractors, the Court ruled that the city had shown no direct evidence establishing discrimination *by the city* against minority contractors. Thus, the city of Richmond's plan failed to establish a compelling reason for AA by the city in minority contracting and failed to meet the narrowly tailored test because it could not tie the 30 percent figure to the actual degree of discrimination attributed to the city's actions.

In ***Adarand v. Peña***, a white-owned contractor sued the secretary of transportation over the constitutionality of minority set-asides in federally funded highway projects.[18] In resolving this case, the Court extended its ruling in *Croson* to the federal government. In so doing, it firmly established that the use of race as a preferential category in an employment context would be subject to the strictest judicial scrutiny. In essence, the court reaffirmed and anchored its guidance in *Croson* that whether used for "benign" purposes or not, racial preferences must be justified by a compelling government reason and be narrowly tailored as a solution.

Since *Croson* and *Adarand*, Californians passed an amendment to their state Constitution prohibiting affirmative action by state actors, and the U.S. Supreme Court has agreed to hear another case brought by Adarand. Therefore, it seems that the general trend away from social equity and toward individual rights and efficiency that is reflected in legislation and case law concerning AA is paralleled by case law affirming the right of corporations to compete for contracts without minority set-asides. Whether this shift reflects recognition that equality of opportunity has already been achieved for minority contractors, or simply a turning away from social equity as a dominant value because of changes in the political climate, depends upon one's point of view.

FROM AFFIRMATIVE ACTION TO DIVERSITY MANAGEMENT

Unlike EEO and AA efforts, which have traditionally focused primarily on the selection and promotion processes affecting women and minorities, diversity management efforts are focused on bringing the most out of broadly defined diverse working environments. While EEO and AA efforts were designed to promote access to employment, diversity management has another element. Diversity management, while fostered by the social equity value, is also more explicitly grounded in the value of efficiency. In addition to the example of the friend of the court brief in the Michigan Law School case described above is a private sector one. No one needed to tell McDonald's to hire Spanish-speaking employees in areas where the customer base was Hispanic. It was just good business. As our communities diversify, the public sector workforce has incentives to diversify as well—as long as customer service is valued.

For our purposes, the term *diversity* will include differences in employee and applicant characteristics (race, gender, ethnicity, national origin, language, religion, age, education, intelligence, and disabilities) that constitute the range of variation among human beings in the workforce. Researcher Norma Riccucci describes these efforts accurately, stating that managing diversity "includes the ability of organizations to harness the diverse human resources available in order to create a productive and motivated workforce . . . key here is management's ability to develop ways to address such challenges as communication breakdowns, misunderstandings, and even hostilities that invariably result from working in an environment with persons form highly diverse backgrounds, age cohorts, and lifestyles."[19]

Immigration and Cultural Diversity

The workforce in modern industrialized nations is becoming socially more diverse. In the United States, the workforce is comprised increasingly of immigrants whose primary language is not English and whose primary norms are not those of "mainstream" American culture. In 2000, the Census Bureau estimated that 11.1 percent of the U.S. population was foreign born, and by 2006, this estimate had risen to 12.5 percent. In 1960, foreign-born Americans came mostly from Europe. Today this new wave of immigration is coming mainly from Latin America and Asia—Mexico, the Philippines, China, Cuba, Vietnam, and El Salvador. It results from economic globalization, interminable ethnic and political conflicts in developing countries, and an intense desire among migrants to find a better life for themselves and their families in the United States.

The current wave of immigration is different from others in that increased residential segregation and cultural isolation make it possible for large immigrant communities to thrive as foreign enclaves in this country. In extremely diverse cities such as Los Angeles, Miami, and New York City, it is common to find immigrant communities and neighborhoods where foreign languages such as Spanish and Chinese have become the primary language of choice. In addition, and different from previous waves of immigration, pockets of immigrants can be found outside of the nation's largest cities. In short, we have increased **cultural diversity** in a nation that was formerly considered linguistically and culturally homogeneous. In brief, our image of America has changed from a "melting pot" to a salad bowl. This has not occurred without considerable unrest among native-born U.S. residents. White conservatives frequently voice appeals for "English-only" or seek stricter controls over immigration in an effort to keep out those who might become a burden to health, education, and criminal justice systems. American-born African Americans, already embittered at being economically disadvantaged compared to whites, are newly embittered about being excluded from the burgeoning Latin economy if they are not bilingual. As one said at a university "career day" in Miami several years ago, "Why do I have to learn Spanish to get a job in the country where I was born?" The honest answer, "Because people who are bilingual have better job prospects in a bilingual economy," does not respond adequately to the underlying sense of anger and dispossession that impelled the question.

The Case for Diversity

In the private sector, **workforce diversity** can be attributed to increasing economic pressures for organizations to remain competitive in the new global economy. The general argument that workforce diversity makes good business sense grows out of a fundamental premise—that businesses whose employees "can speak the same language" as their customers/clients will be more successful than those that cannot. The market will sort out the successful from unsuccessful firms in diverse markets, and those that succeed will probably be the ones whose workforce matches the customer base in diversity.

While governments may not face economic pressures to diversify since they may operate as monopolies within a geographic area, they do face continued political and practical pressures to do so. Politically speaking, public sector jobs are public sector resources since they are funded through tax revenues. As such, many have argued that they should be distributed equitably across gender and ethnic groups so that public bureaucracies will be representative of the citizens they serve. Commonly referred to as the theory of "**Representative Bureaucracy**," this rationale is the basis of much of the public sector's push for the equitable employment of women and minorities. The push for equitable representation can also be made on a practical, market-based basis in those cases where public bureaucracies serve constituencies with unique service needs. For instance, the growth of Hispanic, Spanish-speaking communities throughout the nation has prompted many government agencies to increase their Hispanic recruitment efforts to meet the unique demands of serving these communities. Recruitment efforts by the police department of the City of Baltimore, MD, provide a great example of such efforts. To meet the needs of a diverse community for which Spanish is increasingly the primary language of many citizens, the City made a special effort to hire and train Spanish-speaking officers. When efforts to recruit in the local community proved difficult, the City extended its efforts to the territory of Puerto Rico since many residents of the island speak both Spanish and English.[20]

The process by which diverse minorities have been incorporated into the workforce varies dependent upon state and local conditions and laws, and overgeneralizations should be avoided. Nonetheless, examining the evolution of minority groups through several stages of empowerment and protection can show the relationship among economics, politics, and workforce diversity. In the beginning, members of diverse groups were almost automatically excluded from the workforce, except for unskilled positions, because they were outside the "mainstream" culture. This exclusion was based in law as well as custom. Second, as economic development and labor shortages increased (such as in the United States during World War II), these groups were admitted into the labor market (particularly if they possessed job skills in short supply), though they faced continued economic and legal discrimination and were excluded from consideration for desirable professional and technical positions. Third, as economic development and labor shortages continued, and as their political power continued to increase, group members were accepted for a range of positions, and their employment rights were protected by laws guaranteeing equal employment access (EEA). In the United States, for example, applicants' equal employment rights have been protected by Title VII of the Civil Rights Act (1964) and by the Americans with Disabilities Act (1990). Fourth, as these groups became increasingly powerful politically, efforts to reduce the considerable informal discrimination that continued in recruitment, promotion, pay, and benefits led to establishment of workplace policies, such as salary equality and employment proportionate with their representation in the labor market. Voluntary AA programs encouraged achievement of these goals. If voluntary achievement efforts were unsuccessful, conformance was sometimes mandated by AA compliance agencies or court orders. Fifth, continued social and political changes are now leading to the welcoming of diversity as a desirable political and social condition, and continued economic pressures lead to the development of **diversity management programs** for organizations that desire to remain economically competitive or politically responsive.

These stages in the evolution of political power and legal protection for diverse groups in the workforce are shown in Table 7-2.

Distinguishing among EEO, AA, and Diversity Management

Diversity management programs are the current stage of an evolutionary process defined by increased social participation, political power, and legal protection for minorities. Therefore, it is understandable that some people consider these programs to be simply "old

TABLE 7-2 Political Power and Legal Protection for Diverse Groups in the Workforce

Stage	Employment Status	Legal Protection
1	Excluded from the workforce	none
2	Admitted to the workforce but excluded from desirable jobs	none
3	Accepted into the workforce	EEO
4	Recruited into the workforce	AA
5	Welcomed into the workforce	diversity management

wine in new bottles"—a contemporary variant on the EEO or AA that have characterized HRM in the United States for the past thirty years. However, diversity management differs from EEO or AA programs in five important respects.[21]

First, their purposes are different. EEO is based on organizational efforts to avoid violating employees' or applicants' legal or constitutional rights. AA is based on organizational efforts to achieve proportional representation of selected groups. In contrast, diversity management programs originate from managers' objective of increasing productivity and effectiveness.[22]

Second, AA laws protect the employment rights of designated categories of persons only (in the United States, such groups as blacks, Hispanics, native Americans, Asian Americans, workers over forty years old, women, and Americans with disabilities). Diversity management programs are based on recognition not only of these protected groups but also of the entire spectrum of characteristics (knowledge, skills, and abilities) that managers and personnel directors need to recognize and factor into personnel decisions in order to acquire and develop a productive workforce.

Third, AA programs emphasize recruitment, selection, and sometimes promotion because those personnel functions are most closely tied to proportional representation of protected groups. However, diversity management programs include all personnel functions related to organizational effectiveness (including recruitment, promotion and retention, job design, pay and benefits, education and training, and performance measurement and improvement).

Fourth, diversity management programs have a different locus of control. AA and EEO programs are based on managerial responses to external compliance agencies' requirements. However, diversity management programs originate as internal organizational responses to managerial demands for enhanced productivity and effectiveness (although this response is itself a reaction to demographic changes in overall population).

Fifth, AA programs tend to be viewed negatively by managers and employees, because they are based on a negative premise ("What changes must we make in recruitment and selection procedures to demonstrate a good faith effort to achieve a representative workforce, and thereby avoid sanctions by AA compliance agencies or courts?"). In contrast, the most successful diversity management programs tend to be viewed as positive by managers and employees, because they are based on a different question ("What changes can we make in our organization's mission, culture, policies, and programs in order to become more effective and more competitive?").[23]

The Role of Mission, Organization Culture, and Personnel Policy and Practice in Diversity Management

Diversity management requires changes in **organizational culture**—the values, assumptions, and communication patterns that characterize interaction among employees. These patterns are invented, discovered, or developed by members of the organization as responses to problems or sensitivity to client needs; they become part of the culture as they are taught to new members as the correct way to perceive, think, and feel in relation to these problems or needs.[24] Viewed from this perspective, diversity management represents a change in the way organizations do business, rather than just an adaptation of existing personnel policies and programs to meet the specialized needs of minorities and women.

An organization's decision to use workforce diversity to increase effectiveness causes changes in its HRM policy and practice.[25] Policies and practices are the rules and procedures that implement organizational objectives, and they are management's strategic plan for accomplishing its mission. Diversity management programs affect five specific areas of human resource management policy and practice: recruitment and retention, job design, education and training, benefits and rewards, and performance measurement and improvement.

Recruitment and retention policies and programs include those strategies already commonplace in AA programs: increasing the applicant pool of underrepresented groups, increasing their selection rate by developing valid alternatives for tests that have a disparate impact, and developing **mentoring** systems to encourage retention. Yet their purpose is productivity enhancement through a diverse workforce rather than legal compliance through recruitment or selection quotas; they apply to a broader spectrum of applicant and employee characteristics; they include a broader range of personnel activities; their locus of control is internal rather than external; and their tone is positive rather than negative.

Job design options that offer flexibility of work locations and schedules need to be considered to attract and retain women with child- and elder-care responsibilities into the workforce.[26] To attract and retain persons with **disabilities**, reasonable accommodation must be offered to make the workplace physically accessible and to make jobs available to persons who are otherwise qualified to perform the primary duties.[27]

Education and training programs are influenced in two ways. First, there is a need for supervisory training on policies and compliance procedures, as well as identifying harassment. Second, employer concerns with the educational preparation of future workers have led employers to include basic skills unrelated to specific job tasks (such as literacy and English as a second language).[28] There is increasing interest in strengthening federal- and state-sponsored job training programs, and in sponsoring joint business–government policy initiatives such as tax incentives for costs associated with business training programs.[29] *Pay and benefit policies* often become more flexible and innovative: flexible benefits, benefits for part-time positions, parental leave, child- and elder-care support programs, and phased retirement. Employee assistance programs (EAPs) are an effective response to diversity in the workplace.[30]

Performance measurement and productivity improvement programs often change in that managers and supervisors now need to consider the differing values and motivational perspectives of a diverse workforce.[31] Diversity management has also brought about changing definitions of productivity, based on the need for variation in managerial styles and resultant dramatic increases in organizational effectiveness.[32]

The common threads linking these five areas of personnel policy and practice are their common objective of increased organizational effectiveness, and their cumulative impact on organizational culture. Organizations that wish to attract and keep a diversified workforce must change the culture of the organization to create a climate in which persons from diverse groups feel accepted, comfortable, and productive. This is why the tone of diversity management programs differs from their affirmative compliance program predecessors—affirming diversity is different from tolerating or accepting it.[33]

Characteristics of Effective and Ineffective Diversity Management Programs

Diversity management programs typically encounter two types of implementation issues—systemic and situational. Systemic issues arise when AA opponents have succeeded in forcing a premature transition from "forced" compliance to diversity management on the grounds that "we have had too much legalistic, quota-based diversification; it's time to do away with affirmative action and replace it with diversity management"—even though informal but strongly entrenched racism or gender discrimination still exists within the culture of the organization. Operational issues arise when systemic discrimination is not part of the dominant culture, yet minorities and women still confront invisible barriers—a **glass ceiling** that inhibits success almost imperceptibly at each step of the promotional ladder, but with substantial cumulative effect.[34]

To avoid both negative outcomes, experts have proposed a relatively uniform set of criteria for assessing the effectiveness of diversity management policies and programs.[35] These include:

1. A broad definition of diversity that includes a range of characteristics, rather than only those used to define "protected classes" under existing AA;
2. A systematic assessment of the existing culture to determine how members at all levels view the present organization;
3. Top-level initiation of, commitment to, and visibility of workforce diversity as an essential organizational policy rather than as a legal compliance issue or staff function;
4. Establishment of specific objectives;
5. Integration into the managerial performance evaluation and reward structure;
6. Coordination with other activities such as employee development, job design, and succession planning; and
7. Continual evaluation and improvement.

Insufficient top-level commitment or organizational visibility generally renders diversification efforts unsuccessful because the program's long-term impact on organization's mission or culture is inadequate.

Diversity Management and Other HRM Trends

Diversity management programs are consistent with other contemporaneous trends such as employee involvement and participation, employee development, and nonadversarial dispute resolution. Employee involvement and participation are considered essential for maintaining high productivity (at least among employees in key professional and technical positions). Even in the absence of significant financial rewards, employees tend to work happily and effectively when they have the necessary skills, see their work as meaningful, feel personally responsible for productivity, and have firsthand knowledge of the actual results of their labor. As teamwork becomes more important—or recognized as being important—managers are increasingly called upon to demonstrate multicultural competence utilizing a diverse workforce. Employee development is related to diversification, at least for key professional and technical employees, because it (1) focuses planning and budget analysis on human resources; (2) facilitates cost-benefit analysis of current training and development activities; and (3) fosters communication and commitment of organizational goals through employee participation and involvement.

Alternative dispute resolution (ADR) is a philosophy and practice of settling organizational differences by means other than formal and quasi-legal adversarial procedures. It has several specific HR applications, and it will be further discussed as an alternative to traditional employee civil service grievance procedures in Chapter 13, and collective bargaining contract administration procedures in Chapter 14. The challenge of channeling diversity into productivity is complicated by the breadth of expectations that members of diverse cultures bring to their work. Without a method of settling disputes that models the organization's commitment to tolerance and respect, differences lead only to divisiveness that consumes organizational resources without positive results. Traditional adversarial dispute resolution techniques are not particularly effective at resolving organizational conflicts: They build acrimony, harden bargaining positions, and delay the resolution of the original conflict. Therefore, innovative conflict resolution techniques such as "win-win" negotiation and group problem solving are often more effective and have the additional advantage of modeling the organization's commitment to respect, tolerance, and dignity.[36]

Generational Diversity

One aspect of diversity that has received increasing attention over the past decade is the unique challenge of managing employees of different generational backgrounds. Overall, workers across the nation are choosing to remain in the workforce longer than in the past, and as employers bring younger workers into the workforce, work environments in which employees range in age from the mid-sixties to the early twenties have been created. This wide range in employee age groups has meant that managers must adapt to their work strategies to the unique expectations of each generation of employees because research has found that employment expectations are shaped by one's generational experiences.

The four most common generations currently in the workplace are: The Veterans (born prior to 1945), Baby Boomers (1945–1965), Generation Xers (1965–1980), and Generation Nexters (1980–2000).[37] Common perceptions of the values of each generation include the following:

- *Veterans:* dedicated employees; hard workers; value rules, conformity, and authority
- *Baby Boomers:* optimistic; value team work and personal growth and involvement
- *Generation Xers:* pragmatic; self-reliant; value diversity
- *Generation Nexters:* optimistic; technologically savvy; achievement oriented[38]

As researchers have pointed out, the values that each generation brings into the workplace have been shaped by their experiences. For example, Generation Xers have been looked upon as extremely self-reliant because many were raised in households with two working parents and were expected to be responsible at an early age. As a result, they tend to work well independently, without the need for constant supervision. Generation Nexters, on the other hand, have come of age during the rapid growth in technology, and, as a result, are extremely comfortable with technologically sophisticated working environments. Many Veterans and Baby Boomers, however, were trained and socialized in less technologically sophisticated environments, so managers should be aware of these differences when implementing new technologies in a workplace. Overall, the challenge for managers is to understand each generation's values and to foster workplaces that support these values to the best extent possible while recognizing that there will be substantial differences among individuals within generations.

Sexual Orientation and Gender Identification

Another aspect of diversity that has received an increasing amount of attention is the employment treatment of lesbian, gay, bisexual, and transgender (LGBT) persons in both the public and private sector workforce. Unlike prohibitions of discrimination based on race and gender, there is no federal statute prohibiting discrimination based on **sexual orientation**; however, same sex harassment is prohibited under federal sexual harassment guidelines. This lack of protection has effectively allowed public- and private-sector employers to discriminate based on sexual orientation with impunity, and research suggests that members of the LGBT community do experience substantial discrimination in the labor market.[39] However, in recent years, many states and localities, such as the State of Kansas, have made the decision to address this issue independent of the federal government and have enacted local statutes prohibiting discrimination based on sexual orientation.[40] While this aspect of diversity will continue to evolve at all levels of government, it is imperative that public administrators and human resources professionals be aware of needs and concerns of LGBT employees, as well as the statutory guidelines applicable to their employment.

THE ROLE OF THE HR MANAGER IN ACHIEVING PRODUCTIVITY AND FAIRNESS

Conflict over the relative importance of social equity and the appropriateness of alternative strategies for achieving it has caused concern in some specific areas. What has been the actual impact of all these programs on the employment of minorities and women? How can the positive and negative impacts of diversity management programs on productivity and fairness be measured and assessed? What changes does diversification force them to make in how they view their jobs and how they do them?

Effect of AA on Employment of Minorities and Women

Has civil rights legislation and employment discrimination litigation reduced discrimination and opened doors for minorities and women? The quick answer is yes, but closer analysis leads to mixed findings by level of government and ethnicity. Compared to their overall presence in the civilian labor force, women and African Americans are generally well represented at all levels of government, while Hispanics are generally underrepresented. Within local government, women represent approximately 42 percent of all employees, while African Americans and Hispanics represent approximately 19 and 10 percent of all employees respectively.[41] At the state level, women represent approximately 51 percent of all employees, while African Americans and Hispanics represent approximately 19 and 7 percent of all employees respectively.[42] Representation at the federal level follows the same pattern, with women representing approximately 44 percent of the federal workforce and African Americans and Hispanics representing 18 and 8 percent of the workforce respectively.[43]

Legally, the *kinds* of discrimination reported in cases that came before the Court in the 1970s have decreased. It is difficult to conceive today of a case of intentional racial discrimination in employment like that reported in *Griggs* (1971) or *Paradise* (1987). The values of social equity have challenged merit systems to demonstrate that personnel practices once assumed to be job related are, in fact, job related. In this way, AA has benefited all employees, regardless of race or gender. Jobs are advertised publicly and widely; interview questions and tests are tailored to specific jobs; performance appraisal instruments have become more job related; and pay systems have become more equitable and sensitive to gender differences—even if they have not erased them. Over the years, these practices have been instituted as normal parts of human resources systems. In fact, in some cases, the practice has become rigidly adhered to becoming the source of complaints among those seeking reform of civil service systems. For example, managers have challenged the length of time involved in hiring practices designed to insure fairness because organizations can lose talented applicants who receive timely job offers from other employers.

While it is common to see diversity practices embedded in human resources systems, it is equally clear that acceptance of diversity is not yet a part of the value structure of all Americans. While women have joined management ranks in large numbers, a "glass ceiling" inhibits their advancement to top corporate ranks. For example, while women in the federal government represent 44 percent of all employees, they represent 68 percent of those in the entry grade levels and only 28 percent of senior executives.[44] Furthermore, a backlash against AA has developed over the last thirty years. First, opponents of affirmative action state that it is unfair to African Americans because, while it has helped privileged African Americans enhance their jobs status, it has done nothing to alleviate the employment crisis among poor African Americans increasingly plagued by inadequate education, drug abuse, and crime. Second, opponents state that AA is the opening wedge of a comprehensive ideology that threatens the basic American value of equality under the law. They fear it will lead to the "Balkanization" of American society, the creation of a culture in which all public policy decisions are made based on social equity.[45]

In addition to its specific impact on the public personnel manager, AA has a more general impact. Conflicts between social equity and merit result in the application of confusing and contradictory decision rules regulating acquisition. During periods of growth, managers overcome these conflicts by hiring more people from all groups—as long as the pie gets larger, everyone can get a bigger piece. However, in periods of decline, conflicts between social equity and other values result in heightened conflict.

What can we expect in the future? This same tension among conflicting values is likely to continue. On the one hand, political pressures for representativeness and economic pressures for enhanced productivity will result in increased workforce diversification efforts. On the other hand, reactions against these pressures will result in either administrative formalism in the implementation of diversification programs or resistance to them by particular groups that perceive them as threatening to their job prospects. To the extent that economic markets can influence personnel policies and practices, the forecast connecting workforce diversity and productivity seems on target. Nevertheless, the strength of the marketplace contains its weakness as well; it is driven by the value of efficiency, not by concerns of equity, fairness, or justice. While the connection between productivity and diversity may increase representation of minorities in the workplace, history suggests that if it does so fairly, it will be coincidental. In the new millennium, the value of social equity is being carried into the political arena more by demographic reality than by legislation, litigation, and conscience. While the courts will continue to orient themselves to the protection of individual rights, demographic realities will force legislatures and administrative agencies to respond to representation and the broader political concern of workforce diversity. Further, increasing emphasis on customer satisfaction in multiethnic communities may very well connect workforce diversity to productivity.[46]

Summary

EEO, AA, and diversity management programs have greatly affected all personnel functions. They are all based on the value of social equity and individual rights and on the AA laws and procedures used to implement these values. Despite the current eclipse of social equity due to the renewed emphasis on other values, AA will continue to have a profound impact on public administration because the practices designed to advance AA—encouraged by law and managerial innovation—have become part of the daily routine in human resources management.

In the end, it may be helpful to view the struggle over social equity as a continual conflict with many possible solutions. If discrimination is individual, then EEO is the answer. If there is systemic racism or gender discrimination, then AA is required as a political stage America needs to go through on its way to accepting increasing cultural and, therefore, workforce diversity. This distinction is a good way of parsing the values of individual rights and social equity within the broad topic of diversity management and the law. Demographic diversity is accompanied by economic pressures, as technological change and globalization of the economy increase public and private employers' demands for a highly trained workforce. Political pressures by women, minorities, older workers, immigrants, and persons with disabilities have resulted in legal changes in the employment rights of groups formerly excluded by law or custom from desirable professional and technical jobs.

Predictably, conflict over the relative importance of social equity and the best ways of achieving it have led public administrators and officials to reexamine the impact of diversity management programs on productivity and fairness, and on how they do their jobs.

Key Terms

Adarand v. Peña *166*
affirmative action (AA) *160*
affirmative action plans (AAPs) *160*
alternative dispute resolution (ADR) *172*
conciliation agreement *162*
consent decree *162*
court order *162*
cultural diversity *168*
discrimination *161*
diversity management *160*
diversity management program *169*
equal employment opportunity (EEO) *160*
Equal Employment Opportunity Act (1972) *160*
Equal Employment Opportunity Commission (EEOC) *160*
Executive Order (EO) 11246 *161*
glass ceiling *172*
Griggs v. Duke Power Company *163*
Gratz v. Bollinger *165*
Grutter v. Bollinger *165*
Johnson v. Transportation Agency *164*
mentoring *171*
minority business enterprises (MBEs) *166*
minority set-asides *166*
Office of Federal Contract Compliance Programs (OFCCP) *161*
organizational culture *170*
representative bureaucracy *168*
requests for proposals (RFPs) *166*
reverse discrimination *164*
Richmond v. Croson *166*
sexual orientation *174*
strict scrutiny *164*
Title VII (Civil Rights Act of 1964) *160*
underutilization *161*
United States v. Paradise *164*
workforce diversity *168*

Discussion Questions

1. Explain EEO and AA, and point out the difference between them?
2. What federal agencies are responsible for compliance with EEO/AA laws?
3. What mechanisms are associated with voluntary and involuntary AA compliance?
4. Why is the role of federal courts so significant in interpreting social equity legislation?
5. With respect to the fundamental conflict between EEO and AA, how has the Supreme Court endorsed and interpreted social equity legislation from 1971 to the present?
6. Why has service contracting increased conflict between minority businesses and other contractors?
7. Have we had too much affirmative action in the past thirty years, or not enough? Why?
8. How does diversity management differ from both EEO and AA?
9. What do you believe is the relationship among AA, workforce diversity, and productivity in a culturally diverse community?
10. How do diversity management programs affect organizational culture, mission, policies, and programs? Why do some work and others fail?
11. What role do you think the public HR manager should take in advancing AA and workforce diversity in an environment of conflicting values over how best to achieve social equity?

Exercise: Equal Employment Opportunity or Affirmative Action?

Read the following passages from Supreme Court opinions, and then answer the questions:

> It is plainly true that in our society blacks have suffered discrimination immeasurably greater than any directed at other racial groups. But those who believe that racial preferences can help to "even the score" display, and reinforce, a manner of thinking by race that was the source of the injustice and that will, if it endures within our society, be the source of more injustice still. The relevant proposition is not that it was blacks, or Jews, or Irish who were discriminated against, but that it was individual men and women, "created equal," who were discriminated against. And the relevant resolve is that it should never happen again. Racial preferences appear to "even the score" (in some small degree) only if one embraces the proposition that our society is appropriately viewed as divided into races, making it right that an injustice rendered in the past to a black man should be compensated for by discriminating against a white. Nothing is worth that embrace.
>
> Justice Scalia, *Richmond v. Croson*, 57 LW 4132, 4148 (1989)

> A profound difference separates governmental actions that themselves are racist, and governmental actions that seek to remedy the effects of prior racism or to prevent neutral governmental activity from perpetuating the effects of such racism. . . . Racial classifications "drawn on the presumption that one race is inferior to another or because they put the weight of government behind racial hatred and separatism" warrant the strictest judicial scrutiny because of the very irrelevance of these rationales. . . . By contrast . . . [b]ecause the consideration of race is relevant to remedying the continuing effects of past racial discrimination, and because governmental programs employing racial classifications for remedial purposes can be crafted to avoid stigmatization, . . . such programs should not be subjected to conventional "scrutiny"—scrutiny that is strict in theory, but fatal in fact.
>
> Justice Marshall, *Richmond v. Croson*, 57 LW 4132, 4155 (1989)

> Congress has not commanded that the less qualified be preferred over the better qualified simply because of minority origins. Far from disparaging job qualifications as such, Congress has made such qualifications the controlling

factor, so that race, religion, nationality and sex become irrelevant.

Chief Justice Burger, *Griggs v. Duke Power Company*, 401 L Ed 2d, 158, 167 (1971)

Questions

1. Identify the values in each of the passages.
2. Which passages do you agree with most/disagree with most?

Case Study #1: Social Equity vs. Employee Rights

Read the following scenario and complete the assignment in the last paragraph.

In 2002, a group of Hispanic Americans sued the city government for discrimination in employment practices in the police and fire departments. The court encouraged the parties to enter a consent decree, which they did. The consent decree called for the city to cease its discrimination, to identify the victims of discrimination, to make the hiring of the qualified victims a priority, and to establish hiring and promotion goals that would bring the percentage of Hispanic Americans in the public safety departments on par with the number of qualified potential Hispanic-American applicants in the surrounding labor market.

By 2004, although the city had hired a few of the plaintiffs who had not already found other jobs, the city had shown little effort to comply with the consent decree, and the racial imbalances were hardly affected. The Hispanics complained that those who were hired had been kept in lower-paying job classifications longer than their Anglo peers had been and were subjected to racial jokes; they were paired with each other in the police department and assigned to Hispanic-American high-crime areas. In the fire department, they were isolated in the day-to-day informal activities of the department. It was rumored about city hall that the mayor had encouraged the personnel director to "do as little as possible" in complying with the consent decree.

In 2005, the Hispanic advocates went back to the court, requesting judicial intervention. The court summoned the parties, and a revised consent decree was entered. It provided for a court-ordered trustee to monitor the consent decree. In 1996, the city halted all hiring, citing budgetary problems. By 2008, the city began to hire on a case-by-case basis in other departments, but not in public safety, citing the lack of need for additional officers and fire fighters.

The Hispanic plaintiffs returned again to the court, seeking relief. After consulting with the trustee, the judge, citing the court's exasperation and failure to note good faith on the part of the city, was determined to construct a solution that would make a difference. At this point, the mayor announced the hiring of a chief administrative officer and assigned the CAO the responsibility of coming up with a plan to "deal with this mess." The city successfully persuaded the judge to give it six more months to rectify the problems. The judge reluctantly agreed.

You are the CAO. Develop a plan, recognizing that it will have to be approved by a judge who will tolerate no more delays. At the same time, you must understand that the judge is bound to analyze the plan according to the strict scrutiny standard. Thus, you must remedy the effects of the discrimination, but your plan must not place too much of a burden for the remedy on innocent nonminority workers.

Case Study #2: From EEO and AA to Diversity Management

You are a big-city HR director. For years, you and other city administrators have emphasized AA compliance by (1) making it a key organizational objective; (2) taking steps to reduce underutilization of protected classes by targeted programs for recruitment, testing, selection, training, and career development; and (3) establishing separate grievance systems to protect against sexual harassment, racial and ethnic discrimination, and other violations of employee rights.

Now, you hear increasing complaints about the adequacy of these AA compliance policies and programs from managers and employees. Managers ask, "Isn't there a way that we can create a climate of ethnic harmony without resorting to slow and costly administrative proceedings?" Employees in protected categories are unhappy: "Why don't you treat us as employees and human beings, rather than focusing only on gender, race, disability, or ethnicity? Aren't our skills and performance more important than these?" Other employees also dislike AA: "I can't get ahead in this organization because I'm a white male. We're discriminated against all the time, but we don't have any legal protection because we're not members of a protected class."

You decide that the best way to deal with these unsatisfactory conditions is by developing diversity management policies and programs. You prepare a formal presentation to the city manager and other department directors explaining how these policies and programs will help the city run better. They listen to your presentation, and then ask questions. How do you answer them?

Questions

1. How does diversity management differ from EEO or AA? Isn't this just "old wine in new bottles"?
2. Why does diversity management require changes in our mission, culture, or values? It's just a personnel issue, right? Can't we just say we value diversity, and let it go at that?
3. How will diversity management programs affect these specific areas of human resource management policy and practice: recruitment and retention, job design, education and training, benefits and rewards, and performance measurement and improvement?
4. Won't this put the AA office out of business? How will you ever sell it to them?
5. Has anyone else done this before? What results did they see?
6. If we're going to do it right, what are the characteristics of a successful diversity management? Of an unsuccessful one?

Notes

1. http://www.census.gov/Press-Release/www/releases/archives/population/010048.html
2. U.S. Census Bureau (2006). American Community Survey Data Profile Highlights. Found at http://factfinder.census.gov/servlet/ACSSAFFFacts?_submenuld=factsheet_1&_sse=on; http://www.census.gov/Press-Release/www/releases/archives/population/011910.html
3. The Civil Rights Act of 1964, P.L. 88–352, 78 Stat. 241, 28 USC. 1147 [1976].
4. The Equal Employment Opportunity Act of 1972, P.L. 93–380, 88 Stat. 514, 2–0 USC 1228 [1976].
5. U.S. Office of Personnel Management (2008). *Federal Equal Opportunity Recruitment Program Report: Fiscal Year 2007*. Available at: http://opm.gov/About_OPM/Reports/FEORP/2008/feorp2008.pdf
6. U.S. Equal Employment Opportunity Commission (2009). *Laws Enforced by the U.S. Equal Employment Opportunity Commission*. Washington, D.C.: U.S. EEOC. Available at: http://www.eeoc.gov/policy/laws.html
7. Kellough, Edward J. (2006). Understanding affirmative action politics, discrimination, and the search for justice. Washington D.C.: Georgetown University press p. 33.
8. *Griggs v. Duke Power Company*, 401 U.S. 424 (1971).
9. Ibid.
10. Ibid.
11. *United States v. Paradise*, 480 U.S. 149 (1987).
12. *Johnson v. Transportation Agency*, 480 U.S. 616 (1987).
13. *United States v. Paradise*, 480 U.S. 149 (1987).
14. *Gratz v. Bollinger*, 539 U.S. 244 (2003).
15. *Grutter v. Bollinger*, 539 U.S. 306 (2003).
16. Becton, J. W. Jr., Lt. Gen. et. al. (2003) Amicus Brief to the United States Court of Appeals for the Sixth Circuit. No. 02–241, 02–516.
17. *Richmond v. Croson*, 488 U.S. 469 (1989).
18. *Adarand v. Peña*, 515 U.S. 200 (1995).
19. Riccucci, N. M. (2002). *Managing diversity in public sector workforces*. Boulder, CO: Westview Press.
20. Sentementes, G. G. (July 8, 2008). "Baltimore Recruiters Draw Large Crowds in Puerto Rico." *The Baltimore Sun*.

21 Kelly, E., and F. Dobbin (1998). How affirmative action became diversity management. *American Behavioral Scientist, 41* (7): 960–984; and Agocs, C., and C. Burr (1996). Employment equity, affirmative action and managing diversity: assessing the differences. *International Journal of Manpower, 17* (4/5): 30–45.

22. Wallsten, K. (1998). Diversity pays off in big sales for Toyota dealership. *Workforce, 77* (9): 91–92.
23. Roosevelt, T. R. (1990). From affirmative action to affirming diversity. *Harvard Business Review, 68*: 107–117.
24. Schein, E. (1981). *Organizational culture and leadership*. San Francisco, CA: Jossey-Bass.
25. Jamieson, D., and J. O'Mara (1991). *Managing workforce 2000*. San Francisco, CA: Jossey-Bass.
26. Morgan, H., and K. Tucker (1991). *Companies that care*. New York: Fireside.
27. U.S. Equal Employment Opportunity Commission (1991). *Americans with Disabilities Act handbook*. Washington, DC: U.S. Department of Justice, Equal Employment Opportunity Commission.
28. Solomon, C. (1993). Managing today's immigrants. *Personnel Journal, 72*: 57–65.
29. Rosow, J., and R. Zager (1988). *Training—the corporate edge*. San Francisco, CA: Jossey-Bass.
30. Rosow, J., and R. Zager (February 2000). EAPs: An effective response to diversity in the workplace. *IPMA News*. Alexandria, VA: International Personnel Management Association, p. 15.
31. Rubaii-Barrett, N., and A. Beck (1993). Minorities in the majority: Implications for managing cultural diversity. *Public Personnel Management, 22*: 503–522.
32. Loden, M., and J. Rosener (1991). *Workforce America! Managing employee diversity as a vital resource*. Homewood, IL: Business One Irwin.
33. Soni, V. (2000). A twenty-first-century reception for diversity in the public sector: A case study. *Public Administration Review, 60* (5): 395–408.
34. Grolsch, S., and L. Doherty (1999). Diversity management in practice. *International Journal of Contemporary Hospitality Management, 11* (6): 262–268.
35. Denison, D. (1990). Corporate culture and organizational effectiveness. New York: John Wiley.
36. Jahn, K. A. (Summer 2000). Benefits and detriments of workplace conflict. *Public Manager*, pp. 24–26; Allison, J. R. (2000). Five ways to keep disputes out of court. *Harvard Business Review, 78* (1): 166–176; and Carver, T. B., and A. Vondra (2000). Alternative dispute resolution: Why it doesn't work and why it does. *Harvard Business Review, 78* (3): 120–130.
37. Riccucci, N. (2002). *Managing diversity in public sector workforces*. Boulder, CO: Westview Press.
38. Zemke, R., C. Raines, and B. Filipczak (2000). *Generations at work: Managing the clash of Veterans, Boomers, Xers, and Nexters in your workplace*. New York: American Management Association.
39. Klawitter, M. M., and V. Flatt. (1998). The effects of state and local antidiscrimination policies on earnings for gays and lesbians. *Journal of Policy Analysis and Management, 17* (4): 658–686.
40. Riccucci, N., and C. Gossett (June 1996). Employment discrimination in state and local government: The lesbian and gay male experience. *American Review of Public Administration, 26* (2): 175–200.
41. U.S. Equal Employment Opportunity Commission (EEOC) (2003). *2003 Job patterns for minorities and women in state and local government*. Washington, DC: U.S. Government Printing Office.
42. Ibid.
43. U.S. Office of Personnel Management (2008). *Federal Equal Opportunity Recruitment Report: Fiscal Year 2007*.
44. Ibid.
45. Lemann, N. (June 11, 1995). What happened to the case for affirmative action? *The New York Times Magazine*, pp. 36–43.
46. Cox, T. H., and S. Blake (1991). Managing cultural diversity: Implications for organizational competitiveness. *Academy of Management Executive, 5* (3), 45–56; Coleman, T. (October 1990). Managing diversity at work: The new American dilemma. *Public Management, 72*: 2–6.

CHAPTER 8

Recruitment, Selection, and Promotion

The public sector is faced with many responsibilities that distinguish it from the private sector. Insuring public safety, justice, and environmental quality are just a few areas that go beyond the demands placed on private organizations. Recruiting and retaining highly qualified employees to provide the services citizens take for granted is becoming increasingly difficult in a competitive labor market because even though the responsibilities may differ, the private and public sectors are in direct competition for the same scarce qualified applicants. Even when the economy starts to weaken and the unemployment rate increases, the demand for labor in skilled and knowledge-based professions will remain.

Dynamism in the economy has forced many adaptations in the recruitment, selection, and retention of public employees. Nevertheless, much remains the same, anchored by conflicts that frequently characterize debate over the appropriate criteria to use in the recruitment and selection of job applicants and the promotion of employees. In addition to describing some of the technical aspects of recruitment and selection, this chapter reviews the value conflicts and the compromises that take place over the criteria used in the acquisition and planning functions. It discusses how the contemporary labor market affects the view of work and how organizations of the future affect the acquisition function.

By the end of this chapter, you will be able to:

1. Define the acquisition function.
2. Describe the influence different values have on the objectives of the acquisition function.
3. Describe how characteristics of the workforce and the nature of contemporary work influence the acquisition function.
4. Describe ten steps in the recruitment and selection process.
5. Identify six practices that are likely to produce timely and valid hiring processes.
6. Discuss the comparative characteristics of centralized, decentralized, and electronic staffing techniques, and outsourcing.
7. Describe the concept of test validation and validation strategies.
8. Describe the main provisions of the Americans with Disabilities Act and how the ADA affects recruitment and selection.

THE ACQUISITION FUNCTION

The second of the four functions every comprehensive personnel system must fulfill, **the acquisition function**, involves the acquisition of competencies that will enable an organization to fulfill its mission. It may seem impersonal to talk about the recruitment and hiring of people in terms of acquisition. Traditionally, the impersonality of merit systems—the most comprehensive and pervasive personnel systems in government—has been a virtue. In merit systems, personnel decisions are supposed to be made based on an applicant's competencies and the performance that results from the employee's application of his or her competencies to the agency's work, not based on whom an applicant or employee knows. Competencies traditionally have been seen in terms of knowledge, skills, and abilities (KSAs). The knowledge portion deals with the information that allows a person to perform from an informed perspective, for example, theories, facts, and principles. The skills piece addresses the demonstrated abilities or proficiencies, which are developed and learned from past work and life experience. This concept has also been expanded to include **personal attributes** reflected in a person's past effectiveness, for example, attitudes, habits, traits, behaviors, interpersonal skills, and emotional intelligence.

VALUE CONFLICTS AND THE ACQUISITION FUNCTION

Most recruitment, selection, and promotion decisions are not made within a politicized environment. Yet, it would be naive to argue that all are conducted according to routine procedures designed only to reward competence. Tension occurs when the elected leadership believes it could accomplish more to advance its political platform—legitimized through an election—if it had more influence over top-level classified positions. In these cases, partisan pressures crop up either formally or informally to influence career appointments. Over time, if these attempts are successful, the response is that the competencies necessary for informed public policy formulation and implementation are eroded. If the inroads result in notoriety or scandal involving political appointees, counter pressure is felt to strengthen the merit system. A recent example of these conflicting values was brought to light in the summer of 2008 when it was revealed that senior political appointees in the U.S. Department of Justice had systematically attempted to hire new career civil service attorneys based on political affiliation. Shocking to many merit system advocates was the extent to which the appointees examined the political background of applicants when it was clear that selection decisions were legally mandated to be made based on merit.[1]

Not only must merit systems respond to political pressures to accommodate the value of responsiveness, they also must adapt to public policy initiatives and political pressure stemming from the values of social equity and individual rights.[2] Arvey and Sackett write, "Most organizations value productivity; a great many also value cultural diversity. Conflict arises when selection systems known to contribute to the first detract from the second, as in the case of valid selection systems with negative impact on protected groups. No clear solution has emerged, although what is surfacing is a clear sense that **fairness is a social issue** *rather than a scientific one* [emphasis added]."[3] As discussed in Chapter 7, the most direct way of realizing social equity in the acquisition process is through targeted recruitment and the establishment of hiring goals—for veterans, women, or racial and ethnic minorities.

So far, we have talked about issues of political responsiveness and representation, efficiency, and social equity in the staffing process. The value of individual rights enters as protection from partisan political influence. Thus, acquisition routines that include open access and selection criteria based on competencies derived from the job to be performed have the effect of protecting the rights of individual job applicants to fair treatment.

The value of individual rights is also expressed significantly in the promotion process where upward mobility is allocated, or in layoffs, where jobs themselves are allocated through the planning and sanction functions. Collective bargaining systems, seeking to protect the rights and treatment of their members, are particularly oriented toward these kinds of allocation decisions rather than acquisition—recruitment and selection—decisions.

Even though a union may not seek to influence recruitment and selection decisions in nonapprenticeship positions, it will make every effort to convince newly appointed employees to join the union if the job falls within the union's bargaining unit. In Kansas City, Missouri, every newly appointed firefighter joins the union, even though Missouri is a right-to-work state. During the initial training period, peer pressure is applied to accomplish this goal.

One of the ways unions protect their members from management favoritism is by insisting that seniority play a major role in allocation decisions like promotion and layoffs. Similarly, they argue against contracting out of city services if unionized city employees currently perform those services. Again, where merit systems exist alongside collective bargaining systems, compromises are commonly reached. For example, promotion scores are often calculated according to a formula that includes credit for an examination score and for years of service.

A major thesis of this book is that these value conflicts, whether between responsiveness/representation and efficiency, efficiency and equity, or responsiveness/representation and individual rights, cannot be avoided because the values themselves are fundamental to the political culture. As long as public jobs are considered scarce resources, these values will be brought to bear on acquisition and planning or allocation in personnel decisions. This results in merit systems under continual pressure from advocates of values other than efficiency and public policy compromises that eventually are reflected in personnel routines, techniques, and regulations.

What complicates human resource management tremendously is that advocates of individual rights rely on legislation, civil service review boards, and judicial tools to constrain managers, while civil service reformers, organization theorists, and commentators are arguing for flexibility, consideration of contextual factors, and personal attributes in selection decisions. Advocates of these two views may confront each other in legislative arenas. Reconciliation of these perspectives, often determined politically, requires changes in HRM systems and practices with supervisors and managers expected to work out the details.

EXTERNAL INFLUENCES AND CONTEMPORARY CHALLENGES

In addition to the conflict over values in the allocation of public jobs as scarce resources, other factors like demographics of the workforce and the nature of contemporary work also influence the acquisition function.

Workforce Demographics

Without a doubt, demographic shifts taking place within the American workforce represent some of the most critical challenges for public employers seeking to maintain a stable employment base. In Chapter 7, we discussed the rapid growth of women and minorities within the U.S. labor force; however, equally important is the fact that the labor force is becoming tighter and more competitive at a time when the number of employees eligible for retirement is rapidly increasing due to the aging of the Baby Boomer generation. Some have referred to these trends as the basis for a "crisis" in human capital if public sector employers are not able to recruit new talent into the public labor force to replace those who intend to retire in the near future.[4] This "crisis" is especially evident at the federal level. The Partnership for Public Service, a nonprofit research organization, recently reported the following statistics:

- Approximately one third of the federal government's Senior Executive Service is projected to retire by 2012.
- Approximately 27 percent of all federal supervisors will retire by 2012.
- Within key agencies such as the Federal Aviation Administration and the Social Security Administration, 26 to 23 percent of all employees are projected to retire by 2012.[5]

To address this growing challenge, the Partnership has proposed that agencies:

- Develop and implement workforce plans that identify and meet future talent needs
- Modify recruiting strategies to attract new talent, including at the mid-and senior-levels
- Streamline hiring processes, and make greater use of recruitment, retention, and relocation incentives, including student loan repayments
- Focus on retention, including taking steps to improve employee satisfaction, and strategically using workforce flexibilities to help retain experienced talent.[6]

Nature of Work

In addition to strategic considerations resulting from workforce composition, the way work is performed requires rethinking of recruitment and selection functions as well. Most prominently, the increasing reliance on teams and teamwork emphasizes what traditionally are seen as important but nontask-related factors connected to productivity in the work environment. Borman and Motowidlo call them **contextual factors**, which include:

- Volunteering to carry out task activities that are not formally a part of the job
- Persisting with extra enthusiasm or effort when necessary to complete task activities successfully
- Helping and cooperating with others
- Following organizational rules and procedures even when personally inconvenient
- Endorsing, supporting, and defending organizational objectives[7]

To these factors one might add conflict resolution skills and working within a demographically diverse environment. According to Borman and Motowidlo, these activities "do not support the technical core itself as much as they support the organizational, social, and psychological environment in which the technical core must function."[8] Their research shows that the contextual parts of management jobs are substantial, and they should be considered in recruitment and selection processes. Along this line, Guion's literature review shows that social skills and motivation are as important as knowledge in predicting job performance.[9] The challenge is that these and other contextual factors relate to *personal attributes*, complicating recruitment and selection processes, which in the last few decades have increasingly become more formalized and impersonal in order to avoid the risk of civil rights violations in employment decisions. Guion asks, "What are decision makers to do if the people predicted to perform tasks well are not predicted to do very well contextually—or vice versa?"[10]

It seems reasonable to conclude that some of these contextual factors may be more important than others in some situations. In his discussion of privatization of government services, Mintzberg has identified five models for managing government.[11] Each has implications for recruitment and selection. In the normative-control model, attitudes, values, and beliefs significantly influence task accomplishment, and he argues that they should be considered as part of the recruitment and selection process. This is probably truer with regard to social service delivery than other government work, but traditionally the virtue of public service has been found in the dedication of public servants to the collective good.

In their edited volume, Hesselbein, Goldsmith, and Beckhard describe leadership and organizations of the future. The essence of their message is that traditional hierarchical structures will have limited utility because they are best suited to operating in stable environments. In dynamic environments, more loosely structured organizations, composed of individuals with the capacity and willingness to learn continually, are more effective.[12]

Competencies

Of the many changes in HRM that have occurred in the last several years is the addition of the term **competencies** to our vocabulary. A review will find few common definitions of the term and few common lists of what is included as a competency, thus complicating a discussion of the concept. Nevertheless, the thrust is clear. The emphasis on strategic thinking has produced a direct emphasis in selection processes to determine what exactly should a job applicant be able to do and has the job applicant demonstrated that he or she is competent to do what is required. Interviewing has become more interactive as employers probe to identify candidates who have demonstrated valued competencies in the past. Training, the development function, is becoming more targeted toward competencies, and the performance appraisal process is being geared in that direction as well. What is not clear in this movement is whether something truly new in human resources management is emerging and if the use of competencies in selection processes results in the selection of individuals who otherwise would not be selected if traditional criteria were used. Further, does their selection make an appreciable difference in productivity?

STEPS IN THE STAFFING PROCESS

Before proceeding with a discussion of recruitment and selection methods, it will be useful to identify various steps and responsibilities in the staffing process, which includes both planning and acquisition functions:

1. Identify human resource needs as part of the strategic planning process
2. Seek budgetary approval to hire employees
3. Develop valid selection criteria
4. Select a method of recruitment
5. Recruit

6. Test or otherwise screen applicants with methods unique to each position
7. Prepare a list of qualified applicants
8. Interview the most highly qualified applicants
9. Conduct background and reference checks where appropriate
10. Select the most qualified applicant available for the position
11. Extensive new hire orientation and training

Different jurisdictions or agencies will carry out these steps in different ways. The important point to be made here is that the line manager—the person the potential hire will actually be working for—is most heavily involved in steps 1, 2, 3, 8, 10, and 11. The personnel department's job is to assist the line manager in finding and hiring the best applicant (a staffing role) and to ensure that the staffing process takes place without the undue influence of politics or favoritism (a regulatory role).

Every step in this process is important, but in many cases, the first step has become undervalued. It is easy to overlook this step when faced with the replacement of many positions that are embedded in organizational routines and services that go unquestioned. For example, replacing a secretary rarely triggers an examination of unit goals.

Consider a different situation. Those of you reading this book probably are taking a university level course in human resources management. Let's say the department offering the course has a faculty vacancy. Here are some of the questions the department will ask itself:

- What will student demand be in the future and in what kinds of areas?
- How are present faculty members prepared to meet future demands?
- Does the department possess the faculty competencies to teach in technology-supported formats that contemporary students expect?
- To give it flexibility, should the department hire one full-time replacement or one or more part-time faculty as needs arise?

These questions require the strategic thinking outlined in Chapter 3. Without answering these questions, the remaining steps in the staffing process are tools with narrow purpose.

In past labor markets with an ample supply of workers, public agencies had little trouble attracting a qualified applicant pool for vacant positions, but, as the U.S. labor market has tightened, personnel professionals and managers are finding it a growing challenge to attract the applicant pools of the past. This challenge has forced personnel departments to focus more of their efforts on strategic recruitment initiatives, and the growth of Web-based employment search engines has only intensified the need for public agencies to be up-to-date in their efforts. As recent as the early 1990s, it was common for public agencies to post their job announcements on bulletin boards in public buildings or in local print media. However, if agencies were to take this same approach in 2008, they would almost be guaranteed an insufficient applicant pool. Most new entries in today's labor market turn to Web-based job postings as their primary source of employment information, and those public agencies that have not invested in their Web-based presence are surely to operate at a competitive disadvantage. Recognizing the importance of **Web-based recruitment** in its efforts to fill vacancies, the federal government has gone so far as to contract out the design and management of its employment website, *www.USAJobs.gov*, to Monster.com, a leading private sector employment website.[13]

Along with selecting a recruitment method, agencies must establish the minimum qualifications for a position through job analysis. Then, the hiring authority must determine the appropriate method(s) to measure the extent to which applicants or employees possess these qualifications. In a tight labor market, standard qualifications may be called into question. For example, should elimination from the applicant pool of those with criminal records be revisited when public services cannot be adequately provided because of labor shortages?

Nine methods are commonly used to assess qualifications: review of biographical data, aptitude tests, ability tests, performance exams, references, performance evaluation (for promotional assessment of current employees only), interviews, assessment centers, and a probationary period. Four types of written tests are commonly used for selection purposes although the use of written tests has decreased significantly in the past decade: aptitude, characteristics or traits, ability, and performance. Aptitude tests measure general intelligence or cognitive ability (e.g., the federal government's now-discontinued Professional, Administrative Career Entrance (PACE) examination, or the Otis-Lennon). Aptitude tests are both relatively inexpensive to administer and score, and highly reliable. Some commentators are wary of the ease with which responses to psychological tests can be "faked" to match the presumed desired responses to the set of test scores. However, interim reliability checks can reduce the likelihood of this happening. The validity of such tests, however, can range from minimal to moderate, depending on the quality of the job analysis and the resulting **construct validation** of the aptitude as a predictor.

A second type of paper-and-pencil test measures personality traits or characteristics. The resulting personality profiles are then compared against profiles of current employees considered successful in the position or against traits judged as job related through construct validation. Examples are the Edwards Personality Preference Scale (EPPS) and the Minnesota Multiphasic Personality Inventory (MMPI).

Ability tests measure the extent to which applicants possess generalized abilities or skills related to job performance through empirical or construct validation. Examples would be verbal or mathematical ability, such as the Scholastic Aptitude Test (SAT) or the Graduate Record Examination (GRE). The more closely an ability test simulates actual job tasks and context, the more it becomes a performance test. A realistic typing or word processing test would be a good example. A performance test would be position-specific in that it would measure an applicant's ability to type a given kind of material on the specific machine used on the job. Research studies generally confirm that ability tests, which result from job analysis, are logically related to subsequent job performance.[14]

Interviews are a popular selection or promotion method.[15] Most organizations will not hire an employee without one because they believe the interview gives them the opportunity to observe an applicant's appearance and interpersonal skills and to ask questions about subjects not adequately covered on the application form. However, interviews are not recommended as a primary selection method. Not only do they take a good deal of the supervisor's time, but they also require interviewing skills on the part of the supervisor or interviewing panel. Since interviews are a prime method of rejecting candidates who look good on paper but might not fit into an organization, they are subject to scrutiny as potentially invalid selection criteria.

What, then, are some good guidelines to follow concerning interviews? Behavioral interviewing is a method that has become popular in achieving the desire to understand an applicant's competencies including personal attributes. Interview questions are open-ended and the applicant is requested to provide actual occurrences of past employment that address the topic of the question. As an example, "provide a time when you found yourself confronted with an angry customer and explain how you handled this situation." These types of questions allow the reviewer to see how the applicant views a situation, what priorities were held, and what they consider effective actions. Behavioral interviewing relies on predefined questions but is less structured in that questions may be expanded upon based on the response given by the applicant. Panel interviews (those involving more than one interviewer) are more reliable than individual interviews, and can use either style, structured or less structured, though they also increase the cost of this already expensive selection method.

Rodger M. Matthews, Kansas Division of Personnel Services states, "The State of Kansas has improved its recruitment and selection process by eliminating testing and enhancing the registration process with a qualitative approach to measuring competencies. The emphasis has shifted to assessing the level, quality, complexity, and behavioral descriptors performed rather than on the amount of time spent performing a skill or the testing ability of applicants. The qualitative approach allows the state to de-emphasize 'minimum qualifications' and concentrate on the 'competencies' of an outstanding employee throughout the applicant process" (February 2001). In essence, the goal is to identify well-rounded applicants who posses the competencies needed to be successful. Let's say an engineer has outstanding competencies within the field of engineering but is unable to personally interact, contribute, and cooperate with others. This person may be viewed as a liability rather than an asset in an organization needing projects completed under a team approach versus individually. Organizations bear responsibility in becoming familiar with their own work culture, workflow structures, and demands before recruiting, to ensure a proper match and to allow success to both the new employee and organization.

The open-ended and probing nature of some interviewing has replaced the strict, by the book, stick to a specific list of questions approach that prevailed a decade ago. In part, the reason has to do with increased emphasis on finding the right candidate, more acceptability of practices that promote fairness in selection processes, and less prominence of the law as the dominating force in human resources management. However, this more subjective approach to interviewing also necessitates interviewer training to ensure a consistent and reliable approach across the organization.

References are another selection tool. They are usually used to verify educational and employment records or to obtain information about the applicant's skills or personality. Their validity depends upon the opportunity that the writer has had to observe the applicant and upon the relatedness of this relationship to the prospective job. Because recommendation letters are overwhelmingly positive, readers frequently fall into the trap of looking for the smallest of differences as they attempt to distinguish one applicant from another. A better use of reference letters is to stimulate questions that can be asked in an interview. However, reference checks also pose challenging legal questions in today's society. As described in detail in Chapter 12, if past employers fail to reveal damaging yet relevant information about a former employee or if they give out the damaging information but it unfairly harms the employee's chances of obtaining employment, they may become involved in litigation.

Previous performance evaluations are often used to assess potential for reassignment or promotion. They are valid to the extent that the ratings are based on job performance and this performance involves the same skills or abilities required in the prospective job. Their reliability is based on the extent of inter-rater agreement among previous supervisory evaluations.

Assessment centers may be used to stress performance on job-related tasks. They are used in both the public and the private sectors; in the public sector, their use is most prevalent among law enforcement organizations. If performance criteria are validated, they can be useful in selection, promotion, and career development. Candidates may be given an "in-basket" full of documents that an employee might confront in a typical day and be asked how the various items should be dealt with. A panel would then judge the candidates' responses.

The last selection or promotion method is the probationary appointment. This technique possesses the highest possible validity and reliability factors because it measures actual performance on the job. However, it also carries the highest cost and greatest risk to the organization, because a potentially unqualified employee may occupy a critical position until he or she makes enough serious mistakes to be considered unfit. The use of the probationary period places upon supervisors the responsibility of weeding out unsatisfactory or marginal employees before they attain career status (and hence the right to grievance hearings to protest a discharge after they have attained a "property interest" in their jobs); it places upon personnel managers the responsibility of developing valid probationary period evaluation systems. After an employee is no longer on probationary status, their "property right" makes it extremely difficult to dismiss the employee. The "property right" representing individual rights appears to have greater value than efficiency. An employer must show that an employee has been given substantial "due process" before a permanent employee may be dismissed.

Because each of these methods differs in value orientation, cost validity, and reliability, organizations must compare them.[16] Table 8-1 summarizes their comparative advantages.

In this section, we have described steps involved in the staffing process. We have made it sound logical, rational, and uniform. The fact of the matter is that in today's competitive labor market, the most rational and valid recruitment and selection procedures may take the longest time to implement. In a competitive environment, this may mean the loss of good candidates to other employers. Government can no more afford the loss of qualified candidates than can the private sector.

TABLE 8-1 Comparison of Selection Methods

Method	Validity	Reliability	Cost
1. Biodata	moderate	high	low
2. References (letters of recommendation)	low	low	low
3. Aptitude tests	moderate	moderate	low
4. Characteristics of trait tests	moderate	moderate	low
5. Ability tests	moderate	moderate	moderate
6. Performance tests	high	moderate	moderate
7. Interviews	low	low	high
8. Assessment centers	moderate	high	high
9. Probationary appointment	very high	very high	very high

TIMELY HIRING PRACTICES

Acknowledging tight labor markets, the International Personnel Management Association and NAPSE Human Resources Benchmarking Project asked human resources professionals about their hiring habits.[17] Several best or promising practices were identified to foster timely yet valid hiring:

- Decentralization that gives more latitude, authority, and responsibility to hiring managers
- Flexibility, for example, in the number of applicants that must be interviewed
- Technology, especially in the submission of applications and development of databases to select list of qualified applicants
- Tracking and monitoring practices to determine if they are meeting the dual criteria of timeliness and validity
- Use of alternatives to written exams such as skill inventories and résumé screens
- Continuously recruiting for hard-to-fill and high volume job classifications

While these steps will increase the timeliness of the hiring process, Kellough raises the possibility that decentralization and flexibility could undermine merit principles.[18] The fundamental question here is whether merit values and operating principles have anchored themselves strongly enough in human resources management's thinking that decentralization and flexibility pose minor risk.

RECRUITMENT AND SELECTION MODELS

Because both the number of positions agencies need to fill and the conditions under which staffing is conducted may vary, staffing models differ with circumstances. Generally, four types are possible: centralized, decentralized, electronic models, and outsourcing.

Centralized Recruitment

If the agency has several thousand employees, and if different departments recruit large numbers of clerical or technical employees for the same types of positions, **centralized recruitment and selection** may be used based on efficiency.

If recruitment is centralized, the central personnel agency will be responsible for requesting from agency personnel managers periodic estimates of the number and type of new employees needed in the future (the next quarter or fiscal year). The staffing needs of all agencies are entered into a computer, after being classified by occupational code and salary level, and a summary listing of all projected new hiring needs is produced.

In reality, producing an accurate projection of new hiring needs is rarely this simple. To begin with, it is not always possible for agencies to predict their needs a year ahead of time. A political crisis or budget cut can drastically affect recruitment needs, and hence the quality of the estimate. Central personnel agency recruiters also realize that agency personnel managers will tend to overestimate the number of employees they require, just because from their point of view it is better to have too many applicants than too few. Naturally, this conflicts with the need of the central personnel agency to reduce selection costs by reducing the number of applicants to the minimum number needed to ensure that all available positions are filled with qualified applicants. In addition, specialized positions require a greater ratio of applicants to projected vacancies, because a higher percentage of applicants are likely to be rejected by the selecting agency as not meeting the specialized requirements of the position.

While there are many drawbacks to centralized human resources management, two factors argue in its favor. First, the amount of variation in the recruitment and selection process in individual agencies is reduced, thus benefiting the values of social equity and individual rights. Second, it may be easier to advance systemwide human resources management policy—like emphasizing the recruitment and selection of minorities.

Decentralized Recruitment

Decentralized recruitment and selection is traditionally likely to occur in agencies that are relatively small, for which recruitment needs are limited, and where each agency employs different types of workers. Increasingly, it is used in larger units.[19] It is usually used for professional, scientific, or administrative positions peculiar to a particular agency. For example, smaller municipalities may not have enough vacancies to utilize the services of a central personnel department. Alternatively, the department heads may have successfully argued that their particular employees are unique and that it is more appropriate to handle recruitment and selection on a departmental level. Police and fire departments are likely to make this argument at the municipal level.

If recruitment is decentralized, individual public agencies will go through essentially the same steps required for centralized recruitment, except that dealings with the central personnel agency are limited. Agency personnel managers will work directly with the supervisors in their agencies to make periodic estimates of hiring needs. Then agency recruiters will meet with agency affirmative action specialists to determine whether recruitment efforts should be targeted toward specific minority groups. After evaluating both the need for new employees and the diversity goals of the agency, the agency personnel director will determine what recruitment efforts are required. The job announcement process is the same as that of a central personnel agency, except that applicants are requested to send their applications to the specific agency.

The trend in human resources management is toward decentralization.[20] In response to criticisms that personnel practices are burdensome, time-consuming, and unresponsive to sister agencies, the federal government has increasingly decentralized recruitment and selection over the past decade, but Kellough has expressed concern that decentralized personnel processes could lead to more violations of the merit principles.[21] On the other hand, a recent U.S. Merit Systems Protection Board report concluded that the decentralization has occurred with no corruption linked to "spoils," no decline in the quality of federal employees, and increases in diversity.[22]

"I have authority now that I only dreamed of five years ago" is a comment by John Martello, Human Resources Director at the Kansas State School for the Blind, about the decentralization underway within the State of Kansas. He gives the following example of how "Classification Authority" was issued to the agency by the central Division of Personnel Services for the first time in its history. This allows the Kansas State School for the Blind to directly administer FTE and position management in a more responsive manner, with regular audits by the central Division of Personnel Services for compliance within established classification standards.

Some agencies utilize a combination of centralized and decentralized recruitment. For example, a central personnel agency may authorize individual agencies to recruit and test applicants independently, subject to audit by the central personnel agency once they have been hired. This compromise will provide for a greater degree of centralized control than is possible with a decentralized system, while simultaneously providing agencies with timelier and more flexible recruitment available from a central personnel agency.

Electronic (web-based) Recruitment

Until the mid-1990s, touch-tone dedicated phone lines and job posting bulletins allowed agencies to advertise vacancies and to refer applicants to agencies with hiring needs. The contemporary recruitment environment, however, is characterized by an increasing reliance on agency and third-party recruitment websites that permit employers to reach a much larger applicant base. Additionally, these websites allow applicants to search for vacancies, post résumés, apply for positions, and have their qualifications evaluated through the establishment of a "virtual" electronic "hiring hall."[23] Three of the more prominent websites include the federal government's *www.USAJobs.gov*, *www.publicservicecareers.org*, and *www.monster.com*, a leading private sector website that also posts positions for public agencies willing to purchase their services.

In recent years, one of the key questions for human resources professionals has been whether to develop their own recruitment websites, purchase the services of third-party sites, or to do both. Each option has its own set of costs and benefits depending on the size of the agency and type of positions to be filled. For instance, a large agency, such as the U.S. Department of Defense, would likely benefit from using all three options since cost is generally not a concern. However, a smaller agency or locality might want to consider developing their own website if they generally have few vacant positions or need a tailored approach to recruitment. Still, some agencies might find it hard to maintain the internal skills necessary to maintain a website. In these cases, it would likely be prudent to purchase services from a third-party provider.

Additionally, the use of electronic recruitment methods also raises questions of equity and fairness in the application process. For those applicants skilled in information technology, searching and applying for positions electronically will not be a major challenge, but for those potential applicants that do not have access to computers or are not skilled in their operation, electronic recruitment can pose a challenge. Ultimately, employers must be aware of these challenges and, where possible, take steps to ensure that all applicants are able to successfully seek employment. These steps may include the availability of public computers for application purposes or the maintenance of paper-based application procedures.

Outsourcing

Outsourcing and the elimination of personnel services historically provided by government have increased over the last decade.[24] This increased use of contracting to achieve economies of scale without sacrificing core organizational competencies has meant that agencies are increasingly choosing to use outsourcing as a recruitment device. In particular, they are likely to use employment services for hiring temporary employees, or executive search firms ("headhunters") for professional and managerial recruitment.

The efficiency in time of outsourcing for temporary workers is evident. The process is shortened noticeably with responsibility for recruitment and selection resting with the temporary employment agency. While this type of outsourcing seems to make sense, it raises a larger issue: Is it necessary for a government jurisdiction itself to recruit and select for other positions or can these activities be performed just as effectively by private employment agencies under contract? Searches for chief administrative officers and some department heads are now conducted by executive search firms. Why not other positions?

Initially the goal of outsourcing was to save money. Temporary employment agencies are used to aid in locating qualified candidates in a tight labor market to augment the recruitment efforts of the agency. It also allows an organization to concentrate on its mission, that which it can do uniquely. Why not contract with a private employment agency for recruitment and selection with the stipulation that all applicant pools will contain individuals with required competencies and will reflect demographically the appropriate labor market?

In some ways, the challenge here is first to identify what the agency or government jurisdiction considers its core mission and values. Tom Lewinsohn, former personnel director in Kansas City, Missouri, and past president of the International Personnel Management Association, suggests that recruitment and selection are so integrally connected to the concept of merit, a core governmental value, that outsourcing these activities undermines the concept of the public service.[25]

Recruitment and Selection Models

The availability of centralized, decentralized, electronic recruitment methods, and outsourcing means that the actual staffing process followed by public agencies is complex and varies with the nature and context of the agency. Table 8-2 depicts recruitment and selection routines that take place in Lawrence, Kansas, a council-manager city with a permanent population of some 90,000. By reviewing the information, one can find a number of the steps and methods already discussed as well as the influence of the values of efficiency, social equity, responsiveness, and individual rights. Knowledge, skills/abilities, and personal attributes are weighted very heavily in each of the selection processes. For both the nonpublic-safety and public-safety entry-level positions, usually the city administers a test of knowledge or skill supplemented by interviews and reference checks. For all positions in the city, a preemployment physical includes a drug-screening test. Oral interview boards have replaced interviews with individual supervisors, in order to get a broader range of opinion on the suitability of applicants. Interview boards also protect the individual rights of applicants to fair and equal treatment. A review of licenses and certificates is particularly important in screening applicants for technical positions. In the last few years, electronic mail bulletin boards and a dedicated information phone line have expanded recruitment efforts.

No paper-and-pencil testing takes place for department heads or for the city manager, but the national recruitment procedure indicates a desire to secure professionally trained talent. In addition, the interview board usually includes a professional in a related field, one who is not a member of the city staff. For example, selection of a new finance director might include a banker or the city's auditor as a member of the interview board.

Social equity is particularly noticeable in the public-safety positions, where special efforts are made in the recruitment process. Recent *recruitment* efforts for police and firefighters featured a poster advertising the positions and showing minority and female officers and firefighters; special booths at a shopping mall in the metropolitan Kansas City area

TABLE 8–2 Recruitment and Selection Process in Lawrence, Kansas

Entry-Level Positions (NonPublic-Safety)	Public-Safety Positions	Department Director	City Manager (Chief Administrative Officer)	Temporary Employment Agency	Part-Time Positions	Technical Positions
RECRUITMENT						
• City website • Local newspaper • Announcements to eighty local agencies including Jobs Service Center, NAACP, Haskell Indian Nations University • E-Mail Bulletin Boards • Dedicated information telephone line	• City website • Local and regional newspapers • Announcements to eighty local agencies and law enforcement and fire agencies • Special effort to recruit women and minorities • E-Mail Bulletin Boards • Dedicated information telephone line	• City website • Local and regional newspapers • Professional associations (national) • Announcements to eighty local agencies • Dedicated information telephone line • E-mail bulletin boards	• City website • Local and regional newspapers • Professional associations • Announcements to eighty local agencies • E-mail bulletin boards • Dedicated information telephone line	Bid process on key positions	• Local newspaper • Announcements to 80 local agencies • E-mail bulletin boards • Dedicated information telephone line	• Local and regional newspapers • Professional associations national and/or state/regional • Announcements to eighty local agencies • E-mail bulletin boards • Dedicated information telephone line

SELECTION						
• Applications screened by personnel office • Reduced applicant pool reviewed by hiring authority • Test where appropriate • Interview with board • Reference checks • Post-offer physical, including drug screening • Appointment by personnel director	• Written test • Physical fitness evaluation • Interview with board • Interview by chief • Reference checks • Post-offer physical, including drug screening and physiological test for police officers • Appointment by department director	• Applicants screened by personnel/office selection committee/ city manager • Reduced pool reviewed by city manager • Assessment lab • Committee interview • Interview with city manager • Reference checks • Post-offer physical, including drug screening • Appointment by city manager	• Applications screened by consultant/ personnel department/ committee of the governing body/entire governing body • Reference checks • Interview with governing body (may also include visits with depart-ment heads • Post-offer physical including drug screening • Appointment by governing body	Order position as needed for specified time needed	• Applications screened by department • Interview by supervisor • Reference checks • Appointment by supervisor	• Applicants screened by personnel office and department • Reduce pool reviewed by division manager • Assessment lab • Interview with committee • Interview with department director • Reference checks • Test on technical data • Review of certificates • Appointment by supervisor/ department director
LENGTH OF TOTAL PROCESS						
4–8 weeks	3–4 months	2–3 months	3–5 months	1–5 days	3–5 weeks	2–3 months
TRAINING						
On the job	• Law enforcement academy • Fire training program	On the job	On the job	On the job	On the job	• On the job • Technical training as needed to retain certifications

with concentrations of minority populations; special visits to a junior college with a large minority population; and special outreach in the Topeka, Kansas, area working with the YWCA to identify female candidates. No special efforts were made to show preference to women and minorities in any of the four *selection* processes.

The value of responsiveness is apparent only in the selection for city manager. The manager serves at the pleasure of the governing body, and elected officials are heavily involved in all phases of the selection process, whether they hire an executive search consultant or handle the process through their own personnel department. They employ criteria designed to determine whether the manager will work well with the governing body and will fit in with the political and social culture of the city.

While Table 8-2 shows the value of responsiveness isolated to selection of the city manager that is not an entirely accurate portrayal. In many jurisdictions, even though the chief administrative officer legally can hire and fire department heads, it is often wise to consult with the governing body or mayor before doing so. For example, hiring and firing a police chief in most communities is fraught with potential political problems; the same often is true of the planning director.

Finally, the table shows that recruitment for temporary and part-time positions is not nearly as time consuming when compared to other categories of employees. Efficiency is the dominant value with little attention paid to individual rights.

Table 8-2 was developed in 1997. In 2001, we asked the director of administrative services for the City of Lawrence to review the table for accuracy. His comments are entirely consistent with other comments in this chapter that staffing has become a more challenging management function as the supply of labor has shrunk. He said, "I found little has changed from the basic processes found in the table. However, because of the extremely tight labor market and with rapid changes in technology, I found several elements within the model have changed."[26]

These changes include:

- Speeding up the hiring process so as not to lose good applicants to competing employers
- Becoming more aggressive in retention of current employees
- Conducting special recruitment to hire experienced police officers with special rate of pay as opposed to everyone starting at the bottom
- Coordinating with the state employment office
- Enhancing our presence on the Internet including online applications
- Expanding outreach for recruitment with an additional recruiter position.

TEST VALIDATION AND THE ACQUISITION FUNCTION

A test is any device used to separate qualified from unqualified applicants for selection or promotion. Included are written examinations as well as selection methods not normally thought of as tests, including interviews, medical examinations, drug tests, background investigations, and physical requirements.

To be valid, a test must separate more-qualified from less-qualified applicants on the basis of job-related competencies or performance.

Social equity advocates are often associated with promoting preferential treatment of minorities and women. However, their greatest and most lasting contribution to personnel management may prove to be in the area of **test validation**. For in seeking

		Job Performance High	Job Performance Low
Test Score	High	True Positive	False Positive
	Low	False Negative	True Negative

FIGURE 8–1 Relationships between Test Scores and Job Performance

to remove barriers to equal opportunity based on discriminatory hiring criteria (those based on race, religion, or other nonmerit factors), social equity advocates have been responsible for general acceptance of the merit system principle that job applicants are to be chosen on the basis of job-related criteria.

What is a job-related test or selection device? The answer is simple to state but difficult to put into practice. It is a test that does a good job of predicting job performance. For example, an interview process is valid if those who do well on the interview do well on the job, and if those who do not do well in the interview do not do well on the job (or would not do well if hired). To simplify our discussion, we will talk in terms of valid and invalid when in reality we are talking in degrees. No selection device can predict with 100 percent accuracy who will and will not do well on the job. Are undergraduate grades a good predictor of subsequent performance in graduate school? For those who enter graduate school right after their undergraduate education, the answer is probably yes—but it is not foolproof. For those who have been out of school for a long time, they tend to be less reliable, except at the extremes. Then, there is a subsequent question: Are good grades in graduate school a good predictor of good career performance?

Figure 8-1 shows in matrix form the possible relationships between test scores or other selection devices and job performance.

The more valid a test, the more **true positives** and **true negatives** it will produce. In other words, those who do well on the test in fact will do well on the job, and those who do poorly on the test will do poorly on the job. The less valid a selection method, the more likely it will produce **false positives** and **false negatives**. A false positive is a person who does well on the test but does not turn out to do well on the job. The test falsely predicted a good job performance. A false negative occurs where a person fails to do well on the test but does (or would do) well on the job. Social equity advocates are mostly concerned with selection methods that produce false negatives when those clustered in that quadrant are members of disadvantaged classes. An example would be an arbitrary height requirement for firefighters. It is likely that women, who tend to be shorter than men, will be discriminated against with this requirement. The burden is on the employer to show that the height requirement produces a minimum number of false negatives and that those that are produced are not systematically drawn from a disadvantaged population—unless, of course, the test is valid; that is, the height requirement is indeed related to job performance.

TEST VALIDATION METHODS

Three established validation strategies are acceptable: empirical, construct, and content validation. *Empirical validation*, also known as **criterion validation**, requires that a test score be significantly correlated, in a statistical sense, with important elements of job performance. The expectation is that those who perform well on the job would have done well on the preemployment test.

Construct validation involves both identifying psychological traits and aptitudes that relate to successful job performance and devising a test that measures these traits. For example, most insurance companies give psychological tests to applicants for sales positions. These tests purport to measure the applicant's congeniality, outgoing nature, liking for people, and other traits supposedly related to ability to sell. Police departments require a psychological profile on new recruits. In the sales example, tests have been developed by identifying the best salespeople in the organization, giving them a psychological test measuring a variety of traits, and establishing a personality profile of the "ideal salesperson." Police professionals are trying to eliminate individuals with unacceptable traits—overly aggressive and inflexible—from the applicant pool. Profiles are then used as a yardstick against which the characteristics of applicants are measured. Those who approximate this yardstick move on in the selection process; those who do not are more carefully screened.

Content validation requires that the job be analyzed to determine its duties, the particular conditions that make work easy or difficult, realistic performance standards, the competencies required to perform these tasks up to these standards under these conditions, and the minimum qualifications required to ensure that an applicant would have these competencies. For example, it is logical to assume that a prison guard, responsible for transporting prisoners by car from one location to another, would need to know how to drive.

Content validation, therefore, links the functions of affirmative action and job analysis. In addition, it connects them with a third function, productivity. This is because the establishment of a logical relationship between duties and qualifications is not only a defense of validity, it is also a justification for discriminating between qualified and unqualified applicants based on their anticipated performance. It would follow from this that a content-valid job description (such as an ROD) could be used to assess the validity of a selection or promotion criterion by measuring the performance of an employee hired based on that criterion.

Summary

The acquisition function reflects conflict among the competing values of responsiveness, efficiency, individual rights, and social equity as the basis of allocating public jobs. The goal of most public employers is to hire and promote those with the best knowledge, skills/abilities, and personal attributes to perform the job. However, other interests—represented by politics, collective bargaining, and diversity—frequently challenge this goal. Ultimately, the differences in value and policy orientations must be transformed into workable recruitment, selection, and promotion procedures that permit routine, cost-effective application and promise fair treatment for applicants.

As the workforce continues to change and the availability of qualified labor becomes scarcer, the public sector will need to become more responsive and resilient to compete with the private sector for the same resources. The acquisition of resources will become less bureaucratic and more in-line with the private sector. The changing nature of work and organizations affects recruitment and selection processes as well. As organizations become less hierarchical, more is demanded of employees than traditional competencies connected to a narrowly defined job. As the context within which public agencies operate becomes more heterogeneous and unstable, job analyses become less dependable, and recruitment is expanded to include situational skills and personal traits, such as the ability to contribute to a work group. Selection decisions become more tentative as loyalty between employee and employer is weakened by contemporary trends toward downsizing and privatization.

While contemporary trends question traditional approaches to job analysis, recruitment, and selection, legal requirements imposed by the Civil Rights Act of 1964 and the Americans with Disabilities Act are built on traditional assumptions about work and reinforce the status quo of personnel management.

Key Terms

acquisition function *182*
centralized recruitment and selection *190*
competencies *185*
construct validation *198*
content validation *198*
contextual factors *184*
criterion validation *197*
decentralized recruitment and selection *191*
fairness is a social issue *182*
personal attributes *182*
test validation *196*
true and false positives and negatives *197*
Web-based recruitment *186*

Discussion Questions

1. How does one's value perspective influence the objectives of the recruitment and selection process?
2. What does it mean to say that fairness is a social judgment rather than a scientific calculation? What are the implications for the tension between efficiency and diversity?
3. Describe how workforce demographics and the nature of contemporary work influence the acquisition of public employees.
4. What kind of flexible personnel policies are needed to accommodate the caregiving needs of the modern family where both mother and father work? Or where the family consists of children with a single parent?
5. What is meant by contextual factors that influence how well a person performs as an organizational member? How easy do you think it is to recruit and select for these factors? Does an emphasis on contextual factors conflict with an emphasis on recruiting for diversity?
6. Identify eleven steps in the recruitment and selection process. In an organization you are familiar with, which steps are the most difficult to perform? Why?
7. Identify six timely hiring practices and describe how several might be employed to recruit and select for a job category you are familiar with where demand exceeds supply of applicants and service is suffering from staffing shortages.
8. Compare and contrast centralized, decentralized, and Web-based recruitment techniques.
9. Outsourcing or privatization of government services displaces value issues governments deal with in recruitment and selection processes. Which values do you think will be emphasized by private employment agencies? Can the benefits of outsourcing be realized if vendors are required to incorporate the values of responsiveness, efficiency, social equity, and individual rights into their practices?
10. Review the recruitment and selection processes in Table 8-2 and identify the values emphasized in each model. How would you improve these processes?
11. Describe the concept and importance of test validation and three validation strategies. How have affirmative action and advocates of social equity and individual rights advanced the importance of test validation, and therefore the value of efficiency?
12. How might the Americans with Disabilities Act become as important as the Civil Rights Act of 1964? How do the legal requirements for job analysis implied in the two Acts conflict with modern theories about future organizations?

Exercise: Driving Forces of Change in Recruitment and Selection

This exercise is best conducted with mid-career students in class. Depending upon the size of the class, divide into discussion groups.

- Each group should make two lists. First, make a list of how recruitment and selection processes have changed over the last decade. Then, make a list of recruitment and selection processes that have remained the same.
- Share the lists and come up with one agreed-upon list of what has changed and one list of what has remained the same.
- Identify the driving forces behind the changes that have occurred. Are these forces internal organizational forces or forces external to organizations? If external, what conclusions would you draw about the relationship between internal organizational change and external organizational environments?
- Regarding those aspects that have remained the same, which of the four values—responsiveness/representation, efficiency, social equity, and individual rights—seems evident in them? How do the values you have identified compare to the values that underlie the merit principles listed in Chapter 1? We often talk about organizational values that provide anchors for organizations in times of change. Would you say that the values that underpin merit systems qualify as anchor values?

Case Study: Information Technology Recruitment

Recruiting in information technology (IT) and related fields poses a significant challenge to many public sector organizations that do not pay at market rates; and where recruitment and selection procedures take so much time in public sector organizations, qualified candidates may find jobs with other employers.

Let's look at what it takes to recruit and hire employees skilled in IT. Former Federal Reserve Chairman Alan Greenspan once told a business audience in North Carolina, "The United States is currently confronting what can best be described as another industrial revolution. The rapid acceleration of computer and telecommunications technologies is a major reason for the appreciable increase in our productivity in this expansion, and is likely to continue to be a significant force in expanding standards of living into the twenty-first century."[27] Groups such as the U.S. Department of Commerce's Office of Technology Policy have identified what they consider an inability of the United States to meet the market demand for information technology workers..[28]

Even when the economy starts to weaken and companies start downsizing, demand for labor in knowledge-based professions will remain. Unfortunately, an economic downturn hinders governments' ability to attract and retain needed labor. "In a recession, taxes don't necessarily decline, but if they stop growing and your expenses grow, you have a problem," said Donald Boyd, Director of the Fiscal Studies Program at the Rockefeller Institute of Government in Albany, New York.[29]

When budget pressures are combined with a labor shortage, delaying IT capital projects, outsourcing and contracting out more technology is usually the solution. Some government organizations have resorted to simply hiring minimally qualified people with the aptitude and motivation to learn, or identifying motivated staff internally, and then investing in appropriate training for these select employees. Unfortunately, these newly skilled and trained employees are prime candidates for targeted recruitment efforts by the private sector, with more lucrative compensation and benefit packages. To illustrate, the president of an Arizona IT company said, "I am afraid as an employer of getting people who would require an awful lot of training. We have eight hours to learn a new system. We don't have three months or six months." In this environment, many companies have concluded that they cannot afford the time penalty and the uncertainty associated with "making" the employees they need (through training or retraining). Many employers are, instead, pursuing a "buy" strategy, seeking the exact skills and experience they need for a particular project and paying a premium for that.[30] This lack of IT personnel could "pose problems with the increasing number of governments rolling out electronic government applications. Without adequate safeguards, the public likely won't trust electronic government applications."[31]

In response, governments have attempted to become competitive by becoming creative in obtaining and retaining employees with coveted skills, even within the structured Civil Service System. A perfect example of this is reflected in a letter submitted to the Kansas Senate Ways and Means Committee by Charles E. Simmons, Secretary of Corrections, requesting that Senate Bill 96 remove key information technology positions from the classified Civil Service System and place them in the unclassified service. Here's an excerpt of the letter:

> By placing these positions in the unclassified service, the Department will have the flexibility to offer compensation levels needed to retain qualified personnel in these positions. The existing personnel performing these functions do so through designation as temporary project positions, while the authorized FTE are being held vacant. SB 96 would allow the Department to place these individuals into authorized FTE positions.[32]

Secretary Simmons is pointing out that the compensation structure of the classified Civil Service System (merit system) within the State of Kansas is inadequate to appoint needed personnel, resulting in the classified positions remaining vacant. The use of temporary project positions, with flexible compensation provisions, is the method the Department of Corrections utilized to retain these individuals. Temporary project positions are not considered by the Kansas Division of Budget under the FTE funding structure and can have an unfavorable long-term impact on the agency and incumbents, which is why Secretary Simmons is proposing counting the positions as FTE under the unclassified service. This bypass of the classified Civil Service System is an example of just one creative method used by a government organization to meet critical needs while confronted with limited options.

A number of bonuses have been devised to specifically compensate IT incumbents, beyond the rigid salary structure of a merit system. These include signing bonuses for accepting a position, project bonuses for working on a project, skill bonuses for learning new skills, referral bonuses paid to an employee when an IT applicant they referred accepts an IT position, and longevity bonuses for remaining with the agency for a set period of time.[33] Additionally, some states and regions have undertaken efforts to lure people away from other regions of the country.

> For example, the State of Michigan launched its "Come Home to Michigan" campaign to attract IT workers who grew up in Michigan or were educated there. The Minnesota High Technology Association, in partnership with the Minnesota Department of Economic Security, conducted a five month "Upgrade to Minnesota" ad campaign in Silicon Valley to introduce workers there to the advantages of Minnesota living. The campaign reportedly generated thousands of résumés of technical and scientific workers for the sponsoring companies. The loss of skilled IT workers to others is also a concern of economic development officials. For example, the Hudson Valley, New York area is losing IT professionals to contract work for employers in other areas. It was noted at the Hudson Valley town meeting that the northern New Jersey market pays IT professionals 10 percent more and the New York City market pays 25 percent more. Others see information technology as a tool to keep the residents from moving to other states for job opportunities. U.S. Senator Kent Conrad expressed his concern about the isolation of small towns around the country stating, "There is a need to keep the best and brightest in North Dakota. This is the biggest concern of parents. IT is an opportunity to provide these jobs."[34]

In this type of aggressive environment, from both the private and public sectors, governments must be creative and resourceful to ensure that they obtain and retain the necessary skilled workforce to serve their citizens.

Who are these information technology applicants that everyone wishes to employ? They are mainly younger workers (nearly 75–80 percent under the age of 45) who do not remain with the same employer more than four years.[35] Their educational background is much more diverse than the traditional mold of extensive preparatory training and education in a university setting.[36] A growing number are not U.S. citizens. Larger numbers of foreigners with H-1B visas are employed to help supply this competitive labor market. The challenges in recruiting and employing staff with H-1B visas add to the complexity and cost for an employer, in that Immigration and Naturalization documents, timelines, and processes are jointly the responsibility of the employee with a H-1B "non-immigrant" visa and the employer. "In

1995, only about a quarter of temporary skilled foreign workers were in IT-related fields; by 1997 about half were in IT fields. Largely due to the increased use by the IT industry, the H-1B cap was reached for the first time in August 1997. In 1998, the cap was reached in May."[37] In recent years, the issue of H-1B caps has only increased in importance. In 2008, H-1B slots were filled in one day, a record, and recent proposed legislation has sought to increase the cap from 63,000 slots per year to 130,000 slots per year.[38]

The use of temporary workers and consultants is increasing to help fill voids in staffing, or by-pass merit systems that provide inadequate compensation. The benefit of such relationships is that an employer obtains specific skills needed for a short-term project, without the need for training or for a lengthy (time-consuming) recruitment process. The trade-off is that the employer does not retain the talents and skills of temporary worker or consultant beyond the length of the project; the level of compensation paid is higher than that of regular staff; and the level of continuity and commitment on a project is always suspect. As a result, compensation equity among the workforce is a difficult goal to achieve when there are significant external forces requiring competitive responses on a number of fronts.

Discussion Questions

1. What factors make recruiting of IT professionals a challenge?
2. If your organization recruits for IT professionals, what steps has it had to take to get the best-qualified candidates?
3. Are merit principles compromised with hiring practices that short-circuit traditional merit systems administrative routine?
4. While the acquisition function clearly is affected by the shortage of IT professionals, what other functions are affected? How?

Notes

1. U.S. Department of Justice (June 24, 2008). In Investigation of Allegations of Politicized Hiring in the Department of Justice Honors Program and Summer Law Intern Program. Available at: http://www.usdoj.gov/oig/special/s0806/final.pdf (accessed on August 12, 2008).
2. Mosher, F. C. (1982). *Democracy and the public service* (2nd ed.). New York: Oxford University Press.
3. Arvey, R. D., and P. R. Sackett (1993). Fairness in selection: Current developments and perspectives. In N. Schmitt, W. C. Borman, and Associates (eds.). *Personnel selection in organizations.* San Francisco, CA: Jossey-Bass, pp. 199–200.
4. Voinovich, Sen. George V. (2000). Report to the President: The Crisis in Human Capital. Subcommittee on Oversight of Government Management, Restructuring, and the District of Columbia. Committee on Governmental Affairs. United States Senate. December 2000.
5. Partnership for Public Service (2008). *Issue Brief Brain Drain 2008,* pp. 1–2. www.ourpublicservice.org.
6. Ibid., p. 2.
7. Borman, W. C., and S. J. Motowidlo (1993). Expanding the criterion domain to include elements of contextual performance. In N. Schmitt, W. C. Borman, and Associates (eds.). *Personnel selection in organizations.* San Francisco, CA: Jossey-Bass, p. 73.
8. Ibid., p. 73.
9. Guion, R. M. (1993). The need for change: Six persistent themes. In N. Schmitt, W. C. Borman, and Associates (eds.). *Personnel selection in organizations.* San Francisco, CA: Jossey-Bass, p. 491.
10. Ibid., p. 493.
11. Mintzberg, H. (May–June 1996). Managing government and governing management. *Harvard Business Review, 74*: 75–80.

12. Hesselbein, F., M. Goldsmith, and R. Beckhard (1996). *The leader of the future*. San Francisco, CA: Jossey Bass.
13. Llorens, J., and J. E. Kellough (2008). A revolution in public personnel administration: The growth of Web-based recruitment and selection processes in the federal service. *Public Personnel Management, 36* (3); 207–221.
14. Arvey, R. D., and R. H. Faley (1988). *Fairness in selecting employees* (2nd ed.). Reading, MA: Addison-Wesley.
15. Dipboye, R. L., and B. B. Gaugler (1993). Cognitive and behavioral processes in the selection interview. In N. Schmitt, W. C. Borman, and Associates (eds.). *Personnel selection in organizations*. San Francisco, CA: Jossey-Bass, pp. 135–170; Whetzel, D. L., F. L. Schmitt, and S. D. Maurer (1994). The validity of employment interviews: A comprehensive review and meta-analysis. *Journal of Applied Psychology, 79*: 599–616.
16. Arvey and Faley, *Fairness in selecting employees*.
17. Trice, E. (June 1999). Timely hiring. *International Personnel Management Association News*, pp. 10–11. Also see Sullivan, J. (June 1999). Gaining a competitive advantage. *International Personnel Management Association News*, pp. 14–15; and Greene, T. (November 1999). City of Hampton's innovative recruitment efforts. *International Personnel Management Association News*, p. 19.
18. Kellough, J. E. (1999). Reinventing public personnel management: Ethical implications for managers and public personnel systems. *Public Personnel Management, 28* (4): 655–671.
19. Kellough, J. E. (1993). Award winning programs–interviews with the winners. *Public Personnel Management, 22*: 1–5.
20. Hays, S. W., and Sowa, J. E. (2006). A broader look at the "Accountability" movement: Some grim realities. *Review of Public Personnel Administration,* 26 (2): 102117.
21. Kellough, Reinventing public personnel management.
22. United States Merit Systems Protection Board (1994). *Entering professional positions in the federal government*. Washington, DC: U.S. Merit Systems Protection Board, p. xii.
23. Hutchinson, B. (May 2001). Webifying the employment process. *International Personnel Management Association News*, pp. 12–14; Smith, M. (April 2000). Internet recruiting: The next best thing since? *International Personnel Management Association News*, p. 13.
24. Rainey, G. W., Jr. (2005). Human resource consultants and outsourcing: Focusing on local government. In S. E. Condrey (ed.). *Handbook of human resource management in government* (2nd ed.). San Francisco, CA: Jossey Bass, pp. 701–734.
25. Personal correspondence with the author, July 5, 1996.
26. Hummert, R. (April 18, 2001). Letter to the authors.
27. Alan Greenspan July 10, 1998. The Implications of Technological Changes, remarks at the Charlotte Chamber of Commerce, Charlotte, North Carolina.
28. U.S. Department of Commerce (Fall 1997). *America's new deficit: The shortage of Information Technology workers*. Office of Technology Policy. Available at: http://www.eric.ed.gov/ERICDocs/data/ericdocs2sql/content_storage_01/0000019b/80/14/ff/a4.pdf (accessed on May 4, 2009).
29. Dizard, W., III (January 2001). Economic downturn imperils IT funding. *State & Local Government Computer News*, pp. 1, 6.
30. U.S. Department of Commerce (June 1999). *The digital work force: Building infotech skills at the speed of innovation*. Office of Technology Policy, p. 11. Available at: http://www.eric.ed.gov/ERICDocs/data/ericdocs2sql/content_storage_01/0000019b/80/16/36/2a.pdf (accessed on May 4, 2009).
31. Peterson, S. (February 2001). Security lapse. *The Government Technology*, p. 14.
32. Simmons, C. E. (2001) Secretary of Corrections, Memorandum to Senate Ways and Means Committee. SB96, February 5, 2001.
33. Simmons, C. E. (September 1999). Talent deficit: No relief for employers in new millennium; and recruiting techniques. *International Personnel Management Association News*, pp. 16–17.
34. U.S. Department of Commerce (June 1999). *The digital work force: Building infotech skills at the speed of innovation*. Office of Technology Policy, p. 15. Available at: http://www.eric.ed.gov/ERICDocs/data/ericdocs2sql/content_storage_01/0000019b/80/16/36/2a.pdf (accessed on May 4, 2009).

35. Based on the Department of Labor's Current Population Survey data, 1996.
36. U.S. Department of Commerce (Fall 1997). *America's new deficit: The shortage of Information Technology workers*. Office of Technology Policy. Available at: http://www.eric.ed.gov/ERICDocs/ data/ericdocs2sql/content_storage_01/0000019b/80/14/ff/a4.pdf (accessed on May 4, 2009).
37. U.S. Department of Commerce (June 1999). *The digital work force: Building infotech skills at the speed of nnovation*. Office of Technology Policy, p. 16. Available at: http://www.eric.ed.gov/ERICDocs/data/ericdocs2sql/content_storage_01/0000019b/80/14/ff/a4.pdf (accessed on May 4, 2009).
38. Perelman, D. (March 14, 2008). Bills Would Double, Triple H-1B Cap. *IT Management—eWeek*. Available at: http://www.eweek.com/c/a/IT-Management/Bills-Would-Double-and-Triple-H1B-Cap/ (accessed on August 14, 2008).

PART **FOUR**

Development

CHAPTER 9

Leadership and Employee Performance

In Chapters 3–5, we showed how public employers plan and organize the human resources needs of their agencies. These efforts result from policy planning and decisions that elected officials, agency executives, managers, and supervisors take in light of the situations they confront. Depending upon their role, some of these plans are made legislatively and others administratively. Some are made in consultation with interest groups, contractors, NGOs, and citizens, and others with unions and employees.

In addition, we have seen how agencies target recruitment and acquire staff, sorting out priorities among conflicting values. Having looked at the planning and acquisition functions, we now turn to the **development function**. It involves the challenge of applying employee competencies to organizational problems, building those competencies in light of future problems, and then assessing employee performance in light of organizational expectations. In this chapter, we will address issues of leadership and motivation.

By the end of this chapter, you will be able to:

1. Describe the differences between political and administrative viewpoints.
2. Describe how a market-based perspective differs from that of elected officials and public administrators.
3. Describe the concept of the psychological contract and how it can be used to clarify relationships.
4. Describe the basic components of equity and expectancy theory.
5. Describe the ways in which elected officials, managers, and personnel specialists affect an employee's motivation to perform.
6. Discuss the meaning of "spirituality at work."
7. Describe the ways that elected officials, managers, and personnel specialists affect an employee's ability to perform.
8. Identify four innovations to enhance productivity: total quality management, job enrichment, work-life balance, and teamwork.

DIFFERENCES BETWEEN POLITICAL AND ADMINISTRATIVE VIEWPOINTS

We can think strategically as well as practically about leadership and motivation—the development function. Thinking strategically requires that agency managers understand the broad demographic trends outlined earlier that affect the present and future workforce. It also involves understanding and respecting different perspectives that elected officials and administrative specialists bring to their work. Finally, thinking strategically requires that agency managers have an understanding of theories of motivation as a building block for the competence needed to understand and influence employee performance. Let's start with the different perspectives that elected officials and technically trained civil servants bring to their work.[1] Then, we will add a third dimension, how a market perspective differs from that of elected officials and public administrators.[2]

One of the ways to understand the differences between politics and administration is simply to look at them as alternative perspectives, as **political** and **administrative logic**, rather than as behavioral differences. Figure 9-1 attempts to chart those differences in broad terms.[3]

For a politician, the primary value is responsiveness to the will of the people. This means sometimes acting to promote efficiency, social equity, or individual rights; sometimes representing the interests of a few; and sometimes doing what is good for the majority over the long run. The elected official's focus is primarily outside of the organization and into the community or environment of political interests that rally for and against specific policies and solutions to problems. Even when elected officials "meddle" internally, it can be justified in terms of an external role like "oversight," or helping citizens find their way through an administrative agency's labyrinthine procedures.

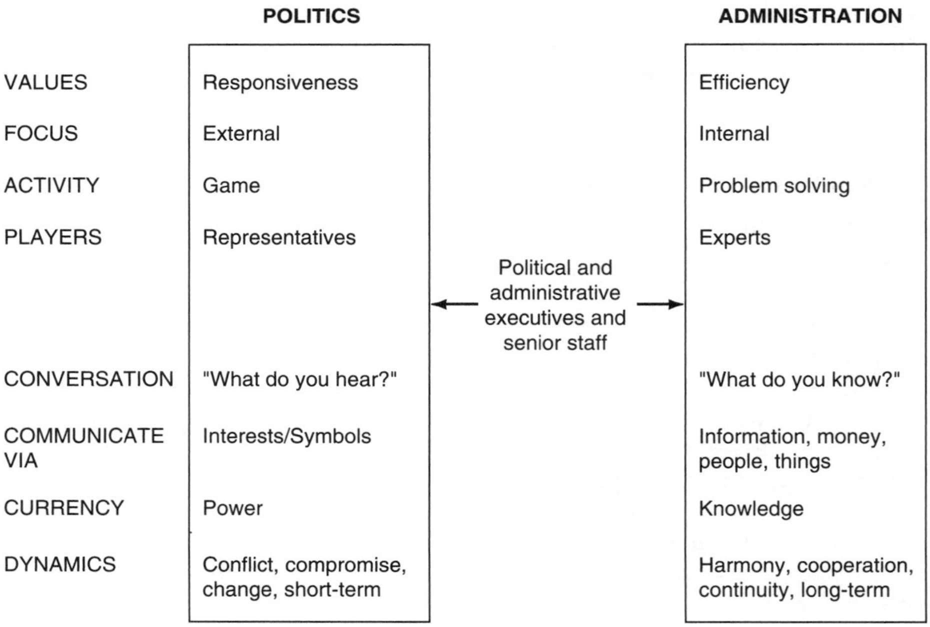

POLITICS
ADMINISTRATION
VALUES
Responsiveness
Efficiency
FOCUS
External
Internal
ACTIVITY
Game
Problem solving
PLAYERS
Representatives
Experts
Political and administrative executives and senior staff
CONVERSATION
"What do you hear?"
"What do you know?"
COMMUNICATE VIA
Interests/Symbols
Information, money, people, things
CURRENCY
Power
Knowledge
DYNAMICS
Conflict, compromise, change, short-term
Harmony, cooperation, continuity, long-term

FIGURE 9-1 Characteristics of Politics and Administration

To some extent, politics differentiates itself from administration in that part of it can only be understood as a game, with its own rules and strategy and tactics. We even refer to the game of politics. Partially, it is a game because the boundaries are so broad and vague. Elected officials must manage their own careers. They cannot count merely on hard work and conscientiousness to keep them in office, and they operate in a world of values where compromise and negotiation are important because "correct" answers are scarce. They come to their office with no special expertise and often without much relevant experience. They are chosen because they represent something their constituents believe will serve them well.

Because the world of politics is a world of conflicting values, communication is often through symbols that convey those values. Politicians love to tell stories and, in return, constituents tell them stories—stories about the (in) efficiency of government, about fairness, about the special needs they want represented. The currency is power. The bottom line for an elected official is the ability to influence other elected officials and build community consensus in order to get things done, and there is no formula for success, especially when referring to amateur politicians like those who serve in most of our governments and school boards. Hierarchy removes so much uncertainty from the lives of administrative officials that it is difficult for them to imagine the uncertainty that elected officials work with. It is hard for an outsider to identify how power is acquired and who is powerful, again because in most legislative bodies there is no hierarchy. In addition, in some governing bodies there is no specialization. The elected official's time perspective is shorter than an administrator's is because, for most elected officials, elected office is not intended to be a career. Even when it is, managing that career requires making short-term, noticeable achievements in an environment of conflicting values.

The administrative world is very different, especially at the level of the personnel specialist, the planner, the engineer, the water plant operator, the scientist at the Environmental Protection Agency, the systems analyst at the Department of Defense, the agronomist at the Department of Agriculture, the budget analyst, and so on. To these people, administration is not a game; it is about the rational, analytical application of knowledge to solve problems. While the problems may have an external origin, the focus is internal; the work is largely internal either to the organization or within professional circles. The water plant operator may never interact with a citizen unless it is on a tour of the water treatment plant; the same holds good for the budget analyst and the personnel specialist. Their professional/technical knowledge and the hierarchy they work in bind their world. They are experts whose knowledge has been acquired over years of education and experience. They were selected for their work based on their knowledge, skills/abilities, and personal attributes, and not because they appealed in some abstract way to a group of voters. In cases where work is contracted out, the distance between administrative and political worlds may be even greater, except in those cases where private firms are politically connected.

"What do you know?" invites a very different response than "What do you hear?" It suggests a factual exchange where those with the most knowledge are the most valued. Usually, this is reflected in a report. Problem solving requires cooperation, and fairness in the implementation of public policy relies on continuity. The administrative specialist thinks in terms of a career, and knowing that he or she is going to be around for the long haul, the vicissitudes of electoral politics are likely to be shunned rather than respected. For every elected official who has bashed a bureaucrat, ten public employees have returned the favor.

The following example illustrates different perceptions of administrators and elected officials.

August 30, 1996

TO: Journal Entry

FR: John Nalbandian, Mayor

RE: Differences in thinking between professionals and elected officials

Last night I was struck by the continuing differences I notice between the ways that staff and the council think about issues. The city and the county are considering a merger between the city's fire department and the county's emergency ambulance service. They would join to form a new city department. Now, the county provides emergency medical service for city residents as well as for residents of the unincorporated parts of the county. The city fire department provides fire service only within the city's boundaries. Townships and other smaller cities in the county provide their own fire protection.

It is clear that the merger would benefit city residents who have first-class fire service, but second-rate ambulance service because the ambulance stations are not co-located with the fire stations, which are strategically placed within the city. Both fire and ambulance personnel are highly trained, and the new proposal would require all personnel to become cross-trained within a designated period.

The chiefs of the fire and emergency medical service initiated the idea of the merger. The governing bodies of the city and county encouraged the effort and left it to staff to work up a proposal and work through the details of merging two personnel systems. The sticking point seems to be the differences in rank. In order to retain their pay and seniority, EMS personnel would have to enter the new organization at a higher rank than some of the firefighters. The firefighters have expressed their concern at having to follow direction from EMS personnel who aren't qualified to fight fires. Most of the firefighters have some level of emergency medical skills. When the issue finally came to the city commission, I asked whether the proposal had been formally agreed to by the three smaller incorporated cities in the county. It hadn't been, although the city administrator of one city said his council would favor it because it would increase accessibility to emergency medical service.

However, the issue for me is whether residents of the unincorporated parts of the county and of these smaller cities really will be satisfied with the biggest city in the county deciding about kinds and levels of emergency medical service for their residents without any provision for them to be represented.

The way I approach the rank question is simply to think to myself, "You (staff) get this straightened out or we'll just mandate something because it is clear this is in the best interest of the residents even if it causes problems for employees."

Well, we will get all this worked out because it really is clear that the public interest would be served by this merger, but we sure do come at it from different directions.

The journal entry describes an incident involving the merging of an ambulance service with a fire department. It shows clearly the different perspectives the elected official and staff brought to this problem. One was looking externally at a broader range of values; the other internally. The elected official was concerned about issues of representation and how the agreement would be seen by the smaller cities in the county. The appointed officials were concerned about how to integrate two personnel systems—the furthest thing from the elected official's mind.

As another example in the human resource area, the police department continually operates under pressure from elected officials who want to know immediately about that incident last night in their district. The elected official is trying to do the best he or she can for the district; to the police department staff, this is just another request that gets in the way of real police work. In addition, the police department draws districts and allocates personnel based on a rational analysis of crime statistics. Downtown interests to increase police presence to "manage" the homeless approach the city council. The mayor needs the support of downtown so the business owners there will not oppose a major suburban economic development initiative. The mayor urges the council to act on the homeless problem. The police department regards the "homeless problem" as minimal compared to their other responsibilities and shows little enthusiasm for the mayor's initiative, angering the mayor and his supporters on the council. Again, the perspectives are very different; and without adequate interpretation and bridge building, these worlds grow farther apart as communities become more politically diverse and problems become more technically complex.

These perspectives differ, but successful governance, including the survival of administrative agencies, requires a blend or at least some understanding of the other perspective. It is too much to expect the politician to understand the world of the budget analyst; nor can the wastewater treatment plant operator be expected to know what it is like to see the world from the council chambers. Those who speak both languages understand both technical and political rationality; they occupy the middle ground. This is one of the crucial roles of the chief administrative officer and other senior administrative officials and political executives or their senior staff. In effect, they are called upon to interpret—to translate the world of administration into value questions and to transform value issues into problems subject to administrative expertise. For example, at an orientation of new county commissioners, the purchasing officer was going over purchasing procedures. She said that staff was authorized to accept bids over the phone for purchases of not more than $5,000. Unnoticed by the purchasing director, the commissioners squirmed. After she had finished, the county administrator said, "I would like to clarify something. The sum of $5,000 may seem like a lot, but in reality staff exercises little discretion in this process. The commission has scrutinized and authorized the programs within which these expenditures will be made. " In adding this policy clarification, the administrator understood that the new commissioners were very concerned about their oversight role and about government spending. He spoke to their unspoken concern that went unnoticed by the purchasing agent, who was more interested in removing responsibility for "minor" requisitions from the hands of elected officials in the mistaken belief that they would welcome this outcome.

While traditionally public administrators have looked at their work in relationship to that of elected officials—the politics/administration dichotomy—the recent emphasis on **market-based values** adds a third element—politics, administration, and markets. In the privatization case at the end of Chapter 4, we saw not only our four familiar political values come into play but also the option of contracting out for the trash services introduced another very important element into the policy-making and administrative process.

We have suggested that thinking politically and administratively involve different mindsets. Thinking from a market perspective involves yet another. Administering a contract with a private vendor involves more than a straightforward contractual arrangement. It involves different ways of thinking. The private sector is not likely to place as much emphasis on individual rights and equity as the elected official or public administrator. Similarly, there is less likely to be much appreciation for the need to conduct business in the open. The need for profit as a driving force is unlikely to be fully appreciated by the public administrator. Elsewhere, we have elaborated on the market perspective.[4]

PSYCHOLOGICAL CONTRACTS

We have identified perspectives held by elected officials, public administrators, and also decision makers in market-driven organizations. In Chapter 3, we contrasted perspectives held by public executives, managers, and line employees. Based on the workforce characteristics described in previous chapters we can see how diversity will challenge agency managers. Since no organization can operate effectively without competent communication among those who view matters from different perspectives, we need a concept that will help one group understand and work with another. That concept is called the **psychological contract**.

A psychological contract is similar to a legal contract but with some important differences. First, let's look at the similarities. A legal contract between two parties sets out what each expects from the other and what each is willing to give to the other. These terms can be referred to as *expectations* and *obligations*. The parties will negotiate these terms, and when they agree, they can sign the contract.

The relationship between any two people or groups can be seen in terms of expectations and obligations. A supervisor has expectations of employees, and employees have expectations of their supervisor. In addition, each party is willing to obligate itself to the other in various ways. For example, the supervisor may expect a lot of initiative from employees and is willing to give employees the freedom needed to express that initiative. If the relationship is troubled, it may be because the supervisor says he or she wants employee initiative, but in practice the supervisor punishes failure.

The same logic holds when we look at the relationship between governing body members and civil servants who find themselves in a working relationship. For example, the elected officials may expect the civil servants to point out problems that need legislative attention. In turn, they may obligate themselves not to criticize the civil servants when they bring bad news to the elected officials. Obviously, this quid pro quo is not always present. If the elected officials "punish" the civil servants when they deliver bad news, they are less likely to have their expectation fulfilled because the civil servants will not feel committed to the obligation. In this case, the contract is not working very well and needs to be discussed among the parties.

While we can use the same terms to describe a psychological contract as we do a legal contract, there are important differences. First, in a psychological contract, many times the terms are not spelled out even though they are the basis for action. In the examples above, the elected officials and the supervisor have said one thing but have acted in ways that send mixed messages. Rarely is the discrepancy articulated in a forum that can lead to some positive action. Second, the terms can change over time, again without spelling out the changes. An employee, when new, will expect more guidance from a supervisor than when experienced. If the supervisor does not realize this, what is seen as helpful behavior to the new employee will be seen as oversupervision as the employee gains expertise.

One way a supervisor or manager can develop a relationship with a group of employees is with discussion that centers on the psychological contract and its terms. The same is true of a public administrator who is managing a contract with a vendor or department heads who are frustrated with a new governing body. At the end of this chapter, we have an exercise that will take you through this kind of discussion. Earlier, we described some demographic characteristics of the workforce of the future. We can expect to see the diversity in the workforce reflected in different expectations and obligations. Younger workers and older workers are at different places in their lives, and the expectations they have of themselves and of others will reflect that. The same can be said of obligations. This can be as simple a matter as how much time each is willing to spend at work.

When expectations and obligations go unfulfilled—whether they are made explicit or not—people can feel like they are being treated unfairly, and their motivation to work may be affected. For all the discussion in books, magazines, and newsletters extolling the need for leadership, there is no area more important for the exercise of leadership than clarifying psychological contracts, starting with supervisors and subordinates. Because mismatches in expectations and obligations can influence perceptions of fairness, we will look more analytically at how people conclude that they are being treated fairly or not. Then, we will examine a framework to look at motivation.

THE FOUNDATION THEORIES: EXPLAINING EMPLOYEE PERFORMANCE WITH EQUITY AND EXPECTANCY THEORIES

Equity Theory[5]

Equity theory helps us understand how a worker reaches the conclusion that he or she is being treated fairly or unfairly. It is crucial to an understanding of the "burned-out" worker, the worker who feels mistreated or feels he or she is being asked to do too much, the worker who feels his or her job is threatened but has no alternatives, the employee who is trying to balance family and work and weighing the consequences. Furthermore, equitable treatment of employees is shown to directly affect employee loyalty, expressions of good will, organizational citizenship, and "going the extra mile" (see Chapter 13).

The feeling of being treated equitably is an internal state of mind resulting from a subjective calculation of what one puts into a job and what one gets out of it, in comparison to some other relevant person. Inputs can include anything of value the employee brings that he or she thinks deserves special recognition in comparison with others—seniority, expertise, type of work, difficulty of work, level of responsibility, and education. Inputs can also include the less formally recognized but still frequently claimed credit for age, sex, race, political influence, and other nonmerit factors like the ability to get along with others and the demands that family life places on the employee. These determinations can be very subjective. Outcome credits have an equally wide range: job security, pay, future opportunity, promotion, recognition, organizational climate, work schedule and flexible work arrangements, autonomy, a reserved parking space, and a certain size and location of office.

Equity calculations involve two types of subjective comparisons: input to output and comparison with other employees. The comparison is important. You may make less money than you think your education warrants, but if friends of yours with similar educational backgrounds are out of work, you may be thankful just to have a job. If they are working and make more than you make, your reaction will be very different.

The theory can be illustrated with the following formula, where one Person compares what he or she puts into a job with what he or she gets out of that job measured against another person—the Other.

$$\frac{\textbf{Person}\ \text{Inputs}}{\text{Outcomes}} = \frac{\textbf{Other}\ \text{Inputs}}{\text{Outcomes}}$$

Equity does not require that all employees receive equal outputs, only that outputs are proportional to inputs, and that employees with comparable inputs receive comparable outputs. For example, managers earn more money (outcomes) than employees do, but generally employees find that equitable because of the added responsibility (inputs) managers have.

There are several ways to deal with an employee's feeling of being treated unfairly. First, the supervisor must recognize that reaching a conclusion that one has been treated unfairly is the product of someone's unique internal logical processes, driven in many cases by a gnawing sense of injustice. The tendency to distort input–output ratios to justify feeling ill treated also impedes simple resolution of equity issues. The supervisor may feel that dealing with an employee's perception of unfair treatment is hopeless because the sense of injustice is part of the employee's character rather than a rational response to the situation. Nonetheless, the supervisor should try to find out what the employee perceives his or her rewards and contributions to be and who an appropriate person for purposes of comparison might be in order to clarify the source of perceived injustice. In effect, the supervisor can try to elicit the terms of the psychological contract that up to that time either have not been articulated or are not being lived up to. Finally, the supervisor can attempt to anticipate equity claims by making clear what inputs justify organizational rewards, consistently applying rewards and punishments, and specifying the reasons behind the actions. Supervisors who establish expectations and provide timely feedback on performance can also prevent unrealistic assessments of the individual's inputs and outputs.

Expectancy Theory

Expectancy theory attempts to reconstruct the mental processes that lead an employee to expend a certain amount of effort toward meeting a work objective. Its premise is that "motivation depends on how much an individual wants something (the strength of the valence) relative to other things, and the perceived effort-reward probability (expectancy) that they will get it."[6] It also augments equity theory in part by showing how employees' feelings of job satisfaction are translated into performance—if they are. Expectancy theory assumes that effort results from three factors:

- The extent to which an employee believes that he or she can do the job at the expected level
- The employee's assessment that identifiable rewards or consequences will occur as a result of doing (or not doing) the job at the expected level
- The value the employee places on these rewards or punishments

In reality, employees do not make these calculations explicitly or formally. Rather, they adjust their level of effort (or change focus from one task to another) based on implicit and intuitive responses to these issues. For example, if an employee is given a task with an indication that a promotion is possible for performing the task well, she will probably do the task well if she believes she has the ability to do so and wants a promotion. Given the same circumstances, another employee who wants to spend more time with his family may turn down the promotion because it means more work (an undesirable consequence), even though he believes he could do the job and might get the promotion.

Expectancy theory helps explain employee reactions to many situations at work including burnout, for example. Burnout results when an employee has challenging work (moderate to high confidence in one's ability to perform the work) but few valued outcomes are associated with doing a good job. Performing the job does not lead to rewarding outcomes. In fact, doing a good job just leads to more work or to punishing consequences without offsetting rewards. The consequences usually are a combination of *extrinsic* and *intrinsic* factors. For example, there may be little positive recognition of the work's value (providing **extrinsic motivation**) by the lay public or elected officials and high-ranking administrators. Successes are so infrequent that self-satisfaction or a sense of achievement (**intrinsic motivation**) is hard to come by. At some point, the person becomes burned-out—the effort just doesn't produce rewarding outcomes.

A temporary employee may expend a lot of effort believing that good performance could lead to a permanent job. If there are no positive outcomes associated with performing well, it is doubtful that over time the employee would do so. An employee who is trying to balance work and family may determine that the outcomes associated with expending effort on family life are more rewarding than overtime. Of course, the difficulty comes when this employee wants to be with the family, but the family needs the money the overtime can earn.

Expectancy theory and equity theory help us understand why the satisfied worker may or may not be productive. People at work can be satisfied for a variety of reasons that may have nothing to do with their performance. For example, an employee may be very satisfied because pay is good, the social environment at work is lively and rewarding, the working conditions are good, and the workload is not too taxing. There is nothing in these elements that would lead one necessarily to expect this person to be a productive worker. The worker may lack some knowledge, skills, or ability, or maybe he or she enjoys the work environment so much that it detracts from work.

In order for the productive worker to be satisfied, high performance must lead to satisfying outcomes. In addition, the recognition or rewards for high performance must be perceived to be distributed equitably. Furthermore, it is easy for a productive worker not to be satisfied. The worker could be very productive and be paid well, but hate the job, be overworked, see no value in the work, and so on. This is why the relationship between satisfaction and performance is not a direct one—that is, not all satisfied workers are productive and not all productive workers are satisfied.[7]

Using These Theories in Human Resources Management

The expectancy model provides an excellent diagnostic tool for analyzing an employee's work behavior because it focuses attention on how the organization affects employee effort and performance in several ways. First, the probability that effort will result in task performance is low if the task is difficult and high if the task is easy. But since easy jobs are usually boring, supervisors must delegate responsibility appropriately by striking a balance between setting a performance level so high as to be perceived as unattainable, or so low as to be seen as attainable but boring. Second, the perceived equity and adequacy of performance evaluation and reward systems have a major influence on the employee's perception that performance will lead to rewards (or punishment). Performance appraisal systems that do not distinguish high and low performers, or that do not result in differential rewards (or punishments) for them, will lead to a downward adjustment of inputs to meet outputs by all workers. Finally, consequences must be desirable to result in effort. A detective, who is rewarded for solving cases quickly and well by the assignment of more cases and more difficult ones, will soon learn to work more slowly, unless other rewards are available to adjust the balance or the cases turn out to be interesting and intrinsically rewarding to work on.

Let's look at how equity theory helps explain one segment in the life of the modern worker. Bill (the Other in the formula above) works very hard and has done work over and above the call of duty (Other's input). One day the nurse at school calls him, says his child is sick, and needs to be taken home. He talks to the supervisor who, wanting to be flexible in order to accommodate the family needs of employees, says to him, "You've been working extra hard (supervisor recognizes Other's input), go ahead and take some time off (Other's outcome) and we won't count it against your vacation time." Other says to himself, "I worked extra hard, it's OK if I take the time off without leave." Bill is a good guy, and this internal logic is important if Bill is not to feel guilty. Bill feels that he has balanced inputs and outcomes and feels no discomfort in what he has done. Sally and Bill work together, and Bill can serve as Sally's comparison other. Sally (Person) feels like she works just as hard as Other (Bill). Sally is young and single, and whenever she has to run an errand, go to the doctor, or take care of her pet she is told to either do it during lunch or take leave. She feels like she is being treated unfairly while having done nothing wrong.

Sally now has some choices to make depending on how strongly she feels the perceived injustice. A very important contribution of equity theory is its proposition that Sally's goal is to get the ratio back into balance. That is, equity theory is based on the concept of cognitive balance. People seek cognitive balance, and when inputs and outcomes are imbalanced, workers will feel motivated to rectify the imbalance. Sally feels like she is putting more into the job than she is getting out of it, at least compared to Bill, her comparison Other. She feels like she is being taken advantage of "just because I am single." She can voice her displeasure to the supervisor and hope that the supervisor will change the policy or treat everyone equally (different sometimes from equitably). Alternatively, she can simply acknowledge a difference between her situation and Bill's and say something like, "Bill really does work hard, as hard as I do, and he has a special situation that deserves the special consideration." If Sally comes to this conclusion, from an equity theory standpoint she has given Bill extra input credit to match the outcome, and now the ratio between Sally and Bill, Person and Other, has been restored.

However, if Sally does not acknowledge that Bill deserves special consideration, she will still feel mistreated. Her ratio of inputs to outcomes is out of balance when compared to Bill's, so she might just cut back on her own inputs saying, "If they won't reward me for working as hard as Bill, I'm not going to work as hard; I am going to sulk." This will work for Sally psychologically, as long as she is willing to accept the consequences of not performing at her former level. If she is working in an organization where she feels her job is in some jeopardy, Sally may not say anything to her supervisor about her displeasure or cut back on her work, but she may simply internalize the displeasure. She can become a disgruntled employee if the injustice is felt strongly enough. From her view, the supervisor acted unfairly; from Bill's point of view, the supervisor acted justly; and from the supervisor's view, he acted with consideration for Bill's special needs. If none of the parties talks about this, it simply gets pushed into an interpersonal underworld where it will affect their relationships, but in ways that will not be easily understood.

Equity theory and expectancy theory lead thoughtful supervisors away from more prescriptive, universal theories of human motivation and performance (such as Maslow's hierarchy of needs or Herzberg's motivator-hygiene theory). In reality, employees are individuals with subjective perceptions of their own needs and abilities. No employee is an unmotivated person. Everyone is motivated to certain behaviors. For example, the employee who expends little effort at work may play his or her heart out for the softball team. The failure of an employee to expend desired effort at work can be attributed to factors identified through equity and expectancy theory. These theories provide useful starting points. Effective human resource managers are those who can develop personnel functions that recognize the impact of organizational climate on employee performance, and good supervisors are those who can use these systems to develop relationships based on open communication and trust.

INFLUENCES ON EMPLOYEES' MOTIVATION TO PERFORM

Both equity and expectancy theories speak to our understanding of employee performance by focusing our attention in part on the willingness of employees to perform and their ability to perform. In this section, we will explore several factors that influence motivation and ability. In addition, we will suggest techniques and alternative work systems that would strengthen motivation and ability. Throughout this discussion, it should be evident that we are discussing the shared roles of personnel managers, supervisors, and appointed and elected officials in promoting effective employee performance.

Increasing Employee Motivation

There is an array of organizational and environmental factors that affects employee motivation or effort. Political leaders, agency managers, and human resource directors are responsible for creating and funding human resource programs that provide incentives for superior performance. With regard to pay for performance, will sufficient money be appropriated so that it actually serves as a reward, or will the amount merely symbolize an effort to make government more like a business?[8] Politicians and agency executives are so engaged externally that sound internal human resource practices often fall beyond their attention span, even though the decisions they might make can have crucial impact on the ability of managers to manage.[9]

Political considerations may require compromises on staffing levels, wages, benefit packages, the availability of incentives, privatization, and contracting out. For most politicians, these compromises are ends in themselves. Their primary goal is to get something done amidst conflicting political objectives, and their work is done when the policy compromise is reached. Many of the nitty-gritty consequences of these decisions are simply left to managers to deal with. Managers trying to promote progressive and comprehensive changes internally face uphill battles in this environment, and their primary task must be to make elected officials and political executives aware of the consequences of the political compromises on their agency's day-to-day operations.

At the departmental level, linking incentives to desired performance will critically affect the employee's belief that high performance will be rewarded and poor performance dealt with. The creation of challenging jobs will tap the intrinsic desire people have to master their work and avoid boring, fatiguing activities that hold few positive outcomes. Moreover, establishing career paths allows employees to look ahead to a future with their employer. Endorsement of fair but streamlined disciplinary procedures will carry the message to managers as well as employees that unsatisfactory performance will not be overlooked. The goal of linking consequences to desired performance is behind many contemporary reforms in public human resources compensation systems.

Perhaps, the greatest influence on employee effort involves the fairness with which employees feel they are being treated. The day-to-day interactions between supervisor and subordinate, the small seemingly inconsequential matters of doing one's job daily, and the cordial relationships between coworkers are the foundation on which employees build trust that they will be treated fairly by those applying the organization's policies and procedures. Thus, the organizational climate in the work unit as guided by the manager will be the main determinant of the perception of fairness for the entire organization.[10] The personnel office, in turn, can influence this climate indirectly by training supervisors on how to create positive working conditions for employees and how to enhance perceptions of equity in the workplace. They can monitor pay and evaluation processes to ensure no obvious abuses are occurring. They can assist departments in the design of challenging jobs and can work toward developing classification and compensation plans that foster innovative work design and work assignments, and the availability of monetary incentives.

Public Service Motive

One way to influence employee motivation is to acknowledge what research is beginning to show—there is something that can be called a **public service motive**. That is, people are drawn to public service, in varying degrees of course, by a desire to serve.[11] Brewer, Coleman Selden, and Facer have shown that this desire can be divided into four more specific motives: Samaritans—guardians of the underprivileged; communitarians—motivated by sentiments of civic duty and public service; patriots—acting for the good of the public; and humanitarians—those motivated by a strong sense of social justice.[12]

Huddleston's interview project with Senior Executive Service award winners corroborates the presence of a public service motive.[13] Perry, Brudney, Coursey, and Littlepage report similar findings based on studies of award-winning volunteers.[14] To the extent that a public service motive exists, its implications for human resources management are clear. The work itself can be motivating, and making a difference can increase employee commitment. Too much emphasis on making government run like a business, with focus on financial incentives to the exclusion of rewards that recognize the **public service motivation**, could have a negative effect on these members of the workforce. Similarly, contracting out for work that attracted public employees to government service may have a negative effect on their motivation and commitment.

Spirituality in Organizations

Recent work by Perry and his colleagues, cited above, not only found the presence of a public service motive among award-winning volunteers, it also showed that spirituality is commonly associated with pubic service motives. Traditionally, we have viewed religion and organizational life as distinct arenas. Nevertheless, while there may be legal reasons to separate church and state, as individuals we have trouble separating our spirituality from our work.

What exactly do we mean by **spirituality in the workplace**? Unfortunately, there is no easy answer to this question that has been explored in some depth.[15] First, the familiar reference to public service as a "calling" evokes a sense of the spirit. Then, we can call upon a couple of descriptions to help us intuitively grasp a further meaning. According to Nash and McClennan, it is the "maintenance of perspective, a sense of calm and confidence, a spark of creativity, a feeling of being anchored and fully operational" (p. 230).[16] Perry cites a passage from an interview with a volunteer exemplar that seems informative as well, "I think it's the most basic . . . social awareness, having to leave the world a better place than they found it. And I think the best way to do that is not by giving money necessarily, although that's nice, but most of the people didn't actually make the money that they give. But I think that it's really putting yourself out there, and doing the work, and getting into the trenches . . . . I think it's a moral issue."[17]

It is clear from the study of spirituality in the workplace that we are not talking about religion at work, although authors disagree about the connections or overlaps. A second observation is that a "belief in the notions of transcendence and compassion for others is more pronounced in public service employees than in their business-oriented counterparts."[18] The issue no longer appears to be whether spirituality plays a role in what kind of work one is attracted to; it now regards what organizational and human resource leaders can do with this information. In part, the answer to the question resides in whether an organization's goal is to create a "culture of commitment" or whether one is satisfied with a "culture of compliance." Pursuing commitment requires attention to job design, what work gets outsourced and what work stays in house, whether employees are regarded as assets or costs, and whether they are being treated justly (Chapter 13).

Increasing Employee Commitment

Employee motivation and effort are demonstrated by **employee commitment** to the organization and its goals. If all a manager had to worry about was increasing employee commitment, the task would be simple—provide incentives, treat employees as assets, provide meaningful work, and recruit people who respond to public service as a calling. However, conflicting forces in today's public organizations make securing commitment a difficult task. On the one hand, managers are encouraged to promote teamwork and participative decision making to give employees more voice in determining how their work life will proceed. They encourage commitment to the work group and its goals, and they provide incentives to work together well. On the other hand, employees see the rising trend for privatization of governmental services and the downsizing of the public workforce in the interests of cutting costs. They see full-time jobs being divided into part-time jobs in order to avoid benefit payments.

Employees can become quite cynical about team building and commitment if they believe their efforts will not stave off the possible loss of their jobs. They may feel the conflict within themselves between loyalty to the work unit and colleagues and the necessity to "look out for yourself" in uncertain times. Increased union membership among public employees over the past several decades may provide evidence of these concerns. Nevertheless, managers need to continue to try innovations to build that commitment, while being honest with employees about the current status of the organization's plans because external political influences on government continue to demand more for less, and one can never be sure whether this is just rhetoric or a real call to action.

Flexible Work Locations and Schedules[19]

Several common innovations in working conditions serve to increase employee commitment. In the past, all employees were expected to have identical working hours and a fixed job location, but this is no longer true or necessary. Changes in technology (primarily telecommunications and computers) have meant that employees can work productively at decentralized workstations, or at home. The need for broader service delivery to clients and the complex child-care and elder-care arrangements necessitated by two-career families have resulted in the development of part-time, flexible, and compressed work schedules that respond to employee needs for **work/life balance**. The focus on employees as resources has led to the development of variable models of resource use that have proved effective at achieving improved performance.

Under **flextime**, all employees are expected to work during core hours (such as 9:30 to 3:00). Depending on agency needs and personal preferences, each employee is free to negotiate a fixed work schedule with different start and end times. Some agencies have flextime programs that enable employees to work longer days in order to have fewer workdays in a week or month (such as ten hours per day, four days a week). Research on flextime experiments in both the public and private sectors generally reveals positive results in employee attitudes and in the reduction of absenteeism, tardiness, and, in some cases, increases in productivity.

Job sharing is the splitting of one job between two part-time employees on a regular basis. There are obvious advantages for employees (part-time work rather than having to choose between full-time work and no work at all) and the agency (lower costs, more skill sets for the job). Job sharing requires clear expectations and precise coordination between employees, with their supervisor, and with clients/customers inside and outside the agency. In addition, the agency must develop policies for contributions to and division of pensions, health care, and other benefits.

Under flexi place, employees may work away from the office provided a suitable telecommuting workstation is available. This works best in knowledge management jobs for professionals who can work independently and yet remain in contact with the agency through a variety of electronic media (such as, conference calls, videoconferencing, and e-mail). Besides attracting competent individuals who value independence and flexibility, the agency can as well save its workspace from becoming overcrowded. The downsides, of course, are predictable things like communication and control, and unpredictable ones like workplace health and safety and workers' compensation claims. Presently, tools that can monitor computer work at a telecommuting station exist.[20]

INFLUENCES ON EMPLOYEES' ABILITY TO PERFORM

In addition to motivation, employees must have the necessary competencies in order to perform well. Legislatures and personnel experts have the most significant effect on the ability of the worker through the wage-setting process. The more money allocated to salaries, the more competitive a governmental employer will become in the labor market and the more talent it will attract. For example, some attributed the problems in the year-long troublesome effort to change a pay system at the University of Kansas to a vendor's failure to attract and hold onto the needed computer programming talent. Similarly, salary level and working conditions affect an employee's intention to stay with an employer. Unfortunately, public agencies often serve as training grounds for the private sector by paying relatively low salaries for experienced employees. For example, social workers hired by a state human service agency are usually paid competitive entry-level salaries, but if they are not given pay increases as they gain experience, they may choose to leave state employment for nonprofit or private sector jobs. This turnover of experienced employees can reduce productivity by making case tracking more difficult, by hampering management development, and by diminishing organizational memory.

Department managers and personnel directors affect productivity significantly through employee selection. If a market wage will attract talented applicants to the public employer, then the hiring process must be able to select the candidates with the best potential to perform current responsibilities as well as learn new skills and possess personal attributes necessary to work in tomorrow's organizations. Other important departmental influences on the employee's ability to perform include the quality of on-the-job training and coaching and the quality and timeliness of feedback regarding performance.

In the area of training, the human resource department has significant effect on the ability factor by conducting training needs assessments and by locating or offering training opportunities. In addition, the department can support managers by emphasizing and researching the validity of selection methods, by working with supervisors and employees to develop performance-based appraisal methods, and by increasing supervisory skill in communicating constructive feedback to employees. In some cases, personnel departments will track labor market conditions and gather data on prevailing wage rates for input into legislative decisions regarding allocation or collective bargaining positions.

ORGANIZING FOR PRODUCTIVITY

Productivity can be discussed in many contexts. In earlier chapters, we have discussed downsizing, strategic thinking, and workforce planning, and ways to calculate efficiency and effectiveness. This section describes additional elements that fall within the category of continuous improvement. In other words, we are looking at productivity as an ongoing or continuing function of management rather than a one-time intervention. These approaches show various ways that productivity can be improved by focusing continuously on human resources. First, we describe the legacy of total quality management, an approach that brought the term *continuous improvement* into popular management thinking. Then, we will look at ways to affect productivity through the design of individual jobs, attentiveness to work/life balance, and the issues associated with this potential conflict, and we finish with a section on teamwork and collaboration that represent ways of organizing to manage work.

The Legacy of Total Quality Management[21]

Total quality management (TQM) is a management philosophy that combines scientific methods for experimentation and continuous improvement of processes with teamwork and participative decision making as the approach for implementing improvement changes. The central theme is the improvement of quality and the gaining of customer satisfaction. While some regard the total quality movement as a management fad whose time has passed, as with nearly all business innovations, there are lessons to be learned even if the buzzwords have lost their currency. There are four key ingredients at the heart of TQM that warrant enduring attention. They are:

- a customer focus
- data-driven decisions
- participative decision making, and
- continuous improvement.

The organization is seen as a complex of systems, with each system made up of interrelated processes that deliver services or goods to "customers." Identifying and understanding these processes is often the starting point to evaluating organizational effectiveness. Finding root causes of quality problems based on observable data collected before and after implementation is often the mundane and difficult aspects of process improvements. In addition to evidence-based decision making, employee participation in diagnosing problems and identifying solutions has become the norm in management literature if not in practice. Finally, the idea that the goal of improvement is a mindset that permeates organizations that want to stay both efficient and responsive has become rooted in managerial lessons.

Job Enrichment

The effort to identify conditions conducive to high performance and employee commitment led in the 1970s and 1980s to research into **job enrichment**. "Enriched jobs" are those where performance of the work itself is rewarding. This classic work is worth reviewing because it conveys the crucial finding that the work itself can be motivating, and designing jobs with that in mind can produce rewarding results not only in terms of productivity but also in terms of commitment. Figure 9-2 illustrates this approach to designing work that leads to high job satisfaction and effectiveness. High internal work motivation, "growth" satisfaction, general job satisfaction, and work effectiveness result when people experience their work as meaningful, when they feel responsible for the quality and quantity of work produced, and when they have firsthand knowledge of the actual results of their labor. These psychological states are likely to result from work designed to incorporate the characteristics of variety, work with a beginning and identifiable end, work of significance, and work characterized by autonomy and feedback.[22]

Jobs that are high in these characteristics are said to be enriched and to have a high motivating potential. Whether high internal motivation, satisfaction, and productivity actually do come about as outcomes for employees depend on their knowledge and skill, their growth needs strength (such as the need for self-esteem or the esteem of others), and their satisfaction with working conditions (such as pay, supervision, and coworkers).

Results of research into this model have been generally supportive. Personnel policy innovations have been adopted first as experiments, and then as options in the "tool kit" the supervisor and personnel director use to match employees with work and to generate good individual and team performance. The design of jobs to enrich them assumes that employees are long-term assets.

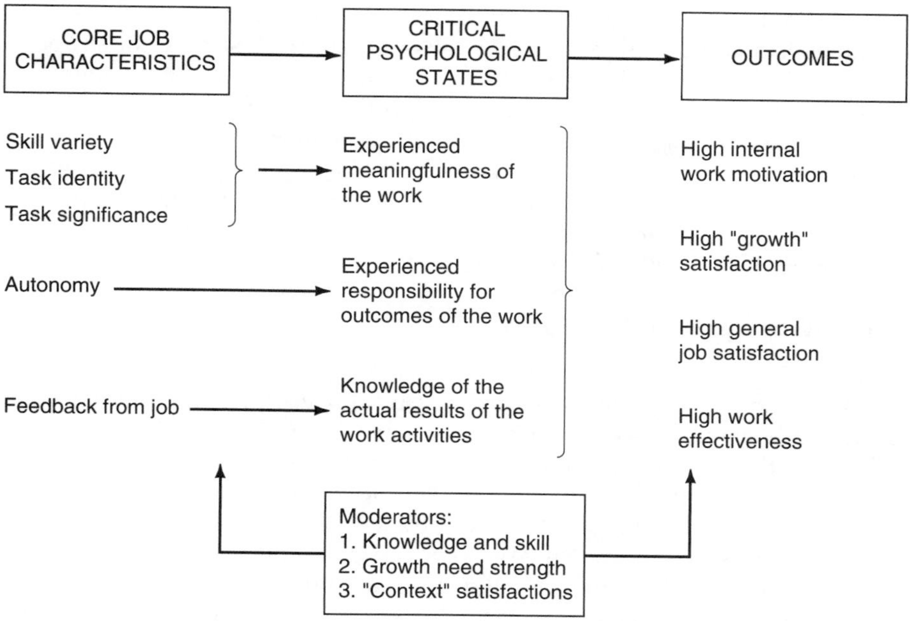

FIGURE 9-2 Job Characteristics Model. (*Source*: Richard Hackman/Greg Oldham, *Work Design,* © 1980 by Addison-Wesley Publishing Company. Reprinted with permission of the publisher.)

Work/Life Balance

The following 2007 statistics from the U.S. Department of Labor indicate the percentage of women's participation in the workforce, and with the number of dual earning couples on the rise, how important dealing with issues of work/life balance are both now and in the future.[23]

- 71 million or 59.3 percent of women aged sixteen and older were labor force participants.
- Women comprised 46 percent of the total U.S. labor force.
- The largest percentage of employed women (39 percent) worked in management, professional, and related occupations.
- Women accounted for 51 percent of all workers in management, professional, and related occupations.
- The higher a person's educational attainment, the more likely he/she will be a labor force participant.

Over the years, organizations have taken a variety of steps to help their employees manage the challenges of working and raising families. These programs are not only important to employees; they are important in attracting labor to an organization. Some of these flexibilities include scheduling flexibility, telecommuting, leave flexibilities, job sharing, employee assistance programs, child- and elder-care assistance, and subsidized transportation.

What factors really matter in reducing work–family tensions? In a recent study, Wadsworth and Owens found that coworker support, supervisor support, and organizational family friendly policies had a positive impact on reducing tensions between work and family demands.[24] Their study is significant, as they note, because it is the first that looked exclusively at public sector employees in this empirical light. In the U.S. Merit Systems Protection Board's 2007 annual employee survey, results show that 85 percent of those surveyed either "strongly agreed" or "agreed" with the statement, "My supervisor supports my need to balance work and family issues." Only 5 percent "disagreed" or "strongly disagreed" with the statement.[25]

Teamwork and Collaboration

Organizing employees into groups to work together on certain projects or on everyday tasks is increasingly the structure that public and private organizations are choosing. There are several reasons for the popularity of **teamwork** as the preferred approach. Organizational problems and issues are so complex today that no one person can grasp all of the information nor have all the skills to adequately and thoroughly analyze and choose the best solutions. The complexity of problems also requires innovativeness and diversity of viewpoints to see all of the options and consequences involved. In addition, today's most serious problems do not fall neatly into our traditional functional departments. For example, to promote economic development a local government must coordinate financial incentives, zoning and site plan issues, infrastructure issues, and code enforcement. In the usual organizational structure, this would involve several different departments: finance, planning, engineering, and public works.

The prevalence of teams coupled with the increasing frequency with which collaboration occurs within and between sectors as well as the emphasis placed on engagement of government with citizens combine to place significant importance on collaborative work and competencies. In fact, words like *boundary-spanning*, *collaborative public management*, *bridge building*, and *facilitative leadership* all attest to the way that contemporary work is conducted.

In a wonderfully creative and important project, Professor Heather Getha-Taylor set out to identify those collaborative competencies that set apart the exemplars from the average performers.[26] She found the following three factors essential to collaborative effectiveness: interpersonal understanding, teamwork and cooperation, and team leadership. Identifying interpersonal understanding as the most basic and critical factor—"which only comes through time and experience"—she poses the provocative question of whether compensation systems that are oriented toward results as opposed to processes are actually working against their goal of encouraging effective collaboration and team work.

Summary

Elected officials, managers, supervisors, and human resource specialists have a significant influence on employee performance. Within the parameters set by legislators and chief executives, human resource systems must be developed that make the fullest use of employee motivation and capabilities. This requires an understanding of what employees need to perform well (such as adequate skills, clear instructions, feedback, and rewards). The external focus of political leaders often deflects their concern for the impact of policy compromises on human resource management within public organizations. Equity theory and expectancy theory provide a useful framework to understand the links between performance and motivation and job satisfaction, as well as diagnostic tools for implementing techniques and methods and for understanding how and why organizational members are responding as they do to higher-level policy and managerial decisions. Those responsible for improving employee effort and performance must be willing to experiment with new approaches and to know how to evaluate their effectiveness in employee performance. The *psychological contract* is a concept that can be used to help explore differences that may be affecting the performance of an employee or work group.

Tomorrow's organization with increased specialization, downsizing, collaborative work, and pay for performance all add challenges and anxiety to the work of elected and appointed executives, managers, supervisors, and employees. Organizing work in this type of environment of change highlights the importance of an organization and its members who are capable of dealing with the resultant ambiguity and who are willing and able to learn from their organizational experiences and make personal and organizational changes based on that learning.

Key terms

administrative logic *208*
development function *207*
employee commitment *219*
equity theory *213*
expectancy theory *214*
extrinsic motivation *215*
flextime *220*
intrinsic motivation *215*
job enrichment *222*
job sharing *220*
market-based values *211*
political logic *208*
psychological contract *212*
public service motivation *218*
spirituality in the workplace *219*
teamwork *224*
total quality management (TQM) *221*
work/life balance *220*

Discussion Questions

1. Identify the differences between political and administrative logic and give examples of each. How important do you think these differences are when it comes to understanding the ways that elected and appointed officials act? What do you think is the most significant difference between market-based logic and political and administrative logic?
2. Describe the concept of the psychological contract and identify a situation you are familiar with where it might be employed to help clarify and resolve differences.
3. Describe the basic components of equity and expectancy theory. How do they help to explain employee performance? Identify an example from your own life where equity theory or expectancy theory helps you understand why you did what you did.
4. Describe the ways that elected officials, managers, and personnel specialists affect an employee's motivation to perform.
5. Describe the ways that elected officials, managers, and personnel specialists affect an employee's ability to perform.
6. How do you think a public employer should regard the issue of spirituality in the workplace? Is it an asset to be explored? Or is it a topic best left undiscussed?
7. Describe four approaches to productivity: total quality management, job enrichment, work/life balance, and teamwork. Select an organization you are familiar with. If you were responsible for

charting a strategy for productivity improvement, which would you focus on and why?

8. Select one or more jobs you are familiar with. Pick from those that you think are very satisfying and rewarding to perform and those that are not. Use Figure 9-2 to help analyze these different jobs. What lessons do you take from this exercise?

Case Study #1: Requiem for a Good Soldier

"How about Rachel Fowlkes?" Gordon asked. "She's certainly in line for the job. Rachel has had all the requisite training and experience to become an assistant director." Harold Nash, manager of the Department of Health and Welfare, rolled a ballpoint pen between his fingers and rocked slowly in his executive desk chair. "I don't know," he said softly. "I really don't know. Give me another rundown on her experience."

Clifton Gordon opened the manila personnel folder and laid it on Nash's desk. "Six years with this bureau, but she'd been with the old Vocational Rehabilitation Department for almost nine years before the reorganization. She started as a clerk, was in line for assistant director at the time we reorganized."

"We had too many chiefs as a result of that merger," Nash said. "As I recall, a few people were bumped."

Gordon smiled. "I remember that, all right. She was one that was bumped and I was the one who took over as assistant director."

"How did she take it?" Nash asked.

"No problem," Gordon said. "She was a good soldier."

"A good soldier," Nash echoed.

"She was very capable and versatile," Gordon said. "In fact I relied on her heavily for new personnel training. Many of those green young men she trained are now directors and assistant directors." Gordon pointed to the personnel folder. "Rachel was made acting assistant director of the information and public assistance section four years ago and apparently was seriously considered for the position of assistant director when Tom Walters retired."

Nash shook his head. "Regrettably, I had a difficult choice then as well. I had to choose between a capable career woman and an equally talented young man. Both were on the cert as bests qualified. In the end I felt Manpower Research was not the right place in which to place our first female assistant director."

"Now would be a perfect time," Gordon said, "especially in view of the governor's recent order on the EEO Act and the stress on the utilization of minorities and women. I think that's what all this talk of affirmative action is all about. Wouldn't promoting Rachel be an affirmative action?"

Nash winced. "Don't remind me. That report to the governor is due shortly! But back to Rachel; promotions must ultimately be based on merit and not on sex or color of skin."

"I agree completely," Gordon replied quickly, "but with all other things being equal, why not select a woman?"

"If that were true, I just might. But all other things are not equal. Not only do I again have several capable candidates along with Rachel on the cert, but there have been problems with Rachel lately."

"I wasn't aware of that. What's happened to Rachel, the good soldier? I can't imagine her causing problems for anybody."

"That's what I'd like to know," Nash said. "For the past six months I've given her several responsibilities and she just hasn't responded the way she used to. Her work output is definitely deteriorating and her attitude is, too."

"What's her complaint?"

"No one seems to be able to put his finger on the problem: I even had her in the office once for a casual chat, but she claimed there was nothing causing her any concern. I mentioned her slipping work performance and she promised to improve."

"And?"

"Oh, she's improved. I guess her work is O.K., but that old spark is gone."

"That's a shame," Gordon said. "Rachel has done so well . . . for a woman."

Nash nodded, "Yes, it is a shame. I'm afraid we'll have to look elsewhere to fill that assistant director position."

Source: U.S. Civil Service Commission Bureau of Training, *The Equal Employment Opportunity Act: Implications for Public Employers.* Washington, DC: U.S. Government Printing Office, 1973.

Questions

1. Using equity theory, analyze how and why Rachel's behavior has changed during the case.
2. What are the important inputs and outcomes from Rachel's point of view? Who is the focus of her social comparison?
3. What factor(s) has Harold Nash given input credit for that Rachel may have overlooked?
4. Utilizing expectancy theory, analyze how Rachel's behavior has changed during the case.
5. How has Rachel's estimation of her ability to perform as assistant director changed? Has the value she places on different outcomes associated with being assistant director changed? Has her expectation changed that good performance in her current job will lead to a promotion?
6. How would you define "old spark" in terms of a performance goal or job standard? How would you feel as an employee if someone failed to promote you justifying it, in part, by your loss of the "old spark"?
7. How do you think Rachel feels at this point in her job? How do you think you might feel? How common do you think the case of Rachel is in modern organizations?
8. Who is responsible for the changes in Rachel's behavior in this case? Who is accountable for them? What is the difference?
9. If you were Harold Nash, would you promote Rachel, given the deterioration of her morale and her apparent competent but lackluster performance?
10. This case study was developed over thirty-five years ago to support affirmative action by illustrating how managerial behavior and organizational culture can affect employee performance. Is this type of discrimination against women as prevalent now as then? If not, what general changes in employment law, organizational policy, and management practice have made it less prevalent? If so, why does the "glass ceiling" still exist in spite of these changes?
11. If you were Rachel, and if you confronted this situation today, what would you do?

Case Study #2: Recruiting a Water Plant Technician

The city of Valdez is recruiting for a water plant technician. Shelly Wong appears to be head and shoulders more qualified than the other candidates. Her knowledge is up to date; she has had enough experience to establish a reliable work record; and she comes with great recommendations as a solid organizational citizen by her present employer. She has outgrown her present job.

Everything seems to be going well with the recruitment and selection process. When Ms. Wong is asked if she has any questions, she responds, "This looks like a great place to work, but we take care of an elderly parent in our home, and we have day-care needs for our children." She continues, "I am looking for an employer who can offer a flexible work schedule. Will I need to take leave each time I have to pick up a sick child from day care? And on occasion my mother, who lives with us, needs transportation to the doctor's, and I like to be there when she talks with the doctor because she doesn't speak English very well."

The personnel officer responds, "I'm sorry, we run a pretty tight ship around here, and the water treatment plant technicians are mostly men who don't seem to have these kinds of needs. We'll try to work something out; we really want you to work for us. But I don't want to mislead you—maybe we aren't where we should be in this area."

Questions

1. Could the personnel director have approached this situation differently?
2. If the city wanted to "get where it should be in this area," what should it do?
3. How might each of the following productivity improvement strategies ease this dilemma (flex-time, job sharing, telecommuting, and teamwork and collaboration)?
4. What possible problems might this organization encounter in implementing any of the strategies you think might be usefully applied here? How might it overcome them?
5. Are work/life issues predominantly issues that female employees must deal with? Are there different issues for women and men?

Exercise: Psychological Contracts

Assume you are working to improve a supervisor–subordinate relationship. (If you like, you may substitute another relationship.) Divide into two groups. One group will act as the supervisor, the other as the employees. Each group should list the expectations it has of the other. The supervisory group should list the expectations that supervisors ideally have of subordinates. The subordinate group should list the expectations they would ideally have of supervisors. Do the same for obligations. Do not include simplistic items on your lists like "honesty" or "open communication." Try to be more specific.

Share your lists. Put the subordinates' obligations next to the supervisors' expectations and the supervisors' obligations next to the subordinates' expectations. Compare the lists. See if what one group expects, the other is willing to give. Can you tell from your lists whether you have the basis for a good relationship? If not, what needs to be altered, added, or subtracted?

Is the ideal relationship you have described oriented toward traditional hierarchy or is it more team oriented? How would you alter your lists to make them more team oriented?

Could you do this exercise at work? If not, what is holding you back? What kind of responsibility could YOU take to help promote this kind of discussion in your work group?

Notes

1. Nalbandian, J. (1994). Reflections of a "pracademic" on the logic of politics and administration. *Public Administration Review, 54*: 531.
2. Klingner, D. E., J. Nalbandian, and B. S. Romzek (2002). Politics, administration, and markets. *American Review of Public Administration, 32*: 117–144.
3. Nalbandian, Reflections of a "pracademic" on the logic of politics and administration.
4. Klingner, Nalbandian, and Romzek, Politics, administration, and markets.
5. Adams, J. S. (1965). Inequity in social exchange. In L. Berkowitz (ed.). *Advances in Experimental Social Psychology* (Vol. 2). New York: Academic Press.
6. Vroom, V. H. (1964). *Work and motivation.* New York: John Wiley.
7. Bowling, N. A. (2007). Is the job satisfaction–job performance relationship spurious? A meta-analytic examination. *Journal of Vocational Behavior, 71* (2): 167–185.
8. Perry, J. L., D. Mesch, and L. Paarlberg (2006). Motivating employees in a new governance era: The performance paradigm revisited. *Public Administration Review, 66* (4): 505–515.
9. Michaels, J. E. (2005). *Becoming an effective political appointee: 7 Lessons from experienced appointees.* Washington, DC: IBM Center for the Business of Government.
10. Salamon, S. D., and S. L. Robinson (2008). Trust that binds: The impact of collective felt trust on organizational performance. *Journal of Applied Psychology, 93* (3); 593–601.
11. Perry, J. L. (1997). Antecedents of public service motivation. *Journal of Public Administration Research and Theory, 7* (2): 181–197; Coursey, D. H., J. L. Perry, and J. L. Brudney (2008). Psychometric verification of public service motivation instrument. *Review of Public Personnel Administration, 28* (1): 79–90.
12. Brewer, G. A., S. Coleman Selden, and R. L. Facer, II (2000). Individual conceptions of public service motivation. *Public Administration Review, 60* (3): 254–264.
13. Huddleston, M. W. (1999). *Profiles in excellence: Conversations with the best of America's career executive service.* Arlington, VA: The Pricewater houseCoopers Endowment for the Business of Government.
14. Perry, J. L., J. L. Brudney, D. Coursey, and L. Littlepage (2008). What drives morally committed citizens? A study of the antecedents of public service motivation. *Public Administration Review, 68* (3): 445–458.
15. Houston, D. J., and K. E. Cartwright (2007). Spirituality and public service. *Public Administration Review, 67* (1): 88–102; King, S. M. (2007). Religion, spirituality, and the workplace:

Challenges for public administration. *Public Administration Review, 67* (1): 103–114.

16. Nash, L., and S. McLennan (2001). *Church on Sunday, Work on Monday: The challenge of fusing christian values with business life.* San Francisco, CA: Jossey Bass.
17. Perry, Brudney, Coursey, and Littlepage, What drives morally committed citizens? A study of the antecedents of public service motivation, p. 453.
18. Houston and Cartwright, Spirituality and public service.
19. Office of Personnel Management (2005). *Work arrangements and quality of work/life.* www.opm.gov/hcaaf_resource_center/assets/TAL_tool10.pdf
20. Baker, S. (2008). *The Numerati.* Boston, MA: Houghton Mifflin Company. Chapter 2.
21. Deming, W. E. (1982). *Out of the crisis.* Cambridge, MA: MIT Press; Hackman, J. R., and R. Wageman (1995). Total quality management: empirical, conceptual, and practical issues. *Administrative Science Quarterly, 40* (2): 309–343.
22. Hackman, J. R. (1986). *Psychology and work.* Washington, DC: American Psychological Association; Hackman, J. R., and G. R. Oldham (1980). *Work redesign.* Reading, MA: Addison Wesley.
23. U.S. Department of Labor, Bureau of Labor Statistics, *Employment and Earnings*, 2007 Annual Averages and the *Monthly Labor Review*, November 2007.
24. Wadsworth, L. L., and B. P. Owens (2007). The effects of social support on work–family enhancement and work–family conflict in the public sector. *Public Administration Review, 67* (1): 75–86.
25. U.S. Merit Systems Protection Board (2007). Annual Employee Survey Results.
26. Getha-Taylor, H. (2008). Identifying collaborative competencies. *Review of Public Personnel Administration, 28* (2): 103–119.

CHAPTER 10

Training, Education, and Staff Development

The need for greater investment in the training and development of public employees in this decade and beyond is widely recognized and is part of the strategic thinking explored in Chapter 3. Several factors, such as increasing retirement rates, are responsible for projected shortages in valued competencies and the resultant need for training. Demographic projections of the future workforce coupled with heightened demand for professional and technical skills suggest critical gaps. Rapid technological change suggests that the knowledge, skills, and abilities of workers today will be obsolete tomorrow. The mismatch is between the education and training received, and the changing knowledge and skills—both in quantity and in kind—demanded by organizations.

A common way of equipping organizations with valued competencies that will position an employer to respond to present and future challenges is to hire new employees, acquiring their competencies. Alternatively, an organization can negotiate with other organizations to purchase or lease required competence. As we have seen in other chapters, it is becoming increasingly common for public employers to contract with other employers—private and public—for both service delivery and staff work. In this chapter, we explore a third way of renewing human resources—working with new and existing employees to tailor, update, and develop new competencies.

Every organization must invest time and money in developing employees. Different organizations fulfill this function to varying degrees and with varying priority, and a survey of public employers conducted by the IPMA-HR and the NASPE found that 86 percent of respondents provided training for 75 percent or more of their employees.[1] Most organizations provide new employee orientation, on-the-job training, and mandated training such as training in safety procedures and preventing sexual harassment. Others have a comprehensive human resources development plan that includes formal and informal instruction, internal and external programs, organizational development, and sophisticated tracking systems connected to organizational goals and objectives for every employee. The **development function** is seen as more important in organizations where employees are considered assets and training is viewed as integral to mission accomplishment than in organizations where it is simply a cost of production.

By the end of this chapter, you will be able to:

1. Identify the relationship between training and strategic planning.
2. Distinguish between training, education, and staff development as part of the development function.
3. Identify issues and methods associated with developing the organization as a whole, new employees, and existing employees.
4. Identify and briefly describe the three roles of the human resources development specialist.
5. Briefly describe training needs assessment, design, and evaluation.
6. Discuss the way the development function is viewed from the perspective of alternative personnel systems.
7. Discuss the role that professional associations play in the training and development process.

TRAINING AS PART OF STRATEGIC PLANNING

Ultimately, when training is a component of the strategic planning process it broadens the development focus to encompass individuals, groups, and the organization as a whole. Furthermore, aligning a development strategy with agency goals has several advantages. First, it helps to clarify budget options in the human resources development area. It provides guidance for determining how much money an agency is going to invest in development. Alternative investments can also be evaluated in terms of how well they advance agency goals. Second, the alignment provides a framework to evaluate whether or not the development activity has actually produced a cost-effective result. Finally, it provides additional resources and mechanisms to clarify and advance agency goals. It facilitates communication about agency goals and can advance commitment to agency goals through participative and team-based discussion, and design and implementation of development activities. Linking training objectives to strategic agency goals presumes consensus among political executives, legislators, senior administrative staff, and union officials regarding agency purposes and objectives. The field of education provides an example where this external environment affects the training of schoolteachers. School districts often face the political reality of low pay for teachers and high demands for increased quality of teaching. Building a training plan to address the strategic goal of upgrading the subject matter knowledge of teachers as well as their teaching skills without acknowledging how the rate of pay affects the quality of the applicant pool is a political reality that undermines the linkage between training goals and agency goals. Similarly, the failure of a teachers' union to acknowledge skill deficiencies among teachers limits ability to connect training objectives and strategic goals. Both of these issues, essentially involving personnel functions such as acquisition and development, relate closely to broader issues of conflict among values and systems.

OBJECTIVES OF THE DEVELOPMENT FUNCTION: TRAINING, EDUCATION, AND STAFF DEVELOPMENT

Nadler and Nadler identify three categories of development activities—training, education, and staff development, which we think is a useful categorization scheme.[2] The development function is most often associated with **training** employees to perform existing jobs more efficiently, effectively, and responsively. But in many organizations, the development function includes more than training for short-term improvement. It is not uncommon for organizations to focus on the **education**, of employees for the longer term, to build the competencies they will need for promotions to specific jobs in the career ladder. For example, the U.S. Office of Personnel Management (OPM) operates a Federal Executive Institute and a number of regional Management Development Centers targeted toward both future supervisors and current supervisors seeking to move up the management ladder. Select training areas offered by OPM include "Emotional Competence: Working with Others for Results" and "Executive Communication Skills: Leading the Process of Change."[3] **Staff development** is designed to open the organization to broader vistas and new ways of thinking. Staff development aims to build the competencies of employees and teams, to enhance the general knowledge base of the organization, and to prepare a cadre of people to think strategically even if strategic thinking is not required in their present jobs.

The primary distinguishing feature among these three development functions is time. Training provides learning for current responsibilities and tasks. Much of this learning focuses on skill building but can also include understanding concepts and theories and increasing self-awareness of one's own personal attributes, perceptions, attitudes, and ways of thinking. For example, supervisory training often includes performance management as a main topic, which can include skills such as setting goals and performance standards, assessing performance, and giving feedback. It can also include learning theories of motivation and understanding one's own communication style and its impact on others. All of this learning is directed toward improving the supervisor's current responsibilities and enhancing managerial competence.

Education is more future oriented. It can include skill building but may put more emphasis on learning that can be generalized to different situations and on preparing the individual for new responsibilities and challenges. A supervisor who aspires to a managerial position may be encouraged to continue his or her formal education by obtaining a college degree at the bachelor's or master's level. A literacy program offered by an organization has specific benefits currently for the employee, but its benefits are more to enhance the overall functioning of that individual once his or her reading skills are improved.

Staff development is also future oriented, but the future is less clear and less defined. The focus is to prepare employees for changes that are not specifically anticipated or clearly known. Employees are being asked to prepare themselves to meet unknown problems and to be ready to face a changing, uncertain future. While skill building may still be a component of this type of development, the emphasis is much more on building attitudes and knowledge that are consistent with the organization's values and changing requirements. The emphasis is also on developing the competencies that will enhance the individual's ability to lead. For example, the U.S. Senior Executive Service has identified the following five core competencies required of its leaders: leading change, leading people, being results driven, having business acumen, and building coalitions/communications.[4] Many leadership programs fall into this category of development in which self-awareness, change management, strategic planning, visioning the future, and becoming a leader who will inspire and build confidence in others are taught.[5]

The distinction between training, education, and staff development is also mirrored in public agencies that have developed comprehensive sets of competencies for first-line supervisors, managers, and administrative executives. This emphasis on competencies, whether in training, education, or staff development, promises to connect the development function more directly to managerial goals for service delivery by focusing on what employees actually are capable of doing and what they will need to be able to do in the future, as opposed to time in grade and what they have been exposed to through experience and training.

We can look at current issues and methods of training, education, and staff development from three perspectives—the organization, new employees, and existing employees. What methods exist to build the capacity of the organization? What methods and issues focus on new and existing employees?

ORGANIZATIONAL APPROACHES TO DEVELOPMENT

Organizations are like individuals in some respects. Just as individuals seek feedback to improve, organizations and organizational units must undergo their own self-assessments. There are many ways to do this, and we identify and discuss some of them in this section.

Organization Development and Planned Change

Managers and supervisors are responsible not only for training individual employees to improve their work skills, but also for helping to make changes in the work environment so that skills are used most effectively. This process is called **organization development (OD)**. It developed in the 1960s as a combination of sensitivity training, a focus on the emotional side of interpersonal work relationships, and **action research**. Action research is based on gathering data about practical problems and feeding the data back to employee participants for interpretation and assessment. An employee-centered problem-solving process follows these phases. OD is similar to training in that both are change oriented. However, OD is usually participant focused rather than trainer oriented; it seeks to increase productivity by increasing employee identification with the objectives of the organization rather than by increasing employee job skills; it focuses on the process variables that comprise human interaction rather than the work product itself; and it tends to be systems- and group-oriented rather than aimed at building the knowledge and skills of individual employees.[6]

One widely used method of organization development is **team building**. Team building activities are designed to assist members of a work group to increase their productivity as a group. Typically, team building begins when a consultant is called into an organization to diagnose and correct a problem in the relationships within a department or between departments. Rather than define the problem alone, the consultant will invite members of the work group(s) to engage in diagnostic exercises aimed at assessing how well the group is working together and where the problem areas might be. Data are collected through questionnaire or discussion, then summarized and fed back to the participants. Work group members are asked to help the consultant interpret the results. The consultant might ask, "What do these data tell you about how well you are working as a group?" "What do you need to be doing more of/less of to increase your team effectiveness?" "If this group were operating at a high performance level, what would we see that now is missing?" Problems are identified, discussed, given a priority, and then a process for dealing with them is devised by the group with the help of the consultant.

Team building is gaining more notice currently because of the emphasis on teamwork, as discussed in the previous chapter, as well as less emphasis on hierarchy in general. It focuses on training individuals to work together in teams as well as enhancing the job skills of individual members because the capacity of teams is what will enhance productivity in many agencies. Thus, it is closely tied to a number of related trends, such as diversity training, 360-degree evaluation, team-based performance pay, issues involving mutual as well as, or instead of, hierarchical accountability, and strategic human resource management.

Diversity Training

The composition of the workforce is changing both demographically and in terms of the number of temporary and part-time workers, and these trends pose several challenges to the human resources development specialist. One of the biggest development challenges for public employers is accommodating administrative processes and human relations to differences in culture and ethnicity. As described in earlier chapters, ethnic minorities are entering the workforce at a faster rate than ever before; immigrants constitute a larger proportion of the workforce than at any time since World War I; and the rate of women entering the workforce is increasing. A generalized tolerance for differences and adherence to procedural rules simply cannot be expected to absorb the organizational shocks these demographic changes are bringing. Norma Riccucci points out that "Perhaps the key to preparing managers, supervisors, and works for diversity in the workforce lies in training, development, and education" and that "Managers and supervisors will need to be trained to learn and understand the culture of the organization and the rules, values, and attitudes that undergird it."[7]

The nature of bureaucracy itself may mitigate some of the differences. That is, job descriptions, work goals, performance standards, and the general impersonality of bureaucracy can be expected to have a homogenizing effect on the workforce. Nevertheless, the remarks of Bellah and associates provide words of caution. They observe, "Americans, it would seem, feel most comfortable in thinking about politics in terms of a consensual community of autonomous, but essentially similar, individuals. For all the lip service given to respect for cultural differences, Americans seem to lack the resources to think about the relationships between groups that are culturally, socially, or economically quite different."[8] The challenge we face today is whether Bellah's remarks are still accurate or are outdated.

It seems reasonable to think that investments will be needed in training and educating employees to understand, deal with, and even appreciate diversity. In some cases, however, training and education will not be enough. Organizations will have to come to grips with prejudice not only among Anglos but also among the minorities themselves. In such cases, organizational expectations will need to be clarified, and rewards and discipline may be required to make the point that, at a minimum, differences are to be tolerated if not valued. Training in team building and in creativity and innovation may serve to reinforce and add to specific diversity training.

Training in workforce diversity should include several components:[9]

- Skilled instructors sensitive to multicultural awareness
- Experiential learning, including role playing, exercises, discussions, and group experiences
- Flexibility and latitude for tailoring to specific work group circumstances
- Clearly identified goals that connect to a larger organizational philosophy and effort
- Evaluative instruments to assess effectiveness
- Follow-up programs and other activities because increasing awareness may occur in a half-day training session, but long-term change of attitudes and behavior takes much longer

Commitment to Continuous Learning

Underpinning many innovations in the development area is the overriding precept that organizations increasingly must prepare themselves to adapt to change. They can do this by seeing themselves as learning systems, with employees serving as both learners and teachers.[10] **Continuous learning** requires that the organization teach its employees new skills, new technology, and new knowledge. It assumes that the more employees know about their equipment and work processes, the better prepared they will be to discover problems and ideas for solutions. The commitment to continuous learning also requires that employees use their knowledge and skills to proactively discover administrative and production problems they can then help to solve. It also requires developing the attitudes of the learner—curiosity, creativity, open-mindedness, willingness to take risks, willingness to learn from mistakes, and willingness to teach others.

At first, the concept of continuous learning seems simple. No one consciously would oppose continuous learning, yet many resisting forces exist. In a classic article on organizational change, Chris Argyris identifies organizational norms like avoiding conflict and "straight talk" that work against questioning an agency's basic assumptions and operating procedures.[11] Managers are more likely to reward workers who solve problems rather than discover them. Further, in a hierarchical system, workers are often reminded that management has the upper hand, and improvements in work methods may threaten job security. In the face of today's external environmental pressures that require organizations to make rapid changes in the least costly way, organizational norms often do not allow for mistakes much less for learning from them.

Finally, history would suggest that organizations are more likely to make technical work simple; they mask its complexity in order to accommodate basic employee skills rather than investing in an upgrade of basic skills so that employees could learn more about their equipment. Rosow and Zager observe, "The amount of training required to profit from a new technology varies directly with the amount of diversity of new knowledge embodied in it."[12] In sum, a commitment to continuous learning takes more than a slogan on the wall or a phrase in a mission statement; it requires a philosophical orientation that challenges many of the ways Americans are used to conducting business and government.

DEVELOPING NEW EMPLOYEES

New Employee Orientation

Easily one of the most neglected areas of training, the new employee orientation can have several valuable purposes.[13] It can:

- Reduce start up costs by providing the employee with basic information in an efficient manner
- Relieve supervisors and coworkers of basic orientation tasks
- Reduce anxiety by familiarizing new employee with information and reducing need to "bother" supervisors and coworkers to obtain basic information
- Reduce employee turnover by showing that the organization values the employee
- Develop realistic job expectations and introduce organizational values and culture.

In conjunction with the new employee-orientation process, recent scholarship has focused on the dynamic of "onboarding" new employees. A report published jointly by the nonprofit organization Partnership for Public Service and Booze Allen Hamilton, a private sector consulting firm, describe onboarding as the "process of integrating and acculturating new employees into the organization and providing them with the tools, resources and knowledge to become successful and productive."[14] As the report points out, the onboarding process is distinct from the orientation process in that it integrates all aspects of the organization, not just the HR office, and has a much more long-term focus aimed at increasing employee engagement, performance, and retention.[15]

Training for Basic Skill Development

Public employers are no different from private employers in their need for job applicants with increasingly sophisticated basic skills. Estimates of the number of Americans whose reading, writing, and computing skills limit their employment opportunities are frightening. A recent report by the U.S. Department of Education found that 14 percent of American adults were "below basic" in prose literacy and 22 percent were "below basic" in quantitative literacy. However, only 13 percent of adults demonstrated that they were "proficient" in prose literacy, and only 13 percent were "proficient" in quantitative literacy. Overall, the report found that the vast majority of American adults operate at a "basic" or "intermediate" level of literacy.[16]

According to the Hudson Institute, while disadvantaged minorities will be entering the workforce in larger numbers, it is not clear whether their economic outlook will improve: "Unskilled and poorly educated workers will face multiple threats on tomorrow's labor markets. Modern technology—especially IT—tends to reduce the demand for unskilled labor. Globalization will increase U.S. consumption of imported goods and services produced by low-skilled workers. As a result, there will be less demand for low-skilled workers who produce comparable goods and services here. A rapidly changing economy will harm low-skilled and poorly educated workers who cannot adapt to changes in the workplace."[17]

The Hudson Institute's report *Workforce 2020* paints a challenging picture, and one that makes training and education not only an organizational problem but also more importantly a public policy problem of significant proportions. Just as many have assumed that government employers should take the lead in promoting social equity, it may be that public agencies will be seen as primary agents of public policy initiatives emphasizing **basic skill development** in the workplace.

In today's work environment, the knowledge of computer operations, especially of word processing and database management, can be considered a basic skill not unlike those of reading and writing. In this area, it is the younger workers, who have been schooled early on in computer technology and are more comfortable with electronic media, who will have the advantage over older workers. Unfortunately, some older employees are reluctant to admit their limited skill in this area and will not seek the necessary training. Their advantage of work experience will not benefit them in an era of rapidly changing technological conditions. However, it is also amazing how some older workers want to learn new technology that builds on what they already know.

Integrating On-the-Job Training (OJT) with Other Training

Sometimes **on-the-job training (OJT)** is carried out simply by directing an experienced worker to "teach Sam your job" or "break Jan in." It is often overlooked as an integral part of the development function, especially since it is directed in each unit idiosyncratically. For this reason, there is wide variability in the effectiveness of on-the-job training. It is among the best and poorest of development activities. It is done informally at all levels most often including new employee orientation and training in job tasks, policies, and procedures. Formal programs include apprenticeships and internships. A good example of a formal progression of skill training on the job is found in many police and fire departments.

OJT can be a highly successful and highly motivating form of training because the individual puts into practice right away what he or she has learned. There is immediate feedback on the level of proficiency attained, and it often occurs when the individual needs and wants to learn a particular skill. For example, a new employee is using the computer and is stuck because he or she doesn't know how to perform a particular function. The employee may ask a coworker who then spends a half hour instructing him or her on that particular function.

One problem associated with OJT activities is that it is not planned in any systematic way to provide a progression of skill development at regular intervals. If conducted haphazardly, there is no way of tracking who has received what kind of training. In addition, often OJT is not seen as a part of the responsibilities of supervisors and other employees and, therefore, they are not given credit or training for performing this function. It may be seen more as an imposition by the coworker selected to "in" the new employee.

Besides tracking and recognition as part of a systematic approach to OJT, evaluation procedures must be incorporated so that individuals will see their progress. Human resource development (HRD) specialists can provide assistance by developing tracking and evaluation procedures, by identifying skill sets which are appropriate for OJT, and by training staff to be OJT trainers. If certain competencies can be well defined, if instructional materials are developed, and if individuals can evaluate their progress, OJT can also be a self-paced, individualized activity with minimal supervision.

DEVELOPING CURRENT EMPLOYEES

Training for Temporary and Part-time Employees

With the increased use of temporary and part-time employees, organizations face the practical question of how much training must be offered to these workers. Since these employees may constitute a significant portion of the workforce, the financial investment could be considerable. Because these employees are often not considered as part of the "regular" workforce, their training needs are forgotten. It is not unusual for someone to be a "temporary" worker for two to three years and not have received any training. If there are too many of these forgotten workers in an agency, productivity will eventually be affected. There will be serious gaps between the competency of full-time personnel and temporary and part-time employees. There will also be a "class" distinction made, which can affect teamwork and feelings of commitment and loyalty. Further, in some cases, temporary appointments can be used as a path to full-time positions. If this is a regular component of acquisition practice, does it make sense to really treat "temporary" employees as temporary when it comes to skill development?

Coaching and Counseling: Whose Job Is It?

Coaching and counseling are often overlooked as training activities—yet every manager, supervisor, and HRD specialist at one time or another does them. Coaching involves a situation- or behavior-specific characteristic that has been identified as needing improvement. Coaching is conducted in one-to-one sessions with either an outside consultant, an HRD specialist, or with one's own supervisor. The latter option has the advantage of being conducted by someone who has seen the behavior in context and who can provide immediate feedback and reinforcement for improved progress. However, because of the inherent authority of the supervisor, the individual may resist revealing shortfalls and skill deficiencies. A crucial predicament for any subordinate is whether or not to share one's perceived needs with a supervisor, knowing that the supervisor can assist, but also knowing that the supervisor can make negative if unspoken judgments ("Shouldn't you know how to do that? Isn't that what we hired you for?") that can affect performance evaluations and subsequent rewards. This predicament is why new employees may seek more guidance from other employees rather than a supervisor. The solution may be to have individual confidential sessions with someone outside the reporting hierarchy but enlisting the individual's boss and peers to provide support, reinforcement, and feedback in day-to-day interactions.

A development activity related to coaching is counseling, a more general approach to helping the employee. It may involve correcting a particular behavior or attitude that is more person-centered than situational. It may involve career counseling to help the individual develop a plan for building that worker's career. It may involve helping a person deal with a personal crisis that is adversely affecting his or her work performance. While no one should engage in doing therapy without the clinical training and knowledge, managers and supervisors are often called upon to work with employees on a personal level. There are several points that should be considered.

Managers and HRD specialists should know their own limits and comfort in this area. A manager may refer a person to the human resource department or specialist for counseling without ever personally attempting it because it is a terribly uncomfortable situation. While it is true that referral in this case to HR or an outside referral may be appropriate, the manager will also need to increase his or her comfort level and skill in this area.

Managers and supervisors should know when and how to make referrals for outside professional help. Whether the referral is to an employee assistance program, to an outside consultant, or to another type of professional, it is important that they recognize what is appropriate and how to suggest this alternative in a way that will not increase the employee's resistance.

Department managers and supervisors should understand the human resources policies when providing coaching and counseling assistance. What is available? For which type of matters? Is training for managers and supervisors offered?

Coaching and counseling sessions should be conducted in private and, to the extent possible, confidentially. A climate of support will enable the individual to more honestly and willingly examine the behavior and issues in question.

Online Interactive and Self-Paced Training

With the proliferation of the Internet into many organizations and individual's homes, new, innovative computer applications allow training to occur wherever Web access can be obtained and whenever an individual chooses.[18] In Chapter 2, we emphasized the Internet as providing access to continuing education opportunities for human resources professionals, and that extends to all managers. Every professional association has a website and most post newsletters, documents, publications, and training and education opportunities. The availability of online journal databases promises to make research easier for students and professionals alike.

Distance learning between people geographically dispersed allows organizations the ability to provide timely training with minimal interruption to each person's professional and personal life, by eliminating the need to travel to and from a physical training site.[19] At a Training 2001 Conference and Expo in Atlanta, Mr. Tom Kelly, Vice President, Internet Learning Solutions Group, Cisco Systems stated, "E-learning will not put trainer out of business. On-site learning is still a good way to learn, but it's not the only way anymore."[20] Additionally, extensive and elaborate training packages for individual study can be downloaded or published on a CD-ROM, providing an individual a comprehensive and self-paced training session. E-learning is often more efficient than traditional training because it allows trainers to divide a program into smaller pieces; users can go directly to a specific part of the course they are interested in and bypass the rest, thereby saving time.

The Unique Role of Professional Associations

As work becomes more technical and professional, the competencies of employees are expected to increase. Associated with this movement is an increasing role for professional associations in the development of their members. In some cases, this involves certification and/or licensure with required investments in training in order to maintain one's good standing as a technician/professional. The International City/County Management Association is a good example of an association that has ramped up its investment in training and development opportunities for its members. It has identified managerial competencies; made skills assessment tools available to its members, the results of which lead to professional development plans; and developed a certification program for managers who invest in a plan of development. Further, the Association provides a daily brief of local government news online; provides informational webcasts; holds an annual conference as well as encouraging regional and statewide professional development conferences; and also sponsors special programs for "emerging leaders" in response to the changing demographics of the city management profession.

THREE ROLES FOR THE HUMAN RESOURCE DEVELOPMENT SPECIALIST

Trends in the development function affect the way the role of the human resource development specialist is envisioned, independent of fluctuations in funding for training, education, and staff development. The trend away from canned training packages to training designs tailored to strategic agency goals places the HRD trainer in a more essential organizational position.

Nadler and Nadler have conceptualized the HRD specialist's role in three ways:[21]

- *Learning Specialist*: facilitator of learning, designer of learning programs, developer of instructional strategies
- *Manager of HRD*: supervisor of HRD programs, developer of HRD personnel, arranger of facilities and finance, maintainer of relations
- *Consultant*: expert, advocate, stimulator, change agent

Although all roles must be filled if the development function is to operate comprehensively and effectively, they can be merged, and one is not necessarily exclusive of the others. The list roughly approximates the historical evolution of the human resource development function. In addition, it is clear that for development to be tied to the agency's goals and mission, the HRD specialist must be well versed in strategic planning theories and processes.

In general, human resource development staff must demonstrate several competencies to fulfill these roles: knowledge of the organization, its purposes, and structure; knowledge of adult learning; knowledge of the relationship between an organization's culture and its learning environment; and knowledge of organizational, group, and individual change.

These competencies and the trends in the development function create a career track for the HRD specialist that requires formal management education and a consultant orientation. It is no longer adequate for the HRD specialist oriented to organizational productivity simply to receive vendors and decide which training packages to buy.

Perhaps, as important as the human resources department enhancing their competence as development specialists is the heightened awareness that an essential generic managerial competence relates to facilitating learning and managing change. Specific competencies include building teams and teamwork, valuing diversity, supporting innovation, facilitative leadership, and empowering employees. Thus, while the human resources department may have a specialist role to play in the development function, the bulk of the daily responsibility for developing employee competencies rests with every manager.

TRAINING NEEDS ASSESSMENT, DESIGN, AND EVALUATION

There are a number of practical issues connected to training that HRD specialists face. For example, when is training appropriate? How does one design and evaluate training development programs? Even though we will concentrate in this section specifically on training programs as opposed to education and development, much of the information will be applicable to all three categories of development nterventions.[22]

Assessment Function

WHEN IS TRAINING APPROPRIATE? Training is frequently used as a solution to a performance problem without considering alternatives. Table 10-1 summarizes the causes of performance problems, the preferred organizational responses to them, and the personnel activity involved.

The first response of many organizations to performance problems will be to ignore them if they are insignificant or if there is no readily apparent solution. The second response involves examining selection criteria to determine if they really reflect the competencies needed to perform the job; and if not, then raising the standards or reexamining the criteria themselves. This involves a trade-off between the higher salaries that must be paid to attract people that are more qualified and the higher cost of on-the-job training after they are hired, plus the greater risk of losing them to a competitor once they are trained. The third response is deceptively simple, for it involves merely clarifying standards by providing orientation or feedback to employees. This assumes, of course, that performance standards have already been established for the job—a big assumption in many cases. The fourth possible solution is to train employees by giving them the job-related skills needed to meet current performance

TABLE 10-1 Organizational Responses to Performance Problems

Situation	Organizational Response	Personnel Activity
1. Problem is insignificant	Ignore it	None
2. Selection criteria are inadequate	Increase attention to selection criteria	Job analysis
3. Employees are unaware of performance standards	Set goals and standards and provide feedback	Orientation, performance evaluation
4. Employees have inadequate skills	Provide training	Training
5. Good performance is not rewarded; poor performance is not punished	Provide rewards or punishments and connect them to performance	Performance evaluation, disciplinary action

standards. Finally, if the problem is associated with the desire to do the work, supervisors may offer greater rewards to employees who meet performance standards, or initiate disciplinary action against those who do not.

Some of these options are more difficult to implement than others. Changing selection criteria or rewards and punishments may be difficult, because these involve changes in job evaluation and flexible compensation plans. Because training is one of the easiest options to implement, the probability is relatively high that it will be used regardless of its appropriateness to the situation and, even though it is problematic, it will produce the desired results. Employers can train their employees and increase their ability to perform the work, but, generally, they are in for a disappointment if they think one can *train* people to expend more energy on the job.

Before designing a training program or a series of training programs, the HRD specialist should conduct some kind of assessment. What problems exist? Are they suitable to a training solution? Then the content of the program is designed. Once the program is completed, an evaluation should be conducted to measure the reactions of the trainees and, where appropriate, the objective impact of the training on the original problem area.

ASSESSING TRAINING NEEDS Management may require training for all employees in a job classification without regard for data concerning a particular employee's performance. For example, all newly appointed supervisors may be required to take training in supervisory methods and delegation; or employees whose jobs require extensive public contact may be required to take communications training. This first type of **training needs** assessment may be called a *general treatment need*.

A second type of training needs assessment is based on *observable performance discrepancies*. These are indicated by problems such as standards of work performance not being met, accidents, frequent need for equipment repair, several low ratings on employee evaluation reports, high rate of turnover, the use of many methods to do the same job, and deadlines not being met. In this case, management's job is to observe the jobs and workers in question and uncover the difficulties. This may be done through observation, interviews, questionnaires, performance appraisal, and by requiring employees to keep track of their own work output.

A third type of development assessment is related not to present performance discrepancies but to future human resource needs. Nadler and Nadler would call these *educational and staff development needs*. For example, an organization contemplating the adoption of a new human resources management information system will need to account for the training necessary for the employees. This type of needs assessment is based on the anticipation of a future discrepancy caused by technological advances and changes in mission and strategic goals. This type of assessment may be self-initiated as employees are asked—sometimes as part of the appraisal process—to create professional development plans based on where they are in their work and where they would like to see themselves headed.

Planning, Delivering, and Evaluating Training Programs

DESIGNING A TRAINING PROGRAM Once a problem area is identified, an intervention can be planned. Often sending someone to training is a naively simple solution. To reiterate, training can only benefit an employee who does not know how to work effectively; it should not be used in cases where employees know how to perform effectively but for other reasons do not perform up to standard.

If training is an appropriate intervention, the appropriateness of a particular **training design** depends upon the target of the change. The simplest distinction in training objectives is whether the change will involve an interpersonal dimension. Traditional training methods, which are more directive, teacher-oriented, and have as their objective transferring knowledge, work best where the trainees are motivated to change, see the value in the change, and where the change can be readily incorporated into the way the employee currently performs the job.[23]

The more significant the change anticipated, the more likely it will involve rejection of something the employee already knows and relies upon. Training techniques appropriate to these situations must be trainee oriented, with the trainer taking a more facilitative role. If the anticipated change is tangible and involves technical training, the trainer must maintain a delicate balance between getting the material across and recognizing that not all the trainees may be eager to reject what they already know and what may still serve them well.

Supervisory training is probably as difficult as any other because it involves a degree of new knowledge, but knowledge that has to be filtered through an interpersonal and cognitive screen unique to each individual. Further, there is no one best way to be an effective supervisor. Mass production supervisory training falls victim to the charge that it is activity oriented rather than results oriented. Results-oriented supervisory training must at some point be tailored to individual supervisors. Regardless of the goal of the intervention, group discussion, case studies, and role play are techniques commonly used to get trainees involved and invested in the learning process. By encouraging the trainee to integrate material presented with his or her own knowledge, and by reinforcing the integration through performance at the training session, the likelihood increases that training will result in the learning of new behaviors.

The steps involved in tailoring a training intervention to a specific agency or work group move through five phases.[24]

- *Problem perception*: sensing that a problem exists because previous work methods or relationships are no longer effective.
- *Diagnosis*: defining the nature of the problem(s).

- *"Unfreezing"*: reducing reliance on unsuccessful methods and exploring reasons why standard operating procedures are not working.
- *"Movement" or increased experimentation*: committing time and money to testing alternatives and working to reduce the forces resisting change.
- *"Refreezing"*: integrating changes into the organization's natural work processes and anchoring them to reward, and other administrative systems.

The likelihood of change occurring depends upon several factors like the nature of the change expected. Does it present a relative advantage to the person who is supposed to adopt the change? Can the person see what the change will produce or is the proposed result vague? Is the change compatible with past practice, competencies, and values? Can the change be adopted gradually and incrementally, or does it need to be adopted completely?[25]

Evaluating Training Programs

Evaluation of training programs takes place at two distinct levels, that of the organization and that of the employee. At the organizational level, it is imperative that managers and human resources professionals demonstrate the utility of training programs or the returns to investments, commonly referred to as return on investment (ROI), in employee development. In an interview with the *Wall Street Journal*, leading ROI expert Jack Phillips states that in order for organizations to realize a positive return on their training investments, it is key for them to match training initiatives to actual needs, gain the support of managers, and evaluate the effectiveness of training efforts.[26]

To be effective at the employee level, training must address an employee's need or be intended to correct a skill deficiency. For optimum learning, the employee must recognize the need and want to acquire new information or skills. Whatever performance standards are set, the employee should not be frustrated by a trainer who requires too much or too little.

Many learning theories resolve around the idea of reinforcement. It is natural for people to repeat behavior that is followed by rewards and to avoid actions they associate with negative outcomes. If employees in a training situation are given no feedback, there is no opportunity to guide the desired learning. It is extremely important that supervisors understand the value of positive reinforcement. Supervisors are in the best position to observe performance problems, show employees the correct work method, provide feedback, and connect subsequent rewards or punishments to performance. Most organizational training is informal and occurs on the job, through precisely this process.

To justify itself, training must demonstrate an impact on the performance of the employee. By determining how well employees have learned, management can make decisions about the training and its effectiveness. The mere existence of a training staff, an array of courses, and trainees do not ensure that learning is taking place. Because development activities consume both time and money, evaluation should be built into any program.

Training can be evaluated at five levels: reaction, learning, behavior, results, and cost effectiveness.[27]

Reaction	How well did the trainees like the training? Do they feel they benefited from the training?
Learning	To what extent did the trainees learn the facts, principles, and approaches that were included in the training?

Behavior	To what extent did the trainee's job behavior change because of the program?
Results	What increases in productivity or decreases in cost were achieved? To what extent were unit or organizational goals advanced?
Cost effectiveness	Assuming the training is effective, is it the least expensive method of solving the problem?

Perhaps the greatest challenge facing those who evaluate training is to recognize that while most development activities are delivered to individual employees, the goal is to get the organization as a whole learning, growing, and pulling together. Modest individual changes directed uniformly toward organizational goals may be highly desired yet difficult to achieve and measure.

DIFFERENT PERSPECTIVES FROM ALTERNATE PERSONNEL SYSTEMS

The development function is viewed differently from the perspective of alternative personnel systems. Political executives are selected for their partisan loyalty and partisan policy orientations. Usually, they receive little training prior to or following their appointment, despite the fact that many have little public policy-making experience and few of the skills required to manage complex public organizations. Because training, education, and staff development represent time-consuming investments in the future, political executives, who frequently spend a short time in government, have little interest in the development function, either for themselves or for those who work for them. The function takes on a special significance, however, if political executives are able to influence the selection of training consultants.

As the permanent bureaucracy, members of the civil service value the development function more than do political executives. In fact, many professionals working for public employers, like those in health-related professions, are required to enroll in a minimum number of continuing education hours annually in order to maintain various certifications or licenses.

By its very nature, the civil service houses an abundance of public-policy-related knowledge as well as the competencies needed to translate public policy goals into service delivery and regulatory actions. The quality of public policy making depends on the knowledge of a government's civil servants. Without the ability to acquire and enhance the valued knowledge, expertise, and experience of government employees, civil service systems lose their credibility and focus as the reservoir of society's knowledge about its own problems. One could argue that because of major cost-cutting measures, the knowledge base of civil service systems has been seriously eroding since the late 1970s.

The development function is also of vital importance in advancing the goals of affirmative action because training and development opportunities that prepare employees for future advancement, such as management development programs, can greatly affect the presence of women and minorities at all levels of the organizational hierarchy. The concern in the next decade is that equity gains will be lost if women and minorities entering the workforce are not afforded an equal opportunity to take advantage of training and development opportunities.

The development function meets with mixed reaction in the collective bargaining personnel subsystem. On the one hand, union members value the continuous development of knowledge, skills, and abilities needed to maintain timely competencies and to involve union members in organizational decisions about work processes. Further, the development function is connected to a long-standing apprenticeship tradition involving structured experiences designed to transform the apprentice into a skilled craftsperson. On the other hand, because of perceived threats to job security, union members have often resisted organizational development efforts designed to improve the quality and efficiency of work processes.

Training is rarely seen as an organizational priority for temporary workers, or when a service is being contracted out. Temporary workers are seen either as sole proprietors, responsible for their own competencies and personal attributes, or as referrals from employment agencies that are accountable for their expertise.

The competencies of private contractors are accounted for through a bidding process where the contract itself specifies expected levels of services. It is important to realize that one of the reasons why an organization or agency would contract out work is because the private contractor has a higher level of skilled employees than the contracting agency. This is especially true in nonrecurring, highly skilled work.

Additionally, for many public organizations, the development and training of volunteers is especially critical to mission success. The U.S. Department of Health and Human Services has noted in its guidance to volunteer-based organizations that volunteer training be "specific to the requirements of the volunteer position, geared to the skill level of the volunteer, ongoing, specific to the needs identified by both the volunteer and supervisor," and "periodically evaluated to determine if it is on track."[28] The guidance also notes that the training of volunteers also has a value beyond just building competencies. Training may also serve as a type of reward system to motivate volunteers.[29]

Summary

Even though training budgets seem the first to be cut in times of fiscal stress, ample evidence suggests that the development function will increase in importance in the coming decade. Seeking quality requires an employer investment in the competences of a workforce that must become intimately acquainted with service delivery systems and committed to a customer orientation. The value of efficiency that is captured in the basic concept of civil service systems provides the foundation for government to face these challenges. However, investments in the development function go beyond traditional training and extend into the areas of education and staff development, where employers indicate their willingness to make long-term investments in their employees. In part, this depends upon whether public employers are able to view their employees as assets rather than costs and whether citizens are willing to do the same.

Strategic thinking in human resources management depends in large part on being able to connect the development function to the organization's short- and longer-term goals and objectives—identifying the competencies needed and then preparing to develop them. In this effort, every manager becomes a development specialist practicing facilitative leadership, developing employees, and managing change.

Key Terms

Discussion Questions

1. Identify the relationship between training and strategic planning. Can you give an example from an organization you are familiar with that illustrates how training is or should be connected to strategic thinking about agency goals?
2. Of the issues and methods associated with developing the organization and training new and existing employees, which should be paid more attention to in an organization you are familiar with? Why? How would doing a better job on the issue/method you selected make the organization more effective?
3. Distinguish between training, education, and staff development as part of the development function.
4. Identify and briefly describe the three roles of the human resource development specialist. Which of these roles or activities do you think general managers should be able to perform?
5. Briefly describe training needs assessment, design, and evaluation.
6. Discuss the way the development function is viewed from the perspectives of alternative personnel systems.
7. Briefly discuss the role and value of professional associations in the training and development of public sector employees.

CASE STUDY #1: Develop a Diversity Training Program

You are the director of the human resource development department of a city with a population of 105,000. Your city provides its citizens with a full array of services, including police, fire, water, sanitation, roads, parks, and recreation. Your city employs some 750 employees, including 150 police officers.

Over the years, there has been an influx of recent Asian immigrants and Spanish-speaking people into this city, which used to be predominantly Anglo, with about a 5 percent African American population. Some of the immigrants are joining the city's workforce and racial/ethnic cliques are developing. Over the years, the African Americans have complained that the police treat them differently than other citizens, and they are being joined by spokespersons for the other minorities.

The values of tolerance, dignity, and fairness were underlying issues in the most recent election for city council. The new council has requested that the chief administrative officer develop a program of diversity training to heighten awareness of the value of differences in the workforce and the community. The CAO calls you into the office and asks you to work on a proposal.

Develop a proposal that includes a plan for assessing the need, designing the program, and evaluating it. What problems do you anticipate with the training program?

CASE STUDY #2: Training Vignettes

What factors would you consider to make a decision in the following situations? Identify these factors from the manager or supervisor's perspective, as well as from the perspective of the HRD specialist who is called in for assistance.

1. Focus on your present work or work you are familiar with. You have an employee temporarily assigned to your area. What kind of training would you have the person go through if the person is assigned for three months? What if the period is uncertain, but you know it will be at least six months?
2. It has come to your attention that an employee who is going through a divorce is having performance problems (lower productivity, absenteeism, and tardiness). What would you do?
3. You suspect an employee has an alcohol problem. What would you do?
4. You are considering promoting a very capable manager to an upper level position, but his abrasive style is causing problems in his working relationships with peers and subordinates. What should you do?

CASE STUDY #3: "How Should this Management Team Work Together?"

The city manager of a suburban Midwestern metropolitan city decided to embark on an ambitious change plan. Hired two-and-a-half years ago, she has committed herself to decentralizing power and to encouraging more initiative and decision making from department heads and their division directors. At about the same time two other initiatives were occurring. First, a strategic plan, developed from a survey of citizens and focus groups and identifying several priority areas, needed to move forward to implementation. Second, upon its return from a national meeting, the governing body—led by the mayor—expressed interest in John Carver's policy governance model. This model structures the council-staff relationship in ways designed to keep the council focused on policy issues while providing broad discretionary responsibilities to staff.

The overriding picture emerging from these three initiatives is that, along with its other work, the council would focus on the policy issues outlined in the strategic plan. The staff would develop policy questions that needed council resolution in order to provide the boundaries within which staff could operate. Work committees that cut across departments would develop the policy statements for the council thus reinforcing the manager's desire to decentralize authority.

Attempts to blend these three initiatives have proven easier in theory than in practice. Several factors have combined in unanticipated ways to create obstacles. No single factor appears unmanageable, but in combination, they have created a lot of uncertainty.

1. With a change in mayor, the council's commitment to the policy governance model appears somewhat uncertain.
2. The organizational culture historically has oriented itself around hierarchy, with considerable focus on the manager's office for overall direction and decisions. This orientation has created a range of commitment from the department heads for the new initiatives.
3. A scandal involving a previous city manager has led to relative instability in the city manager position. Reacting to the relatively short tenure and different styles of the previous city managers, some department heads have decided to go their own way. They believe that they have been fulfilling their responsibilities quite well without the new initiatives. Some may even believe that these initiatives are just the latest in a series that stretch back over many years and see them as a diversion from the real work the departments must perform day to day.
4. A few years ago, one department, exercising its initiative, invested heavily and apparently successfully in modern management techniques and philosophies; it views the new organization-wide initiative with mixed feelings.

5. Lastly, the manager herself is an experimenter, quick to act, and unafraid of bold action. She espouses a desire to decentralize power, but sometimes in practice her assertive style contradicts the message.

Several division directors, department heads, and members of the city manager's office have gathered to discuss the situation. You are among that group. Here are your tasks:

1. Divide into three groups: division directors, department heads, and the city manager's office.
2. Within your group come to some agreement on a definition of the problem that now exists.
3. Once you have described the problem, each group should identify the responsibilities that its members should fulfill as well as the responsibilities it expects the other groups to fulfill if the problem is going to be addressed effectively.

Notes

1. IPMA/NASPE (2001). 2000/2001 IPMA/NASPE Benchmarking Report: Training, p. 2.
2. Nadler, L., and Z. Nadler (1989). *Developing human resources* (3rd ed.). San Francisco, CA: Jossey-Bass.
3. U.S. Office of Personnel Management (2008). The Federal Executive Institute and the Management Development Centers. Available at: http://www.leadership.opm.gov/ (accessed on October 8, 2008).
4. U.S. Office of Personnel Management (2008). Executive Core Qualifications. Available at: http://opm.gov/ses/recruitment/ecq.asp (accessed on October 8, 2008).
5. Examples at the local level include the Senior Executive Institute at the University of Virginia, the Public Employee Leadership Academy at the University of North Carolina, the Rocky Mountain Program at the University of Colorado, the Executive Development Program at Arizona State University, and the Leadership Academy at the University of Kansas.
6. Cunningham, J. B. (1995). Strategic considerations in using action research for improving personnel practices. *Public Personnel Management, 24*: 515–530; Gardner, N. (1974). Action training and research: Something old and something new. *Public Administration Review, 34*: 106–115.
7. Riccucci, N. M. (2002). Managing diversity in public sector workforces. Boulder, CO: Westview Press, p. 50.
8. Bellah, R. N., R. Madsen, W. M. Sullivan, A. Swidler, and S. M. Tipton (1985). *Habits of the heart: Individualism and commitment in American life*. Berkeley, CA: University of California Press, p. 206.
9. Smith, M. (February 2000). The impact of diversity training on workforce discrimination. *International Personnel Management Association News*, pp. 13–14.
10. Willingham, R. (October 2000). The redefinition of training. *International Personnel Management Association News*, p. 16.
11. Argyris, C. (1980). Making the undiscussable and its undiscussability discussable. *Public Administration Review, 40*: 205–213.
12. Rosow, J. M., and R. Zager (1988). *Training—the competitive edge: Introducing new technology into the workplace*. San Francisco, CA: Jossey-Bass, p. 9.
13. Brown, J. (April 2000). Employee orientation. *International Personnel Management Association News*, pp. 10–11; IPMA (April 2000). New employee orientation programs key to starting employees off right. *International Personnel Management Association News*, p. 12.
14. Partnership for Public Service and Booze Allen Hamilton (2008). Getting on board: A model for integrating and engaging new employees, p. 2. Available at: www.ourpublicservice.org (accessed on October 8, 2008).
15. Ibid., p. 2–3.
16. U.S. Department of Education (2005). A first look at the literacy of America's adults in the 21st Century, p. 4. Available at: http://nces.ed.gov/NAAL/PDF/2006470.PDF (accessed on October 8, 2008).
17. Judy, R. W., and C. D'Amico (1997). *Workforce 2020*. Indianapolis, IN: Hudson Institute, p. 49.
18. Hurdy, J. J. (March 2001). E-learning: A new tool for government in the new economy. *International Personnel Management Association News*, pp. 9, 11; Smith, M. (March 2001). E-learning in the 21st

century. *International Personnel Management Association News*, pp. 10–11.
19. Smith, M. (May 2000). Distance learning as a future workplace trend. *International Personnel Management Association News*, p. 21.
20. McIlvaine, A. (May 1, 2001). Training 2001: An e-Learning Odyssey. *Human Resource Executive*, p. 8, 24.
21. Nadler, L., and Z. Nadler (1989). *Developing human resources* (3rd ed.). San Francisco, CA: Jossey-Bass.
22. IPMA (June 2001). Competency based training. *International Personnel Management Association News*, pp. 1, 4–5, 8.
23. Nalbandian, J. (1985). Human relations and organizational change: Responding to loss. *Review of Public Personnel Administration*, *6*: 29–43.
24. French, W. L., and C. H. Bell, Jr. (1990). *Organizational development* (4th ed.). Upper Saddle River, NJ: Prentice Hall.
25. Rogers, E. M. (1995). *Diffusion of innovations* (4th ed.). New York: Free Press.
26. Lorbor, L. (April 3, 2008). Tips for better returns on training. *Wall Street Journal* online. Available at: http://www.wsj.com/article/SB120714281870283259.html (accessed on October 8, 2008).
27. Trice, E. (September 1999). Exercise training evaluation efforts. *International Personnel Management Association News*, pp. 10–11.
28. U.S. Department of Health and Human Services (2005). Successful strategies for recruiting, training, and utilizing volunteers: a guide for faith- and community-based service providers, p. 3-3. Available at: http://www.samhsa.gov/fbci/Volunteer_handbook.pdf (accessed on October 8, 2008).
29. Ibid.

CHAPTER 11

Performance Appraisal

One of the most challenging aspects of human resources management is the switch in emphasis from managing positions to managing performance. Position management, including analyzing jobs, establishing essential duties and responsibilities, determining necessary knowledge, skills, and abilities, classifying jobs, setting a pay scale, and using the "position" as a critical feature of financial management could all be done without a single reference to a real live person. As public agencies have come to view human resources management in more of a strategic light—looking for the connections between human resources policies, management, agencies goals, and objectives, performance management has become at least as important as position management. Whereas the components of position management are clear-cut, the components of performance management range from legislation that creates authority for an agency and its employees and thus channels their performance to supervisory coaching and counseling of employees. Any deliberate act intended to affect employee performance falls under the category of performance management. The goal of the contemporary organization is to orient these acts toward unit and agency goal accomplishment.

Performance appraisal is supposed to play a key role in the development of employees and their productivity. Theoretically, the appraisal of performance provides employees with feedback on their work, leading to greater clarity regarding organizational expectations and to a more effective channeling of employee ability and effort. In these ways, performance appraisal is a crucial aspect of performance management.

When a formal performance appraisal leads to organizational decisions regarding promotion and pay, the process becomes more complicated; it is accompanied by heightened legal scrutiny for civil rights violations and employee demands for reasons behind the decisions. Where the results of an unsatisfactory appraisal lead to disciplinary action or denial of an organizational reward, due process guarantees are invoked through union contracts, merit-system rules, or possibly even through the U.S. Constitution. Often these legal, accountability, and due process considerations overshadow the feedback purpose of appraisal systems, forcing a formalism better suited to litigation than to management and employee development.

Even though the appraisal function is related to employee productivity and employees' desire to know how well they are doing, rarely are supervisors or employees satisfied with the process. On the one hand, in some organizations it is not taken very seriously and is viewed as a waste of time. In others, it plays a major role in the distribution of organizational rewards and compensation, and then it frequently becomes the source of considerable tension in the employee–employer relationship. For example, in the early 1990s the federal government ended a sixteen-year experiment with pay-for-performance for senior executives, because it had contributed to organizational conflict without increasing employee motivation or performance. However, despite this experience, the federal government has since returned to the practice. Most recently, both the Departments of Defense and Homeland Security have begun the gradual implementation of pay-for-performance systems.

By the end of this chapter, you will be able to:

1. Clarify the goals of performance appraisal.
2. Describe the role of appraisal in different personnel systems.
3. Identify contemporary work trends and their challenges to the appraisal function.
4. Differentiate between performance-based and person-based performance evaluation criteria.
5. Distinguish among seven performance appraisal methods; and discuss the comparative validity, reliability, and cost.
6. Discuss the controversy between traditional supervisory evaluation and alternatives (self-, peer, and 360-degree evaluation).
7. Describe the characteristics of an effective rating system.
8. Describe the human dynamics of the appraisal process, including the supervisor's motivation to assess the performance of subordinates.
9. Describe the relationship of performance appraisal to the sanction function and particularly its role in creating a sense of fairness in an organization.

WHY EVALUATE PERFORMANCE?

Performance appraisal is directed toward technical and management goals but rarely toward employee aspirations. The technical part focuses on developing an instrument that accurately measures individual performance in order to identify an individual's strengths and weaknesses and to differentiate one employee from another. Because personnel decisions like promotions and merit-pay increases are connected to individual performance, the instrument used to evaluate performance must withstand serious scrutiny by employees and managers.

Management hopes to achieve several objectives through the performance appraisal process:

1. Communicate management goals and objectives to employees. It is clear that performance appraisal reinforces managerial expectations. After instructing employees what to do, it is management's responsibility to follow through by providing feedback on how performance matches the stated criteria.
2. Motivate employees to improve their performance. The purpose of providing feedback, or constructive criticism, is to improve performance. Appraisal, then, should encourage employees to maintain or improve job performance.

3. Distribute organizational rewards such as salary increases and promotions equitably. One of the primary criteria of organizational justice and quality of employee work life is whether rewards are distributed fairly.
4. Conduct personnel management research. Logic suggests that if jobs have been analyzed accurately, and if people have been selected for those jobs based on job-related skills, knowledge, and abilities, their subsequent on-the-job performance should be satisfactory or better. If not, one might suspect defects in the job analysis, selection, or promotion criteria—or in the performance appraisal system itself.

From the employee's standpoint, the issue is fairness. Title VII of the 1964 Civil Rights Act, as amended (1972), requires employers to validate any personnel technique that affects an employee's chances for promotion. This includes performance appraisal. For this reason, it is strongly suggested that personnel managers adopt one of the performance-oriented techniques discussed later in this chapter. At the federal level, the Civil Service Reform Act of 1978 provided a model for a sound, straightforward approach to performance appraisal. According to Lah and Perry, "the act sought to create objectives-based performance appraisal systems to replace more informal and subjective systems."[1] It is interesting to note the parallel between the Act's focus on objectivity in the appraisal process and the long-standing focus on objectivity in the selection of public employees. This connection was emphasized in a recent report by the U.S. Merit Systems Protection Board stating that "agencies that use performance appraisals as a basis for pay decisions should anticipate the same degree of scrutiny currently given to employment tests and other selection procedures . . . After all, agencies are indeed using a 'selection procedure' in that they are using performance appraisals to *select* employees for pay increases and awards."[2] The common ground is found in the overall mandate that personnel decisions be based on job-related criteria.

PERFORMANCE APPRAISAL AND ALTERNATE PERSONNEL SYSTEMS

Much of the discussion in this chapter focuses on civil service systems. Civil service personnel systems often are called merit systems, frequently confusing even government employees. Personnel systems based on merit are those where a variety of personnel decisions are based on competencies and performance rather than seniority or politics. Merit-pay plans are those that attempt to tie compensation to performance. Performance appraisal and civil service systems go hand in hand, and to the extent they can help distinguish and document employee performance, they advance the goals of personnel systems based on merit.

Affirmative action personnel systems also have a significant investment in reliable and valid appraisal systems. This interest parallels a similar interest in the development of selection devices free of inappropriate or irrelevant judgments. This interest has thrust performance appraisal systems into the judicial arena, subjecting them to standards of validity and reliability that they may not be able to meet when preserving the essential subjectivity involved in one person evaluating another's work.

Performance appraisal systems are largely irrelevant political appointees. Political executives rarely remain on the job long enough to benefit from or suffer formal appraisals. Their superiors are other political executives, often elected officials whose subjective criteria for effective job performance make formal assessments like those in civil service systems difficult to implement. Further, the higher up in an organizational hierarchy one travels, the more likely that the substance of an individual's job will be determined by that individual, with only limited guidance by superiors or the previous incumbent's job description.

Collective bargaining personnel systems generally oppose pay for individual performance and appraisal plans developed as a part of performance-based compensation. Unions prefer to negotiate wages for their workers and see individual incentive or merit plans as ways of pitting one union member against another and introducing conditions where managers can favor one employee over another.

From the perspective of public sector agencies and public managers, performance evaluation systems have limited applicability to those employed by an outside contractor. Where contractors provide public services, contract negotiation, administration, and compliance replace traditional supervisory practices (setting performance standards, providing feedback and arranging consequences). While this process involves many of the same elements as performance appraisal, it has a different basis in law, administrative procedure, and managerial practice. However, this does not mean that contracting organizations should not devote ample attention to their own performance evaluation systems. Ultimately, the performance of their (contract) employees affects their contractual performance, as well as the opportunity to be awarded future contracts.

From the public employer and employee's standpoint, formal performance appraisals for part-time or temporary workers seem much less relevant than for career employees, except for those looking for a permanent, full-time job. In those cases, the employer's interests may differ from the employee's. The employer sees little gain from investing time in performance appraisal. However, the employee may see the appraisal as essential to the search for a permanent, full-time position, in that it results in documentation of performance relative to job standards or other employees in similar positions.

Additionally, the use of volunteer labor also necessitates a unique concern for performance evaluation systems. In many public sector agencies and nongovernmental organizations, there is a strong reliance upon volunteer labor to accomplish agency tasks. To the extent that volunteers are utilized in core functional areas, it is both desirable and necessary for supervisors to evaluate their performance. Sometimes, this may be done to "weed out" volunteers who are incompetent, or those whose behavior creates legal or financial risks for the agency. At other times, the performance evaluation of volunteers may be used to further strengthen the psychological contract between volunteers and a public agency or nongovernmental organization. This is especially important given that their relationship with the organization is less formalized than that of a paid or contractual employee.

CONTEMPORARY CHALLENGES TO PERFORMANCE APPRAISAL

Traditionally, performance appraisal has been regarded as a necessary and basic technical personnel function, even though it has never quite lived up to its expectations.[3] It is not difficult to understand why its stature has remained secure among human resource management advocates over the years. It is difficult to imagine behavior changing without feedback. Therefore, it makes sense that formalizing feedback from supervisor to employee would lead employees to behave in ways their employer valued.

Even though in practice an employee's behavior is influenced by feedback from a variety of sources (most significantly from peers and colleagues), performance appraisal has usually been associated with communication from supervisor to employee. This tradition coincides with the view that organizations are hierarchies of command and control, and the premises upon which employees make decisions should be hierarchically determined.

While formal appraisal systems are comfortably nested in routine administrative procedures and hierarchical structures, several contemporary work trends challenge the utility of the traditional appraisal. These trends are:

- The changing nature of work means less commitment between organization and employee, and therefore less possibility of influencing employee behavior through feedback and rewards.
- Part-time or temporary work makes performance appraisal less important for the employer, but more important for the employee seeking a permanent, full-time job.
- Privatization and contracting eliminate the need for appraisal of individual performance but substitutes the importance of contract compliance monitoring.
- Flatter organizational hierarchies challenge traditional superior–subordinate appraisals and greater spans of control hinder supervisory observation of employee work. Additionally, the shift from individual positions to work teams necessitates multirater evaluations, which run counter to many supervisors' notions of control, and evaluations are technically more difficult to perform.
- For knowledge workers, the shift from physical work locations to virtual work locations and the shift to more flexible working schedules has challenged the traditional norms of employee work expectations.
- Limited organizational rewards and punishments make evaluation ineffective at linking pay or disciplinary action to performance, particularly in personnel systems governed by civil service rules or collective bargaining agreements.

These factors combine to diminish the value of performance evaluation in all but traditional civil service systems, where evaluation systems are legally required to demonstrate the job relatedness of promotion or disciplinary action. Because supervisors must exercise discretion in the allocation of organizational rewards and discipline, the demand for fairness requires organizational focus on the criteria used to make these decisions, the processes used to reach them, and the outcomes or sanctions they produce.[4] In other words, procedural and substantive fairness argue for formalized appraisal systems that encourage rational judgments.

However, even in civil service systems, performance evaluation is widely regarded (in private) as irrelevant by employees and supervisors. The ambivalent status of the performance appraisal function in essence parallels the tension that exists more generally in human resource management between the values of efficiency (the flexibility to manage and control employees) and political responsiveness on the one hand, and individual rights and equity on the other. The future of the appraisal function will evolve out of this tension as well as the rapidly evolving way we organize ourselves to work—whether in teams or individually; whether relatively permanently or temporarily; whether publicly or privately.

PERFORMANCE-BASED AND PERSON-BASED EVALUATION CRITERIA

If we assume that the appraisal function will not disappear, if only because organizational justice demands some formalization of the criteria used to allocate rewards and punishments (as it does in the allocation of jobs through the staffing function), the fundamental question is: What factors should be evaluated? There are two basic sets of criteria, person-based and performance-based, though some appraisal methods must employ a mixture of the two types when person-based traits are deemed an element of organizational performance.

In the **person-based rating system**, the rater compares employees against other employees or against some absolute standard. **Performance-based rating systems** measure each employee's behaviors against previously established behaviors and standards. Each criterion has advantages. Person-based systems are, beyond a doubt, the easiest and cheapest to design, administer, and interpret. Many organizations evaluate employees on the extent to which they possess desirable personality traits—initiative, dependability, intelligence, or adaptability. Ratings are easily quantified and compared with past appraisals or ratings of other people or units through computerization so that frequently overburdened supervisors in a minimum of time can complete the appraisal process. However, person-oriented appraisal systems share the same drawbacks, further discussed below, as trait-oriented job appraisal and classification systems—they have low validity and low reliability and are of dubious value in improving performance.

First, such systems are invalid to the extent that personality characteristics are unrelated to job performance. For example, organizational and environmental characteristics heavily influence the nature of a given position and, by implication, the kinds of skills or characteristics needed for successful performance. It is impossible to specify for all positions in an organization a uniform set of desirable personality characteristics that can be demonstrably related to successful job performance. Second, the reliability of trait ratings is frequently marginal at best; two supervisors may have very different definitions of loyalty, depending on their views of the job or their level of expectation for their employees. Third, comparative trait appraisals are not useful for counseling employees because they neither identify areas of satisfactory or unsatisfactory performance nor suggest areas where improvement is needed. Since an employee's personality characteristics are central to his or her self-concept, it is difficult for supervisors and employees to discuss them without lapsing into amateur psychology and defensiveness. Because of their low validity and reliability, person-oriented systems are not very useful for personnel management research aimed at validating selection or promotion criteria.

For these reasons, most performance specialists advocate the use of performance-based systems that evaluate job-related behaviors. In fact, person-based systems can rarely stand the test of legal scrutiny that examines their reliability and validity in relation to actual job performance. In contrast to person-based systems, performance criteria communicate managerial objectives clearly; are both relevant to job performance and reasonably reliable; and better fulfill the purposes of reward allocation, performance improvement, and personnel management research. If objective performance standards are established between employees and supervisors through some process of participative goal setting, the employee becomes clearly aware of the specific behavioral expectations attached to his or her position.

The fact that desired behaviors are specified makes the evaluative criteria more valid. That is, the job behaviors or expected competencies themselves provide the basis for evaluation, rather than personality characteristics believed to be related to performance.[5] Performance-based appraisals are more reliable because the use of objective standards enables raters, employees, and observers to determine whether predetermined performance standards have been met. As a result, changes in salary levels, promotions, or firings can be amply justified by reference to employee productivity. Reward allocation decisions can be explained to employees by discussing their performance objectively, rather than by arguing about the desirability of changing certain negative personality traits. Areas where performance improvement is needed can be identified for counseling, training, or job assignment purposes. The performance-based system increases job-related communication between employees and supervisors, primarily because performance standards must be altered periodically to meet changes in organizational objectives, resource allocation, or environmental constraints. In short, performance-based appraisal systems are fairer than person-based systems, even though personal qualities of employees are highly valued.

Tziner and colleagues found that performance-based rating systems produced higher levels of goal clarity, goal acceptance, and goal commitment; resulted in greater levels of employee satisfaction with the appraisal process; and were associated with greater improvements in individual performance over time.[6] Taylor and associates found that perceived fairness in appraisal systems results in more loyalty and organizational commitment to and satisfaction with the appraisal process even when employees receive lower evaluations.[7]

However, performance-based systems are considerably harder to develop than person-based systems. In a 2005 survey of federal employees evaluated by five-level appraisal systems, 69 percent of respondents agreed that appropriate standards were used by their managers to rate their performance, but only 52 percent agreed that their performance measures were objective.[8] First, because performance standards will vary (depending on the characteristics of the employee, the objectives of the organization, available resources, and external conditions), separate performance standards must be developed for each employee, or for each class of similar positions. Second, the organization may wish to specify desired methods of task performance as well as objectives. Third, the changing nature of organizations and environments means that employee performance standards may also change, and seldom at regularly scheduled or administratively convenient intervals. As a result, supervisors will need to spend more time working with employees to develop performance standards and subsequent appraisal interviews. Since supervisors are rewarded primarily for improving their work unit's short-term productivity, they may view developmental counseling as an inefficient use of their time.

Fourth, it is difficult to develop objective performance standards for many staff people or for positions that are complex or interrelated in a job series. Job-related, objective measures are more suited to simple jobs with tangible output that can be attributed to employee performance. Attempts to measure performance in complex jobs objectively can focus attention on concrete but trivial factors. Further, an employee's performance is also subject to other influences: the quality of the performance standards-setting process, the relationship with others in the work unit, and environmental factors. An example would be when teachers point out that, in addition to teacher performance, student accomplishments are influenced by home environment, peers, level of ability, class size, and other factors that complicate the assessment of teachers based on student performance. Since evaluative standards are individualized, computerized scoring or interpretation of results is difficult.

Last, it is difficult to compare the performance of employees with different standards. If each of three employees has met previously established performance standards, how does a supervisor decide which of them should be recommended for a promotion?

APPRAISAL METHODS

The criterion question concerns whether personality characteristics or behavior will be the object of appraisal and the difficulty of separating the two; the methods question concerns the format or technique by which the criterion will be evaluated. Seven methods are commonly used:

1. Graphic rating (or adjectival scaling)
2. Ranking
3. Forced-choice
4. Essay
5. Objective
6. Critical incident (or work sampling)
7. Behaviorally anchored rating scales (BARS)

Some of these techniques, primarily the first three, are more adaptable to person-oriented systems. Others are utilized primarily in performance-based systems.

1. **Graphic-rating scales** are the most easily developed, administered, and scored format. They consist of a listing of desirable or undesirable personality traits in one column and beside each trait a scale (or box) that the rater marks to indicate the extent to which the rated employee demonstrates the trait. An example of a graphic-rating scale appears in Figure 11-1.
2. **Ranking techniques** are similar to graphic-rating scales in that they are also based on traits. However, they require the rater to rank-order each employee on each of the listed traits. While they overcome one fault of graphic-rating scales, the tendency of raters to rate all employees high on all characteristics, it is difficult for raters to rank more than ten employees against one another.
3. **Forced-choice techniques** are the most valid trait-rating method. Based on a previous analysis of the position, job analysts have determined which traits or behaviors are most related to successful job performance. Several positive traits or behaviors are given in the form of a multiple-choice question, and the rater is asked to indicate the one that corresponds most closely with the employee's job performance or personality. Because supervisors are unsure which item is the "best" response according to the person who designed the test, forced-choice techniques reduce supervisory bias.

FIGURE 11-1 Employee Rating

Date of Rating ______________ White—Personnel; Canary—Dept./Div.; Pink—Employee

Rating Period: From ______________ To ______________

___Probationary
___Annual
___Special
___Final

Soc. Sec. No.	Activity	Class	Obj.	Employee Name

INSTRUCTIONS

Evaluate employee's performance and behavior to the degree he or she meets job requirements, taking into consideration all factors in the employee's performance. Individual factors under each trait should be designated, where applicable, as (+) high; (✓) average; (–) low. The overall mark for each trait should be indicated by placing an (x) in the applicable columns labeled Outstanding, Above Average, Average, Below Average, and Unsatisfactory. BEFORE RATING EMPLOYEE, PLEASE REVIEW YOUR RATING MANUAL.

TRAIT			Outsdg.	Above Average	Average	Below Average	Unsat.
Quality of Work	___Accuracy ___Completeness ___Oral expression	___Written expression ___Soundness of judgment in decisions ___Reliability of work results					
Work Output	___Amount of work performed ___Completion of work on schedule	___Physical fitness ___Learning ability					

TRAIT			Outsdg.	Above Average	Average	Below Average	Unsat.
Work Habits	___ Organization and planning of assignments ___ Job interest ___ Attendance	___ Compliance with work instructions ___ Observance of work hours ___ Conscientious use of work time					
Safety	___ Care of equipment, property, and materials	___ Personal safety habits					
Personal Relations	___ Cooperation with fellow employees ___ Personal appearance and habits	___ Dealing with the public ___ Ability to get along with others					
Adaptability	___ Performance in emergencies ___ Performance with minimum of instruction	___ Performance under changing conditions ___ Self-reliance, initiative, and problem solving					
	FOR USE IN RATING SUPERVISORS ONLY:						
Supervisory Skills	___ Leadership ___ Acceptance by others ___ Decision making ___ Effectiveness and skill in Planning and laying out work	___ Fairness and impartiality ___ Communicating problems to others ___ Training-Safety					

TRAIT		Outsdg.	Above Average	Average	below Average	Unsat.
General Evaluation	Indicate by an (×) in the appropriate column your own general evaluation of the employee's rating, taking all the above and other pertinent factors into consideration. A written statement must be made on the reverse side of this form if the ratings is OUTSTANDING or UNSATISFACTORY on this item				*	*#

Signature of
Rater: ____________________

Title: ____________________

Signature of
Rater's Supervisor: ____________________

Title: ____________________

*An (×) here indicates loss of annual salary increase
An (×) here indicates employee must be rated again in 90 days.
TO EMPLOYEE: Your signature is required, however, it does not imply that you agree with the rating.

Date ____________ Employee Signature ____________________

Person Evaluated ______________________________

Position ______________________________

Organization Unit ______________________________

Date ______________________________

Instructions: Please place a check on the line to the left of the statement that best describes this employee.

1. This employee
   ___ a. always looks presentable
   ___ b. shows initiative and independence
   ___ c. works well with others in groups
   ___ d. produces work of high quality
2. This employee
   ___ a. completes work promptly and on time
   ___ b. pays much attention to detail
   ___ c. works well under pressure
   ___ d. works well without supervisory guidance
3. This employee
   ___ a. is loyal to his or her supervisor
   ___ b. uses imagination and creativity
   ___ c. is thorough and dependable
   ___ d. accepts responsibility willingly

FIGURE 11-2 Forced-Choice Performance Evaluation Format

Naturally, they are disliked by supervisors, who want to know how they are rating their employees. An example of the forced-choice format appears in Figure 11-2.

4. The fourth appraisal technique, the **essay format**, is among the oldest and most widely used forms of appraisal. The rater simply makes narrative comments about the employee. Since these may relate to personality or performance, the essay method is suitable for person- or performance-oriented systems. However, it has the disadvantages of being time consuming, biased in favor of employees with supervisors who can write well, and impossible to standardize. It is frequently used in conjunction with graphic-rating or ranking techniques to clarify extremely low or high ratings. However, the burden on supervisors is so great that when essay elaboration is required to justify high or low ratings, supervisors have a tendency to rate employees toward the middle of a normal curve.
5. The **objective method** is a measure of work performance—quality, quantity, or timeliness—against previously established standards. It is used most often in private industry by companies with piece-rate pay plans; however, public-sector organizations are adopting a variant of this approach by measuring workload indicators. For example, employment counselors may be evaluated on the number of jobs they fill or on the percentage of placements who remain on the job after three months. An example is provided in Figure 11-3.

FIGURE 11-3 Health Center

HEALTH CENTER

JOB DESCRIPTION

JOB TITLE Primary Nurse

Department Nursing Service

Date ______

Job Code No ______

Job Title of Person to Whom Reporting Head Nurse

Pay Grade ______

Date Revised ______

Job Summary: A professional nurse, who has responsibility, authority, and accountability for quality nursing care for an assigned group of patients.

PERFORMANCE EVALUATION

Probationary Review [ ]

Merit Review [ ] Special [ ]

Present Grade ______ Step ______

Name ______

Date of Hire ______

Evaluation Due Date ______

RESPONSIBILITIES	*PERFORMANCE STANDARDS*	*ATTAINED YES/NO*	*IF NO, HOW CAN SUCH BE ATTAINED*
ASSESSMENT:			
1. Complete the admission procedure to include	Within one hour of patient's admission to the unit, introduces self and identifies the primary nurse's role to the patient and/or the family.		
Orientation	Orients patient/family to the unit.		
Assesses the patient needs	Tentative assessment and nursing judgment, based on the patient's immediate needs at the time of admission to the unit, will be reflected in the initial notation on the nurse's progress notes and/or the nursing history summary		

RESPONSIBILITIES	*PERFORMANCE STANDARDS*	*ATTAINED YES/NO*	*IF NO, HOW CAN SUCH BE ATTAINED*
	Performs assessment within 24 hours of admission to the unit. Assessment is based on subjective and objective data which may include records, consultation, and test data. Physical: breath and bowel sounds peripheral pulses level of consciousness general skin condition and color physical abnormalities		
Completes a nursing history	Completes nursing history within 24 hours of admission to the unit and enters notation on Patient Care Guide.		
PLANNING:			
1. Initiates a patient care guide	Assures that a 24-hour patient care guide is completed within 24 hours of patient admission to the unit. This will define patient/family problems and formulate plan of care that attempts to modify or eliminate each nursing problem.		
2. Includes the patient and family in the planning of the patient's care.	Includes the patient and the family in the planning of the patient's care both initially and throughout the hospitalization and reflects this action via documentation on the patient care guide and verbal feedback from the patient and/or family.		
3. Initiates discharge planning	Describe short and long term goals, as identified by the patient and/or family, beginning at time of admission.		

RESPONSIBILITIES	*PERFORMANCE STANDARDS*	*ATTAINED YES/NO*	*IF NO, HOW CAN SUCH BE ATTAINED*
INTERVENTION:			
1. Performs all independent nursing functions and performs dependent nursing functions as ordered by the physician and documents all nursing assessment, plans, and interventions.	Within the framework of the health center policies and procedures, and documents accordingly on the patient chart.		
2. Communicates patient's status to other health care and family members.	Communicates daily with patient and/or family regarding events of the day and current status. Provides time for questions. Communicates to personnel on her tour of duty verbal and written assignments with deadlines for completion. Communicates patient data to oncoming shift via organized, pertinent, factual walking report and updates Kardex accordingly. Attends doctors' rounds, and communicates with physicians.		
3. Utilizes social service department and resources in order to promote, restore, and maintain optimal health care for patient/family.	Initiates utilization of community health resources with the cooperation of the physicians and communicates these actions.		
4. Utilizes team members appropriately; according to their abilities and position description.	Establishes priorities of nursing care based on assessment of patient needs, reflected on the daily primary nursing assignment worksheet.		

RESPONSIBILITIES	*PERFORMANCE STANDARDS*	*ATTAINED YES/NO*	*IF NO, HOW CAN SUCH BE ATTAINED*
5. Coordinates patient/family teaching, based upon assessment of patient readiness.	Assures that delegated assignments have been completed before the end of the shift. Schedules break and meal times for team members. Patient/family teaching will be reflected in the chart at the time of discharge.		

JOB SPECIFICATIONS

Comments on Work Habits: ______________________________

Supervisor Date Department Head Date

My supervisor has reviewed my Job Description and Performance Evaluation with me. My signature does not necessarily mean that I agree.

Comments ______________________________

______________ Signature______________ Date ______

6. The **critical incident or work sampling** method is an objective technique that records representative examples of good (or bad) performance in relation to agreed-upon employee objectives. It has the same advantages and disadvantages of performance-oriented systems generally. One cautionary note, however: To the extent that the selected incidents are not representative of employee performance over time, the method is open to distortion and bias. Figure 11-4 presents an example of a critical incident appraisal form.
7. The **behaviorally anchored rating scale (BARS)** is a technique that employs objective performance criteria in a standardized appraisal format. The personnel manager who wishes to use BARS develops a range of possible standards for each task and then translates these statements into numerical scores. To be job related, these performance-oriented statements must be validated by job analysis. This approach can also be used within the selection process by developing assessment procedures that measure applicant behaviors based on a behaviorally anchored rating scale.

BARS is handy because it makes use of objective appraisal criteria and is easy to employ. However, it is time-consuming to develop and has not lived up to expectations because the distinction between behavior and traits is not as salient as once thought.[9] Figure 11-5 presents an example of a behaviorally anchored rating form for a primary nurse.

Person Evaluated ______________________________

Position ______________________________

Organization Unit ______________________________

Time Period ______________ to ______________

Employee Objectives	*Examples of Successful or Unsuccessful Performance*
1.	a. b. c. d.
2.	a. b. c. d.
3.	a. b. c. d.

FIGURE 11-4 Critical Incident Performance Evaluation Format

FIGURE 11-5 Behaviorally Anchored Rating Scales (BARS) Evaluation Format

Student evaluated ________________ Course: ________ Dates: ________ to ________

	COURSE GRADE			
Evaluative Criteria	*A*	*B*	*C*	*D*
1. Term paper (75 percent of course grade)	Meet criteria for a grade of B and in addition: Develop new insights, theories, or solutions	Meet criteria for a grade of C and in addition: Analyze and critically evaluate existing knowledge presented in lectures, discu-ssion, and outside reading	Completed by date scheduled in course outline; repeat existing knowledge from lectures and outside reading Follow proper style (grammar, organization, footnotes, and bibliography)	Not completed by date scheduled: not meeting minimum criteria for a grade of C
2. Class participation (25 percent of course grade)	Meet criteria for a grade of B and in addition: 1. Listen to and evaluate the class participation of other students 2. Show ability to analyze and evaluate material presented in lecture and discussion	Meet criteria for a grade of C and in addition: 1. Participate in class discussions 2. Demonstrate correct factual knowledge of concepts and theories from lectures and reading	Attend class as scheduled or notify professor in advance of absences	Not meet criteria for a grade of C

TABLE 11-1 Performance Evaluation Systems

Purpose	Criteria	Methods
Communication of objectives	Performance-oriented	Critical incident (work sampling), objective measures, BARS
Reward allocation	Person- or performance-oriented	Graphic rating, ranking, forced-choice, BARS
Performance improvement	Performance-oriented	Critical incident (work sampling), objective measures, BARS
Personnel research	Performance-oriented	Essay, work sampling (critical incident), objective measures, BARS

So far, our discussion has emphasized that the purpose of an employee appraisal system must be clearly stated and that evaluation methods must be suitable to the evaluative criteria chosen. Table 11-1 summarizes these relationships.

While Table 11-1 points out the uses of each appraisal method, judicial reviews of discrimination cases involving appraisal instruments will be forcing more uniformity in future appraisal systems. Feild and Holley[10] report that, on the basis of their research examining employment discrimination court decisions involving appraisal systems, the following characteristics clearly contributed to verdicts for the defending organizations: A job analysis was used to develop the appraisal system; a behavior-oriented versus person-oriented system was used; evaluators were given specific written instructions on how to use the rating instrument; the appraisal results were reviewed with employees; and the defending organizations tended to be nonindustrial in nature.

WHO SHOULD EVALUATE EMPLOYEE PERFORMANCE?

An employee's performance may be rated by a number of people. The immediate supervisor most commonly assesses the performance of subordinates, and most employees prefer this.[11] Supervisory assessments reinforce authority relationships in an organization and are frequently seen as the primary function distinguishing a superior from a subordinate. Because the superior–subordinate relationship itself is affected by so many factors, supervisory ratings are easily biased. Self-ratings can be employed to promote an honest discussion between superior and subordinate about the subordinate's performance. Nevertheless, self-ratings receive mixed support: Some studies find them inflated; others see them deflated in comparison with supervisory ratings. However, a recent report by the U.S. Merit Systems Protection Board on pay-for-performance states that self-ratings may benefit those supervisors who simply manage too many employees to be aware of each employee's annual accomplishments, a definite consequence of what some have referred to as the "hollowing out" of public management.[12]

Peer ratings, while infrequently utilized, have proved acceptable both in terms of reliability and validity. Peer ratings solve several problems associated with traditional superior–subordinate evaluations. They offer multiple raters who have more access to the employee's behavior, including a more comprehensive view of the person being rated, and they are able to assess collegiality or teamwork, an increasingly salient behavior in today's work environment. However, peer ratings are difficult to sell to employers and employees. Additionally, peer ratings hold the potential for creating employee conflict when paired with pay-for-performance systems.[13] Subordinate ratings are equally rare, and their main function is to provide data to begin discussion of the superior–subordinate relationship in a work group.

One of the challenges these findings on peer and subordinate ratings pose for human resource management is that future trends in the design and philosophy of work point toward the necessity of peer and self-ratings. Working in teams and seeking quality through an organizational philosophy of continuous improvement suggest less emphasis on methods of human resource management that grow out of current assessment techniques. More emphasis on teamwork requires greater emphasis on "getting along with others" and a host of other specific team-related, personal behaviors. Any appraisal system must fit into an organization's larger system of command, control, and coordination. If an organization retains a hierarchical orientation, anything other than superior–subordinate ratings is going to cause friction. One reconciliation is the possibility of retaining allocation decisions and formal evaluative judgments in the superior, while emphasizing the developmental role of appraisals with peer and subordinate ratings.

Nevertheless, it would appear difficult to reconcile the goals of continuous self-improvement with hierarchical control and authority. This observation, frequently made in normative statements during the human relations movement of the 1960s and 1970s, is becoming more relevant as technological changes and pressures for quality and productivity challenge traditional methods of organizational command and control. Table 11-2 summarizes perhaps the most important factor in credible appraisal systems—access to information about the person being rated. Peer ratings stand out as the most useful in this regard.

A significant amount of effort by human resources specialists has gone into creating accurate appraisal instruments and in training supervisors to dismiss inappropriate and irrelevant considerations when making formal assessments—and one wonders if technique dominates purpose in this area. The goal is to minimize rater bias without

TABLE 11-2 Access to Information about Task and Interpersonal Behaviors and Results

	SOURCE				
	Subordinates	**Self**	**Peers**	**Next Level (Supervisor)**	**Higher Level (Upper Management)**
TASK					
Behaviors	Rare	Always	Frequent	Occasional	Rare
Results	Occasional	Frequent	Frequent	Frequent	Occasional
INTERPERSONAL					
Behaviors	Frequent	Always	Frequent	Occasional	Rare
Results	Frequent	Frequent	Frequent	Occasional	Rare

Source: Reprinted with permission from *Understanding performance appraisal*, © 1995 by Kevin R. Murphy and Jeannette N. Cleveland. Published by Sage Publications, Thousand Oaks, CA.

jeopardizing the supervisory discretion necessary in making judgments about employee performance. The difficulty in eliminating rater bias is that people, including supervisors, tend to make global evaluative judgments of others.[14] The fact is that supervisors come to conclusions about employees without the help of assessment instruments. Raters tend to use the performance appraisal process to document rather than discover how well an employee is performing, and tension between human resources professionals and supervisors may result in those instances where supervisors perceive that appraisal instruments impede accurate appraisals and human resources professionals profess that they ensure a level of objectivity. This probably helps account for Milkovich and Wigdor's observation that "There is no compelling evidence that one appraisal format is significantly better than another" and that "Global ratings do not appear to produce very different results from job-specific ratings."[15] This leads them to assign marginal value to the expenditure of more time and money developing more accurate assessment instruments.[16]

The inevitable global assessments that supervisors make acknowledge the complexities of work, the multiplicity of factors causing different levels of work performance, the difficulty of actually describing the constituent elements of a job without trivializing it, and the critical role that who a person is influences the kind of work a person does, both its quality and its quantity. In addition, supervisors know that each employee creates an environment for the work of other employees, and to separate out individual performance artificially distorts what happens in an office.

An effort to meet several of the traditional criteria of performance appraisal with an emphasis on teams, clients, and customers is the **360-degree evaluation**.[17] With this method the person being rated is placed in the middle of a metaphorical circle, and salient members of his or her role set become potential raters, usually with the immediate supervisor either conveying a summary to the person being rated or actually gathering the information and evaluating it individually. This kind of appraisal encourages communication of the employee's goals and understanding of organizational expectations to members of the role set, and it enhances communication with "customers," whether internal or external to the organization. These multiple views give a more accurate picture of the employee's contribution to the organization than a traditional superior–subordinate appraisal would. This approach, however, is time consuming, may challenge the hierarchical nature of an organization, and may bring issues of trust, confidentiality, and anonymity to the forefront among peers. Recent research on the use of 360-degree systems has found that they are best used for the purposes of employee coaching, employee development planning, and employee feedback, rather than as a component of compensation in pay-for-performance systems.[18] In addition, as part of a human resources management information system, there now is available software to help manage the "paperwork," data collection, and consolidation required of a 360-degree system.[19] Figure 11-6 provides an example of a 360-degree rating instrument.

CHARACTERISTICS OF AN EFFECTIVE APPRAISAL SYSTEM

Ultimately, performance appraisal systems should be aligned with an organization's mission and culture, and even though different evaluative methods are likely to identify the same employees as high or low performers, we have already seen in Table 11-1 that different appraisal methods are suitable for different evaluative purposes. Several guidelines follow for the effective use of appraisal systems by public organizations.[20]

Person Evaluated:

Rater Position (subordinate, peer, supervisor):

Date of Rating:

Rating Scale:

Strongly disagree	Disagree	Neither agree nor disagree	Agree	Strongly agree
1	2	3	4	5

Please use the above scale to rate this employee on the following statements:

1. This employee has a firm understanding and knowledge of the organization's goal and mission.	1	2	3	4	5
2. This employee conducts himself/herself professionally in all organizational situations and environments.	1	2	3	4	5
3. This employee interacts well others and contributes fully to the organization.	1	2	3	4	5
4. This employee treats his/her employees fairly at all times.	1	2	3	4	5

FIGURE 11-6 360-Degree Performance Appraisal Instrument

First, it may be wise to utilize separate systems for separate purposes. It seems clear when one looks at the purposes of appraisal systems that two fundamentally different supervisory roles can be detected. If the purpose is allocation of rewards, the supervisor or other rater becomes a judge. If the purpose is to improve employee performance, the supervisor is a counselor, coach, or facilitator. The fact is that supervisors assume both roles in their day-to-day work, but the roles are difficult to integrate successfully. It may well be that different appraisal instruments lend themselves to different functions, just as different times should be set aside to discuss allocation decisions and developmental issues with employees. Furthermore, it may be that peers, subordinates, and customers can better fulfill the developmental function with ratings than by a superior who does not have as frequent access to the employee's behavior or, in some cases, is not as credible.

Second, raters should have the opportunity, ability, and desire to rate employees accurately. Since employee understanding and acceptance of evaluative criteria are keys to performance improvement, it follows that employees should participate jointly in the determination of goals. The performance appraisal system must be job related, must allow the opportunity for interaction and understanding between rater and the person being rated, and must serve the performance improvement needs of both individual and organization.

Third, job analysis and performance appraisal need to be more closely related by developing occupation-specific job descriptions that include performance standards as well as duties, responsibilities, and minimum qualifications. Such job descriptions must specify the conditions under which work is to be performed, including such factors as resources, guidelines, and interrelationships. Necessarily, they will be specific to each occupation and perhaps to each organization as well. If the organization is attempting to structure itself along team lines, traditional, individual-oriented appraisals will become questionable and, where present, will have to adapt themselves to assessing behaviors that make teams work well.

Fourth, appraisal must be tied to long-range employee objectives such as promotion and career planning and more generally capture the employee's motivation for self-improvement. Performance appraisal is not an end in itself; nor should it be driven solely by short-term consequences like pay for performance. While performance improvement is administratively separate from promotional assessment and organizational human resource planning, both employees and organizations realize that performance appraisal relates to rewards, promotional consideration, and career planning. Further, connecting pay to performance places a significant burden on performance appraisal systems.

Fifth, because appraisal systems inevitably attempt to minimize subjectivity there always will be a formalism about them that cannot capture the nuances of behavior and personal attributes that contribute to a full appreciation of employee contributions at work. Supervisors will attempt to fudge their formal ratings to reflect these informal behaviors or behaviors that add value to employee performance but are not included formally because of their subjective nature. At the same time, some jobs defy objective evaluation of employees. This is another case where any formal appraisal system cannot provide a full account of employee performance. The subjectivity involved in any evaluation of employee performance means that the effectiveness of any performance appraisal system rests on a foundation of trust within an organization and open communication, particularly between the person being rated and the rater.

The sixth and perhaps most important characteristic of an effective appraisal system relates to the criteria used to select supervisors. In a report on supervision and poor performers, the U.S. Merit Systems Protection Board makes the selection to supervisory jobs of people who have an aptitude for the human relations aspects of supervisory work its number one recommendation for improving the federal performance management system.[21] In that same report (p. 21), some 37 percent of the managers and supervisors surveyed indicated that it was difficult or very difficult for them to discuss performance deficiencies with their problem performers.

THE HUMAN DYNAMICS OF THE APPRAISAL PROCESS

In light of the attention that appraisal techniques have received over the past years due to the growth of pay-for-performance systems, it should concern human resources professionals that many managers consider the performance appraisal process as one of their most disliked tasks.[22] However, considering that feedback is essential to goal accomplishment and productivity, why were appraisal systems regarded so lightly prior to judicial scrutiny and the emphasis on pay-for-performance?

One reason is that not all employees are interested in productivity. When the caseload of an income maintenance worker in a social service agency is increased because of budgetary constraints to the point where the unspoken emphasis is on *quantity* of cases processed at the expense of *quality*, the individual worker begins to value his or her welfare, working conditions, and equity of the workload more than productivity. A second reason is that multiple sources of performance feedback exist in an organization, with the formal appraisal system constituting only the most visible and tangible. People in organizations are constantly receiving and interpreting cues about others and attributing motives to their behavior. A third reason concerns the human dynamics of the appraisal process as opposed to measurement issues surrounding the reliability and validity of the appraisal instrument itself.

Douglas Cederblom reviewed literature on the appraisal interview—the formal part of the appraisal process where the rater and the person being rated sit down to talk about performance.[23] He found three factors contributing to the success of the appraisal interview. First, goal setting during the interview seemed positively associated with employee satisfaction with both the interview and its utility. Underlying the goal-setting process is the employee's confidence in the rater's technical knowledge about the subordinate's work. Second, the encouragement of subordinate participation in the interview—"welcoming participation," "opportunity to present ideas or feelings," and "boss asked my opinion"—seemed to produce positive subordinate assessments of the interview process. Last, the support of the rater expressed in terms of encouragement, constructive guidance, and sincere, specific praise of the subordinate results in positive feelings about the interview.

Criticism from superior to subordinate produces mixed results. On the one hand, a certain amount of criticism should lend perceived credibility to the superior's assessment. On the other hand, research rarely shows much lasting change in an employee following a supervisory critique. In part, this is because few raters know how to provide a constructive critique of an employee, and when a trait-rating form is used, employees inevitably interpret criticism in personal rather than behavioral terms. The obvious here warrants mention. Anything in the appraisal interview that produces a defensive employee reaction (regardless of the rater's intent) is likely to detract from the subordinate's satisfaction with the interview and is unlikely to have much success in altering an employee's behavior at work.

Palguta observed that while it may be statistically impossible for all employees to perform better than average, the emotional investment of employees in believing they are better than average is significant.[24] When pay is tied to performance, this investment is magnified because pay tangibly reflects supervisory judgments about employees in ways that employees cannot ignore or easily discount. And, even in the federal government where there is no evidence to suggest that the number of poor performers is large or that incompetence is a serious problem, the goal of feedback on below-average performers is to encourage poor performers to quit or to improve.[25] There is some evidence that poorer performers are more likely to leave the federal government than those who rate higher.[26] However, when the results of appraisals are used for allocation decisions like pay, superiors tend to become more lenient in their ratings.[27] While some poorly rated employees may leave, most stay, harboring feelings of inequity and discontent. In the federal government, less than 1 percent of employees receive a rating below "fully successful." In fact, the majority of employees receive a rating of better than fully successful, and a rating of fully successful puts an employee in the bottom 10–20 percent of many occupations in federal agencies.[28] The difficulty with inflated ratings is that the emotional investment of workers in their performance leads them to discount "satisfactory" ratings— which carry few economic rewards—and become disgruntled. They then blame their discontent on organizational factors like supervision and managerial policies and practices.[29]

In looking for reasons why appraisal systems seem to have little real effect as managerial tools despite their theoretical promise, Nalbandian has turned to expectancy theory for an explanation.[30] He argues that the appraisal tool an organization uses may increase a supervisor's ability to assess employees, but many factors affecting the willingness of supervisors to evaluate employees seem easily overlooked. From an expectancy theory perspective, raters anticipate few positive outcomes from an honest attempt to rate subordinates. Most supervisors generally know who their effective and ineffective employees are even if they cannot always articulate their reasoning to someone else's satisfaction. From the supervisor's perspective, then, the formal appraisal process duplicates an assessment the supervisor has already made. Thus, when the supervisor conducts an appraisal, it is seen as benefiting someone else. Further, research in the federal government has shown that for those managers who have attempted to address poor employee performance through performance interventions, such as additional training or performance improvement plans, the overwhelming majority of supervisors have witnessed no effect on employee performance.[31]

In addition, many authors and practitioners have pointed to the emotionally discomforting outcomes, the ones with negative valences, which the rater associates with the appraisal interview.[32] This is where the supervisor's assessment of the employee must be communicated face to face. Behaviorally oriented rating systems are designed to make assessments more objective and thus more acceptable to employees. Unfortunately, bad news is bad news regardless of whether or not it results from an assessment a supervisor feels is objective. When employees argue, sulk, look distraught, bewildered, or disappointed, or threaten to file a grievance because they disagree with the supervisor's assessment, most supervisors will experience such behavior in negative terms. The supervisor is likely, then, to find ways of behaving in the future that will not stimulate these employee responses. Is it any wonder that supervisors are prone to assess employees similarly, with most employees rated at least satisfactory? In fact, because employees take a satisfactory rating as a sign of disapproval, the majority of ratings exceed satisfactory.

The negative experiences supervisors have when rating subordinates appear unappreciated by others. For example, in a survey where federal employees were asked which changes in the performance management system in their agency they believed would advance agency missions, 66 percent indicated that a pass/fail system might help and 55 percent indicated that not using performance ratings as the basis for cash awards might help.[33] Another survey of federal employees showed that the more experience supervisors have with performance appraisal, the less complicated they want it to be.[34]

One of the goals to a successful appraisal is putting the parties at ease as they begin discussing the employee's performance. The city of Irving, Texas, asks each employee to fill out a short questionnaire to begin the process. The following questions are designed to engage the employees and to produce information that will lead to a more productive appraisal.[35]

- In appraising your performance, are there any other persons you work with or around with whom your supervisor should speak to get a more complete picture of how you do your work/get results?
- Of what accomplishments and skills acquired during the last appraisal period are you particularly proud?

- What can be done to make you more effective in your job?
- What can be done to help you provide better service to your customer?

In sum, while a considerable amount of effort goes into the seemingly endless task of producing accurate measurements of performance, the human dynamics of the appraisal process probably remain a greater challenge. Until supervisors experience the appraisal process positively, the underlying motivation to make appraisal systems work will be absent.

PERFORMANCE APPRAISAL, THE SANCTIONS PROCESS, AND FAIRNESS

Discipline is a formal way for an organization to perform the sanctions function by letting employees know they have violated an organizational expectation and by imposing negative consequences. Employees can be disciplined for poor performance or for inappropriate conduct. A performance appraisal is a critical precursor to disciplining an employee for poor performance, unless the discipline involves a performance incident that is a clear policy violation that places the organization at a legal or financial risk. Usually, if an employee gets into a fight, or is drinking on the job, or sleeping on the night shift, a performance appraisal is not required prior to discipline.

An employee who has been disciplined has had something taken away—a suspension involving pay, a demotion, or dismissal—or has been set on this path with a formal warning or a letter of reprimand.

With the consequences of disciplinary action as great as they can be, the issue of fairness in exercising discipline is paramount in the employee's mind. If the organization can withhold an employee's pay or take away a job for poor performance, the employee wants to know what is expected. An employee who is performing below supervisory expectations wants an opportunity to respond to these concerns (so that an alleged performance deficiency is demonstrated in fact to be valid before discipline is imposed) and a chance to improve.

A performance appraisal is essential in this process because it formally serves as a warning device and then as documentary evidence if a third party is called upon to make a judgment about the fairness of the discipline. It is a crucial step in establishing an environment of organizational justice because a valid performance appraisal requires (1) preset expectations, (2) accurate observations of behavior, and (3) a written record of the discussion between employee and employer and a third party or higher up if necessary.

The struggle human resource managers face is this: How far does an organization go in establishing formal procedures, including performance appraisal, to advance fairness and organizational justice when added formality limits managerial flexibility and responsiveness? There is no set answer to this question. It is a values question that is complicated in the case of performance appraisal especially, by contemporary work trends outlined earlier in this chapter—part-time and temporary workers, privatization, organizing into teams, and promoting flatter organizational hierarchies.

Summary

This chapter has identified the purposes and methods of assessing employees as well as the legal framework affecting the appraisal process. The benefits and costs of each method were described, along with the observation that while different methods may be more acceptable to subordinates, they do not seem to produce significantly different ratings of employees.

Does the appraisal process actually fulfill its various functions, or does it represent a triumph of technique over purpose? There is no doubt that the formalism of appraisal systems challenges the essentially subjective nature of one person assessing another's work or even one person assessing his or her own performance. However, as long as the distribution of organizational rewards and punishments is connected to individual performance, the formalism can be expected to remain. The desire for organizational justice and the protection of individual rights require that employees know how and why rewards are distributed and that employees be given an opportunity to appeal these judgments and question the processes. This promotes formal performance appraisal methods and processes. If the technology and design of work and the philosophy of total quality management successfully transfer the appraisal process from the individual to the work group, the formalism associated with individual performance appraisal may diminish, even if the employee's demand for fair treatment does not.

Ultimately, in order to produce effective performance appraisal, for those personnel systems for which appraisal serves a useful purpose, some groundwork needs to be laid:

1. Promoting to supervisory positions people who, among their other qualifications, want to supervise and will not look upon the appraisal of employees as a necessary evil
2. An appraisal tool that has been developed with employee participation and that focuses more on performance than traits
3. Training programs directed at supervisory use of the appraisal instrument and understanding of the human dynamics surrounding the appraisal process
4. Rewards for supervisors who competently and seriously approach the appraisal function
5. An open discussion and understanding of the superior–subordinate relationship at work
6. Consequences that mean something for good/poor performance.

Key Terms

360-degree evaluation *270*
behaviorally anchored rating scale (BARS) *266*
critical incident (work sampling) *266*
essay format *261*
forced-choice techniques *257*
graphic-rating scale *257*
objective method *261*
performance-based rating system *255*
person-based rating system *255*
ranking techniques *257*

Discussion Questions

1. Describe four operational functions of a performance appraisal system. Do you think all four can be accomplished with one appraisal method? Are the four functions complementary?
2. Why is performance appraisal associated most closely with civil service systems? How has it contributed to public perceptions that civil service systems are inefficient or ineffective, in comparison with those systems based on employment at will?
3. Identify the contemporary challenges to performance appraisal. How is the tension between

administrative efficiency and individual rights reflected in the appraisal function?

4. Draw up a list of pros and cons for person-based and performance-based rating systems.
5. Identify the six characteristics of an effective rating system. Which of the six do you believe are the more difficult to implement?
6. Utilize an expectancy theory perspective and analyze the motivation of supervisors to rate the performance of subordinates honestly and accurately.
7. Some research shows that fairness in performance appraisal leads to positive employee behavior, commitment, and satisfaction. Fairness is associated with formality, due process, rules, and procedures. Tomorrow's organizations need to be flexible and adaptable. How can you devise a fair appraisal system that is consistent with the attributes of tomorrow's organization?

Case Study: Evaluating Appraisal Instruments

Figures 11-1, 11-3, and 11-6 present the appraisal instruments used in different organizations. Review the figures and respond to the following questions:

1. Which of the three forms is more job related? Which type would you rather use to evaluate employees? Which type would you rather have your supervisor use to evaluate you?
2. Discuss the forms with regard to the following criteria:
   - Accuracy in measuring employee performance
   - Cost and time in developing
   - Ease of completing
   - Use in counseling and developing employees
   - Use in promotion, pay, or other personnel decisions

Notes

1. Lah, T. J., and J. L. Perry (2008). The diffusion of the Civil Service Reform Act of 1978 in OECD Countries: A tale of two paths to reform. *Review of Public Personnel Administration, 28* (3): 282–299.
2. U.S. Merit Systems Protection Board (May 2008). Bright lights, high stakes: Is your appraisal system ready? *Issues of Merit*, p. 6.
3. Greller, M. (1998). Participation in the performance appraisal review: Inflexible manager behavior and variable worker needs. *Human Relations, 51*: 1061–1084.
4. Freedland, M. (1993). Performance appraisal and disciplinary action: The case for control of abuses. *International Labour Review, 132*: 493.
5. Smith, M. (August 1999). Competency-based performance appraisal systems. *International Personnel Management Association News*, p. 16.
6. Tziner, A., R. E. Kopelman, and N. Livneh (1993). Effects of performance appraisal format on perceived goal characteristics, appraisal process satisfaction, and changes in rated job performance: A field experiment. *The Journal of Psychology, 127*: 281–291.
7. Taylor, S. M., K. B. Tracy, M. K. Renard, J. K. Harrison, and S. J. Carroll (1995). Due process in performance appraisal: A quasi-experiment in procedural justice. *Administrative Science Quarterly, 40*: 495–523.
8. U.S. Merit Systems Protection Board (September 2006). Performance appraisal systems: Quality vs. quantity. *Issues of Merit*, p. 4.
9. Milkovich, G. T., and A. K. Wigdor (eds.) (1991). *Pay for performance: Evaluating performance appraisal and merit pay*. Washington, DC: National Academy Press, p. 143.
10. Feild, H. S., and W. H. Holley (1982). The relationship of performance appraisal system characteristics to verdicts in selected employment discrimination cases. *Academy of Management Journal, 25*: 397.
11. United States Merit Systems Protection Board (June 1990). *Working for America: A federal employee survey*. Washington, DC: U.S. Merit Systems Protection Board, p. 17.
12. U.S. Merits Systems Protection Board (2006). Designing an effective pay for performance compensation system, p. 28. Available at: http://www.mspb.gov/netsearch/viewdocs.

aspx?docnumber=224104&version=224323&application=ACROBAT
13. Ibid., p. 28.
14. Milkovich and Wigdor, *Pay for performance*, p. 50.
15. Ibid., p. 149.
16. Ibid., p. 3.
17. Coggburn, J. D. (1998). Subordinate appraisals of managers: Lessons from a state agency. *Review of Public Personnel Administration, 18* (1): 68–79; Milliman, J. F., R. A. Zawacki, B. Schultz, S. Wiggins, and C. A. Norman (1995). Customer service drives 360-degree goal setting. *Personnel Journal, 74*: 136–142; Milliman, J. F., R. A. Zawacki, C. A. Norman, L. Powell, and J. Kirksey, Jr. (1994). Companies evaluate employees from all perspectives. *Personnel Journal, 73*: 99–103.
18. Rogers, E., C. W. Rogers, and W. Metlay (2002). Improving the payoff from 360-degree feedback. *Human Resources Planning, 25* (3): 44–54.
19. Fried, E. (July 1999). 360-Degree feedback software roundup. *International Personnel Management Association News*, pp. 26–27.
20. Longenecker, C. O., and N. Nykodym (1996). Public sector performance appraisal effectiveness: A case study. *Public Personnel Management, 25*: 151–164.
21. U.S. Merit Systems Protection Board (July 1999). *Federal supervisors and poor performers*. Washington, DC: U.S. Merit Systems Protection Board, p. 31.
22. Heathfield, S. (2007). Performance appraisals don't work—what does? *The Journal for Quality and Participation, 30* (1): 6–9.
23. Cederblom, D. (1982). The performance appraisal interview: A review, implications, and suggestions. *Academy of Management Review, 7*: 219–27.
24. Palguta, J. (May 6, 1991). Performance management and pay for performance. A presentation before the Pay-for-Performance Labor-Management Committee and the Performance Management and Recognition System Review Committee. Washington, DC: U.S. Merit Systems Protection Board.
25. U.S. Merit Systems Protection Board, *Federal supervisors and poor performers*, p. 12.
26. United States Merit Systems Protection Board (July 1988). *Toward effective performance management in government*. Washington, DC: U.S. Merit Systems Protection Board, p. 6.
27. Milkovich and Wigdor, *Pay for performance*, p. 72.
28. Palguta, Performance management and pay for performance. A presentation before the Pay-for-Performance Labor-Management Committee and the Performance Management and Recognition System Review Committee.
29. Gabris, G. T., and K. Mitchell (1988). The impact of merit raise scores on employee attitudes: The Matthew effect of performance appraisal. *Public Personnel Management, 17*: 369–386.
30. Nalbandian, J. (1981). Performance appraisal: If only people were not involved. *Public Administration Review, 41*: 392–396.
31. U.S. Office of Personnel Management (1999). Poor performers in government: A quest for the true story, p. 11.
32. Kikoski, J. F. (1998). Effective communication in the performance appraisal interview: Face-to-face communication for public managers in the culturally diverse workplace. *Public Personnel Management, 27* (4): 491–514.
33. U.S. Merit Systems Protection Board, *Federal supervisors and poor performers*, p. 29.
34. Ibid., p. 17.
35. Grote, D. (2000). Public sector organizations: Today's innovative leaders in performance management. *Public Personnel Management*, 29 (1): 9.

CHAPTER 12

Safety and Health

An employer's first responsibility is to provide workers with a safe and healthy workplace. Various factors have caused an unparalleled demand for workplace safety. Among them are frequent job changes, decreased unionization, immigration, population expansion, and technological changes. Prevention of **workplace fatalities, injuries, and illness (WFII)** is of primary concern to public personnel managers. In addition to the personal pain and suffering caused by these incidents, they cost employers billions of dollars annually. These include not only the direct cost of reduced productivity but also the hidden costs of sick leave, employer payments for disability and worker's compensation insurance, and the costs of processing or contesting employees' claims for disability retirement or workers' compensation benefits.[1]

Given that media news coverage seems to focus on stories about workplace homicides ("going postal" became part of our vocabulary over a decade ago), terrorist threats, construction fatalities, and mine disasters, one would suppose that WFIIs were on the rise in the United States. In fact, the opposite is true. The total number of workplace fatalities in 2006 was 7,703, down from 7,734 in 2005. The overall U.S. workplace fatality rate in 2006 was lower than the rate for any year since the first fatality census in 1992.[2] The number of workplace homicides in 2006 was a series low and reflected a decline of over 50 percent from the high reported in 1994. The most frequent type of fatal work-related accident, accounting for nearly one out of four fatal work injuries, was road accidents. Some jobs are quite dangerous: agriculture, forestry, fishing, and mining have annual fatality rates almost ten times the average.[3] There were 501 public employee workplace fatalities in 2006, a 4 percent decrease from 2005. The overall fatality rate for government workers was 2.1 per 100,000 employees, considerably below the total public–private workforce average of 3.9 per 100,000.[4]

According to estimates by the National Safety Council, employee injury costs totaled \$330 billion in 2004.[5] Nearly 60 percent (\$200 billion) was for injuries to employees who were off the job. According to the Agency for Healthcare Research and Quality, private health insurance spends largely on medical care associated with trauma and poisoning among people of working age than for any other health condition. Health-care workers face accident and illness rates equivalent to those working in transportation, agriculture, mining, or transportation.[6] Risks include not only those to which other industries are susceptible (lifting, chemical hazards, and slips and falls), but also life threatening diseases like AIDS, hepatitis, and tuberculosis.[7] Because of these risks, OSHA and the Joint

Commission on Accreditation for Healthcare Organizations (JCAHO) work together on worker and patient safety and health issues in these organizations.[8]

Private sector employees experienced an illness and accident rate of 4.6 per hundred in 2005, about the same as for the previous three years. Inexplicably and unlike the Bureau of Labor Statistics' annual workplace fatality report, the report on illnesses and injuries excludes public employees.[9] This limits comparative conclusions about workplace safety. On the one hand, data indicate that WFIIs have decreased because society's expectations of environmental health and safety management have risen. Moreover, the self-funded workers' compensation program gives companies a strong incentive to reduce their insurance rates by reducing accidents and fatalities. On the other hand, evidence exists that employers generally underreport workplace illness and injuries (particularly for demographic groups like Hispanics)[10] and that state and federal occupational safety and health agencies generally lack the resources needed for effective oversight and sanctions.[11] From a broader perspective, labor leaders assert that global market competition leads nations to take certain political decisions that threaten worker health and safety.[12]

The general topic of employee safety and health includes a variety of national public policy areas: occupational safety and health laws and regulations, health insurance, workers' compensation, and alcohol and drug abuse. It also includes a number of interrelated organizational programs: accident prevention, risk management, health insurance, health benefits, smoking cessation, stress management, drug testing, life-threatening diseases, workplace violence, and employee assistance.

First, health and safety are a *sanction*-related issue. In other words, they significantly concern the employee–employer relationship because of legal compliance responsibilities and legal liability risks. OSHA regulations protect employees against agency violations of health or safety standards. The Family and Medical Leave Act requires employers to grant employees leave to meet child- or elder-care commitments. Moreover, employers who lack policies and programs to counter workplace violence, or drug and alcohol abuse, risk being held liable in civil lawsuits for the consequences of these problems that result in death or injury to customers or other employees. For example, a major U.S. corporation was found liable in a multimillion dollar lawsuit arising from a fatal auto accident involving an employee. The supervisor asked an employee who showed up for work drunk to go home, rather than calling a cab and sending the employee home in it. Therefore, because the employee was following a lawful supervisory order, and because the supervisor knew the employee was drunk, the employer was responsible for damages arising out of the accident!

Second, this topic is a *development*-related issue because there is increasing evidence that healthy employees are more productive and happy than unhealthy ones. Investments in employee health programs increase productivity and decrease health-care and disability retirement costs. Considering how much money employers may have invested in training skilled technical and professional employees, it makes sense to develop programs that help employees manage stress, reduce drug and alcohol abuse, stop smoking, and make other positive **lifestyle choices**.

Third, because of the increasing cost of health care, health and safety are an *allocation* or *planning* issue for the employer. Programs that reduce WFIIs also reduce health benefit costs and workers' compensation insurance rates. Because healthy employees use less sick leave and have lower rates of accidents and injuries, employers must be concerned about health and safety even if they are hiring only temporary and part-time employees. High health-care costs and legal liability risks offer employers a powerful incentive to "weed out" applicants and employees whom they consider to be at unacceptably high risk for WFIIs. These legitimate employer objectives (legal compliance, risk management, and cost control) often conflict with employee rights to privacy and job retention. Moreover, this dilemma gives employers a powerful incentive to rely more heavily on contractors, who are not considered employees in most workplace situations.

By the end of this chapter, you will be able to:

1. Discuss the legal framework of safety and health protection for U.S. workers.
2. Summarize personnel policies and programs that increase workplace health and safety.
3. Discuss what HR managers can do to reduce or respond to workplace violence.
4. Discuss the HR role in more disaster preparedness.
5. Assess the impact of tobacco, alcohol, and illegal drugs on the workplace.
6. Discuss the impact of AIDS and other life-threatening diseases on personnel policy.
7. Describe the role of employee wellness programs as an organizational response to workplace health and safety issues.
8. Show how HR managers balance employers' concerns for productivity and cost containment with employees' concerns for job rights, privacy, and health care.

THE LEGAL FRAMEWORK FOR WORKPLACE SAFETY AND HEALTH

The legal framework for workplace safety and health involves OSHA regulations, a workers' compensation system, the Americans with Disabilities Act, and the Family and Medical Leave Act. It also requires that HR managers and supervisors be aware of the specific issues posed by independent contractors and health-care professionals.

The Occupational Safety and Health Act of 1970

Organized employer concern for work-related accidents and injuries combined with public concern for their social consequences led the federal government to pass legislation regulating private and public employers. The **Occupational Safety and Health Act (OSHA)** was passed in 1970 to ensure that working conditions for all Americans met minimum health and safety standards. Under the provisions of this Act, the **OSHA** sets health and safety standards, inspects public agencies, and levies citations and penalties to enforce compliance.[13] This Act does not establish standards for state and municipal agencies. Instead, it gives states the option of complying with federal standards or of establishing and enforcing standards through a designated state agency. Most states have chosen this second option. If so, the state must develop standards at least as effective as those promulgated by OSHA under federal law, must staff the agency with qualified employees, and must submit periodic reports on agency compliance to the U.S. Department of Labor.

While most of the OSHA regulations apply to industrial plants and private industry, many apply to government agencies as well. Typical regulations for office buildings include standards for number and size of entrances, lighting, ventilation, fire protection, and first-aid facilities. However, there are two major limitations on public agency compliance with OSHA regulations. First, OSHA generally has insufficient resources to investigate complaints. Second, while private contractors providing services through public agencies are subject to fines for OSHA violations, public agencies operating under civil service or political personnel systems are generally not subject to fines. Administrative sanctions like letters of reprimand simply do not have teeth.

Workers' Compensation

Workers' compensation systems began a century ago because of dissatisfaction with the previous practice of discharging injured employees without any employer responsibility for treatment or rehabilitation, or of relying on the civil litigation system to recompense employees for the costs of accidents or injuries. Unlike with Medicare and Medicaid, "workers' comp" is regulated by state laws with no Congressional oversight. Each state's system compensates employees for job-related injuries and illnesses. Workers' compensation is an insurance system with variable payment rates for employers based on the historical risks of accident or injury their employees have suffered. Employers may self-insure, buy private insurance, or seek universal coverage through a publicly chartered insurance agency in each state. The agency pays death benefits, hospitalization expenses, and expenses for a caregiver if an employee is injured or permanently disabled on the job. Workers' comp reimburses employees on an actual cost basis, based on decisions rendered by an administrative hearing body that decides whether the injury or illness is job related, and what compensation from the fund is to be awarded for it. The system is self-supporting, funded by employer contributions based on the number of employees and historical data about the nature and severity of occupational hazards (illness and injury) associated with particular types of work.

The workers' compensation system has worked fairly well in providing a routine system of treatment and rehabilitation for job-related injuries. However, nationwide, the average cost of workers' compensation insurance rose 50 percent from 2001–2003.[14] This increases two types of fraud and abuse. The first is claimant fraud—collusion among health-care providers and employees to increase reimbursable health-care costs excessively by lengthy and unnecessary treatments, and by requests to cover time away from work as compensated time. The second and far more serious problem is premium fraud by employers. Because in some dangerous jobs (such as roofing) the cost to employers for workers' comp insurance may equal the cost of wages themselves, employers often cut costs by fraudulently classifying employees in less-dangerous occupations.

The Americans with Disabilities Act

The **Americans with Disabilities Act (ADA)** prohibits employment discrimination based on ability. Between 1981 and 2004, about 8 percent of noninstitutionalized adults in the United States (about 14 million) reported a work limitation.[15] The ADA gives employment access rights to qualified persons whose disabilities do not adversely affect their work performance, or for whom employers can make reasonable accommodations that will allow them to work productively. Enforcement is through the EEOC. The number of EEOC charges brought under the ADA peaked at 19,798 in 1995 and have dropped thereafter, ranging from 14,893 in 2001 to 16,470 in 2006.[16]

Public personnel directors generally report that the ADA has had no significant impact on their agencies, particularly because the Rehabilitation Act of 1973 had already covered most public personnel practices.[17] However, there have been noticeable impacts on specific HR functions like job analysis and affirmative action compliance.[18] Specifically, employers continue to struggle with the question of when an employee with a disability is covered by the ADA (and thus eligible for accommodation through a **differentiated work assignment**), or is subject to discharge for inability to perform the essential functions of a position.[19] Disabled employees do have a greater risk of workplace injury. One medical study indicated that work disability is associated with a 36 percent increased risk of occupational injury.[20] Common disabilities such as blindness more than triple the risk for injury, and deafness more than doubles it. While this study did not advocate excluding such workers because of elevated risk (because they are indeed protected by the ADA), it emphasized that employers should not hesitate to deny employment—as the law allows—when the applicant's disability is a direct threat to his own health or safety. Older employees—those least likely to be affected by civil service system workforce cuts because of their greater seniority—also have higher health-care costs and rates of workplace illness and injury.

Finally, coverage for mentally disabled employees is perpetually problematic.[21] Mental illnesses are generally harder to diagnose, and accommodations are generally less obvious, than is the case with physical disabilities. While treatment of physical disabilities often requires physical modifications, treatment of mental illnesses often requires changes in the nature or context of the job that are beyond the employer's capacity. Employers may run into ADA conflicts when they attempt to enforce work regulations[22] or provisions against bizarre or hostile employee behavior as part of a program to detect and prevent workplace violence.[23]

The Family and Medical Leave Act

Congress enacted the **Family and Medical Leave Act (FMLA)** in 1993 to respond to growing concerns over job security for people with health problems, and to assist working parents. The Act is an attempt to promote family integrity by balancing the demands of the workplace with family needs.[24] It was originally intended to allow employees with a "serious health condition" to retain their job rights if they need to take time off to care for himself or herself or a family member. However, administrative interpretations of the FMLA have made it difficult, in many employers' opinion, to comply with the law. "Serious health conditions" may include illness such as colds or flu if they are incapacitating and require continued treatment; and the statutory twelve weeks of leave (paid or not) can be taken in increments as small as fifteen minutes per week.[25] Some employees misuse FMLA leave as they might misuse sick leave.[26]

The complexity of legal requirements and interaction among laws (such as ADA and FMLA) are compelling reasons for employers to seek expert advice, to contract out their benefits adjudication policies and procedures, or to avoid ADA compliance issues entirely by using outside contractors instead of employees.

Emergent Issues Posed by Independent Contractors

Two emergent and interrelated issues also affect employers' ability to manage employee health and safety—working at home and part-time work "on the side." First, changes in the nature of work—especially computerization and communications—have made it easy for employees whose jobs comprise "knowledge management" rather than manufacturing or services to work together in virtual networks without being in the same physical location. **Telecommuting** allows employees to increase the flexibility of work schedules or locations, and to thus better balance personal and work needs, by communicating through networked computers, Internet, phones, and faxes. Yet at-home or distant work locations are virtually impossible to monitor for health and safety concerns. So, as employee preferences and employer practice encourage more work at home, how will the lack of safety standards or enforcement affect employer responsibility for the costs of accident or sickness?

A second troublesome issue is "**moonlighting**." Americans work longer hours than their European counterparts and still work "on the side." This can be both legal and of little concern regarding health and safety, as in the case of accountants who prepare individual tax returns for supplemental income. However, it may be illegal (if payments are accepted in cash or as barter and not declared as taxable income) or dangerous for the moonlighting employee (if it involves jobs such as trimming trees or delivering appliances). Employers can avoid collusion and comply with federal income tax laws by reporting all payments to contractors on Form 1099, just as they report all employee wages on Form W-2. As independent contractors, moonlighting workers are supposed to provide their own social security, workers' compensation, and other "hidden" payroll costs. They are also responsible for their own health-care costs and health insurance. The predictable risk management consequence for their "regular" employer is workers' comp fraud. Employees injured while "moonlighting" often seek to claim workers' compensation coverage from their "regular" employer.

The workers' comp system also has difficulty handling psychological and environmental illnesses (such as depression) or stress-related illnesses (stroke and heart attack), where it is difficult to separate the effect of job stress from other stressors. These problems have led to efforts to reform the system in many states. Typical reforms include substitution of light-duty positions for full-time disability, on the theory that paying an employee to work productively in some job is better than paying temporary or permanent disability benefits to that employee, and hiring another person to take his or her place.

IMPROVING WORKPLACE HEALTH AND SAFETY

Improving unsafe or unhealthy working conditions is a legal requirement. In addition, it is also a desirable policy to protect employees and their continued productivity. Human resources directors, risk managers, and other professionals can exert great influence on occupational health and safety through audits and risk assessment, correcting unsafe facilities and workplace conditions, re-designing jobs, providing orientation and training, and using feedback and incentive systems to strengthen a culture of safety among employees and supervisors.[27]

Audits and Risk Assessment

Together with facilities managers and safety engineers, HR directors and risk managers can correct unsafe facilities or working conditions reported by employees or supervisors. Two types of audits are useful. Management audits evaluate whether the occupational safety or health management system fulfills the needs of the organization; compliance audits monitor the organization's compliance with regulatory provisions.[28] Typical elements included in the occupational safety and health audit are program elements (such as safety, ergonomics, and medical care) to environmental factors like resource availability, organizational structure, and accountability.[29] Risk assessment requires understanding federal regulatory agency policies and guidelines with respect to four types of risks that may be present in the workplace:[30]

- Hazardous agents: biological agents, chemicals, disinfectants, antibiotics, hormones, and medications and hazardous waste
- Physical hazards: noise, temperature extremes (including burns caused by heat and freezing), mechanical injuries, radiation, violence, and slips and falls

- Ergonomic hazards: lifting (strains or back injuries), standing (for long periods), and poor lighting (eyestrain)
- Psychological hazards: boredom, discrimination, technological change, shift work, downsizing, and other adverse working conditions.

Improving Job Design

In many cases, high rates of injury and illness are due to faulty job design. A job that is alternately boring and stressful, or that requires the use of dangerous equipment, increases the risk to the employee. Perhaps the personnel department can redesign the work procedure to reduce these factors. For example, many nurses are physically unable to lift and move heavy patients, so hospitals have assigned this duty to male nurses' aides or orderlies. Yet hospitals are frequently understaffed, particularly on the night shift, so nurses often end up doing this lifting themselves. The result can be a disabling back injury that could have been prevented by greater recognition of the costs of *not* filling nurses' aide positions.

Ergonomics is the design of jobs and tools to fit human physiological and psychological needs. The issue has become important because the incidence of so-called "repetitive strain injuries" due to repeated motion, vibration, or pressure has increased rapidly over the past ten years. The worst jobs are in meatpacking and poultry processing plants, garment manufacturing, and automobile repair. However, office equipment like computers and video display terminals also causes many such injuries. In response, OSHA issued regulations in 2000 that required employers to adopt **musculoskeletal disorders (MSD)** policies, including programs to identify and provide medical treatment for injured workers, eliminate or substantially reduce workplace causes, and train employees and managers.[31] The growth of training and orientation programs as a means of increasing employee health and safety is an outgrowth of risk management.[32] These programs should contain information on work safety, potentially hazardous job conditions, emergency evacuation procedures, the location of fire extinguishers and alarms, and procedures for reporting job-related injuries or illnesses. This will reinforce the importance of health and safety for supervisors and employees. It will also minimize the employer's financial and legal liability. If employees have read and signed policies for timely reporting accidents, they will be ineligible for disability benefits based on accident or injury claims not reported in correct or timely fashion.

Training programs need to be comprehensive yet specific to the job. It is no coincidence that employees in high-risk occupations such as public safety and health are required to undergo the most training.[33] For example, firefighters who are qualified as paramedics need technical training in both fields, as well as training to improve their ability to provide complex services in a multiethnic urban environment. Employers cannot expect illiterate employees to use equipment or supplies properly, even if they have explicit written instructions for their safe use.

Feedback and Incentive Programs

Feedback and incentive programs that reward employees and supervisors for safety can support the two-way communication process needed to maintain a culture of occupational safety. Over the past thirty years, repeated results have shown that reward programs for such safety behaviors as use of seat belts and mandatory protective equipment are effective at increasing safe work practices. Since most local governments are self-insured, it makes sense to pass on some of the savings from safety to responsible employees through incentive programs. For example, some cities award savings bonds to employees whose job duties require the use of a city car, and who drive for a year or more without any chargeable accidents (those attributable to traffic violations).

It is important to reward not only employees for safe work habits but also their supervisors for recognizing, evaluating, and controlling occupational health and safety hazards. This means publicizing the agency's record of time lost through work-related accidents or injuries, comparing this with other work units or over time, and using compensation and disability payouts as one measure of the supervisor's performance evaluation. Granted, supervisors cannot control all the unsafe conditions inherent in a job. However, they can work with employees on safer ways of handling jobs, and with top management on ways of designing work so that it can be performed with less risk to employees. Increased safety generally requires not only occupational safety and health programs, but also an informal organizational culture that supports employee perceptions about the personal and organizational value of workplace safety.[34]

WORKPLACE VIOLENCE

According to the Bureau of Justice Statistics, workplace assaults injure an estimated 1.7 million workers each year; in addition, violent workplace incidents account for 18 percent of all violent crime in the United States. Liberty Mutual, in its annual *Workplace Safety Index*, cites "assaults and violent acts" as the tenth leading cause of nonfatal occupational injury in 2002, representing about 1 percent of all workplace injuries and a cost of $400 million. During the thirteen-year period from 1992 to 2004, an average of 807 workplace homicides occurred annually in the United States, according to the Bureau of Labor Statistics (BLS) Census of Fatal Occupational Injuries (CFOI) [BLS 2005]. The number of workplace homicides ranged from a high of 1,080 in 1994 to a low of 551 in 2004, the lowest number since CFOI began in 1992.[35]

Ours is a violent society, and it is not surprising that this violence carries over into the workplace. In recent years, organizational scholars have increasingly focused on various forms of bad behavior in the workplace, including deviance, aggression, antisocial behavior, and violence. OSHA and the Department of Justice classify victims of **workplace violence** as follows:[36]

- *Stranger violence:* Victims have no business relationship with the perpetrators. This includes cab drivers, sales clerks, gas station attendants, and police. The main motive is robbery. About 80 percent of workplace homicides are of this type.
- *Client violence:* A current or former client, customer, or patient attacks victims. Common settings are hospitals, psychiatric facilities, mental health clinics, drug abuse centers, long-term care facilities, prisons, and schools.
- *Employee violence:* Victims are current or former employers, spouses, or significant others of the perpetrators.

Workplace Violence and Public Employees

Public employees are at particular risk from client violence. They must serve all segments of the population, including many who are mentally ill, have convictions for violent crimes, or are under the influence of drugs or alcohol. Further, they must enforce laws, rules, and policies that are unpopular. Potentially violent "customers" are not inclined to distinguish between levels of government or types of agencies. They can resent local government officials simply because they dislike the national government's policies.[37]

A 1997 Department of Justice survey indicated that although public employees made up only 16 percent of the U.S. workforce, 37 percent of the victims of workplace violence work in local state and federal government![38] Women are likely to be victims of employee violence.[39] Workplace homicide was the greatest cause of death among female workers from 1980 to 1985.[40] A **National Institutes of Occupational Safety and Health (NIOSH)** report found that homicides accounted for 12 percent of workplace deaths among men and 42 percent among women.[41] Some workplace violence is attributed to domestic violence: husbands and boyfriends commit 13,000 acts of violence against women in the workplace every year. Abusive husbands and lovers harass 74 percent of employed battered women at work—either in person or over the telephone—causing 56 percent of them to be late at least five times a month, 28 percent to leave early at least five days a month, and 54 percent to miss at least three full days of work a month.[42] This **domestic violence** costs employers an estimated $3 to $5 billion annually in lost productivity, increased health-care costs, absenteeism, and workplace violence.[43]

Beyond these costs, workplace violence has a less measurable impact on employee stress and organizational climate. Organizations that are already working to establish principles of objectivity and fairness as part of alternative dispute resolution procedures under a workforce diversity program will find these efforts undermined by workplace violence or the threat of it.

Employers' Legal Liability for Employee Violence

Employers may be reluctant to confront workplace violence because they fear that if they know that an employee is being abused and do nothing, they will be sued.[44] Nevertheless, this may happen in any event. Under the traditional doctrine of *respondeat superior*, an employer is "vicariously" liable for the violent actions of its employees as long as (1) the employee is acting within the scope of his employment, (2) the employer authorized the employee's action, or (3) the employer ratified the employee's actions subsequent to the occurrence.[45] Courts have also held employers liable to victims under the theory of negligent hiring, retention, and referral. Under these theories, courts have established that there is a duty that the employer owes its employees, customers, suppliers, and other individuals who meet its employees. An employer can be liable for acts of violence committed by current or former employees: for (1) **negligent hiring** if it failed to verify references or employment gaps which could indicate the applicant had spent time in prison; (2) **negligent retention** if it is aware that an employee has dangerous or violent tendencies but takes no action to reclassify or discharge the employee; or (3) **negligent referral** for terminating an employee for violent behavior and then failing to disclose the violent behavior to prospective employers during reference checks, or providing a positive letter of recommendation to the employee. To establish employer liability, a victim generally must show that the employer breached the duty it owed to the victim and the employer's breach of that duty "caused" the victim's injury.[46] The principal means of limiting or expanding employer liability for negligent hiring and retention claims is the requirement of "foreseeability." The stronger the connection between the information known or available to the employer and the harm ultimately suffered, the greater the likelihood that the employer will be found liable in negligence.[47]

Employers who attempt to screen job applicants for violent tendencies run the risk of violating applicants' civil rights. For example, Title VII of the 1964 Civil Rights Act prohibits employers from refusing employment or discharging employees based on (1) an arrest record (since an arrest is not a conviction); or (2) a criminal conviction[48] unless the prospective employer can establish that the conviction would indicate that the applicant poses "a substantial and foreseeable threat to the safety of individuals or property."[49]

Liability issues are not limited to the hiring process. Employers who attempt to discharge an employee for violent outbursts, threatening staff, or demonstrating odd and erratic behavior can also be sued under the ADA. Under this law, employees who exhibit these behaviors may have a legally protected disability, for which the employer must make a reasonable accommodation prior to considering termination. However, given the human, legal, and financial risks of workplace violence, there is widespread agreement that employers should institute a zero-tolerance policy for direct physical assault or the threat of assault.[50]

Employer Responses to Workplace Violence

In 2005, the BLS and NIOSH conducted a comprehensive survey about workplace violence policies, covering 7.4 million employers with 128 million employees. Survey results indicated that 5 percent of all employers had had an incident of workplace violence in the past year. The rate for state and local government agencies was three times this average. Although about a third of the employers reported that the incident had a negative effect on their workplace, 9 percent still had no policy on workplace violence.[51]

What precautions can employers take to protect themselves and their employees from workplace violence?[52] First, employers should examine hiring policies and procedures to be sure that information about gaps in employment, disciplinary action from former employers, use of illegal drugs, and previous criminal convictions are available to those making a hiring decision. References should be checked with at least two prior employers and document everything that is said about the prospective employee in the event they were not disclosing all the relevant facts. A criminal background check may be worthwhile depending on the position.

Second, profiling is not an effective risk management technique. The characteristic profile of the violence-prone employee is a middle-aged white male with a seniority of five to fifteen years who collects guns and has few social ties.[53] Because many nonviolent employees also fit this profile, employers should work to create an employee culture that makes violence unthinkable. They should take verbal and physical violence seriously and establish a "**zero tolerance**" policy that sets consequences for perpetrators. An employer who moves immediately to stop dangerous behavior at the first instance cannot be blamed for allowing it to continue past the point at which when a reasonable person might conclude that the violence-prone employee was placing coworkers or clients at risk. Furthermore, it is usually easier to discipline or separate an employee for misconduct than it is for poor performance. All incidents of workplace violence should be reported to the police for investigation and possible criminal prosecution.[54]

Managers should be aware of the link between workplace violence and a deteriorating organizational culture.[55] If people communicate freely with each other and with management, threats will be reported more readily and agency values will be transmitted more clearly. Supervisors should be trained in how to handle verbal violence. The best form of prevention is to remain calm and decide on the best course of action, listening carefully and being interested in what the angry person is saying. The objective is to let the angry person calm down and lead him or her to focus more on facts rather than on opinions or personality dynamics.

Workplace violence often results from layoffs, particularly in a paternalistic agency where employees have come to expect that they will be taken care of. Yet if employees feel protected, appreciated, and respected, there is less chance that they will become violent. Potential violence can be prevented and downsizing somewhat humanized if the manager has the opportunity to explain and clarify the company's actions. For example, companies that use layoff criteria that de-emphasize recent performance in favor of long-term performance history will find that they eliminate many rationalized motives for disruptive behavior.[56]

Employers should create a plan that describes how the organization would deal with warnings from employees about other potentially violent employees.[57] They should consider establishing a "threat management team" comprising legal staff, security personnel, the personnel director, psychological experts, union representatives, and employee assistance workers to respond to threats of violence or an actual incident. They should take special precautions when terminating an employee for threats or violence. The termination should be conducted in private with at least two supervisors present; security should be immediately available yet unobtrusive; the last paycheck should be provided by mail so that the discharged employee is not required to return to the premises after termination; and HR should work with the employee on such post-termination issues as accrued leave benefits and unemployment compensation.[58]

DISASTER PREPAREDNESS

Since 9/11, the **Department of Homeland Security (DHS)** has been responsible for national policy with respect to hazards, natural disasters, and terrorist incidents. State and local governments have established offices of homeland security or reorganized their emergency management departments to include this function.[59] In general, these changes have involved creating administrative structures and policies in four areas: (1) preventing terrorist incidents through coordination with law enforcement agencies, (2) preparing for disasters and terrorist incidents by developing flexible and responsive plans for dealing with a range of possible scenarios, (3) responding effectively based on these plans, and (4) ensuring that they can continue to provide essential government services to the public.

First, while national policy-making responsibility for disaster response lies with the U.S. Department of Homeland Security (DHS), actual policy implementation will be by "first responders" (law enforcement and fire-rescue paramedics and EMTs) and the public health network working together in "incident management" teams. These organizations are responsible for effectively communicating with one another to respond to disasters, and with the public about these responses. Experience with earthquakes and fires in southern California and the World Trade Center attacks of 9/11 indicates that public demand for information and services will increase dramatically, and often continue for months.[60]

The second step is for individual employers to develop their own response plans for dealing with a range of incidents. Given the difficulty organizations had confronting workplace violence at a relatively minor level a decade ago, it is not surprising that most are not well prepared to respond to natural disasters or terrorist incidents.[61] The primary reasons for this are the difficulties of preparing for the varied contingencies involving a range of hazards, disasters, and terrorist scenarios, and risk managers' arguments against allocating scarce funds to prepare for things that have a small risk of occurring. HR managers are at a particular disadvantage here, given that it is difficult to demonstrate, through cost-benefit analysis based on prior experience, that investments in disaster preparedness are worthwhile.[62]

Third, response data are difficult to find. The one major disaster that would test the effectiveness of this planning was Hurricane Katrina that struck New Orleans in 2005. This disaster was of unprecedented magnitude, with damage estimates ranging from $70 billion to $200 billion. Nevertheless, the general conclusion in government reports and academic journals is that governments were completely overwhelmed by this disaster and faced major problems with intergovernmental communications, decision making, public communication, and service provision, and extended operations.[63]

Although these realities exist, there are things organizations can do to prepare for disasters. First, local organizations coordinate themselves and connect to the federal and state **National Incident Management System (NIMS)**. This is a general template for coordinating responses to disasters across levels of government, with NGOs, and with the private sector.[64] Second, each organization should develop disaster response plans based on both the characteristics common to a locality and those unique to the organization. This includes staffing plans for getting the right people in the right place and with what they need to be safe, comfortable, and productive.[65] They can minimize staff injuries by disaster drills that teach managers and supervisors how to respond appropriately to various scenarios.[66] One of the most troublesome issues is reconciling agency needs for increased staffing through overtime and the use of volunteers with employee needs to locate and care for their own families. Finally, helped by professional associations and working with risk managers and budget directors, HR managers can make data-driven decisions about health insurance, life insurance, and re-insurance policies covering human and financial losses incurred from disasters and terrorist incidents.[67]

TOBACCO, ALCOHOL, AND ILLEGAL DRUGS

Tobacco, alcohol, and other drugs are widely used in our society. It is important to examine three critical areas of research: effects of these drugs in the workplace, legal requirements for employers, and recommended workplace policies and practice.

Effects on Health, Safety, and Productivity

Thirty years ago, smoking was considered a personal habit rather than a workplace policy issue. Today, over twenty states have comprehensive bans against indoor smoking in public places.[68] Most public employers ban smoking in the workplace as a violation of employees' right to a safe and healthy workplace.

The cost of **alcohol abuse** is high, measured in impaired performance, absenteeism, injuries, and fatalities. According to the National Institute on Alcohol Abuse and Alcoholism estimates alcohol abuse results in a yearly $117 billion loss in productivity along with $13 billion in employee rehabilitation expenses.[69] The institute concluded that alcoholism accounts for about 105,000 deaths each year, and an estimated $136 billion in lost employment, reduced productivity, and health-care costs in 1990.[70] Alcohol abuse increases liability risks for employers because of the increased chance of performance impairments that will affect customers, coworkers, or the public. Moreover, employees do not like to work with alcohol abusers because this tends to reduce their own morale and productivity.

Drug abuse is a serious public health problem, and the workplace is obviously not immune from its effects.[71] The National Clearinghouse for Drug and Alcohol Abuse estimated that drug abuse cost U.S. employers $7.2 billion per year in productivity losses. A large-scale longitudinal study of 5,465 postal employees found higher rates of absenteeism and turnover for employees who tested positive for drugs (59.3 percent and 47 percent, respectively).[72] **Substance abuse** also results in higher health insurance costs for employers.

However, because estimates of drug use in general population are not valid indicators of drug use among employees, there is also considerable controversy over the nature and severity of employee drug abuse. Alcohol is the workplace drug of choice, followed by marijuana.[73] A large sample of high school graduates indicated that in 1991, 8 percent of women and 5 percent of men have used alcohol on the job. The next most abused drug is marijuana with 5 percent of men and 1 percent of women reporting use while at work. All other drugs (amphetamines, barbiturates, and cocaine) are used by less than 1 percent of employees surveyed.[74] Therefore, there is little support for concluding that drug and alcohol abuse is rampant in the workplace.[75] A large survey conducted by the National Institute of Mental Health found that casual drug use does not normally influence work performance.[76] However, drug-related accidents are significantly underreported because twenty states deny any compensation claim if drug or alcohol use is present.[77]

Legal Requirements for Employers

Tobacco is legal. However, most employers ban smoking in the workplace because of the health and liability issues raised by exposure to secondhand smoke.[78]

Intoxication by alcohol or illegal drugs is illegal for federal agencies or contractors under Executive Order 12564 (Drug Free Federal Work Place). Alcohol is legal and socially accepted. However, employers may be liable if employees are hurt or cause injury to others at organizational functions where alcohol is served. In such cases, the issue comes down to the extent of the employer's knowledge of, or control over, things like "happy hour" receptions as part of conferences or training seminars.[79] The most common response of organizations that wish to limit their risk exposure is to allow employees to purchase alcohol at off-site locations like conferences or restaurant meetings, but not to reimburse these costs or provide it at the workplace or at employer-sponsored offsite events.

In the past, courts have routinely upheld **drug testing** for cause when there was evidence of impaired performance or misconduct. In deciding whether drug testing of employees without such evidence represents an unreasonable search, courts must balance the degree to which the search is an intrusion upon the individual's privacy rights and the degree to which the search reflects a legitimate government interest. Several Supreme Court decisions clarify this balance. In ***National Treasury Employees Union v. von Raab*** (1988), it upheld the government's right to require drug testing for Customs agents carrying guns and seizing drugs because of the security-sensitive nature of their positions. In ***Samuel Skinner v. Railway Labor Executives' Association*** (1988), it upheld mandatory post-accident testing of railroad workers on grounds that this was a closely regulated industry where the government had a responsibility to protect public safety. Subsequent federal court decisions have clarified, but not substantially changed, these two landmark cases.[80] Most public employers have instituted some form of pre-employment drug testing policy for job applicants, who have a reduced expectation of privacy, because as applicants they are not compelled to seek the job.

The **Omnibus Transportation Employee Testing Act of 1991** does require drug and alcohol testing of employees required to have commercial driver's licenses as a condition of employment (including drivers of trash trucks, dump trucks, buses, and street sweepers). Several types of testing are required under U.S. Department of Transportation guidelines: pre-employment testing of all applicants, post-accident ("critical incident") testing for all employees involved in an accident, random testing of a specified percentage of the workforce annually, and "reasonable suspicion"—testing of employees who appear to be under the influence of alcohol or drugs.

Workplace Policies and Programs

Sixteen states and more than 340 localities require at least some smoking restrictions in private businesses; thirty-two states regulate smoking by public employees in the workplace.[81] In some cases, employers may forbid employees to smoke because of the increased health-care costs and liability risks that smokers impose on coworkers and on their employer. For example, many municipal fire departments are refusing to hire smokers as firefighters because smoking increases the likelihood that firefighters will subsequently be eligible for workers' compensation or disability retirement based on heart or lung disease. In 1994, the city of North Miami (Florida) won a state Supreme Court case prohibiting any new employee from smoking, on similar grounds of increased health-care costs. Usually, an exploratory survey by the personnel department to assess employee attitudes toward smoking will show that relatively few people smoke, and that many who do are willing to limit their use of tobacco on the job. In fact, the pendulum has swung so completely against workplace smoking that some researchers are concerned that the objectivity of smokers' performance appraisals may be affected by this stigma.[82] Employee cooperation with smoking policies can best be achieved by managerial compliance, union involvement, the availability of **smoking cessation programs** offered by the employer, and passing some of the savings along to nonsmoking employees in the form of lower health insurance premiums or health benefit costs. In cases where consensus and voluntary compliance are ineffective, it is sometimes necessary for the agency to discipline employees who violate no-smoking policies or to defend its no-smoking policies in court.

Given the lack of consensus on the magnitude of illegal drug and alcohol use as a workplace problem, there is considerable disagreement on the appropriateness of drug testing as a workplace policy response.[83] In the absence of a legally defined mandate, employers are generally reluctant to institute random drug testing.[84] In the end, they conclude that it is more effective to focus on employee performance, and then to use selective testing as the basis for referral to an EAP or documentation of disciplinary action.[85]

The ultimate solution is education and changing the norms and values of the workplace through employee education programs. The elements of an effective program include cultivating a shared responsibility between labor and management for reducing drug and alcohol abuse, a comprehensive drug education and awareness program, supervisor training on identifying drug use, clear employee policies on drug and alcohol abuse, a fully functioning employee wellness program, and a focused and limited drug and alcohol testing program. However, a recent survey of personnel directors indicated that while an overwhelming majority believe that treatment programs are effective and easily accessible, one in four companies is less likely to hire a candidate recovering from drug addiction.[86] For the most part, courts have not considered alcoholism as a covered disability under ADA. When they have, accommodation has been minimal, such as allowing time off for treatment and rehabilitation.[87]

AIDS AND OTHER LIFE-THREATENING DISEASES

AIDS and other life-threatening diseases pose a risk for employers and employees in general, and especially for those in the public sector. **Acquired immune deficiency syndrome (AIDS)** is a progressive disease. Infected individuals fall into four categories: (1) those who carry and can transmit the virus but display no physical symptoms (**HIV+**); (2) those who experience some AIDS-related symptoms such as night sweats, weight loss, swollen lymph nodes, or fatigue; (3) those who have developed opportunistic infections but do not require hospitalization and are physically able to work; and (4) those who are weakened by multiple infections (and are thus unable to work and may require hospitalization). As patients survive longer because of earlier detection and increasingly effective drug combinations, life spans have increased indefinitely. This means increased costs of prescription drugs and health care because professional providers must supplement family members and volunteer social service agencies as caregivers.[88]

AIDS is a workplace problem for two distinct groups of employees. The group that runs the greatest risk of contracting human immunodeficiency virus (HIV) is the health-care workers (doctors, dentists, nurses, dental hygienists, laboratory technicians, paramedics) whose jobs involve working with the body fluids of HIV+ patients. Transmission of bloodborne pathogens like HIV can be controlled through education, training, and what health-care professional call **"universal precautions"**—preventing blood-to-blood contact (either from an infected patient or worker to an uninfected one) through the use of gloves and other specialized clothing, and safe techniques for handling and disposing of contaminated "sharps" (needles, etc.).[89] This also bypasses the troublesome legal issue of whether health-care professionals should be tested for life-threatening diseases (including AIDS) when circumstances often make it impossible to conduct the same sort of test on incoming emergency patients whom health-care professionals are routinely asked to treat without regard to their own safety.[90]

Employees in other work settings are in no danger of contracting HIV from a coworker under normal working conditions. However, their weakened immune systems make HIV+ employees more susceptible to catching infections from other employees. The solution is to educate employees about the remote possibility of contracting the HIV virus in the workplace. Employers should offer **reasonable accommodation** to HIV+ employees as long as they are healthy enough to perform the primary duties of the position, and then offer sick leave, **disability retirement**, and dependent benefits once failing health forces the employee to leave the workforce.

In reality, health-care professionals—and patients or hospital visitors—are at much greater risk from airborne bacteria that cause tuberculosis ("TB"), staphylococcus ("staph"), and streptococcus ("strep") infections. These spread easily due to closed buildings with mechanical ventilation and air conditioning systems. As overuse of antibiotics causes the evolution of drug-resistant strains of these diseases, and they will probably spread into the general population. Moreover, airborne viruses like influenza ("flu") are immune to antibiotics and are equally dangerous to those with weakened immune systems because of very young age, old age, or illness.

Concern for health-care costs exerts tremendous pressure on employers. Although this is a clear violation of the ADA, it is obviously in their best interest to identify carriers of the AIDS virus prior to employment, and to have AIDS or AIDS-related diseases excluded from coverage as pre-existing conditions. Some employers who would want to treat AIDS as an exclusionary precondition may also discriminate against homosexuals in hiring on the basis that they are members of a high-risk group. These pressures indicate fundamental conflict between the values of individual rights (for AIDS victims, homosexuals, and their coworkers) and efficiency (health-care costs and productivity).[91] Other employment-related AIDS issues have not yet been addressed by the Supreme Court: (1) does mandatory AIDS testing of employees in health-care agencies violate constitutional privacy protection? (2) Is testing prison inmates a civil rights violation? (3) Is it a violation of federal law for a company to reduce the health-care benefits of an employee with AIDS, and (4) does barring an HIV+ medical assistant from participating in surgery violate the ADA?

EMPLOYEE WELLNESS PROGRAMS

Consider the following statistics, and you will understand why employers have adopted **employee wellness programs** (or **employee assistance programs—EAPs**, as they are also called) to deal with a range of employee issues that can interfere with work performance.[92] From the employee's viewpoint, the objective is to treat personal problems before they have an irreparable effect on job status. From the employer's viewpoint, the objective is to rehabilitate employees whose personal problems are a threat to productivity, health-care costs, or legal liability; and to lay the groundwork for possible disciplinary action and discharge (if the employee cannot be rehabilitated) before these threats become a reality. Hard evidence confirms that wellness programs save much more than they cost—according to one recent study, $2.45 for every dollar invested.[93] They also result in improved morale, positive lifestyle changes, improved medical claims and insurance rates, and reduced turnover.

Over time, both the functions of wellness programs and the role of the supervisor have changed substantially and rapidly. The traditional program focused almost exclusively on alcohol abuse. Contemporary programs also address drug abuse, AIDS education, and other personal problems that may affect job performance (family problems, emotional and psychiatric problems, legal counseling, and financial counseling).[94] Wellness programs also treat employee stress caused by economic pressure, increased family responsibilities, and the weakening of the social safety net of institutions.[95] Stress increases the possibility of poor or erratic work performance, causing risks to productivity and risk management. It is a leading cause of absenteeism: a recent study reported that two out of every five unscheduled absences were the result of worker stress and time-off policy abuse.[96] Stress leads to physical disabilities such as high blood pressure, stroke, and heart disease. It can result in increased alcoholism and drug abuse, because employees often use these as stress-reduction mechanisms.[97]

Managers can help employees recognize and manage stress by promoting good health habits, substituting meditation, exercise, or work breaks for unhealthy stress reducers, and providing health counseling.[98] Managers can also recognize that organizational culture can stress employees: downsizing, inadequate training and feedback, or management pressures for unreasonable productivity increases, or mandatory overtime to cope with economic competition. Then they can exert influence within the organization to reduce organizational policies that contribute unreasonably to job stress.

The development of EAPs means that responsibility for the diagnosis and treatment of personal problems is no longer a supervisory responsibility, if indeed it ever was. Today the supervisor observes and records changes in employee behavior and job performance as documentation used to discipline employees and to refer them to the program for professional diagnosis and treatment. Moreover, it poses an ethical issue for personnel directors and employees to consider. Have employers endorsed the concept of the wellness program for its value in **rehabilitation** and productivity, or as a sort of legal insurance policy against employee grievances and lawsuits arising out of disciplinary action?

Finally, wellness programs are also subject to the provisions of the ADA and the privacy requirements of the **Health Insurance Portability and Accountability Act of 1996 (HIPAA)**.[99] If group insurance plans include incentives or disincentives, HIPAA prohibits discrimination based on health status. However, this does not "prevent a group health plan from establishing premium discounts or rebates or modifying otherwise applicable co-payments or deductibles in return for adherence to programs of health promotion and disease prevention."[100]

BALANCING ORGANIZATIONAL EFFECTIVENESS AND EMPLOYEE RIGHTS

Implementation of the ADA, FMLA, Title VII, and workers' compensation laws usually requires balancing organizational effectiveness and employee rights.[101] Employers have always used job-related medical criteria (such as a history of back injuries in an applicant for a job requiring heavy lifting) to exclude applicants who cannot perform the essential functions of a job, and for which no reasonable accommodation exists. This is legal under the ADA. Employers also face considerable pressure from insurance carriers to exclude otherwise qualified applicants by using more generalized genetic[102] health indicators that may indicate that an applicant is a long-term health risk because general health indicators are outside normal limits.[103] Examples are abnormal weight to height, abnormal electrocardiogram, abnormal blood chemistry (such as cholesterol levels), history of heavy drinking (as determined by liver enzyme activity), history of substance abuse (as determined by urinalysis), likelihood of developing AIDS (as determined by HIV antibody tests), or diabetes.[104]

While this is certainly justified from a risk management perspective (one recent study indicates that obesity-related conditions such as heart disease, stroke, and high blood pressure account for 43 percent of health insurance dollars),[105] excluding otherwise qualified applicants is a clear violation of the ADA.[106] The Supreme Court overturned selection standards under which chemical companies refused to employ females of childbearing age in positions in which there was risk of exposure to chemical toxins that could cause birth defects in unborn children.[107] Lower courts had held that the risk to the employer outweighed the right of the individual applicant to be considered for jobs for which they are interested and qualified, holding that these risks were relatively slight compared to the employment rights of the affected individuals. Faced with such dilemmas, it is understandable why finding job-related reasons to disqualify high-risk applicants is a clandestine but routine practice among many personnel directors.[108] Nonetheless, despite enjoying Eleventh Amendment immunity from money damages under Title I of the ADA, states may be liable for money damages under Title II (physical exclusion).[109]

Summary

Employee health and safety are important from the viewpoint of maintaining human resources as an asset and reducing the health-care costs and liability risks generated by unsafe or unhealthy workplace conditions. Personnel directors must appropriately accommodate qualified persons with disabilities, where such practice does not compromise health, productivity, and safety. Personnel directors are also responsible for providing employees with a safe and healthy workplace by addressing such concerns as occupational safety and health, smoking, drug and alcohol abuse, and life-threatening diseases.

Many public personnel directors justifiably view controversial topics such as workplace violence or substance abuse policies as *risks* because they raise unavoidable conflicts among key human resource management values—responsiveness to elected officials, administrative efficiency, and protection of employee rights. In fact, these issues also present personnel directors with *opportunities* to play a critical role in the resolution of emergent public policy.

Key Terms

Acquired Immune Deficiency Syndrome (AIDS) *293*
Americans with Disabilities Act (ADA) *282*
Department of Homeland Security (DHS) *289*
differentiated work assignment *282*
disability retirement *293*
domestic violence *287*
drug testing *291*
employee wellness programs (Employee Assistance Programs—EAPs) *294*
Family and Medical Leave Act (FMLA) *283*
Health Insurance Portability and Accountability Act of 1996 (HIPAA) *295*
lifestyle choices *280*
National Incident Management System (NIMS) *290*
National Institutes of Occupational Safety and Health (NIOSH) *287*
National Treasury Employees Union v. von Raab (1988) *291*
negligent hiring, retention and referral *287*
Occupational Safety and Health Act (OSHA) *281*
Omnibus Transportation Employee Testing Act of (1991) *291*
reasonable accommodation *293*
rehabilitation *295*
Samuel Skinner v. Railway Labor Executives' Association (1988) *292*
smoking cessation program *292*
substance abuse *291*
universal precautions *293*
workers' compensation *282*
workplace fatalities, injuries and illness (WFII) *279*
workplace violence *286*

Discussion Questions

1. What is the relationship between employee health and productivity?
2. What is Occupational Safety and Health Act (OSHA)? What does it require of employers?
3. What can personnel directors do to improve workplace health and safety?
4. What can employers do to reduce or respond to workplace violence, and to more generalized dangers like natural disasters or terrorist incidents?
5. How does employee substance abuse affect productivity, liability, and risk management?
6. What policies and programs have employers adopted to combat workplace substance abuse?
7. Why is AIDS a workplace health issue for public agencies? for health-care employers?
8. What are employee wellness programs (EAPs)? What is their role with respect to workplace substance abuse and AIDS?
9. What dilemmas do public personnel directors face in designing selection, development, and disciplinary action policies and procedures that balance agency concerns for productivity with employee concerns for privacy and individual rights? How should they resolve these dilemmas?

Case Study #1: Developing a Workplace AIDS Policy

You are the personnel director of a state government agency. Top management and employees have both been putting pressure on you to develop a comprehensive agency policy for AIDS and other life-threatening diseases. Because the agency does not provide health-care services, there is no risk of blood-to-blood contact in the course of employees' job duties.

1. What would be the major components of your policy?
2. How would you "sell" it to employees and management?
3. What would be the role of the employee assistance program? How would you evaluate the effectiveness of its services?

Case Study #2: Workplace Violence—"In Hindsight, We Could See it Coming"

The Event

In the predawn hours on February 9, 1996, a disgruntled former park and recreation department employee, Clifton McCree, burst into the maintenance trailer where six of his former coworkers were starting their day's work. In five minutes, six people were dead of gunshot wounds: Clifton McCree had killed five of the six coworkers, and then had turned the gun upon himself; one coworker escaped to tell the story of horror and death.

The Background

After eighteen years of employment, Clifton McCree had been discharged from the City of Ft. Lauderdale in October of 1994 after failing a drug test. After this, he had been unable to find steady work, and he had grown increasingly depressed and angry over what he saw as racial discrimination and retaliation by white employees and supervisors.

Mr. McCree had a history of workplace confrontations with coworkers. In the past, other employees had complained about his occasional threats to kill them. His supervisors had counseled him informally about the need to control his temper. Although he frequently went into rages, and coworkers were afraid of him, his supervisors and other employees had avoided formal complaints and tried to handle the problem internally because they did not want him to lose his job. Despite his temper, he continued to receive satisfactory performance evaluations for nine years, and there was no formal record of his problems. Finally, in 1993, after a screaming match with a white coworker, McCree's supervisor counseled him formally.

Personnel Policies and Procedures

Ironically, the problem came to a head just days after the City issued a new policy on workplace violence in 1994. This policy grew out of another tragedy—the murder of two lawyers in a downtown office building earlier that year. The City's policy was designed to raise awareness of what a potentially violent worker might do, and it set up a procedure for handling such incidents.

Immediately after the policy was issued, the supervisor came to the park and recreation department director, who had just come on the job a few weeks before, and told her about Clifton McCree. Within days, she had interviewed other workers and prepared a chilling memo detailing McCree's threats and racial slurs against his coworkers. The memo indicated that McCree exhibited at least five of the warning signs of potential trouble, including threats, paranoid behavior, and a fascination with workplace violence.

City officials acted quickly, ordering a psychiatric evaluation and a drug test within days. By the end of the month, McCree had been suspended without pay; he flunked the drug test and his firing was in the works. Until the day of the murders, eighteen months to the day after his discharge, he never returned to his workplace.

The Postmortem: Should the City Have Done Anything Differently?

In hindsight, it is difficult to find fault with anyone's actions. Most coworkers and supervisors would initially attempt to counsel a troubled employee informally because they were his friends and they knew he needed the job. With no formal counseling taking place, there would be no written record of previous performance incidents upon which to base a negative performance evaluation. When formal counseling finally occurred in 1993, it was only because coworkers had exerted pressure on management to do something. The City developed a clear and responsible policy on workplace violence in 1994. This policy led to a strong and immediate response by the park and recreation department, and it was the department director's memo that led the City to take action. Appropriately, Clifton McCree was removed from work pending psychiatric evaluation and drug testing. He tested positive and was discharged.

Yet six people died. In addition to the human tragedy, the City will undoubtedly face civil charges from the victims' families, alleging that the City knew that Clifton McCree was violent but did not take adequate precautions to protect coworkers against violence.

1. In hindsight, what do you think the City could have done differently (if anything)?
2. Under the standard of "foreseeability," do you think the City can be held liable for failure to take more timely action against Clifton McCree?
3. Did the City's prompt and responsible action (to discharge Clifton McCree under its new workplace violence policy) in fact increase the chance of workplace violence?
4. HRM usually takes place in communities affected by racial or ethnic unrest, alcohol or drug abuse, and disgruntled employees with easy access to weapons. What can HR managers do to lessen the chances of these factors resulting in workplace tragedies such as this one?

Notes

1. Bureau of Labor Statistics (2008). Occupational illnesses and injuries: Rates, counts and characteristics, 2005. Available at: http://www.bls.gov/iif/oshbulletin2005.htm (accessed August 21, 2008).
2. Bureau of Labor Statistics (2007). Census of Fatal Occupational Injuries (CFOI)—Current and Revised Data. Available at: http://www.bls.gov/iif/oshcfoi1.htm (accessed August 21, 2008).
3. Bureau of Labor Statistics (August 9, 2007). *National Census of Fatal Occupational Injuries in 2006*. Washington, DC: U.S. Department of Labor, USDL 07-1202.
4. Ibid.
5. National Safety Council (February 6, 2006). Off-the-job injuries outpacing gains in workplace safety. Available at: http://www.nsc.org/news/nr020606.aspx (accessed August 21, 2008).
6. Bureau of Labor Statistics (October 7, 2006). Workplace accidents and illnesses in 2006. Available at: http://www.bls.gov/iif/oshwc/osh/os/osnr0028.txt (accessed August 21, 2008).
7. Chiappetta, Tina Ott (December 2006). Food service worker with hepatitis C "regarded as disabled." *IPMA-HR News*, p. 20.
8. Orr, G. (1999). JCAHO and OSHA partner to protect health care workers. *Job and Health Safety Quarterly, 10* (3): 36–40.
9. Bureau of Labor Statistics (October 16, 2007). *Workplace illnesses and injuries in 2006*. Washington, DC: U.S. Department of Labor, USDL 07-1562.
10. Herbert, R., and P. Landrigan (2000). Work-related death: A continuing epidemic. *American Journal of Public Health, 90*: 541–545.
11. Barstow, D. (December 22, 2003). US rarely seeks charges for deaths in workplace. *The New York Times*, National news, pp. 1–8.
12. Morgenson, V. (2006). *Worker safety under siege: Labor, capital, and the politics of workplace safety in a deregulated world*. Armonk, NY: ME Sharpe; and Heath, R., and M. Palenchar (2008). *Strategic issues management: Organizations and public policy challenges*. Thousand Oaks, CA: Sage, pp. 1–4.
13. US Department of Labor, Occupational Safety and Health Administration (1970). OSH Act of 1970. Available at: http://www.osha.gov/pls/oshaweb/owasrch.search_form?p_doc_type=oshact (accessed August 21, 2008).
14. Treaster, J. (June 23, 2003). Cost of insurance for work injuries soars across U.S. *The New York Times*. Available at: query.nytimes.com/gst/fullpage.html?res=9B06E2DF153BF930A15755C0A9659C8B63 (accessed March 3, 2008).
15. Houtenville, A. J., W. A. Erickson, and C. G. Lee (April 4, 2005). *Disability statistics from the Current Population Survey (CPS)*. Ithaca, NY: Cornell University Rehabilitation Research and Training Center on Disability Demographics and Statistics (StatsRRTC). Retrieved August 21, 2008 from www.disabilitystatistics.org
16. Chiappetta, Tina Ott (November 2007). House holds hearing on ADA restoration Act. *IMPA-HR News*, pp. 1, 11.
17. Kellough, J. E. (2000). The Americans with Disabilities Act: A note on personnel policy impacts in state government. *Public Personnel Management, 29* (2): 211–224.
18. Ibid.

19. Massengill, D. (Summer 2004). How much better are you? Impairments, mitigating measures and the determination of disability. *Public Personnel Management, 33* (2): 181–199; Chiappetta, Tina Ott (November 2005). Sanitation worker with night blindness should be allowed to proceed with ADA suit. *IPMA-HR News*, p. 21; Chiappetta, Tina Ott (February 2005). Allergy to office building not covered by ADA. *IPMA-HR News*, p. 20; and Chiappetta, Tina Ott (October 2005). Employer must accommodate an employee who is "regarded as disabled." *IPMA-HR News*, p. 23.
20. Chiappetta, Tina Ott (July 1998). Disabled employees have greater risk of injury in the workplace. *IPMA News*. Alexandria, VA: The International Personnel Management Association, p. 15.
21. Schott, R. L. (Summer 1999). Managers and mental health: Mental illness and the workplace. *Public Personnel Management, 28* (2): 161–183; Chiappetta, Tina Ott (February 2004). First Circuit rules ADD not a disability but allows retaliation claim to proceed. *IPMA-HR News*, p. 19; and Chiappetta, Tina Ott (April 2007). Mentally disabled man may be victim of disability discrimination. *IPMA-HR News*, p. 23.
22. Chiappetta, Tina Ott (April 2007). No disability discrimination—termination was based on misconduct. *IPMA-HR News*, p. 25.
23. Chiappetta, Tina Ott (October 2006). Tenth Circuit Court rules employee's speech disruptive. *IPMA-HR News*, p. 24.
24. Kalk, J. (September 2000). What every employer should know about the Family and Medical Leave Act. *IPMA News*. Alexandria, VA: International Personnel Management Association, pp. 7–8; and Chiappetta, Tina Ott (April 2007). No vacation/sick time for employee on FMLA receiving disability payments. *IPMA-HR News*, p. 23.
25. Chiappetta, Tina Ott (November 2007). FMLA leave—holidays have no impact. *IPMA-HR News*, p. 21; Chiappetta, Tina Ott (November 2007). FMLA leave properly denied. *IPMA-HR News*, p. 23; and Chiappetta, Tina Ott (January 2006). Tenth circuit narrows definition of "serious health condition." *IPMA-HR News*, p. 25.
26. Chiappetta, Tina Ott (January 2006). Employee caught driving and exercising properly fired under FMLA. *IPMA-HR News*, p. 25.
27. Macik-frey, M., J. C. Quick, and D. L. Nelson (2007). Advances in occupational health: From a stressful beginning to a positive future. *Journal of Management, 33* (6): 809–840; Schuman, S. (April 2006). Just as with other sectors, public sector at risk for safety, health Hazards too. *IPMA-HR News*, pp. 1ff.
28. Blotzer, M. J. (1998). Safety and health program audits. *Occupational Hazards, 60* (5): 27–28.
29. Mitchell, C. S. (1998). Evaluating occupational health and safety programs in the public sector. *American Journal of Industrial Medicine, 34*: 600–606.
30. NIOSH (1996). Federal Register notice/Health care workers guidelines. *Federal Register, 61* (243): 66281–66282. Available at: www.cdc.gov/niosh/hcw-fr.html
31. Occupational Safety and Health Administration (November 14, 2000). *Final rule on Ergonomics Program* (29 CFR 1910.900).
32. Occupational Safety and Health Administration (September 2000). From injury prevention to increased productivity. *IPMA News*. Alexandria, VA: International Personnel Management Association, p. 16.
33. Wilson, K. A., C. S. Burke, H. A. Priest and E. Salas (2005). Promoting health care safety through training high reliability teams *Quality and Safety in Health Care, 14*: 303–309.
34. Mansdorf, Z. (1999). Organizational culture and safety performance. *Occupational Hazards, 61* (5): 109–110; and McMahon, S., and J. Kuang (1999). Merging health promotion and protection: A unified philosophy toward employee health. *Professional Safety, 44* (7): 38–39.
35. National Institutes of Occupational Safety and Health (2006). Workplace violence prevention strategies and research needs. NIOSH Publication No. 2006-144. Available at: http://www.cdc.gov/niosh/docs/2006-144/#a11 (accessed August 21, 2008).
36. *Workplace Violence Defined*. Available at: www.osha.gov/oshinfo/priorities/violence.html
37. Burnett, S. (May 1997). Protecting against workplace violence. *IPMA News*. Alexandria, VA: The International Personnel Management Association, pp. 22, 24.
38. Burnett, S. (May 2000). Developing an effective plan to prevent violence in the workplace. *IPMA News*. Alexandria, VA: The International Personnel Management Association, p. 23.
39. Johnson, P., and J. Indvik (Fall 1999). The organizational benefits of assisting domestically abused employees. *Public Personnel Management, 87* (3): 365–374.

40. Kelleher, M. (1996). *New arenas for violence.* Westport, CT: Praeger.
41. Ibid.
42. Solomon, C. M. (April 1995). Talking frankly about domestic violence. *Personnel Journal, 74* (4): 62–69; and Patton, E., and G. Johns (2007). Women's absenteeism in the popular press: Evidence for a gender-specific absence culture. *Human Relations, 60* (11): 1579–1612.
43. Swanberg, J. E., T. Logan, and C. Macke (2005). Intimate partner violence, employment, and the workplace: Consequences and future directions. *Trauma, 6* (4): 286–312.
44. Pereira, J. (March 2, 1995). Legal beat: Employers confront domestic abuse. *The Wall Street Journal*, p. B-1.
45. Feliu, A. G. (1994). Workplace violence and the duty of care: The scope of an employer's obligation to protect against the violent employee. *Employee Relations Law Journal, 21*: 381–403.
46. Martucci, W. C., and D. D. Clemow (1994/1995). Workplace violence: Incidents—and liability—on the rise. *Employment Relations Today, 21*: 463–470.
47. Braverman, M. (1999). *Preventing workplace violence: A guide for employers and practitioners.* Los Angeles, CA: Sage Publications; Labig, C. E. (1995). *Preventing violence in the workplace.* New York: American Management Association; and Denenberg, R., and M. Braverman (1999). *The violence-prone workplace: A new approach to dealing with hostile, threatening and uncivil behavior.* Ithaca, NY: Cornell University Press, pp. 165–169.
48. DiLorenzo, L. P., and D. J. Carroll (March 1995). Screening applicants for a safer workplace. *HR Magazine*, pp. 55–58; and Chiappetta, T. O. (February 2006). Employer liable for firing worker who lied about violent past. *IPMA-HR News*, pp. 25–26.
49. Feliu, Workplace violence and the duty of care, p. 393.
50. Griffin, R., and Y. Lopez (2005). "Bad behavior" in organizations: A review and typology for future research. *Journal of Management, 31* (6): 988–1005.
51. Bureau of Labor Statistics (October 27, 2006). Survey of workplace violence prevention, 2005. Available at: http://www.bls.gov/iif/oshwc/osnr0026.pdf (accessed August 21, 2008).
52. Nigro, L. G., and W. Waugh, Jr. (Fall 1998). Local government responses to workplace violence. *Review of Public Personnel Administration, 58* (3): 5–17.
53. Barrier, M. (1995). The enemy within. *Nation's Business, 83* (2): 18–24.
54. Trice, E. (October 1997). Can (and should) HR help calm domestic violence? *IPMA News.* Alexandria, VA: The International Personnel Management Association, pp. 15, 17.
55. Lawrence, T. B., and S. L. Robinson (2007). Ain't misbehavin: Workplace deviance as organizational resistance. *Journal of Management, 33* (3): 378–394; and Hoobler, J., and J. Swanberg (Fall 2006). The enemy is not us: Unexpected workplace violence trends. *Public Personnel Management, 35* (3): 229–246.
56. Johnson, D. L., J. G. Kurtz, and J. B. Kiehlbauch (1995). Scenario for supervisors. *HR Magazine, 40* (2): 63–68.
57. Smith, M. (October 1998). Violence in the workplace: Are you protected? *IPMA News.* Alexandria, VA: International Personnel Management Association, pp. 12–13.
58. Fox, J. (March 13, 1995). Security: Keeping the homicidal employee at bay. *Forbes, 155*: 24–27.
59. U.S. General Accounting Office (2003). *Bioterrorism: Preparedness varied across state and local jurisdictions.* Washington, DC: US Government Printing Office.
60. Silverstein, K. (2003). Rethinking disaster assistance. *American City and County, 108:* 12.
61. Fowler, K. L., N. D. Kling, and M. D. Larson (2007). Organizational preparedness for coping with a major crisis or disaster. *Business and Society, 46* (1): 88–103.
62. Kondrasuk, J. N. (2004). The effects of 9/11 and terrorism on human resource management: Recovery, reconsideration, and renewal. *Employee Responsibilities and Rights Journal, 16* (1): 25–35.
63. The White House (February 2006). *The federal response to Hurricane Katrina: Lessons learned.* Washington, DC: US Government Printing Office; and US House of Representatives (February 15, 2006). *A failure of initiative: Final report of the Select Bipartisan Committee to investigate the preparation for and response to Katrina.* Washington, DC: Government Printing Office.
64. McKee, K. (August 2008). How prepared are you when disaster strikes? *HR News.* Alexandria, VA: IPMA-HR, pp. 8–9, 13–14.
65. Lowery, J. (August 2008). Ten necessities of disaster planning. *HR News.* Alexandria, VA: IPMA-HR, pp. 6–7, 10–12.

66. Perry, R. W., and L. D. Mankin (2005). Preparing for the unthinkable: Managers, terrorism and the HRM function. *Public Personnel Management, 34* (2): 175–193.
67. Chiappetta, Tina Ott (August 2008). Coping with disaster. *HR News*. Alexandria, VA: IPMA-HR, p. 15.
68. Smith, S. (November 2007). The right to breathe clean air. *Occupational Hazards*, p. 6.
69. Evans, D. (1994). Employers face difficult questions in initiatives against alcohol abuse. *Occupational Health and Safety, 63*: 58–60.
70. Nazario, S. (April 18, 1990). Alcohol is linked to a gene. *The Wall Street Journal*, p. B-1.
71. Newcomb, M. D. (1994). Prevalence of alcohol and other drug use on the job: Cause for concern or irrational hysteria? *The Journal of Drug Issues, 24*: 403–416.
72. Normand, J., S. D. Salyards, and J. J. Mahoney (1990). An evaluation of preemployment drug testing. *Journal of Applied Psychology, 75*: 629–639.
73. Klingner, D., G. Roberts, and V. Patterson (Summer 1998). The Miami Coalition surveys of employee drug use and attitudes: A five-year retrospective (1989–1993). *Public Personnel Management, 27* (2): 201–222.
74. Crow, S. M., M. F. Villere, and S. J. Hartman (1994). Planes, trains, and ships: Drug testing is no substitute for drug supervision: Part II. *Supervision, 55*: 14–16.
75. Kaestner, R., and M. Grossman (1995). Wages, workers' compensation benefits and drug use: Indirect evidence of the effect of drugs on the workplace. *American Economic Review, 85*: 55–60.
76. Gillian, F. (1995). Recreational drug use may not be the biggest threat. *Personnel Journal, 74*: 21–23.
77. Pouzar, E. (1994). Drug and alcohol abuse present RM challenge. *National Underwriter, 98*: 13.
78. Community Guide (2000). *The guide to community preventative services: Effect of smoking bans and restrictions on reducing exposure to Environmental Tobacco Smoke (ETS)*. Available at: http://www.thecommunityguide.org/tobacco/environmental/smokingbans.html (accessed April 25, 2009).
79. Community Guide (September 2000). Alcohol in the workplace causes headaches. *IPMA News*. Alexandria, VA: International Personnel Management Association, p. 18.
80. Goldstein, C. (July 2000). Employee drug testing in the public sector. *IPMA News*. Alexandria, VA: The International Personnel Management Association, pp. 13–15; Chiappetta, Tina Ott (May 2007). Random drug testing legal. *IPMA-HR News*, p. 29.
81. Trenk, B. (April 1989). Clearing the air about smoking policies. *Management Review, 78* (4):32–34; and Community Guide. *Reducing exposure to environmental tobacco smoke: Smoking bans and restrictions*. Available at: http:// www.thecommunityguide.org/tobacco/ environmental/ smokingbans.html (accessed April 25, 2009).
82. Gilbert, R., E. Hannan, and K. Lowe (Fall 1998). Is smoking stigma clouding the objectivity of employee performance appraisal? *Public Personnel Management, 27* (3): 285–300.
83. Crow, S., and S. J. Hartman (1992). Drugs in the workplace: Overstating the problems and the cures. *Journal of Drug Issues, 22*: 923–937.
84. Chiappetta, Tina Ott (November 2004). Random drug testing upheld by Sixth Circuit. *IPMA-HR News*, p. 23; and Chiappetta, Tina Ott (January 2005). County drug testing upheld. *IPMA-HR News*, p. 24.
85. Troubleshooter (February 27, 2007). *The problem; the solution*. Available at: www.people-management.com (accessed March 3, 2008).
86. Troubleshooter (April 2004). Hazeldon survey: One in four companies is less likely to hire a candidate recovering from drug addiction. *IPMA-HR News*, p. 18.
87. Massengill, D. (Fall 2005). Walking a straight (and fine) line: Alcoholism and the Americans with Disabilities Act. *Public Personnel Management, 34* (3): 283–297; and Chiappetta, Tina Ott (April 2004). Alcoholic not disabled, says First Circuit. *IPMA-HR News*, p. 19.
88. Jacobs, S. (December 11, 1995). New AIDS drugs' aim is "buying time." *The Miami Herald*, pp. C-1, 5.
89. Schottmuller, G., and J. Rover (1999). Managing employee exposure. *Surgical Services Management, 5* (9): 37–42.
90. Oswald, E. M. (April 22, 1996). Why all employers should manage AIDS-HIV risk. *National Underwriter (Property & Casualty/Risk & Benefits Management Edition), 100*: 16–18.
91. Burris, S. (1993). *AIDS law today: A new guide for the public*. Connecticut: Yale University Press; and Chiappetta, Tina Ott (August 2006). HIV-positive candidate for Foreign Service Office allowed to proceed with disabilities suit. *IPMA-HR News*, p. 26.

92. Chiappetta, Tina Ott (February 2000). EAPs: An effective response to diversity in the workplace. *IPMA News.* Alexandria, VA: International Personnel Management Association, p. 15.
93. Kramer, T., and E. Shults (March 2008). Wellness programs: ADA and HIPAA Issues. *HR News,* pp. 6,7ff.
94. Carroll, C. (June 1999). Opening doors to ability: A time of transition: EAP alternatives for the 1990s. *IPMA News.* Alexandria, VA: The International Personnel Management Association, pp. 23, 24.
95. Wharton, A. S., and R. J. Erickson (1993). Managing emotions on the job and at home: Understanding the consequences of multiple emotional roles. *Academy of Management Review, 18*: 457–486.
96. Wharton, A. S., and R. J. Erickson (December 1999). More workers checked out due to stress, even as work/life programs showed progress. *IPMA News.* Alexandria, VA: International Personnel Management Association, p. 3. Available at: www.cch.com
97. Harris, M. M., and L. L. Heft (1992). Alcohol and drug use in the workplace: Issues, controversies and directions for future research. *Journal of Management, 18*: 239–266.
98. Smith, M. (January 1999). Coping with employee stress. *IPMA News.* Alexandria, VA: International Personnel Management Association, p. 17. Also available at: www.ipma-hr.org/cprserie.html
99. US Department of Health and Human Services, Office of Civil Rights (May 2003). *Summary of the HIPAA privacy rule.* Available at: www.hhs.gov/ocr/privacy/hipaa/understanding/summary (accessed April 25, 2009).
100. Internal Revenue Code, as cited in Kramer and Shults, *Wellness programs,* p. 7
101. Rushing, J. (April 2004). Legal issues and HR: An overview of the FMLA, ADA, Title VII and workers' compensation. *IPMA-HR News,* p. 1ff.
102. Chiappetta, Tina Ott (April 2007). Anti-discrimination law: Is genetic discrimination law necessary? *IPMA-HR News,* p. 5.
103. Kramer and Shults, Wellness programs, pp. 6, 28.
104. Chiappetta, Tina Ott (February 2005). Diabetic poses question of direct threat. *IPMA-HR News,* p. 19.
105. Centers for Disease Control and Prevention (2004). *Physical activity and good nutrition: Essential elements to prevent chronic disease and obesity.* Washington, DC: US Department of Health and Human Services.
106. Bradbury, M. (March 2007). The legal and managerial challenge of obesity as a disability. *Review of Public Personnel Management, 27* (1): 79–90.
107. Chiappetta, Tina Ott (May 2005). Six circuit finds poor performance not pregnancy discrimination. *IPMA-HR News,* p. 19.
108. Chiappetta, Tina Ott (March 2005). Court recognizes "hostile environment" in ADA case. *IPMA-HR News,* p. 21.
109. Chiappetta, Tina Ott (March 2004). Seventh circuit rules that compensatory/punitive damages are not allowed in ADA retaliation claims. *IPMA-HR News,* p. 19; Chiappetta, Tina Ott (August 2004). Individuals may sue state under Title II of the ADA. *IPMA-HR News,* p. 25; and Chiappetta, Tina Ott (March 2006). Supreme Court rules that states may be liable for money damages under Title II of the ADA. *IPMA-HR News,* p. 27.

PART **FIVE**

Sanctions

CHAPTER 13

Organizational Justice

In 2008, in response to allegations of improper consideration of ideological and political affiliation of candidates for entry-level employment of attorneys with the U.S. Department of Justice (DOJ), the DOJ Office of the Inspector General and Office of Professional Responsibility conducted an investigation. They found the claims to be substantiated contrary to requirements of federal law that prohibit consideration of political affiliation/ideology in hiring of permanent civil service employees. DOJ had established in 2002 a "screening committee" whose members reviewed candidates that various offices in DOJ had recommended be interviewed for permanent positions. Analysis of those deselected by the screening committee showed that the committee had clearly used politics as a criterion in their selection process. The screening committee was composed entirely of political appointees.[1] If this occurred in another department of the federal government, you could have been one of these candidates. How would you feel about being selected or not based on your affiliations in school?

By the end of this chapter, you will be able to:

1. Define the sanction function.
2. Identify the ways an organization establishes and maintains the terms of the employment relationship between employee and employer.
3. Describe the ways different personnel systems view the sanction function.
4. Discuss the balance the Court examines when deciding whether a public employer has violated an employee's constitutional rights to free speech, freedom of association, or privacy rights.
5. Describe the role of property rights and due process in establishing and maintaining the terms of the employment relationship.
6. Define the concept of organizational citizenship and relate it to employee perceptions of fairness.
7. Discuss how discipline and grievance procedures are connected to the sanction function.
8. Diagram a typical disciplinary procedure and describe various steps in a grievance procedure.
9. Define the terms *reasonable accommodation* and *undue hardship* in the Americans with Disabilities Act and show the value conflict implied in these terms.
10. Describe how modern technology raises privacy concerns.

11. Describe the rights of employees who have been sexually harassed or who are considered whistle-blowers.
12. Discuss the transition from sovereign immunity to qualified immunity for public employees.

THE SANCTION FUNCTION

Every organization, public, private, or nonprofit must establish and maintain *terms of the relationship between employee and employer.* This is the **sanction function**, the last of the four core functions. These terms in an employment relationship are captured in expectations employees have of their employer and contributions employees are willing to make in order to have their expectations fulfilled. Similarly, employers have expectations of employees and contribute to them so those expectations are fulfilled. While the expectations and obligations may informally comprise part of a **psychological contract** (see Chapter 9), many are also captured formally in policy documents and in the law itself. The heart of the sanction function involves the interplay of these various expectations and contributions or obligations.

ESTABLISHING AND MAINTAINING EXPECTATIONS

Employee expectations and obligations come from numerous sources, ranging from the law to casual conversations with friends or acquaintances in similar jobs. Employer expectations and obligations are similarly diverse, coming from the law, organizational needs, comparisons with other organizations, and the character of the workforce. Regardless of where they originate, there are several formal mechanisms by which these tangible terms, and sometimes the intangible ones as well, are recognized. The first is the personnel manual, which contains the policies, rules, regulations, procedures, and practices that constitute a particular personnel system. For example, there may be a policy giving priority to promoting from within. There may be rules limiting political activity of employees while on the job. There may be a policy about bonuses or pay for performance. These policies and rules constitute some of the terms of the employment relationship.

Second, in some jurisdictions, the **terms of the employment relationship** are established through collective bargaining between employer and union. These terms are contained in working rules mutually agreed upon by employer and union membership. Third, various local, state, and federal laws establish expectations and obligations of employees and employer. For example, local ordinances may authorize merit personnel systems and policies; legislatures establish pay rates for public employees; the Fair Labor Standards Act describes required compensation policies; the Civil Rights Act of 1964 proscribes various forms of discrimination in employment; the Hatch Act and its counterparts in state and local governments proscribe political activity by employees. These and other laws contain provisions that affect the expectations and obligations that employees and employers have of one another.

It may be of interest to see the extent to which the law does play a role in establishing and maintaining the employment relationship. The total number of charges brought in 2007 under federal discrimination statutes was around 83,000 (72,000 in 1992). Of those, 37 percent (41 percent in 1992) were charges of racial discrimination; 30 percent (32 percent in 1992) for gender; and 32 percent (15 percent in 1992) for claims of retaliation. While these numbers may seem large at first glance, the U.S. Equal Employment Opportunity Commission (EEOC) only filed 362 lawsuits in pursuit of claims, with the other claims either being remediated in some other way or dismissed. Of the lawsuits filed, the large majority was Title VII of the Civil Rights Act of 1964 claims—meaning they were mostly race and gender claims, including harassment.[2]

Last, the sanction function in public employment differs fundamentally from private employment because public employees have certain rights conferred upon them by the U.S. Constitution. Citizens are protected from government action by the Bill of Rights, including the Fourteenth Amendment. When citizens become employees of the government, they give up some of those rights in their role as government employees, but they still have substantially more protection in speech, association, privacy, and equal treatment than do employees of private employers. We will discuss these protections later in the chapter.

Maintaining Expectations

Various processes maintain and enforce the terms established through these four mechanisms. Commonly, we think of employees suing their employer for violating some employee right. However, more realistically, an organization's discipline and grievance procedures maintain the terms of the employment relationship or contract. This is what they are designed to do! Most disagreements are handled informally between supervisor and employee, but when informal channels are inadequate, formal discipline and grievance procedures involving due process are invoked. Sometimes, if those prove ineffective in resolving differences, the employee may complain directly to elected officials or take judicial action.

An employee is disciplined when the employer believes the employee is not living up to the terms of the employment "contract." Usually, this means that the employee is not contributing to the organization in the way the employer expects. On the other hand, when the employee believes the employer has violated its obligations, the employee "grieves" the employer's action, setting in motion some review. In large measure, the quality of the grievance processes due an employee subject to discipline determines whether employees believe they, and their coworkers, have been treated equitably and with dignity. (We will discuss discipline and grievance procedures in more detail later in the chapter.)

The notion that organizational justice is derived from balancing expectations and obligations suggests that the processes which establish and maintain expectations and obligations are as important as what those expectations and obligations actually are—their substance. In the following sections, we will discuss the sanction function in alternate personnel systems, and then we will review both the substantive and procedural rights of public employees and how those rights are balanced by the values of organizational efficiency and political responsiveness.

THE SANCTION FUNCTION IN ALTERNATE PERSONNEL SYSTEMS

We have talked in general about organizational justice, the mechanisms for establishing the terms of the employment relationship, and various processes for maintaining or enforcing those terms. However, there truly are significant differences in the sanction function, depending upon which personnel system the employee is part of. This is because with the sanction function, the rules of the personnel game are established and maintained. This is where the expectations and obligations of employee and employer are determined and enforced. Every so often, one group or another will test its power to influence the rules. This is what inevitably happens with a strike. Regardless of the outcomes on wages and working conditions, a strike gives the adversaries the opportunity to see where they stand with regard to setting expectations and obligations of employee and employer. Taking a case to court or arbitration can serve the same purpose. Battles between the legislature and executive branches of government are often fought over who has the discretion to set the rules.

The reason why unions were so successful in early years of this century was that they held out the promise of organizational justice for employees. One of the first objectives of a union is to negotiate a grievance procedure that includes a third-party decision-making process—one that takes the employee's grievance *outside* the managerial chain of command.

Civil service systems similarly value individual rights as a way of protecting employees from partisan political pressure. The first objective of civil service reform in the late nineteenth century was to legislate the elimination of politics from administration through the creation of systems in which employees could be dismissed only for performance deficiencies, not because they belonged to the wrong party or failed to pay voluntary dues. With regard to the sanction function, however, civil service systems differ from collective bargaining, because civil service systems are founded on dual values—individual rights and efficiency. Thus, even though we often see elaborate due process protections for public employees, we also hear complaints from managers, many covered by the same civil service protections, about the red tape and due process that hardly makes it worth the effort, in their eyes, to discipline employees.

Affirmative action personnel systems are driven by the value of social equity and, depending upon the context, individual rights. The expectation in affirmative action systems is that each person will be treated on his or her own merits and performance. Nevertheless, the benign use of racial classifications benefiting minorities at the expense of the individual rights of nonminorities is rarely rejected by affirmative action advocates. Affirmative action personnel systems strongly advocate due process as a way of ensuring fair treatment in organizational systems suspected of bias.

When it comes to political personnel systems and to contracting out, the value of individual rights diminishes in favor of responsiveness and efficiency, respectively. Due process may not be highly valued. Political executives who serve at the pleasure of elected leaders enjoy virtually no employee rights. Their positions do not fall under merit system provisions, and they are hired, moved, and dismissed largely based on a calculation of the political value they bring to an administration. Consequently, they may be less respectful of the rights of others and see them as impediments to political and administrative action.

Contracting out is often seen as a way of circumventing personnel systems where individual rights have become entrenched at the expense of efficiency and responsiveness. Once a service is contracted out to a private employer, employees will find themselves operating under a new personnel system, usually with fewer employee rights. Depending upon the service, the constitutional protections that employees enjoy under a public personnel system are less likely to apply, and the due process public employees generally enjoy may be sacrificed to the goal of administrative efficiency and profit.

THE CONTEMPORARY SCENE

Employee rights occur within the context of broad political forces and specific organizational cultures. As we have seen in the previous chapters, the value of efficiency coupled with an emphasis on market-based administrative approaches has truly affected the sanction function—the expectations and obligations of employees and employers. Three issues dominate contemporary discussions of organizational justice. The first is outsourcing. The second is at-will employment. The third is the impact that outsourcing has on constitutional rights of employees. Each of these issues has been described below.

Outsourcing

The case for outsourcing has strong political headwind. That force is driven in part by general dissatisfaction in the sanction function, with lengthy and cumbersome processes necessary to take adverse actions against public employees. Why not just transfer the service delivery to the private or nonprofit sectors and let them deal with the issues, usually in settings where at-will employment is the norm?

In May 2003, the U.S. Office of Management and Budget (OMB) issued a directive requiring federal departments and agencies to implement **competitive sourcing**. Competitive sourcing gives public employees the opportunity to provide their own bid to continue providing services. Annually, each department is required to identify inventories of personnel activities that can be classified as "commercial." These activities are then subject to competitive sourcing. This approach is rooted in a market-based human resource policy framework. While this effort has been significant, the results over a five-year period have been modest, attributable in part to administrative support for federal employees to prepare their bids, Congressional action that stacked the deck in favor of public employee bids, and employee and union protest.[3]

At-Will Employment

In addition to **public–private partnerships (PPP)**, another initiative that is being taken especially at the state level is to create **at-will employment**. This is done legislatively by removing positions from the permanent civil service and reallocating them to an unclassified or at-will position. According to Hays and Sowa's 2005 survey of state human resources directors, this action is commonly occurring. Driven by the same kind of dissatisfaction with the way that employee protections have hindered management prerogatives and in the name of efficiency coupled with market-based solutions, at-will employment strips employees of many of their rights, including job security. At the same time, even if positions have not been reclassified to at-will status, statutory action is being taken throughout state personnel systems to restrict employee ability to grieve supervisory decisions and to streamline appeal procedures.[4] This is very similar to private sector practice.

It is easy to dramatize the effect of this kind of change, but the fact of the matter is that no complex organization—public or private—can survive without some measure of employee rights *if* employee commitment and retention are valued. Who would remain working for an organization where a supervisor could fire an employee because the supervisor did not like the color of the employee's hair, or for some other ridiculous claim? In effect, the organization would be conveying a message to its employees: "Do not rock the boat; do not take risks; figure out your supervisor, and say and do what he/she likes." This, of course, is exactly the fear that public administration scholars voice, especially if it sends the message that politics—message, loyalty, and agenda—is more important than competence, experience, and professional/technical analysis. The question is not whether employees will have rights, it is the extent of their applicability, their effect on managerial prerogatives, and the behavioral cues that employees receive when those prerogatives are exercised.

Hays and Sowa's research also shows that activist governors pushing an antibureaucratic agenda are behind this movement to restrict employee rights and replace them with supervisory and managerial prerogatives. These initiatives, coupled with legislative term limits, can negatively affect long-standing relationships between legislative and executive branches, which can lead to relationships of respect and trust.

PROTECTING EMPLOYEES' CONSTITUTIONAL SUBSTANTIVE RIGHTS

Despite these powerful trends toward decentralization and limitations on employee rights, public employees do have rights that cannot be legislated away. These are constitutional rights. It is accurate that some of these rights do depend upon the status of the employee—for example, permanent employees are likely to have property rights in their job and temporary employees or unclassified employees probably would not. But it would be a mistake to dismiss the importance of constitutional rights of public employees not only because there still are millions for whom these rights pertain, but also for what these rights tell us about democratic government and the relationship between political and administrative arenas.

In some instances, knowledge of the decisions reached in particular cases is less important than the reasoning the court employed in reaching a decision. The way that managers and judges reach their decisions is not necessarily the same because in the balance between individual rights and efficiency, the court places much more value on individual rights than managers do. In a court of law, what may be good for the organization as a whole but bad for some individual employees may not serve as an adequate justification for administrative action. Furthermore, the court has said that failure to know the law may put administrators in legal jeopardy.[5] However, awareness of the court's decision is less helpful to managers than awareness and understanding of the court's reasoning. The judiciary is by far more explicit—in the publication of its decisions and in the debate that is reflected in them—about the four values than either the legislative or the executive branches.

Let's now look at some of the legal protections that are incorporated as terms of the public employment contract. Once known to employees, these protections affect their expectations and employer obligations. The degree to which the expectations and obligations are mutually accepted will affect the employee's sense of organizational fairness. However, as in so many matters affecting fairness and rights, the formal rules that protect employees may create tension with the flexibility that supervisors need to manage effectively.

Freedom of Speech and the First Amendment

The First Amendment to the Constitution states, "Congress shall make no law respecting an establishment of religion, or prohibiting the free exercise thereof; or abridging the freedom of speech, or of the press; or the right of the people peaceably to assemble, and to petition the Government for a redress of grievances." This amendment protects citizens from government's intrusions on the free exercise of religion, speech, political beliefs, and political association.

Commonly, we think that the purpose of the First Amendment is to protect a speaker's right to expression—as an end in itself. Actually, the value of the First Amendment may have more to do with issues of transparency and the robust exchange of ideas, leading to an informed deliberative public than any individual's right to speak.[6] While citizens often endorse the First Amendment uncritically, the Court faces a difficult task when applying it to public employment situations. The First Amendment provides the vehicle for classic confrontations between advocates of administrative efficiency and the rights of public employees. On the one hand, government has a duty to conduct its business efficiently, which means requiring respect for hierarchy and organizational loyalty. On the other hand, no one knows better how taxes are being spent than civil servants, and if they feel their jobs will be jeopardized if they speak out, is the public being deprived of information vital to its understanding of government?

The way the Court decides free speech cases regarding public employees is first to ask whether the employee has expressed himself or herself on a *matter of public concern.* Therefore, when a manager thinks about disciplining an employee for speaking out angrily or writing a critical letter to the editor, that is the first question the manager ought to consider as well. If the answer is "yes," the Court looks to see how much the administrative efficiency of the agency has been or is reasonably anticipated to become disrupted. It then tries to balance the two considerations, asking if the disruption is sufficient to outweigh the individual's right to free speech.[7] The more clearly the matter addresses a significant public concern, the more difficult the employer's defense becomes.

Here is an example. In ***Connick v. Myers*** (1983),[8] a 5-4 Court decided that Sheila Myers was appropriately discharged for insubordination when she refused a transfer and then distributed a questionnaire to colleagues regarding the way Harry Connick, the elected district attorney in New Orleans, ran his office. The Court's deference to administrative efficiency is seen in two ways in this case. First, the Court tempered its decision on whether Ms. Myers was speaking out on a matter of public concern by noting that she was a disgruntled employee. In other words, her aims and motives were considered, as well as the content of the information she was providing with the questionnaire results. Further, the majority dismissed the importance of most of the information itself, suggesting that matters of internal agency operations are not a matter of public importance in judging the performance of the district attorney.

Because the Court acknowledged that a few of Myers' questions addressed matters of public concern—the Court's threshold question—they turned to the government's argument on why she should be dismissed. As in all cases, the court always looks for reasons why an action was taken or not taken, and it scrutinizes them. When the court has determined that an employee's constitutional rights are at stake, managerial discretion itself is not a sufficient justification for the disciplinary action.

In this case, the Court concluded: "The limited First Amendment interest involved here does not require that Connick tolerate action which he reasonably believed would disrupt the office, undermine his authority, and destroy close working relationships" (p. 724). Here the Court retreated from previous judgments where *evidence* of disruption would have been required before the employer could have justly considered terminating the employee.

Connick v. Myers points out the difficulty in assessing the whistle-blower's claim. Was Myers a potential whistle-blower who was shut up? Was she simply a disgruntled employee? Does it really matter whether a whistle-blower is a disgruntled employee?

While *Connick v. Myers* involved a public employee's First Amendment rights, in 1996 in the case of ***Wabaunsee County v. Umbehr,***[9] the court held that a private business holding a contract with a public employer has similar rights. *Umbehr* hauled trash for the county and was a frequent critic of the county commissioners. When the county failed to renew his contract, he successfully alleged that they were retaliating for his criticism and thereby violating his First Amendment right to free speech.

Freedom of Association and the First Amendment

Governments have struggled since the early 1800s to draw a balance between a responsive and an efficient government. Advocates of responsiveness have generally favored more political control over public bureaucracies; advocates of administrative efficiency have fought to keep politics out of administration. Political personnel systems fight for the allocation of public jobs based on political loyalty as a reward for service to a political party and as a way of ensuring that newly elected officials can appoint people committed to their goals. This is the point illustrated in the opening paragraph of this chapter. For years, limitations on the political activity of employees as well as constraints on political influence over them have been dealt with in legislatures and executive branches of government.

The courts stepped into this battle in the mid-1970s by limiting the patronage practice of discharging public employees because of political affiliation. The Court argued that patronage dismissals violated a public employee's First Amendment right to freedom of belief and association—to belong to a political party of choice and maintain one's own political beliefs. In ***Rutan v. Republican Party*** of Illinois (1990), a 5-4 Court extended its ruling to hiring, promotion, transfer, and recall decisions.[10] The Court said the government must show a vital governmental interest before it could condition personnel actions on political belief and association. The majority claimed that preservation of democratic processes was not advantaged by patronage enough to outweigh a public employee's First Amendment rights.

In an earlier case, ***Branti v. Finkel*** (1980), the Court decided 6-3 that in trying to determine what positions were exempt from restrictions on patronage dismissals, "The ultimate inquiry is not whether the label 'policymaker' or 'confidential' fits a particular position; rather, the question is whether the hiring authority can demonstrate that party affiliation is an appropriate requirement for the effective performance of the public office involved."[11] In light of *Rutan*, this restriction on patronage dismissals would seem to apply to hiring as well.

In a companion case to *Wabaunsee County v. Umbehr*, the court reviewed the First Amendment rights of contractual and temporary employees in ***O'Hare v. Northlake.***[12] The court ruled that hiring temporary workers based on party affiliation was unconstitutional.

To conclude this discussion of the public employee's rights under the First Amendment, one of the more interesting observations involves the extension of rights to independent contractors and temporary workers. In ***Richardson v. McKnight***, the court ruled that private prison guards charged with violating the constitutional rights of prisoners do not have the same immunity from liability as government prison guards.[13]

However, *Umbehr* and *O'Hare* may be sending a different message. It appears that the practice of contracting out and utilizing noncivil service employees has not yet led to clear-cut conclusions in all aspects of public employment and the constitution.[14]

Privacy, Drug Testing, and the Fourth Amendment

We have seen that public employees in their roles are less protected by the Bill of Rights than when they are acting as ordinary citizens. The Fourth Amendment to the Constitution protects citizens from unreasonable search and seizure and is a crucial foundation for privacy. It does this in law enforcement cases by requiring the searching authority to obtain a warrant prior to the search. A judge, a neutral party, must be convinced that the searching authority has probable cause to believe that the suspected individual has broken the law, before the warrant is issued.

Nevertheless, in some noncriminal cases, the government is able to conduct a search without a warrant. These are cases like border searches, routine searches at airports, and more specifically searches of employee desks and lockers, and searches of individuals themselves—as in drug testing. In these kinds of situations, no probable cause is required. A balance test is performed weighing the government's interest or special need with the individual's expectation of privacy.

For example, Magno Ortega was a psychiatrist working in a state hospital who was suspected of several improprieties, including his acquisition of a computer and charges of sexual harassment as well as taking inappropriate disciplinary action against a resident. While on administrative leave pending an investigation, hospital officials searched his office and seized his property, which it turns out included personal items. Ortega sued, claiming that hospital officials had violated his Fourth Amendment rights. In ***O'Connor v. Ortega*** (1987), the court ruled that the government's interest in maintaining an efficient, effective workplace outweighed Dr. Ortega's privacy interest.[15] This special needs doctrine and balancing test guided the Court's subsequent adjudication of drug-testing cases. In these cases, the public employee's individual right to privacy is balanced against the government's necessity to insure public safety. Over the years, the Court's reasoning has worked its way into administrative procedures relating to alcohol and drug testing.[16] In fact, with the legal reasoning now accepted and incorporated into administrative policy and procedures in public organizations, drug and alcohol issues in the workplace have largely moved from the legal sphere into the health arena, where they become elements of an organizations employee assistance programs.

PROTECTING EMPLOYEES' CONSTITUTIONAL PROCEDURAL RIGHTS

Property Rights and Due Process

Earlier, we suggested that the sanction function is concerned with both the substance of employee and employer expectations and obligations and the processes by which these expectations and obligations are established and maintained. Now, we will look at procedural rights and how they are balanced by the value of organizational efficiency.

The process side of this concern is found in two concepts—**property rights** and **due process**. It has become popular to assert that civil service rules "hamstring" management by making it impossible to discipline or discharge employees protected by civil service systems. In one respect, this statement is correct. Public employees have rights to their jobs that exceed those of their private-sector counterparts. Yet this statement is also incorrect, for these rights are ultimately derived from the constitutional requirement of due process, rather than civil service regulations. Constitutional protections accorded *public* employees are an extension of the government's responsibility to guarantee certain freedoms to its citizens. The key here is that the *government* is bound by the Constitution, whether in its dealings with citizens simply as individuals or citizens as employees.

The Fifth and Fourteenth Amendments to the Constitution require that a government may deprive an individual of substantive rights like life, liberty or property only after ***due process*** of law—a procedural right. Over the years, the courts have come to conclude that public employees have a property interest in their jobs, if they have been led to expect that they will hold their jobs permanently as long as they perform satisfactorily. Courts have found these expectations implied in civil service system personnel policies and manuals that specify an employee will be discharged for good cause only, or where specific grounds for dismissal are identified, or where progressive discipline is endorsed and steps identified. In other words, a job can be considered a public employee's property, and once that is established, the government—the public employer—can take the property/job only after due process.

What is due process? Minimal due process requires that an employer notify an employee of the employee's violation and give the employee a chance to state his or her side of the story. Due process comes in degrees, where the amount depends on the scope of the discipline contemplated. The critical step in linking due process with fairness comes when the person or board hearing the employee appeal or grievance is not in the employee's normal chain of command. This conveys the message that the employee will be heard impartially—by an investigator, board, or arbitrator.

A simple written reprimand might appropriately call for minimal due process, but a contemplated firing that would deprive a public employee of the economic means of supporting him or herself and possibly create difficulty for the employee when seeking another job (infringe on the employee's liberty to seek employment) would require a pretermination hearing.[17] Once again, we see personnel policies and practices growing out of an attempt to balance an employee's expectations of fair treatment (individual rights) with the employer's necessity to manage the public workforce efficiently.

Organizational Citizenship and Employee Perceptions of Fairness

What exactly is **procedural justice**? It consists of both the policies and methods to make organizational decisions regarding the distribution of rewards and punishments as well as an interpersonal aspect—the way supervisors and managers implement the policies and methods. Camerman[18] and Ehrhart's[19] literature review confirms that employee perceptions of substantive justice are influenced by how those decisions are arrived at and carried out. Perhaps most important, the literature on **organizational citizenship**/justice shows that perceptions of fairness emanating from the quality of organizational leadership and supervision are the cornerstones of organizational justice and thus, organizational citizenship.[20] While the goal of due process is to treat individual employees fairly, the consequence is the climate that is set and the larger picture that is drawn for all employees regardless of whether they ever utilize grievance or other due process channels or are the recipients of bad organizational news.

Discipline and Counseling the Unproductive Employee

The employee's sense of fairness is significantly affected by how disciplinary and grievance procedures are carried out, and this puts a premium on the supervisor's role. Disciplinary action is the last step—never the first—in dealing with an employee whose performance is substandard. It will probably not be the last step if it is a response to misconduct—like fighting. It assumes that the supervisor of a poorly performing employee has asked a number of questions regarding job design, selection, orientation, performance appraisal, training, and compensation:

Job design	Are the tasks, conditions, and performance standards of the position reasonable and equitable?
Selection	Does the employee meet the minimum qualifications established for the position?
Orientation and continuing supervision	Were organizational rules and regulations and position requirements clearly communicated to the new employee? Did the employee know the goals to be achieved and what constituted satisfactory performance?
Performance appraisal	Was the employee's performance adequately documented, and was the employee provided informal and formal feedback on the quality of his or her performance?
Training	Does the employee have adequate skills to perform the required tasks at the expected level of competence?
Compensation	Is good performance rewarded, or are there factors in the work environment that make it impossible or punishing to perform well?

Theoretically, therefore, **discipline** represents the last step in supervising employees because it symbolizes a failure to adjust the expectations/obligations of the employment relationship by less intrusive means. It is primarily a supervisory responsibility, since most performance problems are handled informally within the work unit with minimal involvement by the personnel department.

Figure 13-1 shows the sequence of personnel activities that occur prior to disciplinary action. It is the primary responsibility of the employee's immediate supervisor to ensure that each of these steps is followed. Together, they represent the counseling and disciplinary action process.

The personnel manager has three important responsibilities with respect to disciplinary action. Initially, the personnel department is responsible for establishing the process. Once it has been established as part of the agency's personnel rules and regulations, the personnel director is frequently responsible for counseling unproductive employees and for assisting the supervisor in implementing evaluation and training procedures to improve performance or institute disciplinary action. Last, the personnel director is responsible for making sure the system is applied equitably. The following memorandum from the former personnel director in the city of Kansas City, Missouri, to department heads, shows that the personnel director has both a facilitating and a policing role in the disciplinary process.

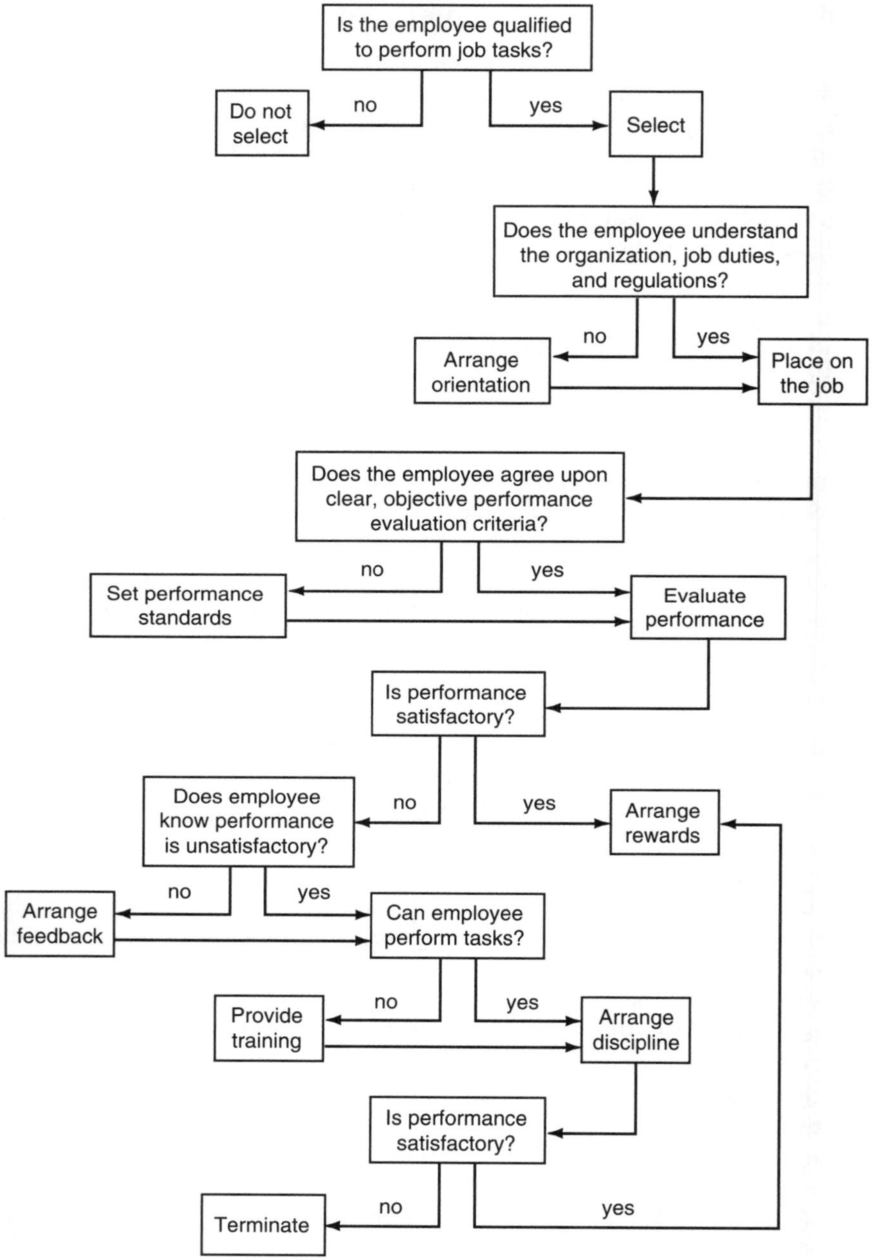

FIGURE 13-1 Disciplinary Action and Other Personnel Activities

To: All Department Heads
From: Tom F. Lewinsohn, Director of Personnel
Subject: Employee Rights and Obligations

In today's world of work, we hear much about employee rights but seldom hear about employee obligations. With our departmental budgets becoming tighter, those employee obligations deserve even more critical attention. For their paychecks, which is only one of their rights, employees can be expected to fulfill obligations such as showing up for work regularly and punctually, taking directions from supervisors, doing their jobs correctly, and following rules.

Too often supervisors do not act soon enough in trying to correct employees not living up to their job obligations. Employees failing to show up for work regularly and/or punctually may be accommodated by giving them status as part-time employees, which more accurately reflects their availability for work. Some employees not living up to their job obligations are tolerated until their supervisors can no longer bear it. Then, by taking disciplinary action, the supervisors may have overreacted to one offense with no back-up data to support their action. Supervisors must be able to justify their disciplinary actions, which may be more often justified and upheld when they acted after having considered the following:

1. Did the employee know that his or her behavior could result in disciplinary action?
2. Was the rule being enforced fairly, and was it applied consistently?
3. Was there an objective investigation of the offense?
4. Does the severity of the discipline reflect the seriousness of the offense and, when possible, take into consideration the employee's service record?

Most of the employees' rights and obligations, listed in the Personnel Rules and Regulations, are sometimes expanded upon by departmental regulations. However, departmental regulations must not conflict with the Personnel Rules and Regulations. Even though departments may become legally bound by their departmental regulations, in cases of appeal of disciplinary action, the departments may lose their enforcement of that disciplinary action if the disciplining supervisor failed to follow departmental regulations.

Employee rights and obligations will become, if they have not already become, a crucial part of managing better with less in the coming austere budget year. It is perhaps the time to rejuvenate the work ethic, "a fair day's pay for a fair day's work," which includes fair and equitable treatment. In addition, it may be time for a reminder that no one has a right to a job, only a right to compete for a job and to retain a job with its rights because of fulfilling job obligations.
TFL: njc

The supervisor and the personnel department play mutually supporting roles for the disciplinary system to work effectively. The personnel manager must help establish a clear and equitable system; the supervisor must provide adequate supervision of employees and enforce work rules fairly. If discipline is required, it is a good idea for it to be handed out by the personnel department based on information provided by the supervisor. This will provide equitable treatment for employees throughout the organization.

Steps in the Grievance Process

Figure 13-2 diagrams a typical disciplinary action and **grievance procedure**. Note that if the employee is a member of a minority group, the equal employment opportunity specialist may be involved in the process.

Management should establish with employees grievance procedures that clearly establish the employee's right to file written complaints concerning alleged unfair management practices and procedures for hearing these complaints in the agency. The specific items that might arise and be subject to a grievance complaint could be defined in personnel rules and regulations. If a collective bargaining agreement exists, the grievance procedure will be defined in the contract. Usually, grievances will be limited to topics in the working rules that an employee believes management has violated. Topics such as the following will probably be included as issues contained in a negotiated contract or in personnel rules enforced by a civil service board. Under each possible area

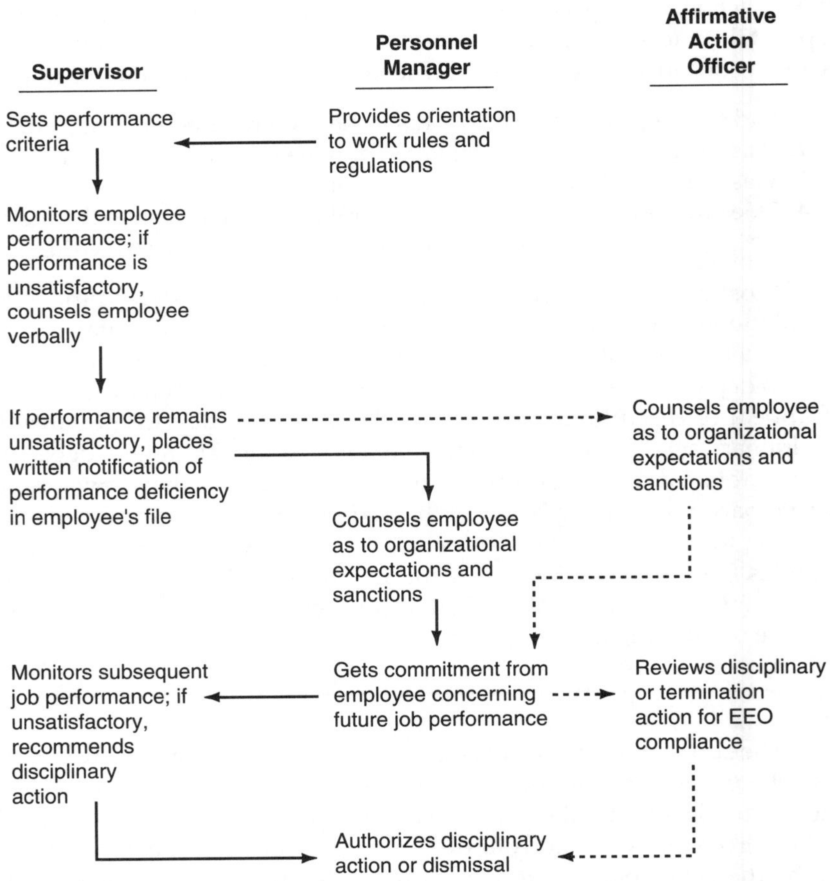

FIGURE 13-2 Disciplinary Action Procedures

of grievance, we have given an example drawn from the exit interview files of a state agency in Kansas.

Work assignments	Employees may feel that work assignments are made subjectively.
Promotion	An employee may feel that the promotional criteria established for a position were not valid or not utilized or that promotional procedures were improper.
Poor supervision	Employees may feel that supervision is inadequate and that supervisors are biased or incompetent.
Political interference	Conflict arises between elected and appointed officials or among supervisors.
Sexual discrimination	Gender inequities and sexual harassment often lead to employee perceptions of unfair treatment.

In any of these instances, it is important that the agency have an established informal and formal grievance procedure that would allow employees to bring their charges to the notice of higher ups and get a fair hearing. The following steps might constitute a typical grievance process:

1. *Informal counseling.* The aggrieved employee should meet and discuss the situation with his or her supervisor or the next higher up if the complaint is about the employee's immediate supervisor. The success of this step depends on an organizational environment that encourages employees to speak openly about their concerns.
2. *Formal grievance.* If informal counseling is unsuccessful, the aggrieved employee should have the opportunity to file a formal grievance in writing stating the problem and what the employee thinks ought to be done to correct the situation. If asked by the employee, the personnel department can help the employee prepare the necessary document.
3. *Consultation between supervisor and personnel director.* After the grievance is filed, the personnel department should consult with the employee to verify the situation and then work with the parties to see if an agreement can be reached.
4. *Investigation/adjudication/arbitration.* A number of steps can follow the attempt by the personnel department to work out a solution between the parties. These might include assigning an impartial person—often from the personnel department—to investigate and make a decision; convening a panel to hear the complaint and make a decision; and securing an outside arbitrator to hear the complaint and render a decision.

Employees can seek redress of grievances by following agency procedures. The more due process afforded the employee internally, the less likely it is that an employee will make a claim of discrimination or unfair treatment.[21] In fact, some legal proceedings will require that internal grievance procedures be followed before undertaking judicial avenues. In other cases, the external investigating agency or court will incorporate the proceedings of an internal process as part of its own review.

ONGOING ISSUES

As might be expected, several ongoing substantive and procedural issues illustrate how judicial interpretation of the Constitution supports conflicting values (primarily employee rights and organizational efficiency). These include:

- state immunity *from federal statues*
- employment eligibility under the Americans with Disability Act (ADA)
- privacy protection of Internet-based communication for public employees
- protection from sexual harassment
- protection for "whistle-blowers"
- employee "comfort" versus workforce diversity programming
- and the extent to which contract employees are covered by constitutional rights

State Immunity *from* Federal Statutes

In the past decade, the Supreme Court has demonstrated its philosophy by emphasizing the importance of states' rights as provided in the Eleventh Amendment. The court held that Congress exceeded its authority when it applied to state employees the Fair Labor Standards Act,[22] the Age Discrimination in Employment Act,[23] and the Americans with Disabilities Act.[24] The majority ruled that Congress had no evidence that states were discriminating based on age or disability when it passed those laws. The rulings do not apply to local governments.

On the one hand, these rulings seem to put other civil rights legislation in jeopardy as applied to state governments. On the other hand, it is not unusual for states themselves to have statutes that parallel these federal laws. For example, California's statute goes further than the ADA in protecting employees with disabilities.[25]

Employment Eligibility under the Americans with Disabilities Act

The Americans with Disabilities Act of 1990[26] is probably the most significant piece of civil rights legislation since Congress passed the Civil Rights Act of 1964. Its purpose is to eliminate discrimination against individuals with disabilities or against those perceived to have a disability. Individuals recovering from drug or alcohol abuse are considered disabled, and those who are HIV infected are also covered. The act parallels the Rehabilitation Act of 1973, but the scope is broader, extending coverage to all employers with fifteen or more full-time employees.

The act, which covers both private and public employers, prohibits discrimination in employment against otherwise qualified applicants and employees and requires that reasonable accommodations in employment conditions and facilities be made for otherwise qualified disabled applicants and employees. Some examples of reasonable accommodation include (1) making existing facilities used by employees readily accessible to and usable by an individual with a disability; (2) job restructuring; (3) modifying work schedules; (4) reassignment to a vacant position; (5) acquiring or modifying equipment or devices; (6) adjusting or modifying examinations, training materials, or policies; (7) providing qualified readers or interpreters.

The requirement that employers make *reasonable accommodations* for the disabled may be mitigated if the employer can show an *undue hardship*—usually financial—would be incurred. Undue hardship is defined by the ADA as an action that is "excessively costly, extensive, substantial, or disruptive, or that would fundamentally alter the nature or operation of the business." In determining undue hardship, factors to be considered include the nature and cost of the accommodation in relation to the size, the financial resources, the nature and structure of the employer's operation, as well as the impact the accommodation would have on the specific facility itself.

The terms **reasonable accommodation** and **undue hardship** represent Congress' attempt to balance employee and employer expectations and obligations and the values of individual rights and efficiency. An employee may expect and an employer is obligated to make a reasonable accommodation for an employee who is disabled but otherwise qualified. However, efficiency tempers this expectation/obligation; an employer is not obligated to make the accommodation if it forces an undue economic hardship or hardship in service delivery. These terms represent a political compromise over conflicting values and expectations/obligations, and they provide general guidance. The particulars of implementation require administrative interpretation and action. Reasonable accommodation and undue hardship are being defined administratively and judicially as the law matures.[27]

Privacy, Technology, and Public Employment

The Fourth Amendment application to drug testing is just one instance that juxtaposes employer interests in productivity and safety with employee interests in privacy. A 2007 survey of its membership by the American Management Association revealed that more than one-fourth of responding employers had fired workers for misusing e-mail and nearly one-third have fired employees for misusing the Internet.[28] Sixty-six percent of the companies use some form of electronic monitoring and/or surveillance. The most frequent reasons for the dismissals had to do with inappropriate content including language used or Internet sites visited. The biggest reason cited are protection from legal liability (e.g., use of e-mail content in litigation). Ninety-five percent of the companies that monitor employees have a written policy.

Public employees have more privacy rights than their private sector counterparts. The Constitution as well as state statutes and federal law like the Freedom of Information Act[29] and the Electronic Communications Privacy Act[30] protect these rights. Important here is the rule of thumb that the more compelling the reason an employer has to monitor employee behavior whether electronically or otherwise, the more likely the court is to defer to the employer. Attempts to prevent behavior like sexual harassment and workplace violence that is injurious to other employees provide a reasonable justification for surveillance. A comprehensive policy that sets out the employer's expectations and is clearly communicated to employees and acknowledged by them provides a crucial base for this aspect of the employer–employee relationship.

Protection against Sexual Harassment

What is **sexual harassment**? The EEOC, responsible for enforcing the Civil Rights Act of 1964, as amended, and various other employment discrimination laws, has issued the following guidelines: unwelcome sexual advances, requests for sexual favors, and other verbal or physical conduct of a sexual nature constitute sexual harassment when (1) submission to such conduct is made either explicitly or implicitly a term or condition of an individual's employment, (2) submission to or rejection of such conduct by an individual is used as the basis for employment decisions affecting such individual, or (3) such conduct has the purpose or effect of unreasonably interfering with an individual's work performance or creating an intimidating, hostile, or offensive working environment.

In simple terms, sexual harassment is not romance although it can certainly grow out of romantic attachments turned sour. It is the coercive and hostile behavior of one person toward another based on gender. The number of cases of sexual harassment filed with the EEOC has increased from 10,500 in 1992 to 12,500 in 2007.[31] The number of males filing suit has increased from 9.1 percent to 16 percent in that same period. However, not all cases are pursued beyond a claim and initial inquiry. Of the 12,500, the EEOC found "no reasonable cause" in 45.5 percent of the cases. Contrary to what one might expect, only a very few complaints actually reach a court. Moreover, an analysis of U.S. appellate court decisions regarding hostile environment claims from 2004 to mid-2005 shows that most fail to make a valid claim.[32]

It is clear that men and women see sexual behavior differently, sometimes markedly so.[33] Rotundo's analysis suggests, "Women perceive a broader range of social-sexual behaviors as harassing. . . . [than men, and] the female–male difference was larger for behaviors that involve hostile work environment harassment, derogatory attitudes toward women, dating pressure, or physical sexual contact than [for] sexual propositions or sexual coercion." (p. 914). While sexual harassment must be ultimately dealt with in the workplace, conflicts involving claims of harassment do find their way into the court system as interested parties seek justice through the law.[34] As in an analysis of other areas of discriminations, the court's analysis may be more important than its actual decisions because the analysis contains the implied guidelines to development of organizational policy and managerial practice. In ***Meritor Savings Bank v. Vinson*** (1986),[35] the Supreme Court established several significant legal guidelines in its interpretation of the Civil Rights Act of 1964, as amended. Mechelle Vinson, who was employed by the bank in 1974, rose through the ranks to assistant branch manager on her merits when in 1978 she was discharged for excessive use of sick leave. Ms. Vinson claimed that during her four years with the bank she had been constantly subjected to sexual harassment. She estimated that over the four-year period she had sexual intercourse with Sidney Taylor, the branch manager, some forty or fifty times. "In addition, [she] testified that Taylor fondled her in front of other employees, followed her into the women's restroom when she went there alone, exposed himself to her, and even forcibly raped her on several occasions." Vinson testified that she was afraid to report the harassment to Taylor's superiors. Taylor denied her charges completely, contending that they resulted from a business dispute.

Even though the conflicting testimony was never resolved, the Supreme Court made several significant legal points in its 9-0 judgment. First, it concluded that an adverse personnel action need not be taken in order to prove that sexual harassment has occurred. It affirmed lower court findings and the EEOC's guidelines that "Title VII affords employees the right to work in an environment free from discriminatory intimidation, ridicule and insult" (p. 59). Further, it affirmed that "a plaintiff may establish a violation of Title VII by proving that discrimination based on sex has created a hostile or abusive work environment" (p. 59). However, it tempered its stance somewhat by saying that in order for a legal violation to occur, the sexual harassment must be "sufficiently severe or pervasive 'to alter the conditions of the [victim's] employment and create an abusive working environment' " (p. 60) (internal cite omitted).

Second, the Court found that when trying to determine the nature of the relationship, "The correct inquiry is whether respondent by her conduct indicated that the alleged sexual advances were *unwelcome*, not whether her actual participation in sexual intercourse was *voluntary*" (p. 60) (emphasis added).

In 1993, the Supreme Court revisited the issue of sexual harassment in ***Harris v. Forklift***.[36] Teresa Harris worked as a manager at Forklift Systems equipment rental company. At issue was whether Harris would have to show that she had suffered psychological injury in order to prevail in her claim that she was working in a sexually abusive and hostile environment. A unanimous Supreme Court found in Harris' favor, indicating that "Title VII comes into play before the harassing conduct leads to a nervous breakdown." A hostile environment exists where a "reasonable person" objectively comes to that conclusion and when a victim subjectively perceives it as such. The Court acknowledged the lack of a cookie-cutter formula for establishing when a hostile environment exists, but it did outline several factors that should be considered: frequency of the conduct, its severity, whether it is physically threatening or humiliating or a mere offensive utterance, and whether it interferes with an employee's work.

As a footnote, in *Harris* the Court rejected a lower court standard that used the "reasonable woman" to determine whether a hostile environment exits. The Court stayed with its frequently relied upon hypothetical "reasonable person." While it is clear that men and women see some behaviors associated with sexual harassment differently, the Court is reluctant to acknowledge that justice should be gender specific—any more than it should be race or age specific.

Recent court cases have made clear that employers are always liable for discriminatory acts by supervisors if resulting in a tangible personnel action. If no tangible personnel action is involved, the employer may mount an effective defense if (1) it can show reasonable care in preventing and correcting promptly harassing behavior and (2) where an employee charging sexual harassment has failed to take advantage of a valid complaint procedure.[37] Finally, in ***Oncale v. Sundowner Offshore Services***, the Supreme Court held that Title VII protects employees from same sex harassment.[38]

However, sexual harassment involves more than issues of power, stereotypes, and litigation. It would be naive to claim that productivity in organizations is disconnected from personal attraction and cooperation. Productivity is often enhanced by close, affectionate working relationships that develop with an organizational culture that encourages respect, dignity, and tolerance. Nevertheless, the proper relationship between sexuality, productivity, and fair treatment is difficult to realize in any organizational context because of divergent and unspoken expectations and perceptions. The relationship between sexuality, productivity, and equity promises to become more complicated with increasing ethnic diversity and accompanying expectations in the workplace.

Protection for "Whistle-blowers"

In spring 2008, it was reported that the Federal Aviation Administration had been developing relationships with airlines that violated standard safety inspection practices. The *Wall Street Journal* reported that the U.S. Office of Special Counsel (OSC) was investigating whistle-blowing complaints from within the Financial Administration Act (FAA) that also included charges of retaliation.[39]

The tendency of public organizations and administrators to withhold self-incriminating information from the public is counterbalanced theoretically by **whistle-blowing**. This form of dissent focuses public attention on behavior the whistle-blower considers illegal or unethical. It is this moral imperative, accompanied by the whistle-blower's knowledge that his or her charges will be scrutinized and possibly met with reprisal, which distinguishes the whistle-blower's actions from a simple act of insubordination for private purposes.

Whistle-blowing is a well-publicized phenomenon because it plays upon the public's desire to expose corruption and increase responsiveness or efficiency in government agencies. The Civil Service Reform Act of 1978, which applies to federal employees, includes as a merit principle: "Employees should be protected against reprisal for the lawful disclosure of information which the employees reasonably believe evidences: (a) a violation of any law, rule, or regulation, or (b) mismanagement, a gross waste of funds, an abuse of authority, or a substantial and specific danger to public health or safety." Several additional federal laws passed since 1978 contain protections for whistle-blowers who disclose specific types of information. There are federal and state laws that cover private sector whistle-blowers in many areas of health, welfare, and safety. However, they are not uniform in coverage.

Despite these protections and similar ones in several state and local governments, employees usually blow the whistle on their employer only as a last resort, when the conflict between their ethical standards and their perception of their agency's behavior is so great as to leave them no choice. In other terms, whistle-blowing results from a perceived gross breach in the employment contract—in this case, the expectations an employee has of his or her employer or coworkers. Often times, this expectation runs counter to the employer's expectation and desire for employee loyalty. Whistle-blowers often exhaust organizational channels for dissent before they "go public" with charges and information.

The U.S. Office of Special Counsel receives and processes complaints—based on issued guidelines and in specific areas of concern—from federal employees. The U.S. Postal Service is excluded as is the military and employees of federal contractors. In FY 2006, the OSC received 435 new claims compared to 555 in FY 2002.[40] Of the 435, thirty-four were seen as warranting formal investigation beyond an initial review within the OSC itself. While the thirty-four may not seem like a large number given the scope of federal work, when compounded with claims that may be processed within federal agencies and not reach the OSC, in the states and local governments that encourage this method of transparency, the number undoubtedly grows.

How should whistle-blowing be evaluated? On the one hand, it divides the agency, undercuts its management, and causes serious organizational harm—sometimes for the self-serving purposes of a disgruntled employee. On the other hand, it may prevent managers from hiding information harmful to the reputation of the agency or its managers, using specious reasons such as security and efficiency. Whistle-blowing represents a classic conflict between individual rights, possibly under the rubric of the First Amendment, and the desire of managers to control the flow of information out of the agency in order to preserve individual careers, administrative efficiency, or political support.

Organizational Justice, Productivity, and Workforce Diversity

Demands on public employers for productivity have resulted in more work with less staff, declining health benefits, and threats of privatization. These contrasting forces place considerable strain on the sanction function and complicate perceptions of organizational justice and organizational citizenship.

Furthermore, there is substantial sentiment among public managers as well as the public at large that the relationship between the rights of public employees and managerial flexibility has tilted toward the side of employees at the expense of government efficiency and responsiveness. Nevertheless, the sanction function is driven by more than demands for individual rights versus productivity or administrative efficiency. Added to this contentious set of factors is the demographic trend toward increasing ethnic diversity in the workforce. Ethnic diversity will complicate employee expectations and what employers can expect from employees. This heterogeneity in expectations and obligations can be expected to place additional strain on the organizational processes aimed at matching them.

It appears that one of the issues that will dominate human resource management is how organizations can effectively manage the relationship between workforce diversity, organizational justice, and productivity. The relationship between any two of these factors might be predictable, but inserting the third adds a dimension of significant uncertainty.

Constitutional Rights of Contract Employees

One of the efficiency arguments for contracting out for service delivery or hiring temporary workers is that their expectations of due process are less than that of permanent civil service employees. With fewer rights, managerial discretion increases and flexibility in handling human resources is enhanced. On the one hand, private-sector employees who handle the contract work have no constitutional rights as employees, and in the case of temporary workers, even if a public employer hires them, there are no expectations of job security.

Rosenbloom and Piotrowski pose several provocative questions raising their concerns about diminished respect for constitutional and administrative law norms conveyed in a commitment to outsourcing:

> Should private contractors' employees have rights to whistle blowing (that match those of public employees), privacy, and liberty that more or less match those guaranteed to government employees by constitutional law? Should freedom of information, open records, and open meetings laws be applied to private contractors? Should the public have the same constitutional and administrative law protections when they deal with private contractors doing outsourced government work as when the interact directly with government agencies?[41]

Without administrative agencies addressing these questions, they are left by default to the federal and state judiciaries. Based on a review of court cases, here are some of the questions the court asks in determining whether constitutional and/or administrative law is applicable to private contractors: "Is the contractor engaged in a public function, acting as a surrogate or adjunct for an agency in an area where constitutional rights are at risk, or so entwined with an agency as to be public in character?"[42] So, for example, a private contractor running a prison for a state could be subject to constitutional and administrative law—which would affect the rights of the employees working for the contractor.

PUBLIC EMPLOYEE LIABILITY

In the 1970s, the Court enlarged the scope of its constitutional inquiry, granting more rights to public employees, clients, or beneficiaries of the government, prisoners, and citizens who otherwise might encounter government officials. It is one thing for the courts to grant new rights; it is another to enforce recognition of and respect for them. One mechanism to advance these ends is the threat that a public official might be held personally liable for violating a citizen's constitutional rights. Traditionally, administrators came to share the same immunity from civil suits arising out of actions connected with their official functions as had formerly belonged only to legislators and judges and other special classes of public employees. However, in order to balance the need to protect the rights of citizens with the need to protect public officials who are required to exercise discretion that affects citizens, the doctrine of **sovereign immunity** gave way to a more limited form of immunity for administrative officials. The revised doctrine, clearly captured now in ***Harlow v. Fitzgerald*** (1982), states that "government officials performing discretionary functions generally are shielded from liability for civil damages insofar as their conduct does not violate clearly established statutory or constitutional rights of which a reasonable person would have known."[43]

The concept of **qualified immunity** outlined in *Harlow* suggests that in order to perform their job effectively and without fear of being sued successfully, public officials must become aware of the constitutional law that impinges upon their work and the work of their agency. The increased use of private contractors to provide public services raises a new set of justice questions. In *Wabaunsee County v. Umbehr*, the court ruled that a private contractor does not relinquish free speech rights when it wins a government contract. We have introduced in this section the concept of "qualified immunity" that protects public employees as they carry out their public duties. Does this practice extend to private business holding government contracts?

In 1997, the Supreme Court answered "no" by a 5-4 vote.[44] An inmate claimed that prison guards had used extreme force in violation of his constitutional rights. The guards claimed qualified immunity in a defense that would mimic that of a public prison guard, arguing that without this protection, every disciplinary action they took would be subject to a lawsuit and the prison's work would suffer.

The court distinguished between public prison guards and those employed by a private contractor arguing that a competitive market place would encourage appropriate actions with regard to prisoners. Too little discipline, cautioned by the fear of lawsuits, would place the private prison management company in a competitive disadvantage with comparable firms. A vigorous dissent argued that the prison function performed was the same whether public or private, and if prison guards employed by the state enjoyed limited immunity, so too should their private management counterparts.

An unrelated development is the potential liability that public employers have for criminal acts of their employees or for acts that violate a citizen's constitutional rights. Lawsuits of this type may claim a failure by the employer to exercise proper vigilance in the hiring, supervision, and/or training of an employee. Thus, in contrast to common practice, the public employer may be responsible for the private actions of an employee. For example, a housing authority unwittingly hires—through a sloppy process—as a housing inspector an individual with a history of theft. The inspector is subsequently found guilty of theft and assault of one of the tenants. The tenant sues the housing authority claiming negligence in hiring. The authority put the tenants at risk, and it should have known about the inspector's criminal history. Some state statutes limit the liability of public employers in this regard.[45] Nevertheless, in cases of gross negligence and where constitutional rights have been violated, a victim may sue under Title 42 U.S. Code 1983, which imposes liability on public employees for "deprivation of any rights, privileges, or immunities secured by the Constitution."

The legal issue in these situations relate to the determination of fault and causation and whether a public employer is guilty of "deliberate indifference." Drawing this conclusion from a single bad decision is very difficult to do.[46] Interestingly, this negligent employee process liability can cause confusion for the human resource manager who is also under notice not to reveal information about discharged employees that might harm their ability to secure another job. Employees have liberty interests guaranteed by the Constitution's Fifth Amendment. The government cannot abridge a person's liberty without due process. The freedom to work is considered a liberty, and if a public employer stigmatizes an employee in the context of discharging or failing to rehire, it may have violated the employee's Fifth Amendment right if due process has not been observed. Sometimes, due process is a simple matter of giving the employee an opportunity to respond in writing to adverse information that may be filed in an employee's personnel records. In other cases, it may require a pre- or post-termination hearing that would allow the employee to respond to any adverse information connected with the discharge.

Summary

In some ways, the sanction function is the most important of the four core functions. Activities designed to fulfill this function aim to establish and maintain the terms of the relationship between employee and employer. These terms consist of expectations and obligations employee and employer have of each other, and they constitute the rules of the game. Expectations and obligations arise from a number of sources. Of these, only public employees enjoy rights stemming from the Constitution. However, practically, these rights are balanced against the duty a public employer has to operate efficiently. In this balance, we can see the inevitable conflict between administrative efficiency and individual rights and resultant perceptions about organizational justice.

Internal disciplinary and grievance procedures are mechanisms to enforce the terms of the employment relationship. Increasing diversity of the workforce will bring a broader array of employee expectations and obligations to the workplace. Relatively, objective disciplinary guidelines and impartial grievance procedures might be expected to ameliorate the negative impact of these differences and provide a foundation of respect necessary to channel the differences into creativity and productivity. The challenge is to accomplish this in a political environment where public employees are seen as entrenched and as obstacles to government efficiency and responsiveness.

Significant effort has been underway at all levels of government, but especially at the federal and state levels, to limit employee rights to advance administrative efficiency. These efforts are fueled not only by an analysis of service delivery options employing private and nonprofit sectors, but also by political ideology where message, agenda, and loyalty may prevail over competence, experience, and analysis.

Key Terms

at-will employment *309*
competitive sourcing *309*
discipline *315*
due process *313*
grievance procedure *318*
organizational citizenship *314*
procedural justice *314*
property rights *313*
psychological contract *306*
public–private partnerships (PPP) *309*
reasonable accommodation *321*
sanction function *306*
sexual harassment *321*
sovereign versus qualified immunity *326*
terms of the employment relationship *306*
undue hardship *321*
whistle-blowing *323*
Branti v. Finkel (1980) *312*
Connick v. Myers (1983) *311*
Harlow v. Fitzgerald (1982) *326*
Harris v. Forklift (1993) *323*
Meritor Savings Bank v. Vinson (1986) *322*
O'Connor v. Ortega (1987) *313*
O'Hare v. Northlake (1996) *312*
Oncale v. Sundowner Offshore Services (1998) *323*
Richardson v. McKnight (1997) *312*
Rutan v. Republican Party of Illinois (1990) *312*
Wabaunsee County v. Umbehr (1996) *312*

Discussion Questions

1. Define the sanction function, and identify the ways an organization establishes and maintains the terms of the employment relationship between employee and employer.
2. Public employees are granted more rights than private-sector employees. Why is this so? Give some examples of rights public employees have that employees in other sectors might not have. Do you think public-sector employees should have fewer rights? Do you think that private-sector employees should have more rights?
3. How does the sanction function differ in alternate personnel systems?
4. Discuss the balance the Supreme Court examines when deciding whether a public employer has violated an employee's First Amendment right to free speech. Why do public employees have a right to free speech? How is the right different from what you have as a citizen?
5. Do you agree with all the provisions of the Fourth Amendment? Do you agree that public employers ought to be able to conduct drug screens of their employees? If you answer "yes" to both questions, how do you reconcile the tension between a literal reading of the Fourth Amendment and conducting drug screens without probable cause? How does the Court reconcile the tension?
6. Why do you think the Supreme Court considers a person's job as property? Describe the role of property rights and due process in establishing and maintaining the terms of the employment relationship.
7. Is it useful to consider employees as organizational citizens? If so, what expectations might they hold of their employer? What expectations might the employer have of them in return? Today, it is frequently asserted that in society at large people seem more concerned with their rights than their community or citizenship obligations. Do you think this is true of organizational citizens as well? How do you think the contemporary employment environment affects organizational citizenship?
8. Some have argued that democratic values must be practiced in order to be learned. If democratic values were practiced in organizations, how would the relationship between employee and employer change? What would be the benefits and the costs in terms of the four values?
9. Discuss how discipline and grievance procedures are connected to the sanction function.
10. Diagram a typical disciplinary procedure.
11. Are the interests of employee and employer the same in establishing a grievance procedure?

Construct a model grievance procedure from the employee's standpoint. Construct it now from the employer's standpoint. Do you have any differences? As an employer, which process would you use to construct a grievance procedure?

12. What rights does the ADA give to employees, and how does it balance those rights with the employer's interests?
13. How has modern technology in the workplace raised new privacy concerns? What do you think is a reasonable approach to an employer having access to an employee's e-mail? To Internet sites visited? What do you see as the similarities and difference between an employer having access to employee e-mail and Internet use and the monitoring of phone calls?
14. Describe the rights of employees who have been sexually harassed or who are considered whistle-blowers.
15. What relationship do you see between organizational justice, productivity, and workforce diversity?
16. Use the various court cases described in the chapter to show how the courts reach a balance among the four values. How does an administrator's understanding of legal reasoning regarding the four values affect policymaking and management in the arena of human resources management?

Case Study: Juan Hernandez v. The County

Introduction

Metropolitan County is the largest local government in the state. County government is divided into about 50 operating departments and employs about 15,000 people. Among the departments is the Office of Data Processing Center (DPC). Juan Hernandez, a Hispanic male, was employed by the DPC on July 15, 1997, as a data processing trainee. On May 10, 1998, he was promoted to the position of Operator I and attained permanent status in that position six months later. He remained in that position until his termination on March 9, 2007. This case study will examine the circumstances leading to his dismissal, his role as a union steward for Local 121 of the American Federation of State, County and Municipal Employees (AFSCME), and the various steps involved in his termination. It will reach conclusions relating to the disciplinary action and grievance process in public agencies in general.

Employment History

From his initial employment until April 2002, Juan Hernandez's record reflected satisfactory and dependable service. On April 25, 2002, however, he received a written reprimand for failing to satisfactorily back up numerous documents that were lost in a power outage. Mr. Hernandez reacted to the reprimand by a letter of rebuttal, which indicated that he disagreed sharply with management's allegations of his lack of general competence.

In October 2002, he received an evaluation summarizing his performance as "in need of attention." His scheduled merit increase was deferred for three months. Although the overall tone of the evaluation was encouraging, it implied incompetence in his ability to grasp the concepts of a larger information technology system. Mr. Hernandez appealed the evaluation but withdrew the appeal when he received a satisfactory evaluation along with his merit increase three months later.

In January 2003, the director of operations for the DPC brought about a reorganization that resulted in Mr. Hernandez being switched from the day to night shift. Despite his objections to this change, Mr. Hernandez's employment continued satisfactorily for the next eighteen months, until he suffered a severe on-the-job injury on July 26, 2004. A portion of the raised computer floor collapsed near his workstation. His resultant knee and leg injuries caused Mr. Hernandez to be absent from work for several months.

Upon his return to work on October 2004, he was presented with a formal record of counseling dated July 29, 2004, just three days after his injury had occurred. This record, which was prepared by his supervisor as a summary of the informal counseling that had occurred with him, cited a number of infractions, having to do with failure to make up time for a long lunch; failure to produce a leave slip for his absence; and for improperly processing various forms needed by other departments.

On June 29, 2005, Mr. Hernandez was given a formal record of counseling citing his involvement in a technical failure that occurred in the computer room at the main console. The essence of the incident concerned Mr. Hernandez's evident unfamiliarity with the software that both he and the operators under his supervision were utilizing.

Shop Steward Election

On July 27, 2006, Mr. Hernandez was elected to the position of shop steward representing the DPC employees with AFSCME Local 121. During his term as shop steward, he aided several employees who were contemplating filing grievances against the DPC because some agency managers were inappropriately assigning work in violation of a collective bargaining agreement.

Termination

On January 9, 2007, Juan Hernandez was himself given an "unsatisfactory" performance evaluation based on his failure to complete certain training courses, designed to insure his knowledge of the hardware and software both he and his subordinates were utilizing. He refused to sign this evaluation.

On January 23, 2007, he was charged one day without pay for calling in sick the day before the start of his scheduled one-week vacation. Upon returning to work, he submitted a doctor's statement excusing him for the absence. This doctor's statement, coupled with other evidence, would later prove the grounds for his termination.

Mr. Robert Hess, an administrative officer for the DPC, began to compile evidence that Mr. Hernandez had falsified doctors' statements that excused several of his absences. He had observed that the handwriting of doctors' excuses dated June 15, 2006, and January 23, 2007, did not match the handwriting of other excuses obtained from the same doctor for the injuries suffered in his 2004 accident. In addition, the excuses in question were written on Pacific Hospital forms, while the others were not.

Interviews were conducted with the physician, Dr. Herman Wilbanks, and with Mr. Vincent Pico, administrative resident at Pacific Hospital. Dr. Wilbanks denied writing the excuses; and Mr. Pico confirmed that Mr. Hernandez had not been a patient at the hospital on the dates in question.

Mr. Hernandez then altered his story by stating that the excuse that he had submitted for the January 23 absence was a copy of the original. He claimed that his daughter, a pre-med student at Long Beach State University, had copied the original one "as practice for her classes," and he had mistakenly submitted the copy. However, the Los Angeles County Crime Laboratory Bureau confirmed that the handwriting was the same on both forms.

On March 10, 2007, Mr. Hernandez attended a scheduled disciplinary action meeting in the office of the deputy director of the DPC. He was represented by the union. At this meeting, he was given a termination letter and a disciplinary action report effecting his dismissal. He signed the form at the union representative's advice.

Appeal Hearing

An appeal hearing was held on May 10, 2007. Mr. Hernandez was represented by AFSCME Local 121; the County was represented by the County Attorney's Office. The impartial hearing examiner concluded that violations 1 through 4 were not substantiated but that the charge of a false claim of leave was substantiated. Mr. Hernandez's termination was sustained (Exhibit A).

Conclusion

Both collective bargaining agreements and disciplinary action procedures provide for progressive discipline of employees for poor performance, and they protect employees against unfair harassment or unsubstantiated allegations.

In the case of Juan Hernandez, the pattern and timing of management's disciplinary action against him are both suspect. A casual review of his record of disciplinary action indicates that it followed on-the-job injuries and his election as shop steward.

On the other hand, it is also clear that Mr. Hernandez's work performance was frequently careless or incompetent. Moreover, his falsification of medical excuses constituted misconduct. Management's efforts to substantiate this required the spending of much time, money, and effort.

The charge of willful misconduct was upheld rather than claims of poor performance. The lesson to be learned from this is that management, in the final analysis, when attempting to terminate an employee who is backed by union and legal representation in front of an impartial examiner, must have documentation that unquestionably establishes poor performance or misconduct.

Questions

After finishing the case study and studying the exhibit carefully, be prepared to discuss the following questions in a small group and to defend your answers in subsequent class discussion.

1. Did the employer (the Data Processing Center) provide Mr. Hernandez with clear performance standards from the time of his employment to the time of his termination?
2. Did the DPC provide Mr. Hernandez with adequate informal counseling concerning his performance discrepancies prior to initiating formal counseling and disciplinary action?
3. Did the employer adequately document Mr. Hernandez's alleged violation of clear performance standards?
4. What is the difference between poor performance and misconduct? Is the distinction important?
5. Who, if anyone, benefited from the outcome of this case study?
6. What functions and values are present in this case?
7. How important is an impartial hearing examiner in developing a sense of organizational justice?

Exhibit A: Hearing Examiner's Report

MONK, MURPHY, TANNENBAUM AND ENDICOTT
ATTORNEYS AT LAW
HEARING EXAMINER'S REPORT

Date: June 20, 2007

To: The Honorable Samuel Shapiro
County Attorney
County
The Honorable Jeremy Irving
Attorney at Law
AFSCME Local 121

On May 10, 2007, the Hearing Examiner heard testimony and considered evidence relative to the termination of Mr. Juan Hernandez from the County, Data Processing Center.

The following charges were advanced to support termination:

1. Alleged violation of time and leave regulations, as described in the formal record of counseling that Mr. Hernandez received on July 29, 2004.
2. Alleged willful negligence in the performance of Mr. Hernandez's job duties in the improper printing of forms, as described in the formal record of counseling which he received on July 29, 2004.
3. Alleged willful negligence in the performance of Mr. Hernandez's job duties in the failure to properly load programs CICS (S337) so as to prevent damage to the System 3000 Data Base on June 9, 2006, as described in the formal record of counseling which he received on June 29, 2006.
4. Alleged failure to complete required training courses (MVS, Payroll system, OMI-CROM OMEGAMON, and OPS-JES2) by January 23, 1992, as required by his performance evaluation of January 9, 2007.
5. Alleged falsification of physician's excuses for sick leave for June 15, 1991, and January 23, 2007, as described in the Laboratory Analysis Report dated March 5, 2007, LACPSD Case #101374.

Having evaluated all evidence and testimony presented relative to these charges, the Hearing Examiner finds that insufficient evidence exists to document discharge on grounds 1, 2, 3, or 4. However, under the terms of the collective bargaining agreement between AFSCME Local 121 and the Board of Supervisors of the County, dated October 27, 2006, sufficient evidence has been presented to document discharge on ground 5.

Discharge is hereby affirmed.

Notes

1. U.S. Department of Justice (2008). An investigation of allegations of politicized hiring in the Department of Justice Honors Program and Summer Law Intern Program. Available at: www.usdoj.gov/oig/special/s0806/final.pdf (accessed on September 28, 2008).
2. U.S. Equal Employment Opportunity Commission (2008). Available at: www.eeoc.gov/stats (accessed on September 28, 2008).
3. Unknown author (2009 forthcoming). Competitive sourcing in the federal civil service. American Review of Public Administration.
4. Hays, S. W., and J. E. Sowa (2006). A broader look at the "accountability" movement. *Review of Public Personnel Administration, 26* (2): 102–117.
5. *Harlow v. Fitzgerald*, 457 U.S. 800 (1982).
6. Piotrowski, S. J., and G. G. Ryzin (2007). Citizen attitudes towards transparency in local government. *American Review of Public Administration, 37* (3): 306–323.
7. *Pickering v. Board of Education of Township High School*, 391 U.S. 563 (1968).
8. *Connick v. Myers*, 461 U.S. 138 (1983).
9. *Wabaunsee County v. Umbehr*, 518 U.S. 668 (1996).
10. *Rutan v. Republican Party of Illinois*, 497 U.S. 62 (1990).
11. *Branti v. Finkel*, 445 U.S. 507 (1980) at p. 518.
12. *O'Hare Truck Service v. City of Northlake*, 518 U.S. 712 (1996).
13. *Richardson v. McKnight*, 521 U.S. 399 (1997).
14. Rosenbloom, D. H., and S. J. Piotrowski (2005). Outsourcing the Constitution and Administrative Law Norms. *American Review of Public Administration, 35*: 103–121.
15. *O'Connor v. Ortega*. 480 U.S. 709 (1987).
16. *Skinner v. Railway Labor Executives' Association*, 489 U.S. 602 (1989); *National Treasury Employees' Union v. Von Raab*, 489 U.S. 656 (1989) at fn 2.
17. *Cleveland v. Loudermill*, 470 U.S. 532 (1985).
18. Camerman, J., R. Cropanzano, and C. Vandenberghe (2007). The benefits of justice for temporary workers. *Group and Organizational Management, 32* (2): 176–207.
19. Ehrhart, M. G. (2004). Leadership and procedural justice climate as antecedents of unit-level organizational citizenship behavior. *Personnel Psychology, 57*: 61–94.
20. Ibid.
21. Goldman, B. (2006). Towards understanding of employment discrimination claiming: An integration of organizational justice and social information processing theory. *Personnel Journal, 54* (2): 361–386.
22. *Alden v. Maine*, 527 U.S. 706 (1999).
23. *Kimmel v. Florida Board of Regents*, 528 U.S. 62 (2000).
24. *University of Alabama v. Patricia Garrett*, 531 U.S. 356 (2001).
25. Giron, L. (December 31, 2000). State law redefines who has disability. *Los Angeles Times*, p. W1.
26. Americans with Disabilities Act of 1990, Public Law 101-336, July 26, 1990; Kohl, J. P., and P. S. Greenlaw. (1996). Title I of the Americans with Disabilities Act: The anatomy of a law. *Public Personnel Management, 25*: 323–332. Available at: http://janweb.icdi.wvu.edu/ (accessed on September 28, 2008).
27. For more information on the Americans with Disabilities Act see: The U.S. Office of Equal Opportunity at http://www.eeoc.gov/types/ada.html (accessed on September 28, 2008).
28. American Management Association and ePolicy Institute (2008). *2007 Electronic monitoring and surveillance survey*. New York: American Management Association. www.amanet.org and www.epolicyinstitute.com
29. 5 U.S.C. 552.
30. 18 U.S.C. 2701.
31. Equal Employment Opportunity Commission (2008). www.eeoc.gov/stats/harass.html
32. Mann, S., and D. Goodman (2008). Sexual harassment isn't always the issue. *Review of Public Personnel Administration, 28* (2): 190–196.
33. Rotundo, M., D.-H. Nguyen, and P. R. Sackett (2001). A meta-analytical review of gender difference in perceptions of sexual harassment. *Journal of Applied Psychology, 86* (5): 914–922.
34. U.S. Office of Equal Employment Opportunity at http://www.eeoc.gov/types/sexual_harassment.html
35. *Meritor Savings Bank v. Vinson* 477 U.S. 57 (1986).
36. *Harris v. Forklift Systems, Inc.*, 510 U.S. 17 (1993).

37. *Burlington Industries, Inc. v. Ellerth*, 527 U.S. 742 (1998) and *Faragher v. City of Boca Raton*, 524 U.S. 775 (1998).
38. *Oncale v. Sundowner Offshore Services, Inc.* 523 U.S. 75 (1998).
39. Pasztor, A., and C. Conkey (May 20, 2008). FAA whistleblower intimidation probed. *Wall Street Journal* (Eastern Edition), p. A3; Conkey, C. (June 12, 2008). Special Counsel has hands full with FAA. *Wall Street Journal* (Eastern Edition), p. A4.
40. U.S. Office of Special Counsel. Annual report to Congress FY 2006. www.osc.gov
41. Rosenbloom and Piotrowski, Outsourcing the Constitution and Administrative Law Norms.
42. Ibid., p. 118.
43. *Harlow v. Fitzgerald*, 73 L Ed 2d 396 (1982) at p. 410.
44. *Richardson v. McKnight*, 117 S.CT. 2100 (1997).
45. *Board of the County Commissioners of Bryan County, Oklahoma v. Brown*, 520 U.S. 397 (1997).
46. Ibid.; also on this subject and for a more legal orientation to many of the topics in this chapter see Lee, Y. S., with D. H. Rosenbloom (2005). *A reasonable public servant*. New York: M. E. Sharpe.

CHAPTER 14

Collective Bargaining

Collective bargaining is primarily focused on the sanction function, in that through collective bargaining the conditions and terms of the employment relationship between employee and employer are determined and maintained. Law and state and federal compliance agencies determine the context for bargaining and resolution of disputes. **Collective bargaining** is a set of techniques under which employees are represented in the negotiation and administration of the terms and conditions of their employment. Because collective bargaining can conflict with other personnel systems, it also focuses conflict over a number of issues: job security with no privatization, employment quotas versus seniority, outsourcing and competitive sourcing, adversarial dispute resolution versus alternative dispute resolution techniques, and win–lose bargaining versus win-win bargaining.

Collective bargaining is a traditional approach to labor relations that has a long and sometimes bitter history in the private sector. In fact, Frederick Taylor's emphasis and devotion to scientific management at the turn of the nineteenth century was due in large part to his belief that it would lead to harmonious labor relations. Over time, unions and collective bargaining became increasingly accepted in the trades and with industrial labor especially—one thinks of auto workers, steel workers, and teamsters commonly as examples of union workers. But times have changed. The past forty years, and especially the 1960s and 1970s, saw a dramatic shift in union activity from the private to public sector, including schoolteachers and employees. In fact, the 4-1 ratio of unionized private-to-public employees has virtually reversed itself. Less than 10 percent of private sector employees are now unionized—an all-time low. In contrast, public employees—teachers, police officers, firefighters, and a variety of other office workers at the state and federal levels—now constitute the bulk of union membership.

The shift away from unions in the private sector can be attributable to several factors, not the least of which is change in the global economy, which places American workers and firms in direct competitive relationships internationally. No directly similar challenge exists for public sector employees. Governments are not going to relocate; and pay and benefits are not going to be determined in the same competitive way as they are in private firms. However, as we have seen throughout the book, at-will employment, competitive sourcing, and the outright sale of public assets like toll roads create challenges for public unions and their members. However, the greatest challenges may be less tangible. According to Riccucci, compared to their predecessors, "The typical American worker is less interested in solidarity and collective action for the good of all workers."[1] As job security for private sector employees continues to be precarious, taxpayers will not support robust pay and benefit packages for public employees who have relatively more secure jobs.

By the end of this chapter, you will be able to:

1. Discuss the history and legal basis of collective bargaining, focusing on differences between the public and private sectors, and between the United States and other countries.
2. Explain the connection between public agencies' legal obligation to protect employees' constitutional rights in the United States, and unions' in their members' individual rights as employees.
3. Describe collective bargaining practices: unit determination, recognition and certification, preparation for negotiation, contract negotiation, contract ratification, and contract administration.
4. Discuss the future of public sector labor relations in terms of partnerships, gainsharing, and alternative dispute resolution.
5. Identify how the value issues underlying contemporary human resources management might affect the future of the field.
6. Identify contemporary and future issues regarding the PADS functions.

COLLECTIVE BARGAINING: HISTORY AND LEGAL BASIS

It is difficult to clearly frame collective bargaining because it evolved differently in the United States than in other parts of the world. Globally, collective bargaining generally evolved as the labor relations aspect of a broader and more ideological political, social, and economic movement. Thus, it is difficult to discuss the history and legal basis of trade unionism in Europe, Latin America, or the Caribbean without first placing it in the broader context of European socialism and the social welfare movement. In the United States, trade unionism initially followed this European model but fundamentally split from it between the 1880s and the 1920s. During that period, general U.S. popular mistrust with European socialism and anarchism and antipathy toward the southern European immigrants who espoused these philosophies led to the development of U.S. unionism as primarily based in the workplace and focused on narrower economic objectives of better pay and benefits. The most fundamental difference resulting from this separate evolution is that in the United States, workers' rights are protected primarily by collective bargaining agreements between employers and unionized employees. Government may facilitate or protect collective bargaining rights, but it has little substantive role in protecting worker's rights through public law. By contrast, under conditions of European socialism, governments took a more active role in protecting employee rights through constitutional safeguards, and unions took a more active role in government. Frequently, these were the basis for political parties or were incorporated into the system by which government institutions represented citizens as both voters and union members.

A related distinction is that in the United States, private sector bargaining is based on a single nationwide body of law and one compliance agency. But in the public sector, bargaining is more complex because there is one law and compliance agency for all national government employees, and separate laws and agencies for state and local government employees in each state—forty-three in all—where collective bargaining is permitted. This section clarifies these complexities.

Private Sector Unions in the United States

In the private sector, collective bargaining began in the late 1800s with the rise of industrial unions (The Industrial Workers of the World and the Congress of Industrial Organization) and craft unions (The American Federation of Labor). In the face of bitter opposition by management, aided in many cases by the federal court system, these unions gained political power and legal protection. The New Deal brought about the passage in 1935 of the **Wagner Act (or the National Labor Relations Act)**, which recognized the right of all private employees to join unions and required management to recognize and bargain collectively with these unions. It prohibited many previously common practices: blacklisting union members, signing "sweetheart contracts" with company unions, and so on. It established a federal agency—the **National Labor Relations Board (NLRB)**—with the responsibility of certifying unions as appropriate bargaining representatives, supervising negotiations to ensure "good faith" bargaining and adjudicating deadlocks (impasses) that might arise during contract negotiations. This law was counterbalanced (at least from management's point of view), by the **Taft–Hartley Act (1947)**, which prohibited labor unions from engaging in **unfair labor practices** and allowed states to pass **right to work laws** (statutes forbidding unions from requiring applicants to be union members in order to qualify for jobs).

With the change from manufacturing to service that began during the 1960s, the percentage of private sector employees operating under collective bargaining agreements has declined steadily from a high point of about 35 percent in 1957 to a low of about 8 percent today. With current economic trends (including **outsourcing**, job export, automation, **two-tiered wage and benefit systems**, and continued growth of service jobs in the secondary labor market), it can be expected that labor unions will not see a resurgence.[2]

The Public Sector—Federal

With the exception of a minor provision of the Taft–Hartley Act prohibiting strikes by public employees, and the **Postal Service Reorganization Act (1970)** that provides for supervision of the U.S. Postal Service collective bargaining by the NLRB, none of these three laws or agencies (the Wagner Act, the Taft–Hartley Act and the NLRB) is involved in public sector collective bargaining. Rather, a complex of laws that apply differentially to federal, state, and local governments regulate collective bargaining in the public sector.

Collective bargaining developed differently in the public sector for two fundamental philosophical reasons. First, in the private sector, the unitary nature of company management makes it possible for a single union to negotiate bilaterally with a single employer. In the public sector, agency managers are accountable to the chief executive, to the legislature, and ultimately to the taxpayers. Thus, it is impossible to negotiate binding contracts at the negotiating table (especially on economic issues) without their being subject to further negotiation and ultimate ratification elsewhere within the political arena. Second, the strike, as an ultimate weapon for exercising collective employee power by withholding services, is more difficult to justify and apply in the public sector because rather than simply affecting corporate directors or stockholders, its direct impact is on the public (possibly involving essential services like police, fire, and sanitation).

Within the federal government, the development of collective bargaining lagged behind the private sector because the types of jobs were different, treatment of employees by employers was better, and federal agencies were relatively small compared to the large industrial firms organized during the 1930s in the private sector. Civil service employees were largely incorporated into the merit system that arose between 1923 and 1945. At the same time, politicians began to lose interest in protecting civil service employees because their jobs were no longer subject to favoritism. Public employees' unions were recognized as legitimate bargaining agents in 1961. Binding grievance arbitration with management was permitted (though not required) in 1969, and the scope of bargaining was broadened in 1975.

In 1978, Congress passed the **Civil Service Reform Act (Title VII)**, which created a labor relations regulatory agency—the **Federal Labor Relations Authority (FLRA)** formally authorized to mediate disputes between federal unions and agency managers. Though this law clarified such issues as unit determination, scope of bargaining, and impasse resolution procedures, federal agency employees may still not strike or bargain collectively over wages and benefits, both of which Congress sets. The act was subsequently amended to create the **Federal Mediation and Conciliation Service (FMCS)**, designed to assist voluntary settlement of collective bargaining issues. Though these acts seemed to have stabilized and advanced formal labor relations in the federal sector, subsequent events have created substantial turmoil.

In 1981, in a signal event, President Reagan's administration fired air traffic controllers—members of PATCO, the union of professional air traffic controllers—who had gone out on strike. The administration hired workers who crossed picket lines and this incident marked a significant blow to unionization in the federal sector. While President Bush attempted to rebuild relationships with federal unions, the number of unfair labor practice charges and grievances nearly doubled for the period 1986–1992.[3]

President Clinton's administration, elected with labor's support, took substantial steps with E.O. 12871 to rebuild labor relations on a platform of partnership. A **National Partnership Council** (NPC) was established to oversee development of partnerships and provide advice to the administration. Unions were to be seen as full partners in organizational problem solving and performance improvement. Unfair labor practice charges and grievances fell by 40 percent during this period.[4]

In 2001, within the first days of his administration, President G. W. Bush revoked the Clinton administration's initiatives, but giving agencies the discretion to adopt labor relationship strategies best suited to their individual needs. While the Clinton administration's partnership approach announced a new age of cooperation, it elevated the status of unions at the expense of managerial flexibility and prerogative. The Bush administration attempted to establish a business model that prizes managerial discretion and responsibility.[5]

A consequence of 9/11, on November 12, 2002, President Bush signed legislation creating the **Department of Homeland Security** (DHS). It combined twenty-two existing agencies and 175,000 federal employees who had been working under eighty separate personnel systems.[6] DHS was given the authority to establish its own personnel system that would be "mission centered, performance focused, contemporary and excellent, generate respect and trust, and be based on merit system principles of fairness."[7] A design team was formed and developed fifty-two proposals, twenty-five of which outlined labor relations and adverse action options. Ferris and Hyde comment, "When the criticism is levied that current personnel systems are not aligned with current strategic mandates of most federal departments, labor relations systems are seen by many as part of that incongruence."[8]

However, after a series of battles with unions and other DHS employee groups, including litigation, DHS withdrew many of the more controversial segments of its plans regarding labor relations and pay for performance.[9] While DHS was not the first federal agency to be exempted from the large federal personnel system (Title V of the U.S. Code), it was not the last either. Most notably, the Department of Defense followed.

The lesson in this brief recent history is that issues of employee rights and solidarity as reflected in unionization seem contrary to contemporary values of efficiency and a market-based orientation although the strength of public sector unions suggests that changes cannot be mandated. Issues regarding organizational structure and change, performance management, flexibility in pay and compensation, timeliness of hiring and staffing decisions, and handling of adverse employment actions—all at one time or another falling generally within the rubric of collective bargaining—are now being viewed in light of contemporary values which downplay individual employee rights, comparatively speaking.

The Public Sector—State and Local

It is more difficult to comprehend and summarize the status of collective bargaining in state and local governments. This is primarily due to federalism, which means that the authorization and regulation of collective bargaining for state and local governments is a state responsibility. Many federal laws (such as affirmative action requirements and the wage-and-hour provisions of the Fair Labor Standards Act) regulate personnel practices in state and local government. Each state is responsible for developing and administering its own laws to regulate collective bargaining by state agencies, and for local governments within the state.

State governments have often gone beyond the federal government in enacting laws to clarify collective bargaining for their employees and for employees of local governments within their jurisdiction. Presently, nearly all states have enacted laws affording at least some public employees the right to "meet and confer" or negotiate on wages and working conditions. Public employees in a few states are not covered by any labor relations laws, with the possible exception of no-strike provisions applicable to public employees.

In our federal system of government, both national and state governments have sovereign powers. Local governments are created and regulated by state governments, so they have no sovereignty. With respect to collective bargaining, this has meant that they cannot enter into collective bargaining agreements with employee organizations unless the state has passed legislation authorizing them to do so. Home rule powers make it possible in some cases for a local government to opt out of the state law or to create its own "meet and confer" ordinances if state law makes it optional. Typically, this has meant that pressure for public-sector bargaining first arose among teachers, police, or firefighters in big cities and spread to other areas of a state once the state statutes or constitutional revisions authorized it. In the states allowing some form of collective bargaining in 2007, over 2 million state employees were represented by unions—some 34 percent of state employees. At the local level, over 5 million were represented by unions—over 45 percent of local government employees including the education sector. These numbers compare to 1 million federal employees—32 percent.[10] The conditions imposed on public sector collective bargaining make the extent of unionization and the growth of collective bargaining understandable. First, the inability of employees to negotiate bilaterally with management has meant that public sector unions have developed primarily as interest groups whose objective is to influence the decisions of the legislatures (Congress, state legislatures, city councils, and school boards) that will have the ultimate authority to ratify or reject negotiated agreements, or to set pay and benefits if these are outside the scope of bargaining.[11] Because the Taft–Hartley Act forbids states from enacting

TABLE 14-1 Public and Private Sector Collective Bargaining in the United States

Sector	Laws	Regulatory Agencies
PRIVATE	National Labor Relations Act Wagner Act (1935) Taft–Hartley Act (1947)	National Labor Relations Board
PUBLIC FEDERAL	Title VII of the 1978 Civil Service Reform Act	Federal Labor Relations Authority
STATE AND LOCAL	Each state has its own law	Each state has its own agency

closed shop provisions applicable to public agencies, public employees are not required to join a union as a condition of employment in a public agency, even though these employees will be covered by the provisions of the collective bargaining agreement negotiated between the union and agency management. These **free riders** benefit from the gains won by the union for its members, but are able to avoid paying dues if they so choose by declining to join the union.

The differences between public- and private-sector collective bargaining laws and regulatory agencies are shown in Table 14-1.

Labor Codes in Europe, Latin America, and the Caribbean

Politically, European democracies tend toward a parliamentary rather than Presidential model, with multiple political parties rather than a two-party system as in the United States. At least historically, European political parties tend to represent smaller and more ideologically unified constituencies than in the United States—including organized labor. So European public- and private-sector unions tend to be more ideological and to have a higher political profile than in the United States. They participate in elections, nominate candidates, and sponsor partisan legislation. Frequently, basic employee rights are included in the national constitution (usually as an appended **Labor Code**), including rights to health care, pensions, annual vacations, and severance bonuses based on years of service. Frequently, these basic rights apply to all employees (whether unionized or not). Because the labor code is highly visible and uniform nationally, employees find it easier to approach government in situations where they feel their rights as employees are being violated. These European traditions carried over to Europe's Latin American and Caribbean colonies during the colonial period, and have largely been retained in the English-, French-, and Spanish-speaking countries of the area.

Imagine, then, the plight of an immigrant worker newly arrived in the United States from one of these countries who has trouble with an employer because, for example, he has not been paid in a month even though he is supposed to be paid weekly, is paid at a lower pay rate than other employees doing comparable work, or is fired for complaining about unsafe working conditions. Rather than a single labor code and a single agency enforcing employee rights, we offer him a variety of federal, state, and private remedies, depending on the situation:

- If you were discriminated against based on a federal EEO/AA law, contact the local office of the appropriate federal compliance agency (see Chapter 8).
- If you were not paid, or not paid for all the hours you worked, and are not a member of a "protected class" (see Chapter 8), contact the state Department of Labor.

- If you have been discriminated against as a "whistleblower" and your employer is a federal contractor (see Chapter 13) contact the U.S. Department of Labor or the Office of Federal Compliance Programs.
- If none of these remedies apply, you may sue your employer in civil court.

Since a large number of workers who experience these employment problems may also face language barriers and immigration issues and since the historical and legal traditions of U.S. collective bargaining differ so fundamentally from those prevalent in their countries of origin, it is not surprising that immigrant workers hold an ambivalent view of economic opportunities in the United States. On the one hand, our higher standard of living and economic development means that it is possible to earn much higher wages here than in most other countries. Our emphasis on market values and our fragmented system for protecting employee rights presents risks that always counterbalance and sometimes outweigh our economic advantages.

COLLECTIVE BARGAINING, INDIVIDUAL RIGHTS, AND THE CONSTITUTION

Collective bargaining is one method by which terms and conditions of employment are determined. Understanding the unique role of collective bargaining in public agencies means understanding the relationship among union power and individual rights, constitutional protection, and political action.

While collective bargaining contracts demonstrate employee influence on some personnel functions (primarily pay, benefits, promotion, and disciplinary action), collective bargaining has no impact on selection (applicants are not eligible for union membership until they are hired and pass their probationary period). Because both managers and unions are required to comply with affirmative action laws, affirmative action has influenced both unions and management much more than collective bargaining has influenced the selection and promotion process.

Public employees' pay and benefits have been particularly affected by collective bargaining. Control over these activities has passed from management to the legislature, which now has three roles in the process: to pass enabling legislation governing contract negotiations, to pass appropriations bills funding negotiated collective bargaining agreements, and to pass substantive legislation incorporating noneconomic issues into the jurisdiction's personnel laws and regulations.

Collective bargaining plays a unique role in the public sector because of its close and interactive relationship with the constitutional rights afforded public employees within civil service systems and because of the union's role in protecting the individual rights of public employees as a dominant value.

In the private sector, only two dominant values are competing in the context of collective bargaining—administrative efficiency and employee rights. Management's legitimate interest is the "bottom line"—protecting profits by keeping production costs (including wages and benefits) low. In the absence of collective bargaining or employment contracts, most employees are hired and fired "at will" (in contrast to the public sector where at-will employment is a relatively new concept). Similarly, pay and benefits are often negotiated on an individual basis, without general awareness by other employees in the company.

In the public sector, government agencies are required to protect the individual rights of employees. This goal originated with the desire of civil service reformers a century ago to protect public employees from partisan political pressure and to promote efficiency. In the last few decades, federal courts have recognized that agencies that are constitutionally required to protect the rights of citizens in general cannot violate the constitutional rights of citizens as public employees. The cumbersome nature of civil service laws regulating disciplinary action, and the need of public managers to maintain efficiency, has meant that elected officials and public managers continue to exert pressures challenging the individual rights of employees. These include contracting, privatization, political appointments, and affirmative action (where the rigidities of civil service or collective bargaining systems based on seniority have had an adverse impact on minorities).

In responding to these pressures, public sector unions have three advantages over their private sector counterparts. First, public agencies are required to provide services to residents of a particular geographic area. This means that with some exceptions (primarily contracting out or outsourcing), the employer is required to remain in a fixed geographic area. Second, union members are not just employees—they are voters as well. Given the key role of legislative action in ratifying negotiated collective bargaining agreements in the public sector, the strength of union members as political action arms and voting blocks is important in understanding their political strength. Third, unions in the public sector have been able to obtain court opinions enforcing the value of individual rights as it is defined and protected by seniority systems.

COLLECTIVE BARGAINING PRACTICES

Collective bargaining has evolved into a formal and technical process, an administrative ritual that involves a number of prescribed concepts: unit determination, recognition and certification, scope of bargaining, contract negotiation, impasse resolution, ratification, contract administration, and unfair labor practices. We will briefly describe each below.

Unit Determination

Before collective bargaining can occur, a primary responsibility of the federal or state collective bargaining agency is to determine appropriate criteria for the formation of unions.[12] The two most commonly used criteria are to divide employees either by agency or by occupation. Agency bargaining establishes each state or local government agency as a separate bargaining unit. While this offers the advantages of working within an existing management structure, it can cause a proliferation of bargaining units and inequities among agency contracts.

An alternative is to group employees into general occupational classes, usually based on the state or local government's job classification system. This will result in the establishment of bargaining units such as health, public safety, teachers, general civil service employees, state university system employees, and so on. This method has the advantage of limiting the number of bargaining units and automatically including employees of new agencies in preestablished units. It also clarifies, on a systemwide basis, which employees are excluded from participation in bargaining units because their jobs are managerial or of a policy-making nature. Its disadvantage is that it lumps workers with different interests and needs into one large bargaining unit, such as all health care workers.

Both agency-based and occupation-based **unit determination** require coordinating mechanisms to ensure that negotiated contracts treat employees equitably.

Recognition and Certification

Once appropriate bargaining units have been established, unions are free to organize employees for bargaining collectively. While no uniformity among state laws exists, **recognition and certification** procedures are generally similar in all states; New York State's Taylor Law was used as a model by many of them. An employer may voluntarily recognize a union as the exclusive bargaining agent for employees in that bargaining unit without a recognition election *if* the union can demonstrate that a majority of the employees in the bargaining unit want to be represented by that union. If voluntary recognition does not occur, the union can win recognition through a representation election. Here, employees are offered the option of approving any union that has been able to show support (through signed authorization cards) from 10 percent of the eligible employees, or declining union representation. Depending upon state law, winning the representation election requires that the union win a majority of the votes cast or a majority of votes from eligible members of the bargaining unit, regardless of the actual number of votes cast.

Once a union has been voluntarily recognized or has won a representation election, it is formally certified by the labor relations agency as the exclusive agent for that bargaining unit. Certification requires that management recognize this union as the legitimate representative of employees and that it engage in collective bargaining over all items required or permitted by applicable law.

Scope of Bargaining

The **scope of bargaining** is simply the range of issues that applicable law requires or permits to be negotiated during collective bargaining. If the laws specify which issues are included or excluded, the scope of bargaining is considered *closed*. If no restrictions are placed upon bargainable issues, the scope of bargaining is termed *open*. Nonetheless, certain issues like agency structure, agency mission, and work methods or processes are usually, but not always, excluded from bargaining because they are management prerogatives. While federal employees do not bargain over wages and other economic issues that Congress deals with, that is not the case in most state and local governments. Yet the distinction between issues included in bargaining—or excluded from it—is not always clear. Issues that management considers excluded, such as adding drug testing to selection or promotion criteria, are frequently considered bargainable by unions because they affect member rights or important public policy issues. In such cases, their bargainability must be clarified by the state labor relations agency.

Contract Negotiation and Preparations for Negotiation

Contract negotiation usually begins immediately following recognition and certification or (if the union has previously been certified) in anticipation of the expiration of an existing contract. Local union officials may represent their own membership, or a professional negotiator who has negotiated similar contracts with other state or local governments may be employed. Management is represented by an experienced negotiator supported by a team of experts that will include the personnel manager, the budget officer, a lawyer, and some line managers who understand the impact of contract provisions on agency operations.

In most cases, negotiation occurs **in the sunshine**. That is, negotiations are conducted in public because states have an open-meetings law that prohibits government officials from determining public policy through back-room deals. Prior to the negotiations, it is important that management's negotiator reach a clear understanding with elected officials concerning their preferred contract provisions and their minimally acceptable contract provisions (particularly with respect to economic issues). It is important to prepare adequately for negotiations by collecting comparative data on other agencies and contract agreements, preparing spreadsheet analyses of the cost of alternative settlements on economic issues, and estimating projected revenues available to pay the price tag on economic items. Good negotiation is impossible without good research.

Negotiation involves both task- and process-oriented issues. Both sides see it as the opportunity to shape HR policy and practice. As in any strategic contest, each side attempts to discover the other's strengths and priorities, while keeping its own hidden until the opposition appears most willing to concede on an issue. Good negotiations depend on the negotiators' ability to marshal facts, sense the opposition's strengths and weaknesses, and judge the influence of outside events (such as job actions or media coverage) on the negotiations. Good faith bargaining requires negotiators to work for the best deal their side can get, while still remaining receptive to the needs of the other party. Experts agree that interest-based bargaining, also called collaborative or **win-win bargaining**, is the most satisfactory.[13]

Impasse Resolution during Contract Negotiations

There are two types of collective bargaining impasses: disagreements that occur during the negotiations over the *substance* of negotiations (such factors as pay or benefits) and disagreements over the interpretation of contract provisions that have previously been negotiated and approved. If management and union are unable to resolve differences through two-party contract negotiations, there remain three procedures involving intervention by a third party: mediation, fact-finding, and arbitration. The order in which these are employed, and whether they are used at all, will depend on the provisions of the applicable collective bargaining law.

Mediation is the intervention of a neutral third party in an attempt to persuade the bargaining parties to reach an agreement. This may be an independent individual or one from a group designated by an agency such as the **American Arbitration Association** or the **Federal Mediation and Conciliation Service (FMCS)**. It is in the interest of both parties to make a good-faith effort to reach a voluntary mediated settlement, as this is the last stage at which they will have full control over contract provisions.

If mediation is not successful, negotiations may progress to the second step—**fact-finding**. A fact-finder appointed by the federal or state collective bargaining agency will conduct a hearing at which both sides present data in support of their positions. After these hearings, the fact-finder releases a report to both parties and to the public that outlines what he or she considers a reasonable settlement. Although this advisory opinion is not binding, the threat of unfavorable publicity may make either side more willing to reach a negotiated settlement.

If fact-finding is unsuccessful, the final stage may be **arbitration**. Essentially the same procedures are followed as in fact-finding. However, the arbitrator's formal report contains contract provisions that both parties have agreed in advance will be binding. In an effort to avoid having to "split the difference" between extreme positions, the arbitrator may decide in advance to take the "last, best final offer" presented by either side, based on either the entire contract or issue-by-issue. Arbitration of substantive items at impasse during contract negotiation is termed **interest arbitration**, to distinguish it from subsequent arbitration over the meaning of previously ratified contract provisions (**grievance arbitration**) during the contract administration process. The cost of third-party interest dispute resolution during negotiations is usually equally borne by both parties.

Contract Ratification

Once representatives of labor and management have negotiated a contract, both the appropriate legislative body and the union's membership must ratify it before becoming law. For the union, **ratification** requires support of the negotiated contract by a majority of those voting. For management, it requires that the legislature (state, county, school district) appropriate the funds required to finance the economic provisions of the contract. Because all states have laws or constitutional provisions prohibiting deficit financing of operating expenses, revenue estimates impose an absolute ceiling on the pay and benefits that may be negotiated through collective bargaining. Nor is it considered bad faith bargaining for a legislature to refuse to ratify a negotiated contract if projected revenues will not meet projected expenses.

The requirement that a negotiated contract be ratified by the legislature is a sore point for union advocates because it limits the application of binding interest arbitration. Courts have uniformly held that the legislature cannot delegate its responsibility for keeping expenditures within revenues. Although union advocates frequently (and justifiably) protest that the legislature is biased toward management, state laws require that the state or local legislature take all interests into account—including those of the union and its members—in deciding whether to ratify a negotiated contract.

Contract Administration

Once a contract has been negotiated and ratified, both union and management are responsible for administering its provisions. Key actors in implementation include the union steward, a union member who will interpret the contract for the employees and serve as their advocate and representative to management; supervisors, who will be implementing contract provisions relating to everyday employee–employer relations; and the personnel manager, who is management's expert on how the contract affects human resource policy and practice.

Conflicts are bound to arise during **contract administration** because reaching compromises during negotiations often requires agreement on what will later turn out to be ambiguous contract language. For example, labor and management may agree during contract negotiations that the shop steward "may spend a reasonable amount of time not to exceed two hours per week on union activities." Subsequently, differences may arise over such issues as whether the steward is in fact spending a "reasonable" amount of time on union business or whether management has the right to approve when this time can be taken. Negotiations will then be needed to determine whether the shop steward's or the supervisor's actions constitute a violation of the contract's provisions.

Part of the contract will therefore outline the process for resolving grievances that occur during contract implementation. The process may begin very informally with discussion between union and management representatives. If the issue is not satisfactorily resolved informally, it is written up as a formal grievance and appealed through channels up to a neutral third party outside the agency. Binding grievance arbitration is the norm (in contrast to the lack of binding *interest* arbitration over contract negotiation impasses).

Management should view the **grievance** process as one more potentially beneficial effort by employees to make the organization more effective by calling attention to inefficient or inequitable supervisory practices. It can serve as an internal evaluation device, a means of instituting planned change and a method of redressing inequitable organizational practices. It is recommended that supervisors and public personnel managers know the contract, maintain open lines of communication with employees, meet and deal informally with union representatives over potential grievances, exhibit uniform and adequate documentation for all personnel actions, and keep the record open to unions and employees. One way to keep both parties honest in handling grievances is to require the losing party to pay for the services of a third-party arbitrator. This discourages unions from pursuing frivolous grievances just to satisfy a disgruntled member, and it encourages management to handle grievances fairly rather than simply opposing the union on every issue.

THE FUTURE OF PUBLIC SECTOR LABOR RELATIONS

While growth in public sector collective bargaining has grown substantially over the past forty years, the future is hardly predictable. Nevertheless, one thing does seem sure. The traditional notion of hard-core adversarial labor management relationships seems very discordant with contemporary public sentiment. One cannot expect private sector employees who see their health and pension benefits pale in comparison to public sector employees stand by as voters and support public sector unions pushing for what may seem arrogant. Thus, we can expect to see the profile of labor relations in terms of partnerships with alternative dispute resolution becoming even more popular and the threat of strike which for teachers, public safety officers, and firefighters less popular among the public.

In fact, binding arbitration and impasse resolution mechanisms have become the norm when compared to strikes and lockouts. This move reflects the growing realization that in today's political environment, labor and management have more to gain from cooperation than from adversarial relationships. While unions traditionally have viewed relationships with management in adversarial terms, the absence of a profit motive and competition in the public sector permit government workers to be treated well and compensated fairly.[14] Much evidence shows that in a union-management setting, collaborative management can exist and can create a positive organizational atmosphere.[15] Calo cites research that concludes union settings can be very conducive to participative decision making and the reduction in traditional autocratic managerial structures.[16] Calo contends that the keys are gaining senior management and union leadership commitment, building mutual trust and respect by choosing to cooperate and working to assess the success of the collaboration, and the third tier of the stool is employing best HR policies and practices.

Diverse organizations oriented toward team-based productivity improvement require methods of resolving disputes that are more appropriate to their culture and structure than traditional grievance resolution. This is part of the movement toward collaborative labor relations. Fortunately, contemporary organizations have been successfully utilizing **alternative dispute resolution (ADR)** techniques that meet these criteria. Generally, these include any procedure, agreed to by the parties to a dispute, in which they call upon the services of a neutral party to assist them in reaching agreements and thus avoid litigation. The most popular variants are mediation and arbitration, but they include a range of procedures:

- *Open door policy:* Encourages employees to bring grievances of any kind to their managers with the assurance that no retaliation will result.[17]
- *Negotiation:* A process of explicit bargaining between parties to a dispute in an effort to reach a settlement without outside intervention.
- *Ombudsman:* Use of a manager with strong communication skills, respected by labor and management, with broad authority to hear disputes and facilitate resolution.[18]
- *Peer review panel:* Use of an informal panel representing labor and management, to determine if existing policy was accurately and equitably applied.[19]
- *Mediation:* Active assistance by a neutral third party in reaching a settlement. Emphasizes informality, confidentiality, and flexibility to resolve a particular dispute or to preserve and improve long-term relationships.[20]
- *Arbitration:* A process by which both sides usually commit themselves in advance to the binding decision of a neutral arbitrator, referee, or private judge, typically through procedures specified by the American Arbitration Association.[21]

This development was spurred by the **Alternative Dispute Resolution Act of 1998**, which encouraged use of alternative methods of workplace dispute resolution throughout the Executive Branch. Every federal agency has an alternative Dispute Resolution policy and the federal Office of Personnel Management provides resources.[22] In addition, the FMCS reports increasing efforts assisting nonfederal governmental units in dispute resolution. ADR results in significant savings in legal fees, quicker dispute resolution, and a decrease in litigation.

Beyond the concrete assertion that cooperative labor relations will be the norm rather than the exception, Adler notes several other trends in public sector unionism.[23] First, he notes the loss of power at the federal level. One of the impacts of the DHS and the Department of Defense creating their own personnel systems is the modification of rights and employee protections provided by the Civil Service Act of 1978. Collective bargaining agreements were also modified. Second, outsourcing and at-will employment have made inroads into employee rights at the state level. Adler reports on research showing that in thirty-one of fifty states, there was a decline in job security. Third, while substantial gains were made in public sector unionism in the past forty years, most of that gain occurred in the 1960s and 1970s. Actually, coverage for teachers, firefighters, and police declined slightly since 1980, while a high level of penetration still exists. Finally, Adler speculates about the impact that the 2005 split among unions in the AFL-CIO will have on the union movement in general. Will the split and the resultant competition among unions for public sector members advantage the labor movement or drain it of resources—both financial and political.

MANAGING THE WORKFORCE OF THE FUTURE

We draw this discussion of labor relations to a close and now speculate on HR issues involved in managing the workforce of the future. We will try to pull together many of the observations made throughout the book, and we invite our readers to compare their observations and experiences with those we offer.

We start with our observations about the values and then aided by Table 14.2, we will discuss the functions.

TABLE 14.2 Managing the Workforce of the Future

Category of Employment				
General	**Specific**	**Personnel Mgmt Function**	**Key Human Resource Management Functions Planning Considerations**	
Payroll Employees	**Full Time—Individual**	Planning	• Hired for the long term (eligible to stay with the organization). • Works more than thirty-five hours per week.	• Usually receives the best benefit packages. • Positions are listed on HRM documents/budgets.
		Acquisition	• Hiring may be a long process. • Individuals should reflect the organization's values for a good organizational "fit."	• Hiring process is tightly controlled. • Promotions can be based on displayed performance and potential.
		Development	• Usually receives high level of professional development and training. • Performance evaluations are focused on professional development and obtaining organizational goals	• Careers are managed by the organization and individual. • Individual development is linked to strategic planning.
		Sanctions	• Employees are viewed as an investment. • Individuals are viewed as investments and may have highest sense of commitment to the organization.	• May expect more beneficial treatment over other types employees. • Receives the most protection under employment laws.
	Full Time—Unionized	Planning	• Collective bargaining determines the terms and conditions of employment. • The political and real power of the union must be considered.	• Positions are listed on HRM documents/budgets. • Works more than thirty-five hours per week.

TABLE 14.2 (*Continued*)

Category of Employment: General	Category of Employment: Specific	Personnel Mgmt Function	Key Human Resource Management Functions Planning Considerations	
		Acquisition	• Collective bargaining agreements can make the recruitment, selection, and promotions difficult. • Individuals should reflect the organization's values for a good organizational "fit."	• Employment expectations are agreed upon with the union and individuals. • Unions will attempt to base promotions on seniority.
		Development	• Usually receives high level of professional development and training. • May be guaranteed certain training and education benefits through collective bargaining agreements.	• Careers are managed by the organization, the union, and the individual. • Individual development is tied to strategic planning.
		Sanctions	• Work expectations can be governed by collective bargaining agreements • Individuals are viewed as investments and may have highest sense of commitment to the organization.	• May demonstrate more loyalty to the union than to the organization. • Worker rights are protected by negotiated agreements and employment laws.
	Part-time	Planning	• Individuals do not expect the same benefits and treatment as full-time employees. • Works less than thirty-five hours per week.	• Traditional part-time workers are included in organizational structures and budgets (such as interns). • Allows flexibility to work employees only when needed.
		Acquisition	• More flexibility in hiring process. • Employees understand that there may be limited possibility for promotion.	• Individuals may not reflect the organization's values to the same extent as the full-time employees.

		Development	• Training and development may include only initial training. • May not require performance evaluations.	
		Sanctions	• Employees expect to have more flexibility in working hours arrangements. • May not have much commitment to the organization.	• Employees may use the job to gain experience or as a stepping stone to full-time employment. • Usually used as a second income, second family income or as limited income during education or retirement.
Temporary Employees	**Temp Service**	Planning	• Can be viewed as a "labor reserve" for times of increased output demand. Usually blue collar or low-skilled labor. • Salary may be more than for full-time employees but savings in benefits, sick pay, vacation pay, etc. make up the difference.	• May work any number of hours, based on contracted agreements. • Minimum human resources management requirements. Personnel support requirements (FICA, Taxes, etc.) may be covered through the Temporary Service Agency.
		Acquisition	• Temp agencies recruit and send out personnel when requested. • No promotions or pay raises.	• Employers save in recruitment and hiring costs. • Agencies can try to select individuals that would fit best in the organization.
		Development	• Training may be limited to integration only • Workers are expected to show up with the prerequisite skills to perform the services contracted.	• Temp service agency may request a critique of service performed.
		Sanctions	• Three-way agreement. Work expectations are negotiated through the temporary service agency.	• Individuals are expected to provide their own professional equipment. • Temp service agency is responsible for legal rights of their employees.

TABLE 14.2 (*Continued*)

Category of Employment				
General	**Specific**	**Personnel Mgmt Function**	**Key Human Resource Management Functions Planning Considerations**	
			• Little loyalty to the organization unless the employee seeks future temporary jobs or full-time employment.	
	Short-term or On Call	Planning	• Can include full-time or part-time employment during peak periods of the year (such as leaf collection period). • Offer flexibility in hours or days worked.	• Usually planned and included in the budget documents.
		Acquisition	• Hiring constraints are not as high as for full-time employees. • Employers may maintain a personnel file on record for returning employees (such as substitute teachers).	
		Development	• Individuals are expected to arrive with prerequisite skills and attributes. Some integration training may be required. • May be required to participate in training to maintain their job certifications (such as police auxiliary).	• Professional development may be managed by the organization but usually is an individual's responsibility. • Routine short-term employees may integrate well into the workforce team.
		Sanctions	• Short-term employees may be perceived and treated as a separate class of worker. • The work output may be less than that of full-time workers due to a difference in commitment and ambition.	• Using short-term employees to counter unions may create conflict between employees. • Short-term employees may have the same legal rights as full-time employees if they are employed over thirty-five hours a week.

Contract Employees	Contracting an Organization for Services	Planning	• Arrangement works well for short term, high skill, requirements (budgets, projects, audits, etc). • Hours/days worked can be contracted based on the requirement (number of hours, flexible or set hours).	• Contracted organization may provide benefits and administrative support to their sub-contractors. • May cost more than in house full-time employees but flexibility and benefit package saving may make the arrangement cost effective.
		Acquisition	• By working though a contracting company, organizations can minimize the time involved in screening and hiring requirements. • Process of hiring services may require more planning time based on the availability of specialty required.	• Contract employees are not eligible for promotions but bonuses can be awarded for exceeding performance objectives. • Should ensure the organization's values are in line your organization to ensure a good "fit."
		Development	• Contracted for their inherent skills and abilities, little or no additional development is required. • Formal performance evaluations are normally not required. Contracting agency may request feedback on performance.	• Some contracting agencies provide training or education that is available at a fee (ICMA). • May be viewed as an "outsider" by the other employees, may have to pull the individuals into the team.
		Sanctions	• Performance expectations are explained in the terms of the contract. • Contractor may display loyalty to their company or contract negotiator and not to the community or government organization.	• Contractors provide their own professional tools. • Changes to job requirements calls for contract renegotiation with the contracting agency.

TABLE 14.2 (*Continued*)

Category of Employment: General	Specific	Personnel Mgmt Function	Key Human Resource Management Functions Planning Considerations	
	Independent Contractor	Planning	• Arrangement works well for short term, high skill, requirements (budgets, projects, audits, etc). • Hours/days worked can be contracted based on the requirement (number of hours, flexible or set hours).	• Individual provides their own personnel administrative support unless specified in the contract (FICA, income tax, health insure). • Individual receives little or no organizational benefits unless specified in the contract.
		Acquisition	• Individual hired through search tools or references. Screening process can take time. • Hiring process involves contracting and legal support.	• Not eligible for promotions but bonuses can be involved as an incentive for exceeding performance objectives. • Should ensure the individual's values are in line with the organization's to ensure a good short-term "fit."
		Development	• Contracted for their inherent skills and abilities, little or no additional development is required. • Formal performance evaluations are normally not required.	• Individuals are responsible for their own continuing education and professional development. • May be viewed as an "outsider" by the other employees, may have to pull the individuals into the team.
		Sanctions	• Performance expectations are explained in the terms of the contract. • Loyalty to the organization is "purchased" through the contract.	• Contractors provide their own professional tools. • Changes to job requirements calls for contract renegotiation.

Note: Table prepared by Major Terrence Ray while a graduate student in public administration at the University of Kansas

Values and Functions

Table 14.2 provides a comprehensive look at various categories of employment and then analyzes each according to the four functions we have been working with throughout the book. While we have talked about these employment categories, we have not systematically placed them beside each other for comparative purposes. The table does this, and the one word that captures an impression of the table is "complexity."

Traditionally, we have looked at **permanent civil service employees**, including those unionized, as the bedrock of government service. As such, temporary workers, part-time workers, contract employees, and outsourced work were seen as peripheral to the centrality of public administration. While we should not lose sight of the millions of permanent public employees in federal, state, and especially local governments, at the same time, we must acknowledge that administering the work of government no longer falls solely upon permanent public employees.

The implications of this observation are enormous if one considers that public employees, more than any other group of people, probably carry the four democratic values into their work. They have to—because "public administration" requires balancing the values in legislative work, implementation, and even in the judicial arena. Without even becoming aware of it, pubic employees inculcate the values into their work. When one of the authors gives policymaking/managerial case studies to groups of public employees who have never actually confronted the case situation, he asks: "Is the case unfamiliar to you?" The answer is always "no; it is familiar"—not the specifics, but the broad contours of issues that will likely be faced, processes that likely will be employed, and the dynamics that will be encountered. The values provide a public service analytical framework for public service professionals, and one wonders what will happen to an appreciation of the values as the permanent public workforce diminishes.

Clearly, what we have seen in recent years is a shift in values toward efficiency and market-based values. The value of responsiveness holds its own but it takes a different shape than in earlier years. While there continues to be issues connected to partisanship and increasing desire to have one's "own" in government jobs, responsiveness today is aligned with efficiency and market-based values. To be responsive today is to be efficient, which in ideological terms means: endorse market-based values.

The value of equity as it was known in the days of affirmative action has yielded to the force of diversity. Increasing diversification of the workforce, in large measure due to immigration, has deflected attention from the initial impetus for racial equality in employment practices. The force of immigration is so powerful that given the generational profile of the future workforce and birthrates among immigrant populations, one wonders when Hispanic workers will take advantage of their political muscle and truly see public employment as a source of mobility.

Diversity itself has become a term that encompasses so many different elements of HR. The different possible combinations of employment status reflected in Table 14.2 provide a glimpse that takes us beyond traditional categories of race and gender. We discussed generational diversity earlier, and one implication of the aging workforce with inevitable retirements is a decline in the value of individual rights in employment. Today's generations are growing up in an environment of globalism where entrepreneurial careers are not only prized but are expected. Those with public service motives who wish to work for the government will find opportunities, but they will come to their work the product of their own generation when it comes to expectations about job security, pay for performance, benefits, and retirement.

Regarding the functions, each contains a challenge for the future. Planning and sanction may see the most dramatic changes brought about on the one hand by a shortage of skilled workers and on the other hand by the mixed employment relationships that affect the psychological and actual contracts between employer and employee.

In the earlier editions of this text, workforce planning was approached technically—as an incremental or comprehensive method. Workforce planning as an imperative has grown with each edition. We used to refer to the military's understanding that tomorrow's generals/admirals are entering the service today. The composition of today's recruits will signal the demographic composition of tomorrow's core of general rank officers. HR planning for the military is an imperative, and now other occupations and employers are coming to the same realization. Every state department of transportation is asking: "Where are tomorrow's engineers going to come from?" At the same time that the demographics of the population and workforce are encouraging workforce planning, people are coming to the realization that "human capital" makes a difference. In Chapter 3, we referred to David Walker's (Comptroller General of the United States) influential observation that organizational transformation depends upon investments in human capital.

As we talk about investments in human capital and as every federal agency now has a Chief Human Capitol Officer, Table 14.2 shows how complex today's employment relationships have become. This complexity is not yet well understood in the HR management area. We have approached the complexity with terms like *governance* and *networks* that have been studied with attendant concern for effectiveness and accountability. Nevertheless, we have not fully studied the dynamics of juxtaposing multiple HR management systems from several organizations. We have seen it work within an agency, and in fact, we argue that organizations must manage internally with civil service, patronage, collective bargaining, and affirmative action systems. Nevertheless, it still is possible, at least theoretically to talk about organizational values and norms within this kind of organization. The **"hollow" organization**—one that primarily manages contracts—challenges the notion not only that human capital is a crucial resource, it also invites uncertainty and conflict when host organizations have invited a multiplicity of other employers along with their HR systems into the arena for the purposes of service delivery. How does one build a base of values in this kind of context? We must wait and see, and we suspect that the private "hollow corporation" may have some lessons for the public sector here.

As a corollary to this discussion, as the hollow state becomes more prevalent, there are dramatic impacts on the sanction function. The expectations of employees will change, especially when it comes to permanence and job security, and employee rights may very well come to be seen as a luxury. The real drama here, however, will be played out in the rights of employees in firms who are contracted with to handle the government's work. The key justification for job security for civil servants is that it gives them the confidence to "speak truth to their politically powerful bosses." The question is whether contract employees will be protected if they attempt to speak "truth to power"—especially in areas that traditionally have been serviced by public employees—like prisons.

Next, demographics are going to force more agility and creativity in attracting and retaining employees. The promise of challenging work cannot be underestimated as a recruitment tool—one of which we expect to employ very creatively both electronically and maybe even by extending recruitment pools beyond our borders. It is difficult to see this happening now with concerns over illegal immigration and terrorism, but private firms utilizing call centers that operate in other countries have tested the waters. Private corporations have only virtual homes with financial capital floating all over the world and work being performed electronically. It may be that some of this will be transferred to the public sector, and we will find increasingly that our engineers will be coming from India. After all, what employer doing technical work would not want a pipeline to graduates from the Indian Institutes of Technology?

Finally, retention of employees is going to depend heavily on investments in the development function. We expect increasing appreciation for the importance of retention as the consequences of retirement make themselves felt. Investing in employees also means investing in their families and in their lives outside of work. Flexible work arrangements, bus passes, on-site day care, days that can be used for elder care, and innovations we do not yet see prevalent in the public sector may become commonplace if retention of employees is valued.

No time in our memory have we seen public administration in more flux. Perhaps for the younger generation of worker, today's employment relationships simply are what they are. What we are concerned about is the institution of public administration as a values-carrying foundation of democracy. As we hollow out the state in favor of more governance, one wonders how the institution of public administration will face the challenges of legitimization. Historically, HR management has been at the core of government reform because it is the core of administrative processes and values. We expect that focus will continue.

Summary

Collective bargaining is law, process, and ritual. As law, it provides the constitutional and statutory foundation that enables employees collectively to negotiate the terms and conditions of employment with managers (and indirectly, with legislators and the public). Second, this collective negotiation takes place by the standardized procedures. Third, employees demonstrate their relative power (through the sanctions process) over employment policy and practice through a ritual.

In the final analysis, the strength of collective bargaining as a public personnel system will be affected by unions' ability to persuade the public and its leaders that strong unions are tied to vital public policy concerns that go beyond the more narrow economic concerns of their current members. The number of union members in the public sector has leveled off, and traditional adversarial relationships are giving way to partnerships and alternative methods of dispute resolution.

In terms of the future of HR management, the emphasis on the values of efficiency and market-based approaches to governing is having a significant effect on the way the functions are being fulfilled. More emphasis on efficiency has meant less emphasis on employee rights, which has an impact on sympathy for unions. In this environment, the functions of planning and sanction become critical, especially the sanction function where expectations and obligations of employer and employee are established and maintained.

Key Terms

alternative dispute resolution (ADR) *345*
Alternative Dispute Resolution Act of 1998 *346*
American Arbitration Association *343*
arbitration *343*
Civil Service Reform Act (Title VII) *337*
closed shop *339*
collective bargaining *334*
contract administration *344*
contract negotiation *342*
Department of Homeland Security *337*
fact-finding *343*
Federal Labor Relations Authority (FLRA) *337*
Federal Mediation and Conciliation Service (FMCS) *337*
free riders *339*
grievance *345*
grievance arbitration *344*
"hollow" organization *354*
"in the sunshine" (negotiations) *343*
interest arbitration *344*
labor code *339*
mediation *343*
National Labor Relations Act (Wagner Act) *336*
National Labor Relations Board (NLRB) *336*
National Partnership Council *337*
outsourcing *336*
Permanent civil service employees *353*
Postal Service Reorganization Act (1970) *336*
ratification *344*
recognition and certification *342*
right to work laws *336*
scope of bargaining *342*
Taft–Hartley Act (1947) *336*
two-tiered wage and benefit systems *336*
unfair labor practices *336*
unit determination *342*
win-win bargaining *343*

Discussion Questions

1. Why is the history of collective bargaining in the public sector different from that in the private sector?
2. Why is the legal structure of collective bargaining more complex and confusing in the public sector than in the private sector?
3. What are the reasons for the current crisis among public sector unions?
4. Should management's strategy toward collective bargaining be (a) opposition to unions and avoidance of collective bargaining or (b) acceptance of unions' legitimacy and participation in collective bargaining? What factors will influence which option management chooses to pursue?
5. Give an example of mediation or arbitration that you are familiar with and discuss what you consider the costs and benefits to the parties involved. What conditions do you think are necessary before mediation or arbitration can be successful?
6. Which of the values issues discussed in the last part of the chapter do you agree with most? Which do you disagree with most? Why? What have the authors missed in terms of values questions that you think are important to the future of public HR management?
7. Which of the four functions, PADS, do you think are going to be most important in the next five years? Why?

Case Study: Good Management or Bargaining in Bad Faith?

Background Information

You are the new city manager for Sunbelt City. It is small (50,000 population) but growing at about 10 percent annually, as retirees and business owners move south seeking warmer winters and lower taxes. The City currently employs about 100 sworn police officers. The city charter classifies police officers as within the civil service system. Because public sector collective bargaining is authorized for local governments in this state, those officers in nonsupervisory positions are also represented by the PBA (Police Benevolent Association).

Sunbelt is governed by a five-member elected city council. Last November, three incumbent council members were defeated by newcomers who ran on a platform of keeping taxes down by making government more effective and efficient. The two remaining council members also favor this objective.

The council has enthusiastically supported your strategy of reducing the city budget by bargaining hard with unions over salary and fringe benefits. By using the veiled threat of privatization or outsourcing as a "hammer," you have successfully renegotiated contracts for the City's solid waste and public works employees. Under the new contracts, trash collectors now work a full eight-hour day instead of being allowed to go home when their routes are finished. The public works department is now operating under a two-tiered contract that protects salaries and benefits for current employees but requires new employees to enter at lower salaries and to pay a higher proportion of their health benefit costs.

Now you face a challenge. A new council member suggests that you use the same strategy in renegotiating the contract with the PBA, up for renewal this year. You immediately sense trouble ahead as other council members have indicated a similar interest. Threatening solid waste and public works employees with privatization is one thing—it has been done all over the country, and many private trash haulers and maintenance companies do a thriving business. What are the alternatives to police officers hired through a civil service system? Will any alternative satisfy voters and the rest of the council, given that Sunbelt residents want both lower taxes and high-quality police protection? You hire a collective bargaining consultant and labor negotiator to provide you with expert advice in the matter. The consultant recommends that you consider three options: (1) hard bargaining with the PBA, (2) contracting for police services with the county sheriff's office, or (3) contracting with a private security firm.

Your Choices

Hard bargaining means taking bargaining positions that reduce pay and benefit costs, such as: (a) proposing a tiered contract offering lower pay and benefits to new officers than current ones; (b) routinely challenging police officer requests for disability retirement and workers' compensation for injuries suspected of being caused by outside employment; (c) hiring civilian employees to do office work and putting all sworn police officers on the street; and (d) proposing early retirement provisions to reduce lower personnel costs by reducing the number of senior officers. This is politically the least risky option, but it will work well only if citizens are convinced the quality of law enforcement will not suffer and if PBA negotiators fear that one of the other two options will be imposed if they do not agree to "giveback" contract provisions that reduce pay and benefit costs.

Contracting with the county sheriff's office means changing the city charter by abolishing the police department and contracting with the county sheriff's office for police services. The contract would need to be carefully negotiated to include (a) reimbursement to Sunbelt for any capital equipment (such as police buildings or vehicles) sold to the county; (b) qualitative and quantitative measures of service (such as number of officers, response time, and responsiveness to the council); and (c) provisions for city police officers to join the county sheriff's department (this would involve complex negotiations over seniority, pay, and benefit packages for both organizations). This option offers probable dramatic short-term cost savings. The downside is less control over quality of service, no assurance that costs for contracting will remain lower than the cost of the Sunbelt police department, and a large one-time lump-sum payment of accrued annual leave to those Sunbelt police officers who elect to retire rather than join the county sheriff's department.

Contracting with a private security firm offers the greatest potential benefits and risks. Private security corporations already provide security at many condominiums and public facilities, operate county and state correctional facilities, and are starting to move into municipal law enforcement. Informal negotiations with officials in private security firms lead you to believe that they will offer to provide sworn law enforcement officers at less than half the cost of the current police department's budget, largely because of lower pay and benefit costs. Not only will payroll costs be lower, but also administrative expenses are capped by the contract, and legal liability risks are covered by the contractor's bond. The risks are also great. Public opinion will probably be against hiring "rent-a-cops" to replace sworn police officers, and the PBA will use this opposition to build a firestorm of political opposition to the proposal. Certainly, the quality of service will be in doubt and the training and fitness for duty of sworn officers may be questionable if, as rumored, the security company hires retired police or corrections officers because they are already certified.

The Outcome

You decide on the first option (hard bargaining), backed by credible statements that if hard bargaining is unsuccessful you intend to pursue council approval for either of the other two options. The PBA fights back hard, stirring up public opinion against you, directly lobbying the council against your proposal, and filing an unfair labor practice charge with the state collective bargaining regulatory agency, alleging that your purported threat to contract out for law enforcement services is in fact a refusal to bargain in good faith. Several weeks later, the hearing officer decides that you have not violated the requirement for good faith bargaining. In the meantime, PBA and public pressure have forced two council members to publicly come out against the contracting option. The county sheriff's department becomes the subject of investigation by the State Attorney General's office and the State Department of Law Enforcement, when it is alleged that sheriff's deputies are guilty of widespread bribery and extortion efforts to protect drug dealers and gambling interests in the county. The PBA agrees to a contract that is essentially the same as the previous one, with a cost-of-living increase in pay and no changes in benefits. As a condition of ratification, the PBA insists privately to council members that you be fired. The council fires you at the same time it approves the collective bargaining agreement with the PBA.

Questions

1. What does this case study show about the current strengths and weaknesses of public-sector collective bargaining as a public personnel system?
2. Looking back at the situation, are there any options that would have been better for you to select than the three you were offered by the consultant?
3. What arguments could you have presented to make a stronger case for hard bargaining or contracting out?
4. Is there anything else you could have done to handle this situation better, or were you simply a victim of bad timing and corruption in the county sheriff's department?
5. At what stage might you have sought out union leadership to discuss a partnership approach to the bargaining? How easy do you think it would be to move from an adversarial approach to a partnership approach?

Notes

1. Riccucci, N. (2007). The changing faced of public employee unionism. *Review of Public Personnel Administration, 27* (1): 72.
2. United States Department of Labor, Bureau of Labor Statistics (2008). Available at: http://data.bls.gov/cgi-bin/surveymost?lu (accessed on September 25, 2008).
3. Ferris, F., and A. C. Hyde (2004). Federal labor-management relations for the next century—or the last? The case of the department of homeland security. *Review of Public Personnel Administration, 24* (3): 216–234.
4. Ibid.
5. Cited in Ferris and Hyde, Federal labor-management relations for the next century—or the last? The case of the department of homeland security, p. 225.
6. Ibid., p. 217.
7. Ibid.
8. Ibid., p. 220.
9. Barr, S. (February 20, 2008). DHS Withdraws Bid to Curb Union Rights. Available at: www.washingtonpost.com (accessed on September 25, 2008).
10. Department of Labor, Bureau of Labor Statistics (2008). Union affiliation of employed wage and salary workers by occupation and industry. Available at: www.bls.gov (accessed on September 25, 2008).
11. Chandler, T., and R. Gely (December 1996). Toward identifying the determinants of public-employee unions' involvement in political activities. *American Review of Public Administration, 26* (4): 417–438.
12. A good general reference for public-sector unit determination is Gershenfeld, W. (1985). Public employee unionization: An overview. In Association of Labor Relations Agencies (1985).

The evolving process: Collective negotiations in public employment. Ft. Washington, PA: Labor Relations Press.

13. Fisher, R., and W. Ury (1991). *Getting to yes.* New York: Penguin Books.
14. Calo, T. J. (April 2008). Collaborative management: A positive approach to public sector employee relations. *HR News Magazine*, pp. 11–14.
15. Martin, E. J. (2003). Labor-management relations, collective bargaining, and public sector: Collaborative solutions in Alameda, California. *LaboPublic Administration and Management: An Interactive Journal, 8* (2): 54–68.
16. Calo, Collaborative management, pp. 12–13.
17. Barrier, M. (July 1998). A working alternative for settling disputes. *Nation's Business, 86* (7): 43–46.
18. Hayford, S. L. (January 2000). Alternative dispute resolution. *Business Horizons, 4:* 111–118.
19. Verespej, M. A. (February 2, 1998). Sidestepping court costs. *Industry Week*, pp. 68–72.
20. Mareschal, P. (Fall 1998). Providing high quality mediation: Insights from the Federal Mediation and Conciliation Service. *Review of Public Personnel Administration, 18*: 55–67.
21. Carver, T., and A. Vondra (May–June 1994). Alternative dispute resolution: Why it doesn't work and why it does. *Harvard Business Review, 70*: 120–130.
22. The federal Office of Personnel Management provides a ADR resource guide at http://www.opm.gov/er/adrguide/ (accessed on September 25, 2008).
23. Adler, J. (Winter 2006). The past as prologue? A brief history of the labor movement in the United States. *Public Personnel Management,* 35 (4): 311–329.

INDEX

Note: locators with letter 'f' denote a figure and locators with letter 't' denote a table on that page

D

E